Nomenklatura

Nomenklatura
The Soviet Ruling Class

Michael Voslensky

TRANSLATED BY
Eric Mosbacher

PREFACE BY MILOVAN DJILAS

DOUBLEDAY & COMPANY, INC.
GARDEN CITY, NEW YORK

Editor's Note

Two forms of transliteration from Cyrillic to Greco-Roman lettering appear in the text which follows. Russian words appearing in the text of the chapters are transliterated using the common journalistic form of sound transliteration. In the notes to each chapter, Russian words appear using the Library of Congress transliteration system, which is more frequently utilized by scholars.

Library of Congress Cataloging in Publication Data
Voslenskiĭ, M. S.
   Nomenklatura.
     1. Government executives—Soviet Union. 2. Elite
(Social sciences)—Soviet Union. 3. Civil service—
Soviet Union. 4. Social classes—Soviet Union.
I. Title.
JN6549.E9V6813   1984   305.5'24'0947

In memory of my father
Sergei Ivanovich Voslensky
and his indomitable love of liberty

Contents

Acknowledgments

Preface

1 A Concealed Class   1

2 A Ruling Class Is Born   14

3 Nomenklatura in the Driver's Seat   68

4 Exploiting Class   112

5 Privileged Class   178

6 The Dictatorship of the Nomenklatura   243

7 The Claim to World Hegemony   319

8 A Weakness of the Nomenklatura:
   Change at the Top   356

9 Parasitic Class   386

Conclusion   441

Index   445

Acknowledgments

Let me begin by expressing my great thanks to the individuals and institutions who helped me write this book and made its publication possible.

It is with deep gratitude that I think of Dr. Gustav W. Heinemann, President of the German Federal Republic, Frau Hilda Heinemann, his wife, and Dr. Walter Wodak, Secretary-General of the Austrian Foreign Ministry, all three of whom are dead, alas. My heartfelt thanks go to Professor Carl-Friedrich von Weizsäcker, the founder and head of the Max Plank Institute at Starnberg, where I wrote this book; they go also to Herr Walter Hesselbach and Countess Marion Dönhoff.

Preface

Voslensky's *Nomenklatura* belongs to the very rare books that need not wait to join the treasury of political reflections. Its time is right now, both due to its actuality and to its extraordinary qualities.

First of all, the book is well and perspicuously created. Step by step it guides the reader into special sectors of the Soviet system without losing sight of the system as a whole. The final picture develops successively, by itself, so to speak.

As a starting point, Voslensky offers the thesis: Even with the revolution in the Soviet Union, through the party a monopolistic privileged stratum was established, which through various phases of development has fortified and legalized its position. This stratum, which not only separated itself from society, from the people, and from the rest of the world, but also inwardly established hierarchical ranks and barriers—this is the Nomenklatura.

Other writers have called it "partyocracy," a "caste," the "new class," the "political bureaucracy" or "party bureaucracy." All refer to the same presence. No doubt the term "nomenklatura" is justified if one refers to the established hierarchical régime within the Soviet bureaucracy, the party bureaucracy, and the bureaucracies concomitant therewith.

Voslensky develops this thesis in detail, historically, statistically, theoretically, and on the basis of personal experience. He presents a comprehensive and complete picture of the Soviet system—a picture that is exhaustive, meticulous and well informed, one of the most complete, if not the most complete ever. In any case, it is the most up-to-date picture of the Soviet system, and therefore—in the light of the tense international situation—very instructive.

The book has special value due to its analytic quality and due to the objective, though not totally disengaged, spirit with which it is leavened. Voslensky does not hate, he does not accuse; even less does he curse or predict.

He describes and analyzes, simply, clearly, and in a documented manner. Voslensky is not driven by ideology or religion, but by realism and striving for the truth. Voslensky's *Nomenklatura* indisputably belongs to the best that has ever been written about the Soviet system.

Through its analytical and realistic manner, *Nomenklatura* gives cause for reflection and apprehension: *how* is the Soviet system constructed, *where* is it leading, and *what* dangers, particularly for Europe, does it bring in its train?

From the very beginning, the idea of power or dictatorship is innate to the Soviet system, in all its expressions. Lenin defines the state as a cudgel, an instrument for the creation of the new socialistic state and the "new socialist man."

This theory of course is based on Marx—on his doctrine of productive capacity and conditions as a foundation not only for the community but also for man and his existence. However, it digresses from Marx as it considers the revolution and the power—"the dictatorship of the proletariat"—as being the foundation of Marx's doctrine and not the abolition of inhuman, debasing, and depressing conditions.

With the principle of power as foundation of everything in the society, and the legalization of violence (Lenin: the dictatorship is a power that is not limited by any laws whatsoever), it was not possible to establish a society that would not turn those in power—the party bureaucracy, the nomenklatura—into a privileged and monopolistic caste. Lenin surely thought it would only be a temporary form that would disappear when the state "withers away." Already in 1918 Lenin —in a conversation with a labor delegation—approved of the fact that party activists received extra rations of food.

So, together with the power, the privileges increased and the state showed no signs of "withering away"; on the contrary, it grew stronger. Even after the "encirclement from the outside" during Lenin's time, a long time ago, had ceased and the "developed socialist society" had been established, the privileges grew stronger.

Bureaucracy does not limit its own privileges, instead it increases them and strengthens its dominance. This in itself should be sufficient, time and again, to be the source of discontent, even if as a human community, human beings as they are can exist and develop only by being different, by finding new ideas and taking new initiatives.

From the start, the Soviet system showed an innate enmity—as well an ideological as a general enmity—both toward "alien" inner social groups and to the world at large, to other social orders and regimes. Contained in itself, the Soviet bureaucracy is negative toward everything, be it outside or inside occurrences, which are distinct from its own restricted ideology, from its pretensions, its provisos, and its practices.

The Soviet system, personified in the party bureaucracy, has no capacity to accept the idea of a world that would not be hostile. Through the system that it has created, the Soviet bureaucracy has condemned itself to thinking conspiratorial thoughts and to living in fear for its existence.

Those in power do not live in a real world; they do not even think of a real world, but a hostile world, convinced that everybody is out to get them; they trust no one, not even those who belong to their closest hierarchical circle.

Such a system cannot be economically productive, and that is not its aim; the objective of the system is the power and supremacy practiced by the leaders, i.e., the party's oligarchy. Actually the system is developed on misery and inactivity, and it is dependent on a power that in itself is privileged and a part of the ruling party: the ruling caste.

Naturally this does not mean that the Soviet bosses would strive to keep their country behind the times and the people ignorant and inactive. On the contrary, not even the leaders are totally void of good intentions. But they do only so much, and that means, in the best of instances, to "complete," to patch the existing state of affairs.

Under oppression and terror, the system has succeeded in achieving an industrial transformation—a process with all the insufficiencies of a superficial ideological and political planning, lacking coordination between the various branches of the economy. It has proved to be ineffective with regard to production, quality, and competition.

The system has no criteria for these characteristics, as it has "put an end" to the market, replacing it with administrative distribution. The system does not produce quality, but quantity only. The ruling class, the nomenklatura, is not interested in economic profitability but only in maintaining its power, its monopoly. For these reasons, what is produced is not of good quality, it is a production that contributes to fortifying and strengthening the position of power. No end to this is in sight.

Naturally it takes care—in order to protect its power from any eventual threat—that the people, the unprivileged, will get sufficient for their existence and for keeping their capacity for work. Nevertheless, inasmuch as this cannot be planned with exactness, even if its priority were high, in the Soviet Union a lack in distribution is unavoidable, as is the queueing in stores and, naturally, the special shops for the leading officials.

The Soviet system produces good quality only in weapons and war matériel, even if here, too, it is behind the Western powers, as the war in Lebanon has shown. The Soviet system brings about quality in weapons for reasons neglected in the rest of their production: weapons mean competition; weak and insufficient weaponry could threaten the power and thus the supremacy by the ruling caste.

Voslensky has not categorically defined the Soviet system. To me, it seems as if he has the conception that it is a form of state capitalism. No doubt there are state-capitalistic elements in the Soviet system. To me, it seems principally to be a kind of industrial feudalism. Be it that or be it something else, one single definition cannot explain the problem. In any case, Voslensky has analyzed the system in detail and given a brilliant description.

In step with establishing its postwar hegemony in Eastern Europe and in step with the strengthening of its military power according to plan—assuredly in this connection both plans and goals exist—the Soviet Union is occupied with carrying out a system of imperial relations and pressures. Most recently the preferred method—for instance in Eastern Europe—is being perpetrated by giving support to national party bureaucracies who guarantee that the control and the "leading role" will be in the hands of the Soviet bureaucracy.

In countries where the Soviet oligarchy is not able to exercise military control, more flexible methods are used, with "agreements" and indirect dependency—first of all military (examples: Cuba, Vietnam). The world is full of backwardness, violence, and plundering; revolutions are unavoidable. The Soviet Union carries on its expansion by supporting revolutions and making the revolutionary movements dependent on it for support, first of all armed support.

In this manner the Soviet influence is widened, as well as Soviet ties and pressures all over the world, particularly in undeveloped areas and among divested, desperate social groups. Internationalism and Communist ideology finally have been transformed into a cover-up for the Soviet state and the expansionism of the Soviet bureaucracy.

The Middle East with its oil fields and Europe with its industrial and scientific potentialities, the way I see it, have been targets for Soviet expansionism. These targets are not separated from each other. The aim is integrated: a Europe cut off from deliveries of oil and other raw material and through military pressures forced into a position of dependency.

The Soviet bosses are aware of their system's organic, and above all economic, lack of efficiency—and the strength of the competition. They cannot eliminate this organic weakness in any other way than by military dominance or, more exactly expressed, by exploitation, through military power, of developed areas. First of all Europe, as it is the "weakest link" in the West: hence the nuclear pressures and blackmailing.

The Western powers both in Europe and in the U.S.A. in my opinion have made fatal mistakes: the U.S.A. in that it has oriented its defense mainly on nuclear weapons, and abolished the compulsory draft system, and Europe in not having strengthened its independence, first of all militarily.

In the meantime, the Soviet Union has achieved nuclear balance, if not superiority. Inasmuch as the Soviet Union also is superior in conventional forces, Europe has been exposed to blackmail and threats, and the U.S.A. to unforeseen tensions and difficulties.

Finally I would like to join Voslensky in saying:

The Soviet system within itself has no important or promising powers of reform, and the dilatoriness and corruption drive it inexorably to expansion, particularly military expansion. A long time has gone by since the Soviet system ceased being a dilemma for critical, political thinking, yet the increase in the expansionistic power cannot be restrained, neither by nice words and good intentions nor by scholarly made and exact analyses in whatever manner these may be useful and necessary.

Milovan Djilas

The books of today are the deeds of tomorrow.
Thomas Mann

Nomenklatura

1
A Concealed Class

This division of society into classes must always be clearly borne in
mind as a fundamental fact of history.
Lenin, *Collected Works,* Vol. 29, p. 475

1. WHAT IS THIS BOOK ABOUT?

What does the Latin word *nomenclatura* mean in the Soviet Union?
The third and latest edition of the Great Soviet Encyclopedia defines it
as follows: "Nomenklatura (Lat. *nomenclatura:* list, index of names). 1.
System (totality) of technical terms and phrases used in a particular
field of science, technology, etc.; 2. System of conventional signs that
constitute the most convenient way of designating certain things."[1]
The encyclopedia goes on to mention the use of the term in connection with various sciences: Is this, then, a book about these sciences?
No. It is about a historical and political phenomenon.

The Soviet Historical Encyclopedia contains entries for *nom* and
nomokanon, but not for *nomenklatura.* It is also absent from the Soviet
Political Dictionary.[2]

Another, not scientific meaning of the term can be found in the
editions of *Administrative Management* of 1964, 1968, and 1971. After
these mentions, the catchword disappeared. The entry stated:
"Nomenklatura. List of positions whose ranks are confirmed by higher
authorities."[3] This entry does not reveal much, since it does not specify
which higher authorities are involved. It is obvious that all positions are
filled on the authorization of higher and not lower authorities. Also
established is that the term "nomenklatura" is used from time to time
in Soviet publications pertaining to the party. The discrepancy between
the political meaning of the "nomenklatura" phenomenon in the Soviet Union and the unusually rare use of the term reveals clearly that
the leadership of the U.S.S.R. wants to reveal as little information as
possible about the nomenklatura. In this they are successful: in the

early 1970s the soviet neological dictionary defined "nomenklatura as a verbal formulation of the 1960s."[4] In reality the concept was about fifty years old. One can find the definition of the nomenklatura in *Structure of the Party*, the manual for party functionaries and students at the party schools and the Marxist-Leninist universities: "The nomenklatura is a list of the highest positions; the candidates for these positions are examined by the various party committees, recommended and confirmed. These nomenklatura party committee members can be relieved of their positions only by authorization of their committees. Persons elevated to the nomenklatura are those in key positions."[5] The previously mentioned neological dictionary emphasizes that the lists of positions and "the functionaries who occupy them" of the nomenklatura are to be described.[6] Thus the concept "nomenklatura" covers not only the list of key positions but also the functionaries who serve in them.

Academician Sakharov writes:

Although the appropriate sociological studies either have not been carried out in our country, or have been classified as secret, it may be affirmed that as early as the 1920's and 30's—and definitively in the postwar years —a special Party-bureaucratic stratum was formed and could be discerned. This is the *nomenklatura*, as its members call themselves; or the "new class," as Milovan Djilas has named them.[7]

Is this book about that new class? Yes. The book is about the "new class," the cornerstone of the system of so-called real socialism. A nonantagonistic society? Official Soviet handbooks describe that system as follows: two classes between whom friendly relations prevail, the working class and the kolkhoz peasantry, as well as an intermediate social stratum, the intelligentsia. There are no class antagonisms and no class struggle in this society. The dictatorship of the proletariat proclaimed after the October Revolution, in 1917, accomplished its historic mission and transformed itself into a state of all people. The Soviet Union is now at the stage of developed socialism and is firmly advancing along the path leading to the Communist classless society.

Is that the real situation?

The Program of the Communist Party of the Soviet Union (CPSU) contains a solemn assurance that the classless society would in all essentials have been attained in the U.S.S.R. by 1980. In reality, not only was it not attained, but Brezhnev himself declared that the period of "developed socialism" is to continue for a long time to come. The Twenty-sixth Party Congress decided to "amend" the Program. Maybe the Program's promise was Khrushchev's error? No, the unfulfilled promise dates back to Lenin, who announced at the second Komsomol (Communist youth) congress, in 1920, that those who were then fifteen would undoubtedly live and work in a Communist age. Those same fifteen-year-olds celebrated their seventy-fifth birthdays in 1980. It is hardly worth mentioning that to Marx and Engels it would have been inconceivable that communism would not yet have been established sixty-six years after the triumph of the proletarian revolution.

The "developed socialism" is hardly better off than the "march toward communism." The concept of developed socialism is not to be found in Marx or Lenin; there are many non-Soviet Communists who consider that "real socialism" as it exists in the Soviet Union is primitive and undeveloped. Only the open enemies of socialism agree that the Soviet Union is a developed socialist society.

As for the "state of all people," Marxism rejects that idea with especial vigor. Engels regarded it as sheer nonsense. Lenin added that "a 'people's state' is as much an absurdity and as much a departure from socialism as the 'free people's state.' "[8]

> every state is a "special force" for the suppression of the oppressed class. Consequently, *every* state is *not* "free" and *not* a "people's state."[9]

Marxism regards any kind of state as an apparatus of the ruling class that exists for the purpose of repressing the other social classes. This idea underlies Marx and Engels's belief that with the advent of the classless society the state will wither away: when there is no more class rule, the state cannot but disappear.

Strangely enough, in the Soviet Union it is not disappearing. On the contrary, there is no country in the West or in the Third World that has a state machine as powerful as that of the U.S.S.R. and the other countries of "real socialism."

What does the growth of the power of the state in the Soviet Union reveal? From the Marxist standpoint, the only possible answer was given by Lenin, who wrote, "The state is a product and a manifestation of the *irreconcilability* of class antagonism."[10]

The power of the Soviet state demonstrates the existence of irreconcilable contradictions in Soviet society. Yet why do the antagonisms arise? In reality the present class friction in the Soviet Union is not between workers and peasants; on the contrary, these two classes are growing closer to each other, both in conditions of work and in standards of living. This means that a third class exists in Soviet society: the not officially mentioned new class.

2. DJILAS AND THE "NEW CLASS"

The "new class" is a phrase often used by Lenin: "The dictatorship of the proletariat means a most determined and most ruthless war waged by the *new class* against a *more powerful* enemy, the bourgeoisie."[11] In one of the last things he wrote, in August 1921, he says, "Everybody knows that the October Revolution actually brought new forces, a *new class*, to the forefront."[12]

The New Class is the title that Milovan Djilas, the Yugoslav political leader and writer, gave to the book in which he analyzes the problem of the ruling elite in socialist society. His career provided him with unique experience. Not only did he belong to this elite for many years, but he was even a member of the Politburo of the Central Committee, the holy of holies of every Communist Party. "I have travelled . . . the entire road open to a communist: from the lowest to the highest rung of the hierarchical ladder, from local and national to international forums, and from the formation of a true communist party and the organisation of a revolution to the establishment of the so-called socialist society," he writes.[13]

His theory can be summed up as follows: After the victory of the socialist revolution, the Communist Party apparatus turns into a new governing class. It monopolizes the power in the country and appropriates all its wealth under the slogan of "nationalization." By appropriating all the means of production, this new class becomes an exploiting class, tramples down all morality, and establishes its dictatorship by terror and total ideological control. As soon as they achieve power, those who fought hardest for the revolutionary ideal and the greatest liberties turn into reactionaries. The only factor to the credit of the new class is the raising of the economic level of underdeveloped countries by massive industrialization and a general improvement of the cultural level. But its economic system is characterized by enormous waste and its culture is indistinguishable from political propaganda. "When the new class leaves the historical scene—and this must happen—there will be less sorrow over its passing than there was for any other class before it," Djilas concludes.[14]

His book has certain peculiar features. It is based solely on Yugoslav experience, and Yugoslavia is not a typical "real socialist" country. Nevertheless Djilas' book suggests a critical analysis of the elite in socialist societies.

3. SOVIET RULING CLASS EXISTS

Djilas was the first to devote a book to the subject, but the question whether the new social stratum emerging in the Soviet Union was not a new ruling class was raised as early as the twenties.

I. Z. Steinberg, a left-wing social revolutionary who was People's Commissar for Justice in Lenin's first government, described the rulers and the ruled in Soviet Russia as follows: "On the one hand there is intoxication with power, unpenalized arrogance, contempt for humanity, and petty malice, small-minded vengefulness and sectarian mistrust, ever-increasing contempt for subordinates, in a word, a new tyranny. On the other there is despondency, anxiety, fear of reprisals, impotent anger, silent hate, sycophancy, continual deception of one's superiors. The result is two new classes divided by a profound social and psychological gulf."[15]

Statements of the same type soon appeared from other political camps. In the thirties, Hermann Pörzgen, Moscow correspondent of the *Frankfurter Zeitung,* referred to the "privileged new social grouping that now governs in the U.S.S.R."[16]

During the same period, the Russian philosopher Nicholas Berdyaev, then an *émigré,* wrote: "The dictatorship of the proletariat, reinforced by the power of the state, develops a huge bureaucracy that holds the whole country as in a spider's web and subjects everything to itself. This new Soviet bureaucracy, which is stronger than the czarist bureaucracy, is the new privileged class that is able horribly to exploit the popular masses. That is precisely what is happening."[17]

In 1946 George Orwell published *Animal Farm*, in which he describes the birth of a "real socialist" society in allegorical form. Animals carry out a revolution against the human beings (not seen through rose-tinted spectacles, either) and take over management of the farm. But the animals' republic soon succumbs to the domination of the pigs and their cruel guard dogs. The animals are forced to carry out the heaviest labor to fulfill the plan laid down by the pigs, who proclaim that they are no longer working for human beings, but for themselves. Meanwhile the pigs have assumed ownership of the farm. The dispossessed human beings note enviously that "the lower animals on Animal Farm did more work and received less food than any animals in the county."[18]

Orwell's story was banned in Communist countries, as was his novel *Nineteen Eighty-four.* In the latter, the society is divided into three classes: the inner party, i.e., the party apparatus that has become the ruling class; the outer party, i.e., the intellectuals subordinate to it; and finally the proles, the class lowest in the social scale.

Some advocates of world revolution are no less virulent in their criticism than are bourgeois authors. Trotsky drew attention to the bureaucratization of the party apparatus and pointed out that instead of the dictatorship of the proletariat a "dictatorship over the proletariat" prevailed.[19] After his murder, by an emissary of the NKVD, his followers continued their analysis of Soviet society. Ernest Mandel describes it as "a degenerate bureaucratic society"[20] and claims that the bureaucracy deprived the workers of their political power as early as the twenties and rapidly developed into a privileged social group. But the Trotskyists do not consider the bureaucracy to be a class.[21] The Italian Marxist Bruno Rizzi criticizes them for this.[22]

The existence of the dominant bureaucracy in the Soviet Union was known in the West long before the publication of Djilas's book, but was not universally accepted. Some authors hesitate to use the term "class"; they prefer to speak of a "caste" or "governing elite." Others take a different view of its composition, associating the intellectuals with it.[23]

In the West the idea that the controlling group in the Soviet Union includes the intellectual class as a whole has actually found its way into schoolbooks. "Instead of the promised classless society, it is claimed, three clearly distinguishable social strata formed in the Soviet Union. Above the peasants and workers there arose a new leading group that is better paid and better fed. It is marked off from the rest of the population by its technical and university education, and it seeks to ensure the latter for its children. This 'new class' is numerically preponderant in the leading positions in party and state, in the economy, and in the cultural sector. Its numbers have increased sixfold since 1926; according to the latest statistics the intelligentsia is fifteen million strong. It has greater and greater influence on developments in the party and the state; Brezhnev and Kosygin are products of this social group."[24]

The view that the leading social group in the Soviet Union does not include the whole of the intelligentsia is of course also to be found in Western literature. The Italian Antonio Carlo regards "the central political bureaucracy" as the leading class.[25]

This view is largely shared by Soviet émigré authors, including G. F. Akhminov[26] and Jacob Sher.[27] According to Roman Redlich, the "Soviet nobility" created by Stalin has been transformed into "a new ruling class" that controls "the levers of power in the state and in production."[28]

Dimitry Panin, who was a camp companion of Solzhenitsyn's and is now an émigré, writes that "the new oppressors" are "the class of the highest party officials." Those "who share power in all departments of the administration" are also members of it, as well as army and KGB officers, managers and senior staff in the major economic sectors, and party officials on regional committees.[29]

In the socialist countries a great deal has also been written, both legally and illegally, about the new ruling class.

Two young assistants at Warsaw University, now well known because of the part they played in Solidarity, Jacek Kurón and Karol Modzelewski, examined various questions connected with the economic foundations of real socialism in the sixties.[30] They, too, had firsthand experience of the new class, though this was less extensive than Djilas's. Kurón was a member of the committee of the Socialist Youth association in Warsaw University, Modzelewski was the son of a Polish Foreign Minister, and both were members of the party. Both in terminology and method of presentation their work strictly conformed with Marxist models. They did for Poland what Djilas had done for Yugoslavia, and sought to demonstrate the existence of a new ruling class, which they described as "the central political bureaucracy."

The Yugoslav philosopher Svetozar Stoyanovič claims that a "ruling state class" has come into existence in the Soviet Union.[31]

The Czech Ota Šik, who was Economics Minister under Dubček and is now a professor of economics in Switzerland, accepts Djilas's analysis: "The party bureaucracy has become the only dominant social class in countries in which state monopoly prevails."[32]

The East German Rudolf Bahro writes that "the last remnants of the illusion that these political and administrative bureaucrats are merely superficially bureaucratized or commissaried Communists should finally be dropped. . . . Bureaucracy has become the natural political way of life, as it were, of a large group of people with marked special interests. . . . This social group essentially includes the holders of the principal positions in the whole political, state, and social power pyramid. . . . From the politico-economic point of view its interests . . . are opposed to those of the primary producers."[33] Bahro insists that the party leadership "works for the consolidation and perpetuation of this late class society of ours."[34] The Chinese Communist press often stigmatized "the handful of neo-capitalist elements sitting on the neck of the Soviet people."[35]

As we see, the greater the inside knowledge of the authors, the more acutely do they raise the question of the ruling class in the Soviet Union. And what have Soviet citizens to say about it?

The *Program of the Democratic Movement of the Soviet Union*, established in 1969, states: "In the course of the past half century it is neither workers nor peasants nor intellectuals who have become the ruling class, but a fourth group: the new exploiting class that reigns autocratically and holds all the threads of power in its hands, their majesties the bureaucratic party elite."[36]

The *Leningrad Program*, which appeared in 1970 in samizdat (clandestine) form, states: "The party and state apparatus represents the one and only political force in the whole country. . . . We see before our eyes what the ruling class in our society really consists of."[37]

In his *Will the Soviet Union Survive until 1984?* Andrei Amalrik speaks of the "existence of a privileged bureaucratic class" and compares Soviet society to a "triple-decker sandwich of which the top layer is the bureaucracy."[38]

The same standpoint is to be found in the posthumous writings of Academician Evgheni S. Varga, a great personality of Comintern.[39] "There are ordinary employees, whether members of the party or not, who are not equipped with power, manage nothing and nobody, give no orders, and issue no legally enforceable decrees. And there are other employees who have power, manage factories, offices, and whole branches of the economy and sectors of political and cultural and ordinary life and ultimately the whole country, both its foreign and domestic affairs, and direct the governing and administrative activity of the whole party; they are persons who are able to give orders and issue instructions and decrees that have legally binding force. They are the ruling class in socialist society, who make the vital decisions that affect its whole life, and they enjoy the plenitude of power. The supreme power is exercised by the heads of the party bureaucracy, to whom all the levers of the party and government apparatus are subject."[40]

Boris V. Talantov, who became well known in the Soviet Union for his activity on behalf of freedom of religion and was persecuted accordingly, wrote in his *Soviet Society 1965–1968:* "A new governing class called the CPSU governs the country."[41]

The Truth About the Present, a samizdat publication that appeared under the pseudonym of R. Medvedev, refers to "the class that is the enemy of the people" that reigns over the Soviet Union.[42]

The author of the samizdat publication *To Speak Is Also to Act* recalls Bukharin's warning that "it is not to be excluded that social classes may transform themselves completely and that new classes may rise from their ruins."[43]

S. Razumny, author of another samizdat publication, writes: "The new governing class emerged from the higher echelons of the party management and in the course of the fifties spread to the middle grades of the bureaucracy."[44]

The journal *Sejatel (The Sower)* speaks about "the administrative class" ruling the Soviet Union.[45]

Reference to the new class is also made in samizdat publications that appear in the various Soviet republics. An *Appeal of the Communists of the Ukraine to the Communists of the whole world* (1964) speaks of the "dictatorship of the Central Committee that carries out all the wishes of the new governing class—the party bureaucracy."[46]

4. THE CONTROLLERS AND THE CONTROLLED

Are these voices of dissidents and of *émigrés* only? No. Even Soviet official sociology contains rare but significant hints of the existence of a special group in Soviet society. *Classes, Social Grades, and Groups in the U.S.S.R.* informs us that "the first thing that counts is the difference between organizers and organized. It is not intellectuals as a whole who have a special position in the organization of socialist labor, but a certain number of persons who in the name of society, on its behalf and under its control, exercise organizing functions in production and all other spheres of social life."[47] This idea is further defined in *The Structure of the Soviet Intelligentsia*, which explains that "to the intelligentsia, or more exactly to one of the sections of which it consists, administration is a special form of professional activity. By reason of its nature and social significance, the work of administration puts intellectuals whose job it is in a special position in relation to those who carry out tasks."[48]

Soviet literature significantly refers to this mysterious "section" of the intelligentsia and those subordinate to it as the controlled and the controllers.[49] Note that the former are only a section of the intelligentsia, while the latter are the rest of the Soviet population.

What are these "controllers" if considered from the Marxist-Leninist standpoint?

Lenin formulates the following definition of class: "Classes are large groups of people differing from each other by the place they occupy in a historically determined system of social production, by their relation (in most cases fixed and formulated in law) to the means of production, by their role in the social organisation of labour, and, consequently, by the dimensions of the share of social wealth of which they dispose and the mode of acquiring it. Classes are groups of people one of which can appropriate the labour of another owing to the different places they occupy in a definite system of social economy."[50]

Every point of this definition fully applies to the group of the "controllers" in Soviet society.

The controllers unquestionably form a large group distinct from everyone else, due to their place in a historically determined system of social production and their role in the social organization of labor. Naturally their share in social wealth and their way of securing it is also different. In other words, these administrators completely comply with Lenin's definition of a class. And because this class plays the leading role in Soviet production and all other fields of social life, it is the ruling class, and the one by which all other classes are oppressed—whence comes our class antagonism. This is the truth about Soviet society.

It is precisely by applying Marxist-Leninist criteria that the "controllers" are seen to be a ruling class. And what other criteria should be applied to the Soviet Union pretending to follow the Marxist path? That is why we shall use Marxist categories in this book; the Marxist analysis, the class approach to the phenomena of social life should not stop at the frontiers of the Soviet Union.

The long, self-sacrificing struggle of Marxist revolutionaries, the revolution, the civil war, the physical extermination of whole classes of society, the unparalleled efforts and the innumerable sacrifices—all in the name of a just, classless society devoid of class antagonism—led ultimately to the establishment of a new antagonistic class society. The previous ruling class of property owners in Russia was succeeded by a new ruling class. The society of real socialism in the Soviet Union is no exception in the history of mankind—it is antagonistic, like all earlier class societies.

As in all real socialist countries, a great deal in the Soviet Union is kept secret. There are state secrets, party secrets, military, economic, and other secrets. But the biggest and most basic secret of all is this: the antagonistic structure of the real socialist society. Everything else is merely part and parcel of that secret, the labyrinth, through which we shall now try to find our way.

NOTES

1. *Bol'šaja Sovetskaja Enciklopedija*, 3rd Ed., Vol. 18, p. 95.
2. *Politicheskij Slovar'*, Moscow, 1958.
3. Kratkij političeskij slovar'. Moscow, 1964, 1968, 1971.
4. Novyje slova i značenija. Slovar'-spravočnik po materialam pressy i literatury 60-ch godov. Moscow, 1971, S. 320
5. Partijnoje stroitel 'stvo. Učebnoje posobije. Moscow, 1981, S. 300.
6. Novyje slova i značenija, S. 320.
7. Andrei D. Sakharov, *My country and the world*. New York, 1976, p. 25.
8. Lenin, *Collected Works*, Moscow, 1963–70, Vol. 25, p. 441.
9. Ibid., p. 398.

10. Ibid., p. 387.
11. Ibid., Vol. 31, pp. 23–24.
12. Ibid., Vol. 33, p. 26.
13. Milovan Djilas, *The New Class*, London, 1946, p. 14.
14. Ibid., p. 72.
15. I. Z. Steinberg, *Nravstvennyj lik revoljucii*, Berlin, 1932, quoted from P. Miljukov, *Rossija na perelome*, Vol. 1, Paris, 1927, p. 191.
16. Hermann Pörzgen, *Ein Land ohne Gott*, Frankfurt, 1936, p. 69.
17. N. Berdyaev, *Istočniki i smysl russkogo kommunizma*, Paris, 1955, p. 105.
18. George Orwell, *Animal Farm*, Penguin, London, 1972, p. 117.
19. Leo Trotsky, *The Revolution Betrayed*, New York, 1937.
20. Ernest Mandel, *Über die Demokratie*, Hamburg, p. 52.
21. *Sozialwissenschaftliche Information für Unterricht und Studium*, 173, No. 1.
22. Bruno Rizzi, *Il collettivismo burocratico*, Imola, 1967.
23. V. V. Kurski, "Class Stratification in the Soviet Union," *Foreign Affairs*, New York, 1953, No. 1, p. 145; Barrington Moore, *Soviet Politics: The Dilemma of Power*, Cambridge, Mass., 1951, p. 280f.
24. *Kletts geschichtliches Unterrichtswerk für die Mittelklassen*, Vol. 4, Stuttgart, 1970, p. 149.
25. Antonio Carlo, *Politische und ökonomische Struktur der UdSSR (1917–1975). Diktatur des Proletariats oder bürokratischer Kollektivismus*, West Berlin, 1972, p. 75.
26. G. F. Akhminov, *Die Macht im Hintergrund*, Grenchen, 1950. *Die Totengräber des Kommunismus. Eine Soziologie der bolschewistischen Revolution*, Stuttgart, 1964.
27. Jakob Sher, *Kuda idti?* (Kniga dlja tekh, kto khotčet izmenit'mir), Paris, 1970.
28. Roman Redlich, *Sovetskoe obščestvo*, Frankfurt, 1972, p. 89.
29. Dimitrii Panin, *O revolucii v SSSR. O prirode ekspluatacij*, Frankfurt, 1973, p. 7.
30. Jacek Kurón and Karol Modzelewski, *Monopolsozialismus*, Hamburg, 1969.
31. Svetozar Stoianović, *Kritik und Zukunft des Sozialismus*, München, 1970, pp. 52–53.
32. Ota Šik, *Das kommunistische Machtsystem*, Hamburg, 1976, pp. 257, 259.
33. Rudolf Bahro, *Die Alternative. Zur Kritik des real existierenden Sozialismus*, Cologne and Frankfurt, 1977, pp. 283–84.
34. Ibid., p. 285.
35. *Nieder mit den neuen Zaren!* Peking, 1969, p. 30.
36. *Programma Demokratitcheskogo dviženija Sovetskogo Sojuza*, Amsterdam, 1970, p. 69.
37. S. Zorin and N. Alexeyev, *Vremja ne ždet. Naša strana nakho-ditsia na povorotnom punkte istorii*, Frankfurt, 1970, pp. 8, 10.
38. Andrei Amalrik, *Will the Soviet Union survive until 1984?*, London, 1970, New York, 1976, pp. 43, 40.
39. In spite of official denials extorted from the Varga family, there is every reason to believe that this document is genuine.
40. *Grani*, 1968, No. 69, p. 138.
41. *Posev*, 1969, No. 9, p. 36.
42. Ibid., 1970, No. 1, p. 40.
43. Quoted from Roy Medvedev, *Sowjetbürger in Opposition. Plädoyer für eine sozialistische Demokratie*, Hamburg, 1973, p. 290.
44. Archiv Samizdata (henceforward referred to as AS), No. 370, p. 4.
45. AS No. 1139, p. 16.

46. AS No. 912.
47. Klassy, socialnye sloi i gruppy v SSSR, Moscow, 1968, p. 147.
48. Struktura sovetskoj intelligencii, Minsk, 1970, p. 155.
49. Problemy izmenenia socialnoi struktury sovetskogo obščestva, Moscow, 1968, p. 122.
50. Lenin: *Collected Works*, Vol. 29, p. 421.

2

A Ruling Class Is Born

The sun of freedom shone on us through the clouds,
And Lenin the Great illumined our path.
Then Stalin raised us, Patriots without doubts,
Inspired us to toil and to heroic wrath.
                    Soviet national anthem (pre-1977 version)

Every Soviet history student is taught that the formation of classes is a slow and laborious process. The course on the history of primitive society, which is merely a paraphrase of Engels's *The Origin of the Family, Private Property, and the State*, deals at length with the withering away of the primitive community, beginning with the patriarchate and lasting for thousands of years. The appearance of classes is presented as a phenomenon extremely remote from the present. We who were at school in 1936–38, the bloody years of the great Stalin purge—how could we appreciate that we were nothing more than the terrified witnesses of the birth of a new ruling class?

1. THE PRACTICAL PURPOSE

All the books on the history of the CPSU begin by mentioning the first Marxist organization in Russia, the Emancipation of Labor group, which was founded in 1883 and which translated Marx into Russian and disseminated his and Engels's ideas. It consisted of a few persons only, but their names are engraved in letters of gold in the history of the Russian labor movement. They were G. V. Plekhanov, P. B. Axelrod, V. J. Zasulich, V. N. Ignatov, and L. G. Deutsch.

Chance willed it that in my school days I met Lev Grigorievich Deutsch, who was then nearly eighty, and I often went to see him. My grandfather was an engineer in the Siberian railway administration and helped Deutsch when he was a deportee in the eighties. Not without risk to himself, he found him work, with the result that Deutsch became greatly attached to our family. The result was that I was able to rouse the bitter envy of my schoolfellows by going to see a man who had known Engels. Lev Grigorievich kept up a vast correspondence with various countries and, not content with giving me exotic stamps, talked to me about the past. In his tiny, two-room flat in the House of the Veterans of the Revolution,[1] he used to talk to me about the early days of the Russian social democratic movement. After my compulsory diet of official history at school, I was delighted by his stories, in which Lenin, Plekhanov, and Trotsky were live human beings with human characteristics, moods, weaknesses, doubts, and hesitations instead of the dismal stereotypes in which the first was invariably the great leader, the second an opportunist, and the third a traitor. It was thus that the atmosphere of the early years of the Russian Marxist movement reached me through half a century.

Listening to Deutsch, I began to appreciate the great problem of the Russian Marxists of the time, namely, the extreme backwardness of the country in relation to the rest of Europe. The heart of the problem was that Russia, which had just taken the first steps along the capitalist path, could not advance to the postcapitalist phase in a single leap.

"You and your friends, Misha, would like to be airmen or arctic explorers," he said, "but with the best will in the world it is impossible, because you are still children, and you can no more skip your age than I, unfortunately, can become a schoolboy again. It is not we who determine the various stages of our life, it is those various stages that determine us. And that is true not only of individual human beings, it also applies to human beings in general, to human society. Could Russia, or any other country at the same stage of social development, by a mere act of will take a single leap that would put it ahead of the most advanced countries? Marx said it could not, and it was obvious. That was the problem that we Russian Marxists were faced with at that time. Do they tell you about that at school?" No, they did not. They briefly mentioned that opportunist allies of the bourgeoisie had propagated the dirty slander that Russia allegedly was not ripe for the proletarian revolution, but that the loyal Marxist Lenin had unmasked the opportunists' game. It did not occur to us that Marx himself was the first of those opportunists.

To a Russian Marxist who was totally convinced of the correctness of Marx's theories and did not try to twist them to his own advantage, the problem was acute.

Russia at that time had several things in common with Russia of the present day. It was a huge empire, with a huge police apparatus, strong traditions, and an oppressed population. How were the revolutionaries to overthrow that colossus? On what were they to base themselves? The Narodniki, the populists, put their hopes on the peasantry, who disappointed them. They turned to terrorism and got rid of a number of individuals, but not of the system. Then it was learned that in distant, industrialized Britain, Marx and Engels had declared the working class to be the only revolutionary force. But Britain was an advanced industrialized country, in complete contrast to Russia, which had no real proletariat, but only a few workers who had hardly emerged from the peasant world. So what were the Russian Marxists to do? All they could do was to spread Marx's and Engels's ideas, educate the workers, gradually prepare them for future struggles, and wait. . . . It was of course not easy to reconcile oneself to the idea of awaiting the natural unfolding of a historical process. Historically, the wait might be short; individually, one lifetime would not be enough. It was painful to realize that one would not live long enough to see the commune of St. Petersburg and the classless society in Russia.

But there could be no accelerating the laws discovered by Marx. He warned the impatient in the Preface to his *Critique of Political Economy:* "No social order ever perishes before all the productive forces for which there is room in it have developed."[2]

Revolution was not something that could be organized; a social revolution could not result from a conspiracy or a seizure of power. It was not the affair of a single class, still less of a single party. "Communists know only too well," Engels wrote, "that all conspiracies are not only futile but even harmful. They know only too well that revolutions are not made deliberately and arbitrarily, but that everywhere and at all times they have been the necessary outcome of circumstances entirely independent of the will and the leadership of particular parties and entire classes."[3]

The proletarian revolution would not begin in Russia or her East

European neighbors. Engels noted that in Russia, Poland, and Hungary medieval serfdom still survived.[4] The proletarian revolution would take place in the "civilized countries": Britain, the United States, France, and Germany. The speed with which it occurred would depend on the degree of development of each of those countries, "according to whether the country has a more developed industry, more wealth, and a more considerable mass of productive forces. And even if the proletarian revolution were successful in those countries, it would not spread to the backward countries, but "will merely provoke a significant reaction and greatly accelerate their previous manner of development."[5]

If the ideas of the young Marx and Engels corresponded to the requirements of the most radical section of Western European youth on the eve of 1848, all they had to offer the Russian revolutionaries, disillusioned with the peasantry and the failure of individual terrorism, was the prospect of a long wait. Such was the state of affairs when a young man from Simbirsk named Vladimir Ulyanov began to attract attention. He started his career as one of Plekhanov's numerous admirers. But it soon became evident that he was less interested in the logical consistency of Marxist theory than in political practice. He denied neither the truth nor the importance of Marxist theory; rather, he devoted himself with unprecedented polemical vigor to defending the purity of the Marxist doctrine. But to young Ulyanov the purpose of theoretical disputation was not the pursuit of truth, it was the discomfiture of political opponents. In 1923, looking back on his career when he felt his end approaching, he wrote: "The practical purpose was always important to me."[6] Those words can be said to be the key to the role of Lenin and Leninism in Russian history.

The practical purpose was to make the revolution in Russia, no matter whether material conditions for new production relations were present or not. The fact that Russia was backward and that its proletariat was still in its infancy, that the productive forces of Russian capitalism were far from exhausted, did not seem to him to be an obstacle. All that mattered was to make the revolution. The young Ulyanov wrote: "We think that an *independent* elaboration of Marx's theory is especially essential for Russian socialists; for this theory provides only general *guiding* principles, which, *in particular*, are applied in England differently than in France, in France differently than in Germany, and in Germany differently than in Russia."[7]

Why did Lenin become a Marxist? That is an unusual, even a sacrilegious question, but it is not devoid of interest. Lenin was not at all interested in Marxist theory until his eighteenth year, and then his interest in it was not whether it was sound or not. What mattered was that it could be used as the basis of a revolutionary ideology. To Lenin it was not a matter of principle, but a useful tool. Why was it an ideological tool more suitable than any other? Because it was the only theory that foresaw a *proletarian* revolution. The failure of the Narodniki had shown that the peasantry would not be the principal revolutionary force and, as the failure of the terrorists had demonstrated, a handful of revolutionary intellectuals could not possibly overthrow the czarist colossus. The only large class that could be counted on in Russia at that time was the proletariat, which at the beginning of the twentieth century was rapidly increasing in numbers. Because of its concentration in industry and the discipline imposed by severe working conditions, the working class was the social group best adapted for use as a battering ram against the existing order.

Millions of persons have solemnly filed past the bald, red-bearded little man in his mausoleum—a yellow mummy from which the brain has been extracted. A much more interesting subject for contemplation would be the brain, preserved at the Academy of Medical Sciences of the U.S.S.R., for it was in that substance of indefinite color and deep convolutions that, three quarters of a century ago, there was born an extraordinary plan that changed the face of the world.

2. "WHAT IS TO BE DONE?"

Lenin developed this plan in *What Is to Be Done?* He took the title from a book by Chernyshevsky that had been the bible of the Russian democrats in the 1860s—and this was a gesture of polemic against Chernyshevsky's ideas. Lenin insisted that a new age had dawned and that the task was no longer to devote oneself to popular education or the seeking out of heroic individuals. What was required now was totally different. Every single point he made was an unprecedented novelty in the political thought of the nineteenth century, Marxism included.

His first point was that Marxism must be transformed into dogma and that freedom of criticism must be dropped. Now, ever since the age of French rationalism, dogma had been considered reactionary and freedom of criticism progressive. The French Revolution and the revolutions of the century that followed had made that idea axiomatic, and at the end of the nineteenth century it was accepted as such by all shades of left-wing opinion. Imagine the sarcasm with which Marx and Engels would have denounced the reactionary nature of a ban on freedom of criticism.

In his chapter "Dogmatism and 'freedom of criticism,' " Lenin tackled the difficult task of defending in Marxist terms an idea that is in complete conflict with Marxist dialectics. According to the latter, there can of course be no standing still in any historical process; the old is displaced by the new, which grows old in its turn and is displaced by something better adapted to the age. But Lenin claimed to develop Marxist thought while congealing it into an infallible dogma that tolerated no criticism.

He knew that critical analysis of Marxism could be dangerous. Who could tell where it might lead? Lenin was well aware that half a century had passed since the publication of the *Communist Manifesto* and that, since the proletarian revolution that it announced was not in sight, Western Marxists were discreetly distancing themselves from it.

Now, Lenin was not a dogmatist, but an adroit pragmatist, even in the field of ideology; under the banner of the dogmatization of Marxism, he quietly subjected it to a radical revision, as is well illustrated by the second point in his plan. Marx formulated the basic principle of historical materialism in his Preface to *The Critique of Political Economy* in the following words: "It is not the consciousness of men that determines their being, but, on the contrary, their social being that determines their consciousness."

In flagrant contradiction with this principle Lenin states: "We have said that *there could not have been* Social-Democratic consciousness among the workers. It would have to be brought to them from without. The history of all countries shows that the working class, exclusively by its own effort, is able to develop only trade-union consciousness, i.e., the conviction that it is necessary to combine in unions, fight the employers, and strive to compel the government to pass necessary labor legislation, etc."[8]

In other words, in the absence of external stimulus the working class does not spontaneously turn to revolution.

Now, Lenin wanted revolution. So "scientific socialism"—i.e., Marxism transformed into unassailable dogma—must be taken to the workers, who, he claimed with a rather forced oversimplification, could not be expected to develop a theory of "scientific socialism" on their own. "The theory of socialism, however, grew out of the philosophic, historical, and economic theories elaborated by educated representatives of the propertied classes, by intellectuals. By their social status, the founders of modern scientific socialism, Marx and Engels, themselves belonged to the bourgeois intelligentsia."[9]

The argument does not ring true. Ideology, in the Marxist view, is not the product of an individual brain, but is developed by and embodied in a whole class and then formulated by an individual. From a Marxist point of view, can one imagine bourgeois ideology being created in the working class and taken to the bourgeoisie by workers? Obviously not. Nevertheless the idea of "introduction from the outside" was extraordinarily important to Lenin. As early as 1899 he wrote in relation to the party: "The task . . . is to bring definite socialist ideals to the spontaneous working-class movement, to connect this movement with socialist convictions that should attain the level of contemporary science, to connect it with the regular political struggle for democracy as a means of achieving socialism—in a word, to fuse this spontaneous movement into one indestructible whole with the activity of the *revolutionary party.*"[10] The sole purpose of "introduction from the outside" was to transform the workers' movement into a minor appendage of the party.

From the point of view of historical materialism, the idea of introduction from the outside does not stand up. Engels, who was also concerned with the question of the acquisition of consciousness by the working class, wrote in 1891: "To drive the possessing classes from the rudder, there must first be a change in the heads of the working masses such as is now—relatively slowly—taking place; to bring this about, we need a still faster pace in the change in methods of production, more machinery, more repression of workers, more ruin of peasants and petty bourgeoisie, more tangible and large-scale evidence of the inevitable consequences of modern big industry."[11]

That is the Marxist position on the question of working-class consciousness. The Leninist idea of introduction from the outside is completely different. Let us imagine the situation in practice.

Intellectuals, having transformed Marxism into an untouchable dogma, appear among the workers and say to them, Your standpoint is not that of your class. We intellectuals will now teach you what your class interests really are. What the workers are interested in and willing to fight for are higher wages and better working conditions. But that, the intellectuals explain, is trade unionism and a betrayal of working-class interests. Now, on which side does the betrayal really lie? Surely on that of the intellectuals, who are aiming at the seizure of power. Will they seize it in their own interests or in that of the workers?

Of course they assure the workers that they will do away with low wages and that they want power only for the sake of the working class and that, when they have it, milk and honey will flow. But if the workers have their wits about them, they will realize that any milk and honey available will not flow for them, but for the intellectuals. And as for the intellectuals, the poor wretches do not yet suspect that, after their victory, it will not be milk and honey, but their blood that will flow like water. But let us not anticipate.

The idea of introduction from the outside and of a fusion between the spontaneous workers' movement and socialism is anti-Marxist, but was a vital link in the chain of Lenin's argument; for if he succeeded in persuading the working class of its interest in supporting the handful of intellectuals, he would have at his disposal an army that could very well put him in power. In *What Is to Be Done?* Lenin frankly refers to the usability of the working class as shock troops for a seizure of power for the benefit of another social group, indicating that "The revolutionary path of the working-class movement might not be a Social Democratic path."[12]

In Lenin's view, a number of factors favored the carrying out of a plan of this kind in Russia. Russian capitalism was at the very outset of its development, and the workers were cruelly exploited, just as they had been in the initial stages of Western capitalism. Lenin realized that in these conditions the Russian proletariat was just as responsive to the idea of revolution.

The catastrophic cultural level of the Russian workers was in Lenin's eyes an additional asset. He wrote:

There is no other country so barbarous and in which the masses of the people are *robbed* to such an extent of education, light and knowledge— no other such country has remained in Europe; Russia is the exception.[13]

From this he concluded, in flat contradiction to Marx, that Russia was just the place for the proletarian revolution. Lack of popular education was no obstacle; instead, it would make it easier to suggest to the working class where its "interests" lay.

From Lenin's standpoint, turning Marxism into a dogma was valuable, "introduction from the outside" was indispensable, but the most important factor for a seizure of power was what is to follow.

3. TWO ORGANIZATIONS: PROFESSIONAL
REVOLUTIONARIES AND THE PARTY

Lenin said that the important thing in politics was to find the key link that would enable one to pull the whole chain. He believed that establishing an organization of professional revolutionaries would make it possible to pull it quickly. "Give us an organization of revolutionaries and we will overturn Russia,"[14] he said, paraphrasing Archimedes.

There had already been revolutionary organizations in Russia and elsewhere in the past, so where was the novelty? It lay in the idea of the *professional* revolutionary. That was the nub of Lenin's plan.

A terrorist organization, the Narodnaya Volya, which lived on funds provided by its supporters, already existed in Russia in the nineteenth century, but the overwhelming majority of revolutionaries were revolutionaries by inclination and not by profession. Lenin dismissed this as "amateurism." The place of these "amateurs of the revolution" must be taken by a team of professionals who would undertake all the preparations necessary for the revolution. Lenin obviously had no faith in personal conviction or selfless devotion to a cause. He believed that preparations for a revolution were possible only if the professional revolutionaries were totally subordinate to their leaders; he remained faithful to that principle to the end. At the Eleventh Party Congress, in 1922, he said:

History knows all sorts of metamorphoses. Relying on firmness of convictions, loyalty, and other splendid moral qualities is anything but a serious attitude in politics.[15]

Moreover, these professional revolutionaries were to be superior in rank to ordinary party members, who must be content with aiding and abetting them, for they were the experts. It was to be the duty of the latter to spread the Marxist dogma among the working class and to organize the masses and prepare them for the proletarian revolution.

Was the organization to consist of workers who had found the strength and the means to rise above their primitive condition, raise their heads, and study Marxism on their own account—even if it had congealed into dogma?

By no means. Though Lenin spoke of a proletarian revolution and of a dictatorship of the proletariat, he did not want the organization of professional revolutionaries to consist of workers.

In *What Is to Be Done?* he contrasts the organization of professional revolutionaries with the workers' organization. Workers were certainly to provide the membership of the latter. On the other hand, the organization of the revolutionaries must consist first and foremost of people who make revolutionary activity their profession (for which reason I speak of the organisation of *revolutionaries,* meaning revolutionary Social Democrats). In view of the common characteristic of the members of such an organisation, *all distinctions as between workers and intellectuals,* not to speak of distinctions of trade and profession, in both categories *must be effaced.*"[16] Moreover, a worker who joined the organization of professional revolutionaries should not remain a worker. Lenin made no bones about it: "A worker-agitator who is at all gifted and "promising" *must not be left* to work eleven hours a day in a factory. We must arrange that he be maintained by the party."[17]

So the "vanguard of the working class" was not to consist of workers. In Lenin's view, the organization that was to bring about the victory of the working class had no need to be a workers' organization.

Its internal structure was similarly paradoxical. Although it struggled for democracy, there was no reason why it should be democratically organized. "The only serious organizational principle for the active workers of our movement should be the strictest secrecy, the strictest selection of members, and the training of professional revolutionaries. Given these qualities, something even more than "democratism" would be guaranteed to us, namely, complete, comradely, mutual confidence among revolutionaries. . . . They have not the time to think about toy forms of democratism (democratism within a close and compact body of comrades in which complete, mutual confidence prevails), but they have a lively sense of their *responsibility,* knowing as they do from experience that an organization of real revolutionaries will stop at nothing to rid itself of an unworthy member."[18]

Thus there was no place for democracy in the revolutionary organization. On the contrary, it must be a kind of revolutionary mafia, in which everything was to be based on conspiracy and mutual trust. A mafioso considered unworthy by the organization, i.e., the management of the organization in the absence of any democracy, was to be liable to the death penalty. "The thing we need is a military organization of agents,"[19] Lenin frankly stated.

Members of the organization were to feel themselves bound by a kind of contract. "We are marching in a compact group along a precipitous and difficult path, firmly holding each other by the hand. We are surrounded on all sides by enemies, and we have to advance almost constantly under their fire. We have combined, by a freely adopted decision, for the purpose of fighting the enemy."[20]

Such lyrical outbursts did not solve the problem of money. Where were the professional revolutionaries' funds to come from?

In the official records of the party, complete silence prevails on that point. True, it was not an easy problem; none of the socialist states that nowadays finance revolutionary organizations in capitalist countries existed yet. Funds came from two sources, the first of which was "expropriation," i.e., bank robbery. Maxim Litvinov, a future Commissar for Foreign Affairs, was arrested abroad while trying to change money stolen from a Russian bank. Soon afterward, Leonid Krassin, a future Soviet diplomatic representative in London, began forging banknotes. Stalin turned out to be an excellent organizer of bank raids.

In 1910, however, the Central Committee decided that "expropriation" was no longer necessary. An alternative source of revenue had been discovered; it was donations. Where did they come from? The party was small, and not much money was to be raised from its members. The proletarian revolution was subsidized by capitalists. Official Soviet history gives little information about contributions to the party made by the millionaire Savva Morosov, or Maxim Gorky's activities in raising funds from Russian and foreign capitalists. A great deal has been written about the financing of the Nazi Party by German capitalists, which was regarded as evidence of collusion between capitalists and the Nazis. But it should certainly be possible to discover at least as much documentary evidence to show that the alleged party of the working class, the Bolshevik Party, was similarly financed by capitalists.

So much for the establishment of the organization of professional revolutionaries. Was that organization identical with the party? It was not. Lenin had other ideas.

The party was to be built up by means of a clandestine political newspaper to be circulated throughout Russia. Lenin discussed this in his article "Where to Begin?"[21] in March 1901. *Iskra (The Spark)*, printed abroad and smuggled into Russia, was to be not only a journal of agitation and propaganda, but also the expression of a central, coordinating will. It must make its readers clandestine members of the party scattered throughout the country, and it must support the work of the organization of professional revolutionaries.

The idea was psychologically sound: The mere fact of regularly reading a clandestine journal led the reader into opposition and plunged him into a group in which the ideas developed in *Iskra* automatically became a platform for action.

That, in Lenin's view, was how the party was to be born, and that in fact was how it was born. Lenin saw to it that it was a "party of a new type," highly organized and strictly led.

As we have already indicated, he did not believe that a revolutionary would really support the party unless he was paid. Also he did not believe that a member of the party would work effectively unless he was under permanent supervision by the party. He thought it highly improbable that anyone would do anything purely on principle. Hence his quarrel with L. Martov the leader of the left-wing Mensheviks. It led to the famous schism between Bolsheviks and Mensheviks at the second congress of the Russian Social Democratic Workers' Party. Martov and his followers wanted to admit to the party anyone willing to cooperate with it in any way, while Lenin and his followers were willing to grant membership only to those who belonged to the organization and were ready to work under its close control. It was an illegal party and the police were on its heels, which obviously required courage on the part of its members, but Lenin and the Bolsheviks favored the principle so well expressed by Yevtushenko:

> The basis of heroism,
> Control, control.

Control of the members of the party won over to the cause by *Iskra* became a task of the professional revolutionaries.

Two organizations came into existence in accordance with Lenin's plan: the organization of professional revolutionaries and the party subordinate to it. Not only did they work differently; their origin and their future differed too. Nevertheless they are referred to as "the party." They correspond exactly with what Orwell called the inner and outer parties in *Nineteen Eighty-four.*

The readers of *Iskra,* organized into a homogeneous organization, provided the nucleus of the future "new-type" party, a mass organization led with a rod of iron, which would carry out orders and acclaim its leaders. The organization of professional revolutionaries formed the nucleus of the future party apparatus.

4. EMBRYON OF A NEW CLASS

Was an organization of professional revolutionaries a good way of preparing the revolution?

If the object was to overthrow the existing order and seize power, the answer was yes. But if you believed that the proletarian revolution was a historical necessity, a dialectical leap from one kind of society to another; if the objective was the breaking of bonds, the bringing about of a change in production relations in favor of new productive forces; if you accepted the theory that this was the inevitable result of the class struggle, the answer was no. There was no place in the Marxist view of history for the classless mafia of professional revolutionaries.

It must be admitted that Lenin never claimed that his plan was a development of Marxist doctrine. He frankly admitted; ". . . the magnificent organisation that the revolutionaries had in the seventies . . .

should serve us as a model."[22] That model was the terrorist organization of the *narodovoltsy,* the populists.

Lenin continued: "The mistake the Narodnaya Volya committed was not in striving to enlist *all* the discontented in the organisation and to direct this organisation to resolute struggle against the autocracy; on the contrary, that was its great historical merit. The mistake was in relying on a theory which in substance was not a revolutionary theory at all, and the Narodnaya Volya members either did not know how, or were unable, to link their movement inseparably with the class struggle in the developing capitalist society."[23]

That argument is very instructive. Lenin was not in the least troubled by the fact that the *narodovoltsy* were not a class organization; their mistake, in his view, was failure to construct an appropriate ideology for turning the class struggle to their own advantage.

After considering all the aspects of Lenin's plan, let us sum up what he has to say about the relations between the professional revolutionaries and the working class.

The former represent the interests of the latter. What do these interests consist of? Not higher wages or an improvement in living and working conditions (which would be trade unionism), but the victory of the proletarian revolution. What was to be the result of that victory? Lenin says that the most important thing in a revolution is the question of power. After the revolution, power was to pass to the proletariat, represented by its vanguard, the nucleus of which was the organization of professional revolutionaries. So, if the latter came into power, they would claim that they represented the interests of the working class, on the pretext that their assumption of power was in the latter's interests.

Communist propaganda repeats Lenin's slogans *ad nauseam* that the party is the party of the working class and the vanguard that struggles for its interests. There has never been an ounce of truth in these slogans, and there never will be. As mentioned, neither the Leninist party as a whole nor its core of professional revolutionaries have ever been the vanguard or even a part of the working class.

To what class did this organization of professional revolutionaries belong? To none. From the outset, Lenin placed it outside the society of the time; it was to become an independent social organism obeying its own rules. Its sole role consisted of overthrowing the existing system of production and the existing social order.

Nevertheless, that small group had a very definite future. If the revolution that it was preparing was successful, it would automatically become an organization of professional rulers.

This was the embryo of a new ruling class.

The Bolsheviks later liked to repeat that the Russia of that time was pregnant with the revolution. It would be more exact to say that Russia was pregnant with a new ruling class that could gain power only by way of revolution.

5. THE DICTATORSHIP OF THE PROLETARIAT AND THE TRANSITION FROM THE BOURGEOIS TO THE SOCIALIST REVOLUTION

If Russia was pregnant with the revolution, the question was, What kind of revolution?

In *The Foundations of Leninism,* Stalin gives the answer: the bourgeois revolution,[24] i.e. the likes of which occurred in Germany in 1848, in France in 1789, and in England in 1643. Of these revolutions, bourgeois democracy was born—not immediately, but after periods of dictatorship of the Cromwellian or Napoleonic type, followed by periods of restoration and more revolution.

But neither in the event of a bourgeois revolution nor in that of a Romanov restoration would Lenin and his followers be able to take power, for there was no hope of persuading the bourgeoisie or the feudal aristocracy that only the Leninists were capable of governing the country.

To Lenin and his professional revolutionaries this problem was acute. The idea of revolution became more than ever bound up in Lenin's mind with that of the seizure of power by his professional revolutionaries. That is the meaning of the tirelessly repeated proposition that the most important thing in a revolution is the question of power. The only kind of revolution in which he was interested was one that would give power to him and his "vanguard of the working class."

How could Russia be made to give birth to a proletarian revolution when the revolution with which it was pregnant was antifeudal? Lenin made two attempts to find an ideological solution to that problem. The first, in 1905, was the theory of the "hegemony of the proletariat"; the second, in the spring of 1917, was that of the "transition from the bourgeois to the proletarian revolution."

With the former, Lenin tried to show that, in spite of opposite experiences in other countries, in a bourgeois revolution in Russia the bourgeoisie would be a counterrevolutionary force, because it would be afraid of the proletariat and where the revolution might lead. If that had been the case, the Russian bourgeoisie would have demonstrated singular perspicacity in anticipating a theory that Lenin put forward only in 1917.

His second theory was that the bourgeois revolution would lead, not to capitalism, but directly to the socialist revolution. This also conflicted with experience in other countries. Lenin's explanation of these two paradoxes, though confused, was categorical. He believed that that was how things were bound to happen in the epoch of imperialism.

That kind of argument is difficult to answer. But, from the Marxist standpoint, Lenin's two propositions were a complete aberration. It was natural that the proletariat should take part in the bourgeois revolution, for all revolutions are made by the popular masses. If Lenin had said that the proletariat would take an active part in the bourgeois revolution, it would have corresponded with reality. But what a strange bourgeois revolution, undertaken by the proletariat against the bourgeoisie! Why call it bourgeois? What did it have in common with a bourgeois revolution in the Marxist sense of the term?

These questions merely reveal the many contradictions in the Leninist theory of revolution. The most important characteristic of a revolution, according to Lenin, was the transfer of power from one class to another. In a proletarian revolution, power would be transferred to the proletariat. But in a bourgeois revolution, would it be transferred to the bourgeoisie? No, said Lenin, it would pass to the proletariat and the peasantry; it would be the dictatorship of the proletariat and the peasantry.

And what would the aim of a proletarian revolution be? If it were the dictatorship of the proletariat, the joint dictatorship of the proletariat and the peasantry would have to be superseded by that of the proletariat alone. So was the proletarian revolution to be directed not against the bourgeoisie but against the peasantry?

In short, Lenin's theory of the hegemony of the proletariat in the bourgeois revolution is hopelessly confused. The idea of transition from a bourgeois to a proletarian revolution is no less confused. In the first place, it is a complete departure from the "hegemony of the proletariat in the bourgeois revolution," since, according to this theory, it was the proletariat and not the bourgeoisie who would seize the state power after the overthrow of czarism. Thus it conflicts with Lenin's own theory. And from the Marxist point of view there is something even more surprising about this.

According to the theory of historical materialism, the bourgeois revolution takes place when the productive forces that have matured in feudal society break their intrinsic bonds. This is the opening of a new historical period in which the productive forces freely develop until they reach the limits set up by capitalist production relations. No "socialist consciousness" can affect the unfolding of this objective process.

In his preface to *Das Kapital*, Marx writes: "Even when a society has got upon the right track for the discovery of the natural laws of its movement . . . it can neither clear by bold leaps, nor remove by a legal enactment, the obstacles offered by the successive phases of its normal development."[25]

Thus, according to historical materialism, it is impossible to pass directly from the bourgeois to the socialist revolution, for in between there is necessarily a long process of growth and development of the productive forces. Passing straight from one to the other is as unthinkable as laying the foundations of a house and putting on the roof without first building the walls.

Lenin was of course perfectly well aware that from the point of view of Marxism his theory of the transition from one revolution to the other was an aberration. But he had nothing else to suggest. It was difficult to find a Marxist formula for his practical purpose that was so remote from Marxism. It does not mean that Lenin's ideas were illogical. But theirs was another, not Marxist, logic. The phrase "working class" when used by Lenin does not mean the proletariat, but merely the organization of professional revolutionaries. He states specifically: ". . . the hegemony of the working class is the political influence which that class (and its representatives) exercises upon other sections of the population."[26] The representatives are Lenin's professionals.

Starting from this premise, Lenin very logically laid the foundations for a maximum as well as a minimum program, as indeed he often did.

In the first event (hegemony of the proletariat), he assumed that he and his followers would undertake the leadership of the revolution and as a matter of course lay their hands on the controlling levers of the state in collaboration with representatives of the peasantry—as was inevitable in an antifeudal revolution ("revolutionary democratic dictatorship of the proletariat and the peasantry").

The minimum program ("transition from the bourgeois to the socialist revolution") was meant for a less favorable alternative course of events: should the Bolsheviks fail to seize power immediately after the fall of czarism, they would have to fight the new bourgeois government and seize the power of the state from it before it was firmly established.

Lenin's hope of establishing his party in power in any event was well understood by his power-hungry professional revolutionaries. Like Lenin himself, they cared little whether or not this ambition was consistent with the idea of the proletarian revolution as conceived by Marx and Engels.

It was of his maximum program, "the hegemony of the proletariat in the bourgeois revolution," that Lenin spoke most often. To what extent was it realized in practice?

6. REVOLUTION WITHOUT THE PARTY

Strange though it may seem, Lenin first learned about the February revolution from the Swiss newspapers. This is his first mention of it, in a letter to his dear friend Inès Armand:

> We here in Zurich are in a state of agitation today: there is a telegram in *Zürcher Post* and in *Neue Zürcher Zeitung* of March 15 that in Russia the revolution *was victorious* in Petrograd on March 14 after three days of struggle, that 12 members of the Duma are in power and the ministers *have all been arrested.*

The leader of the revolution mistrustfully added: "If the Germans are not lying, then it's true." But he quickly went on to cover himself by saying, "That Russia has for the past few days been *on the eve* of revolution is beyond doubt."[27]

In the last sentence he was bluffing. During "the past few days" he had received no news whatever about the situation in Russia. Two days before, on March 13, 1917, he had written to the same correspondent: "From Russia—nothing, not even letters!!!"[28] But he had had no news from Russia for weeks or even months. He was not even reading the Russian newspapers at that time. In September 1916 he wrote to his brother-in-law M. T. Elizarov, in Russia: "If you can, please send Russian newspapers once a week after you have read them, because I have none at all."[29] In November 1916 he wrote to his sister Maria Ilinichna, in Petrograd: "If it is not too much trouble send me three or four times a month the Russian newspapers after you have read them— tie them up tightly with string or they will get lost. I have no Russian newspapers here."[30]

For the "leader of the Russian proletariat," this was a rather primitive method of keeping in touch with the situation in Russia.

Whether the string was insufficient to protect them or whether they were not sent, the fact remains that in the months before the January revolution Lenin received no news from Russia. At the end of January he wrote, again to Inès Armand, saying that he had had a talk with two Russian soldiers who had escaped after a year in a prisoner-of-war camp in Germany, and how glad he was to have some recent information about the events in Russia.[31]

When Alexandra Kollontai asked him for instructions, he had to confess his lack of information. On March 17, 1917, he wrote to her as follows:

> Dear A.M.,
> I have just had your telegram, worded so that it sounds almost ironical (just imagine thinking about "directives" from here, when news is exceptionally meager, while in Petersburg there are probably not only effectively leading comrades of our Party, but also formally commissioned representatives of the Central Committee!).[32]

Actually this was wrong. The first member of the Central Committee of the Bolshevik Party to appear in Petrograd was Stalin, and he had no instructions. He arrived there a week after Lenin's letter.

Perhaps the most striking thing was not that Lenin had no idea what was happening in Russia, but that the revolution was totally unexpected by him. A reading of his works shows that he was taking an active interest at the time in the affairs of the Swiss Social Democrats; about that he was writing once or twice a day to Inès Armand.[33]

Lenin was also very interested in the labor movement in Scandinavia. On March 5, 1917, a week before the revolution, he wrote as follows from Zürich to Alexandra Kollontai, in Sweden:

Really, we must (all of us, the Left in Sweden and those who can get into touch with them) unite, bend every effort, help—for the moment in the life of the Swedish party, the Swedish *and Scandinavian* labour movement, is a *decisive* one.[34]

The *émigré* Lenin had obviously lost touch with what was happening in Russia; a slight increase in the pulse rate of peaceful Sweden sounded louder in his ears than the roar of the approaching revolutionary storm in Russia. He did not feel it coming. Six weeks before the February revolution in Russia he concluded his speech in a meeting of the Swiss Young Socialists with words that seemed to him stirring at the time but in retrospect are comic:

We of the older generation may not live to see the decisive battles of this coming revolution. But I can, I believe, express the confident hope that the youth which is working so splendidly in the socialist movement of Switzerland, and of the whole world, will be fortunate enough not only to fight, but also to win, in the coming proletarian revolution.[35]

That and many other things show that the February revolution was not organized by Lenin's party and, what is more, that the party, Lenin included, did not expect it. Those continually reiterated statements about the "hegemony of the proletariat in the bourgeois revolution" and the "leading role of the vanguard of the working class," the Bolshevik Party, turned out to be empty verbiage.

Lenin's idea that the bourgeoisie would be a counterrevolutionary force in the bourgeois revolution was not confirmed either. He later admitted that the success of the February revolution was to be attributed not only to the proletariat and the peasantry but also to the bourgeoisie. He added, "Hence the easy victory over tsarism."[36] It was to that, and not to the hegemony of the organization of professional revolutionaries, that victory was due.

Does this mean that that organization did not justify its existence? As an organizer of the antifeudal revolution, it failed completely. Neither the revolution of 1905 nor that of February 1917 was launched by the organization of professional revolutionaries. In 1905 it took part only in the quickly suppressed rising in the Presnya district of Moscow, and in February 1917 it took no part at all.

Soviet propagandists continually reiterate that a revolution can take place only under the leadership of a revolutionary party. In the course of time people get used to the idea and end by believing it. But it is wrong. What party led the Great Rebellion in England, in the seventeenth century? Or the French Revolution in 1789 and the risings all over Europe in 1848? What party directed the 1918 revolutions in Germany and Austria? Or that in Hungary in 1956? None of these were the work of a single party, but the revolutions took place all the same.

Though the "new-type" party took no part in overthrowing czarism, it does not follow that setting up the organization of professional revolutionaries was a mistake. Having failed as the organizer of the revolution, it proved to be very efficient as the organizer of the seizure of power.

Lenin had not been able to carry out his maximum program ("hegemony of the proletariat in the bourgeois revolution"), but the energy with which he now devoted himself to carrying out his minimum program ("transition from the bourgeois to the socialist revolution") was all the greater for that.

During the agitated weeks of March 1917, while Lenin was cooped up in Zürich like a caged lion, and during the famous journey in the "sealed" railway coach that took him back to Russia, Lenin developed the theoretical foundation of his plan to overthrow the new revolutionary government in Russia. Though his ideas were improvised and in sharp conflict with Marxist doctrine, their abstract formulation in Marxist terms masked their real meaning. It was only after dotting the i's and crossing the t's of this document that he climbed onto the armored car at the Finland Station on April 3, 1917, to announce the imminence of the socialist revolution. Seven months later, there took place the "Great Socialist October Revolution," as it has officially been called since Stalin gave it that name in 1934.

This time it was not through the newspapers that Lenin was kept informed; he timed the insurrection himself. "We must at all costs, this very evening, this very night, arrest the government—the matter must be decided without fail this very evening, or this very night," he wrote in a letter to the members of the Central Committee of the Bolshevik party on the evening of October 24 (November 6, new style), 1917.[37]

Unlike the revolutions of 1905 and February 1917, the October Revolution was organized and carried out from beginning to end by Lenin's professional revolutionaries. Of that there is no doubt. But there is doubt about another point.

7. PROLETARIAN REVOLUTION?

The visitor to the Smolny Palace, in Leningrad, makes his way down lofty corridors to a long hall with white columns and a big platform. Many films and innumerable paintings record the historic episode that took place there when Lenin, with his celebrated beard and little mustache and fist raised in his characteristic manner, began his speech to the second all-Russian congress of soviets with the following words: "Comrades, the workers' and peasants' revolution, about the necessity of which the Bolsheviks have always spoken, has been accomplished."[38] Lenin's colleagues, transfigured with delight, can be seen behind him. The persons illustrated change from picture to picture according to the fate reserved for them.

In fact, on November 7, 1917, the platform had not yet been installed, Lenin was clean-shaven, and it was not there but at the Petrograd soviet that he made the speech that became historic. He made it at 2:35 P.M., before the insurrection was over. What matters is not that, but whether the revolution in progress was really that of the workers and peasants, as he claimed. Strangely enough, the question has not been settled yet. It was still being discussed fifty-five years later, in 1972, at the Institute of History of the U.S.S.R. and the Department of Social Sciences of the Academy of Sciences.[39]

The issue is not easy, indeed.

The revolution had to be proletarian, i.e., a workers' revolution; at any rate, that was what the Bolsheviks had always proclaimed. On the other hand, since Stalin's time the rule has been that the October Revolution was made by the workers together with the poorest peasants. But Lenin went still further: "In October 1917 we seized power *together with the peasantry as a whole.*"[40] "When we were taking power, we relied on the support of the peasants as a whole."[41] A fortnight after these revolutionary events Lenin wrote: "The peasants of Russia are now faced with the prospect of taking their country's destiny in their own hands."[42] And what about the dictatorship of the proletariat?

Lenin's description of the revolution as being that of the workers and peasants cannot be ignored, and it is confirmed by the composition of his first government, in November 1917. The Bolsheviks were of course well represented, but its membership also included the Left Socialist Revolutionaries, whom future official history was to describe as the party allied to the kulaks (rich peasants). But did the October Revolution really result in a "democratic revolutionary dictatorship of the workers and peasants"?

That was the kind of dictatorship envisaged by Lenin as the consequence of a successful bourgeois revolution. The revolution of February 1917 was a bourgeois revolution. Was the October Revolution its final phase, or was it an independent proletarian revolution? Are we to assume that it was a revolution carried out by the workers alone?

As we see, the confusion is complete. Let's find an answer.

Lenin stated clearly what he meant by revolution. "The passing of state power from one *class* to another is the first, the principal, the basic sign of a *revolution*, both in the strictly scientific and in the practical political meaning of that term."[43] He also said, "The key question of every revolution is undoubtedly the question of state power. Which class holds power decides everything."[44]

Let us consider the question from that angle. That the Winter Palace, in Petrograd, and the Kremlin, in Moscow, were stormed by armed workers and peasants is an undisputed fact. As Lenin had foreseen, they served as effective shock troops against the non-Bolshevik government. In that sense it certainly was a revolution of workers and peasants.

But who came into power? Workers or peasants? There is an old photograph of the first meeting of the Council of People's Commissars. They are all there, seated around a table, looking at us. They include members of the nobility—Lunacharsky and Lenin himself—and intellectuals, scions of the bourgeoisie. Except for Aleksandr Shlyapnikov, who had been a professional revolutionary for many years, there are no workers or peasants. The Bolshevik people's commissars had only one thing in common: independently of their origin or social position, they were all leading members of the organization of professional revolutionaries founded by Lenin. That was the organization that had taken over the state power.

What class did that organization represent? As we have already said, it represented only itself, and it was itself the embryon of a new ruling class.

8. THE DICTATORSHIP THAT NEVER WAS

The dictatorship of the proletariat is one of the basic principles of Marxism. In 1852, Marx wrote that he had not discovered the class struggle, but had been the first to show "that the class struggle necessarily leads to the *dictatorship of the proletariat*" and that "this dictatorship itself only constitutes the transition to the *abolition of all classes* and to a *classless society.*"[45] Marx believed that that was his greatest contribution to the theory of the class struggle.

He worked on the idea throughout his life. In 1875 he wrote in his *Critique of Political Economy:* "Between capitalist and Communist society there lies the period of the revolutionary transformation of the one into the other. There corresponds to this also a political transition period in which the state can be nothing but the revolutionary dictatorship *of the proletariat.*"[46]

Marx and Engels could quote an example of this. Engels was the author of the frequently quoted statement "Do you want to know what the dictatorship of the proletariat will be like? Study the Paris Commune. That was the dictatorship of the proletariat."[47]

Western Communist parties nowadays follow one another in disowning the dictatorship of the proletariat, and no thunder from Moscow makes the rebels tremble. This is disconcerting to the observer. How can Marxist-Leninists so lightheartedly repudiate what Marx and Engels considered to be their principal theoretical contribution? How do these Communists propose to establish communism without the necessary intermediate period? Why did Moscow so modestly avert its eyes, whereas Czech reformers, guilty of much smaller revisionist sins, were summarily called to account?

The suspicion arises that the dictatorship of the proletariat has turned out to be less necessary than the classics expected.

How about the dictatorship of the proletariat in Russia? Let us quote Lenin's definition: "If we translate the Latin, scientific, historicophilosophical term "dictatorship of the proletariat" into simpler language it means just the following: Only a definite class, namely, the urban workers and the factory, industrial workers in general, is able to lead the whole mass of the working and exploited people in the struggle to throw off the yoke of capital, in actually carrying it out, in the struggle to maintain and consolidate the victory, in the work of creating the new, socialist social system and in the entire struggle for the complete abolition of classes."[48]

It could not be clearer: leadership of the revolution and the state to be established in its wake is to be in the hands of the factory workers; that is what dictatorship of the proletariat means.

But in Russia the leadership neither of the revolution nor of the state that succeeded it has ever been in the hands of the factory workers. The only leaders were the professional revolutionaries. What evidence is there that in spite of that there was a dictatorship of the proletariat?

The following evidence was provided in 1955, shortly before the "dictatorship of the proletariat" was succeeded by the "people's state" (we quote from an economics handbook written under Stalin's supervision): "The existence of the working class in the U.S.S.R. is based on state ownership and socialist labor. It is the most progressive class and the driving force of the development of the state. That is why the political leadership of the U.S.S.R. belongs by right to the working class (dictatorship of the proletariat)."[49]

That is not very convincing. In a capitalist state the existence of the working class is based on state or private capitalist ownership and on capitalist labor (there is no socialist labor). Here too, from the Marxist standpoint, the working class is the most progressive class and the driving force of the development of the state. But does that mean that the working class runs the capitalist state? The same argument could be applied to a slave state. Slaves were the driving force of slave-owning society, but the dictatorship was that of the slave owners and not that of the slaves.

Let us look at what Lenin wrote: "The rule of the working class is reflected in the constitution, the ownership, and in the fact that it is we who are running things."[50] Here "we" stands for the organization of professional revolutionaries, whose identity with the working class is what we were trying to prove. Everything is indeed state property, but the state itself belongs to the professional revolutionaries. The dictatorship of the proletariat is certainly enshrined in the constitution, but what does that prove?

Neither Lenin nor Stalin is convincing, so will Soviet reality perhaps provide us with the evidence we are seeking?

If the Council of People's Commissars included no workers, surely there was an absolute majority of workers in the victorious Communist Party? There was not. In Lenin's time the number of workers in the party did not reach 50 percent.[51] Did workers at least constitute a majority on the Central Committee? They did not; professional revolutionaries constituted the majority. Workers were of course included from time to time. The practice of admitting a few workers to the Central Committee for show has survived to the present day. I had the opportunity of meeting some of them, e.g. the textile worker Valentina Gaganova, Hero of Socialist Labor, in 1961–71 member of the Central Committee. These workers are typical representatives of the working-class aristocracy; they are elected to presidiums and are included in delegations sent abroad, but they have no real influence in the Central Committee. They are well aware of this, and they know their place.

Did not the workers secure any advantages for themselves after seizing power with their own hands for the benefit of the professional revolutionaries? In some ways they did. Marx's solemn prophecy that "the hour of bourgeois property has struck. The expropriators will be expropriated" was translated into the Russian vernacular as "Steal what was stolen from you." Expropriations of the bourgeoisie were organized from time to time; armed members of the Cheka led workers to bourgeois apartments and permitted them to take away whatever took their fancy. A small number of working-class families were moved from the cellars in which they had previously lived into bourgeois apartments, and a transparent vagueness prevails about the fate of the previous occupants. The proletariat was given the place of honor in newspapers and speeches and on streamers. The apotheosis was the introduction of workers' control in factories and offices.

It is by studying the development of workers' control that Lenin's strategy after the October Revolution can be followed. Lozovsky, head of the Trade Union International (the Profintern), who was later murdered in prison under Stalin, tells us that Lenin's draft decree on workers' control struck him as too drastic, so much so that he protested: "If you leave it in this state, every group of workers will interpret it as authorization to do whatever it likes," he wrote to Lenin, who impatiently replied: "The important thing at the present moment is to establish workers' control. Later on, depending on experience, we shall be able to think about the form to be taken by workers' control at the national level."[52] The appropriate form was quickly found: workers' control was simply abolished, because it proved to be "contradictory" and "incomplete," as Lenin explained.[53]

Workers' control was abolished, the fur coats taken from the bourgeoisie wore out, and the new norms for the residential space to which individual citizens were entitled transformed the apartments into cramped living quarters smaller than the cellars of the old days.

Thus, though the dictatorship of the proletariat is a basic principle of Marx and Engels, no trace of it is to be found in Soviet reality. It had neither a beginning nor an end.

Now, the end of a dictatorship, whether that of feudal lords or the bourgeoisie, is always a major event in a country's life. The end of an individual dictator invariably causes a sensation, as happened not only with Hitler, Mussolini, and Franco, but also with Primo de Rivera, Dollfuss, Horthy, and Antonescu. Nor did Stalin's death pass unnoticed. But the end of the dictatorship of the proletariat in the Soviet Union left no trace except in theoretical treatises, and to the present day no one can say when it took place, whether it was before the 1936 constitution or, twenty years later, at the time of the proclamation of the "people's state."

This lack of evidence and theoretical muddle are a certain sign of the politically fictitious. That is why Western Communist parties have been able so easily to repudiate the dictatorship of the proletariat; they were renouncing, not a reality, but mere verbiage. If a Western Communist party succeeded in establishing the kind of regime they want, they would call it a "people's state," just as the regimes established after the end of the Second World War were called people's democracies.

There has never been a dictatorship of the proletariat in Russia or anywhere else. Trying to take a serious look at this dictatorship-that-never-was is as pointless as looking at the emperor's new clothes.

9. "DICTATORSHIP OVER THE PROLETARIAT"

Nevertheless there was a dictatorship, a "dictatorship over the proletariat," as Trotsky so rightly called it a little later. Lenin was well aware of this; it was not by chance that he tried to find an ideological justification for it.

In *The State and Revolution*, which he wrote just before October 1917, he discussed postrevolutionary society in a tone very different from that usually used by Marxists. Instead of the idyllic prosperity to be enjoyed by workers and peasants finally liberated from the exploiters' yoke, he insisted on "accounting and control."[54] It suddenly appeared that the workers who were to be the victors in the forthcoming revolution would have to be controlled and disciplined.

Immediately after the October Revolution, Lenin loudly insisted on the necessity of the "inculcation of a new discipline" which he called "the new form of the class struggle."[55] This was not a good omen, for in the matter of the class struggle the Bolsheviks were pitiless.

Lenin clearly explained that potential class enemies were "the groups and sections of workers who stubbornly cling to capitalist traditions and continue to regard the Soviet state in the old way: work as little and as badly as they can and grab as much money as possible from the state."[56] The class enemies now were workers who did not want to be exploited, even by the Soviet state. Lenin explained that, after the October Revolution, "working people . . . know no yoke and no authority except the authority of their own unity, of their own, more class-conscious, bold, solid, revolutionary and steadfast vanguard."[57] This flood of striking adjectives did not alter the fact that the only power was that of what he called the vanguard. That was the reality of the situation.

Lenin recognized the necessity of stimulating the vanguard. "The more profound the revolution, the greater the number of active workers required to accomplish the replacement of capitalism by a socialist machinery," he stated less than six weeks after the events of October, and added that the proletariat, therefore, "should not think of improving its position at the moment, but should think of becoming the ruling class."[58] Talented organizers should come to the fore in practice and be promoted to work in state administration. It and it alone, with the support of the people, can save Russia and the cause of socialism.[59]

He made it clear that these people must "try to become the ruling class." This managing elite was not a provisional creation necessary for an intermediate period, but a distinct social group. Lenin explained to the workers: "The rule of the working class is reflected in the constitution, the ownership, and in the fact that it is we who are running things, while management is quite another matter: It is a question of skill, a question of experience. . . . In order to manage, one must know the job and be a splendid administrator. . . . Administrative experience does not fall from heaven and is not a gift of the Holy Spirit. And that is why the most progressive class is not automatically that which is capable of administering. . . . For the administration and construction of the state, we need people who are masters of administrative technique, who have political and economic experience."[60] Lenin's idea was "a ruling class of administrators." The working class had played the part of army of the revolution that had devolved upon it, and enjoying the pleasures of dictatorship was no longer its prerogative; it must work, be controlled and administered.

In Lenin's *How We Should Reorganise Workers' and Peasants' Inspection* there is no more talk of workers' control. On the contrary, a privileged and specialized bureaucratic organization should be set up. "The . . . employees of the Workers' and Peasants' Inspection that are to remain, according to my plan, should, on the one hand, perform purely secretarial functions . . . and, on the other hand, they should be highly skilled, specially screened, particularly reliable and highly paid," he wrote.[61]

The only particularly reliable employees whom Lenin could think of for these responsible positions were his old comrades, the tried and tested members of the organization of professional revolutionaries. Though he had risen to giddy heights from which he looked down at them with a sense of absolute superiority, he still esteemed and trusted them; and that is why he regarded the latest developments in Soviet society with growing anxiety.

10. A NEW ARISTOCRACY

These developments were the rapid growth of the state and party apparatus and its increasing claims to govern the country.

Its rapid and irresistible growth was due to the transformation of the social structure—the nationalization, centralization, and party monopoly—out of which it was born. The Leninist old guard, men exhausted by long years of hard, militant labor, were suddenly threatened by a mounting wave of careerists. In their zeal to become the "employees," the administrators, of whom Lenin spoke, Communists of recent date crowded at the gates of power, attracted by the prospect of appointment to responsible positions. Lenin could, of course, dismiss any of these ambitious individuals or have them arrested or shot, but their numbers left him helpless. The nature and dimensions of the social changes taking place, the rapid growth of the party, and the enormous size of the country meant that it was impossible for the small group of professional revolutionaries to occupy every key position and keep control of the whole administration. Neither Marx nor Engels nor Lenin himself had foreseen such a development. Lenin was ill and was faced with a totally unexpected situation. His last works show clearly that he was baffled by the problem. Sometimes he tries to blame the czarist heritage; he talks of "the threat of the Russian apparatus taken over from czarism . . . and only slightly lubricated with Soviet oil." But no words could stop what Lenin distinctly saw as "the onslaught of that really Russian man, the Great-Russian chauvinist, in substance a rascal and a tyrant, such as the typical Russian bureaucrat is." The extent of this invasion frightens him. "There is no doubt," he goes on, "that the infinitesimal percentage of Soviet and sovietised workers will drown in that tide of chauvinistic Great-Russian riffraff like a fly in milk."[62] "The need for honest men is desperate," he notes sadly.[63]

Later he admits it was not the czarist bureaucracy that was seizing positions of power. "Our worst internal enemy is the bureaucrat—the Communist who occupies a responsible (or not responsible) Soviet post and enjoys universal respect as a conscientious man,"[64] he notes in 1922. So it was Communist and not czarist officials who were the trouble. Even more serious was the invasion of party organizations by the bureaucracy. In his last article, Lenin refers anxiously to "our Soviet and Party bureaucracy." He notes bitterly that "we have bureaucrats in our Party institutions as well as in the Soviet institutions."[65] The state and party bureaucracy are developing before his eyes into an oppressive totalitarian system, and he can only note helplessly that their work "is apparently suffering from the general conditions of our truly Russian (even though Soviet) bureaucratic ways."[66]

The rising tide of the omnipotent new bureaucracy already represented a threat to the Bolshevik old guard. The careerists had all the important posts in their sights and already constituted a force able to influence Kremlin policy. What course would these power-hungry parvenus follow? Would they pursue the prudent and difficult balance between Marxist dogma and the improvisation necessitated by the special situation of Russia that Leninists had worked out during their years as *émigrés?* Or would they take a more brutal course masked by a Marxist terminology emptied of all meaning? Would it be a reactionary dictatorship exercised over all those at the bottom of the social scale?

On March 26, 1922, Lenin wrote these remarkable words: "If we do not close our eyes to reality we must admit that at the present time the proletarian policy of the Party is not determined by the character of its membership, but by the enormous undivided prestige enjoyed by the small group which might be called the Old Guard of the Party. A slight conflict within this group will be enough, if not to destroy this prestige, at all events to weaken the group to such a degree as to rob it of all power to determine policy."[67] He does not dare even to hint clearly what the result would be.

We find this hint in the works of Shulgin, a White Russian *émigré* whose anti-Communist books *1920* and *Days* were printed in Soviet Russia by Lenin's orders. His third book, *Three Capitals: A Journey Through Red Russia,* sums up Lenin's impact on the country—not without a certain grim pleasure—as follows: "Inequality has returned. Moribund communism is retreating to the field of theory: hollow words and stupid speeches. But life has conquered. And, just as no two blades of grass are identical, there are a multitude of intermediary stages between rich and poor. A new social ladder has formed, and with it hope has returned: every single individual's hope of rising in society." He also wrote this: "Power is a profession like any other. When a coachman gets drunk and does his work badly, he is sacked. That is what happened to us, who were the masters. We drank too much and sang too much. We were thrown out, and other masters were chosen in our place—this time the Jewish clique. They will of course soon be liquidated. But not before a new dynasty has been formed that will have passed through a hard school. It will have to know how to govern; otherwise it will be thrown out too.

"Communism is a mere episode. Communism ('steal what was stolen from you') and other talk of the same type was nothing but a lever that made it possible to put new masters in the place of the old. Soon they will be sent to the museum (the museum of the revolution) and life will resume its former course. The masters will have changed, that's all."[68]

One finds in these words the prophetic idea of two strata in the Soviet ruling class. The social class that the anti-Semite Shulgin calls "the Jewish clique" is the organization of professional revolutionaries. It was true that Jews—whom the Shulgins, the masters of czarist Russia, had so thoroughly oppressed—were not exactly absent from its ranks; but it was also true that the professional revolutionaries would not be able to maintain themselves in power for long. These internationalist intellectuals were too remote from the Russian masses. On the eve of the forthcoming struggle within the new ruling class, it was there that the weakness of the professional revolutionaries lay in relation to the new arrivals on the scene; these latter were much more deeply rooted in the population. History was getting its own back on the sorcerer's apprentices.

Lenin and his professional revolutionaries disappointed the workers, whom they had promised a dictatorship of the proletariat. They started a rapidly developing process of establishing a new governing class. But the process soon escaped from their control. The old Bolsheviks, weakened by remnants of idealism and the illusion that they were serving the interests of the working class, turned out to be helpless. They found themselves up against new forces, devoid of idealism, whose only clear aim was to creep into the bed of power.

By a bitter irony of fate, three weeks after the reference to the dangers inherent in the apparatus, Stalin was elected Secretary-General of the Central Committee. It took place on Lenin's recommendation. Lenin was afraid of "a small internal struggle" that might weaken the authority of the Bolshevik old guard, and he brought to power the man whose plan was just to foment internal struggles and do away with that authority.

11. CREATION OF THE NOMENKLATURA

Lenin the revolutionary created the organization of professional revolutionaries; Stalin the apparatchik created the nomenklatura. Lenin's creation was the lever that enabled him to overturn Russia, and it was soon put in the museum of the revolution, as Shulgin had foreseen. Stalin's invention was the apparatus that enabled him to rule Russia. It turned out to be infinitely more durable.

We have already mentioned that the organization of professional revolutionaries was numerically too weak to govern a huge empire by itself and fill all the responsible positions in the growing party and state apparatus; careerists rushed in to fill the vacuum. For an applicant to have some chance of success, not much was required of him; he must not be of bourgeois or noble origin, and he must be a member of the party (or of the Komsomol if he was under age). Service in the Red Army during the civil war was recognized as service to the revolutionary cause.

Selection was obviously necessary, but with which criteria? The most important qualification was not professional, but political. If Albert Einstein (not a member of the Party) applied for a job at the same time as Ivan Stupidov, a young sailor from the Baltic Fleet and a member of the Party, Ivan Stupidov had to be appointed.

The obvious stupidity of this arrangement did not mean that those who imposed it were naïve. When it was vital to have real specialists in key positions, they were found. During the civil war against the Whites, the Red Army was commanded by military specialists, former czarist generals and other officers. The triumph of political qualifications in peacetime is explained by a rule that is incomprehensible to the Western mentality steeped in the spirit of competition: though it has been never openly admitted, it seems to be necessary to socialism to give jobs to people with little or no qualifications for the work involved. Why?

There is a perfectly rational explanation for this phenomenon, which is to be found everywhere in all the socialist countries. Everyone has to be aware of the fact that he has his job not by right but as a favor done to him by his superiors, and that he can be just as easily replaced if that favor is withdrawn. That is the principle underlying Stalin's saying (assiduously repeated to the present day) that "with us no one is irreplaceable."

During the many years that I lived in the Soviet Union I rarely came across anyone who was really qualified for his job. And it was persons with ability who suffered most: as they failed to meet the usual selection rule, they—and not the others—always seemed to be in the wrong jobs.

This principle of political selection produced in those lucky enough to get good jobs complete submission to the will of their superiors. Might it not be the way to make themselves irreplaceable? Aspirants to social promotion were animated by a genuine desire to carry out the slightest whim of those who had appointed them.

The key to Stalin's historic ascent lay in that trivial fact; he succeeded in concentrating all appointments to key positions in the country in his own hands and those of his apparatus, and it was by this use of political qualifications that he assured himself of the complete devotion of the whole of the new ruling class, the nomenklatura.

Stalin's Western biographers have so overplayed the conflict between Stalin and the other members of the Central Committee that it has become a commonplace: on the one hand Trotsky, Bukharin, Zinoviev, spellbinders intoxicated by their own eloquence, and on the other that plebeian, taciturn, and obstinate Stalin. Seen from the outside, that was plausible enough. But the heart of the matter lay elsewhere, in the work done by Stalin at the Secretariat of the party's Central Committee. At the time, this earned him the nickname of "Comrade File Cabinet" (tovarishch Kartotekov). He and his staff indeed concentrated on personal files and records. "The staffs are of decisive importance," he said later. He studied the personnel problem in depth, passing it through the sieve of his interests and calculations, placing men in the various fields of his nomenklatura like a composer arranging the notes of the symphony he is composing. He was said to have kept up to date from the early twenties his file of people who might interest him under any particular heading and to have never allowed his secretary to go near it.

It would of course be naïve to suppose that the nomenklatura was successfully established only because Stalin and his staff were skilled in the use of files. Stalin invented the system that made possible the successful selection of personnel to run the state and the party.

He made some comments on his system of selection at the Twelfth Party Congress, in 1923: "It is necessary to choose staffs in such a way," he said, "as to fill the various posts with people who are capable of carrying out the directives, able to understand the directives, able to accept these directives as their own, and capable of putting them into effect. Otherwise the policy becomes meaningless, becomes mere gesticulation." Thus the basic idea was to have men in responsible positions who would be willing to obey instructions. Hence "the qualifications of every single individual must be thoroughly scrutinized."[69] *Stalin dixit.*

This was done. In 1920, departments of the Central Committee and of the regional committees were created, responsible for the registration and appointment of officials. This was the *"uchraspred."* The uchraspreds were the first organizations formed for the specific purpose of making appointments to important posts in the party. They were also responsible for dismissals; they drew up lists of those who would "return to the workshop or the plow."[70]

Stalin became Secretary-General of the Central Committee in April 1922. At the Twelfth Party Congress, in August that year, figures were published for the first time showing how many officials were employed in the party apparatus. There were 325 in Moscow, 2,000 in the regions, 8,000 in the districts; 5,000 others were permanently employed in big industrial enterprises and local administrations. Altogether there were 15,325, a pretty impressive figure.[71]

In his report to the Twelfth Congress, Stalin said, "Until now this department has confined itself to registering and distributing comrades for *uyezd* [part of a 'government'], *gubernia* ['government'] committees, and regional committees. Beyond this, to put it bluntly, it did not stick its nose. . . . The Registration and Distribution Department . . . must not confine itself to the *uyezd* and *guberniya* committees. It must now cover all branches of the administration without exception, and the entire industrial commanding personnel. . . ."[72]

This, too, was done. After the Twelfth Congress, when it was clear that Lenin would not be returning to power, the registration and appointment of leading officials "in all fields of the administration and the economy without exception" was handed over to Uchraspred.[73]

The uchraspred of the Central Committee was the most active. Stalin said of it that in the future it would have "immense importance."[74] By 1922 Uchraspred had made more than ten thousand appointments,[75] and it expanded its activities in 1923. Seven Commissions were created within the Uchraspred to supervise the staffing of the most important branches of the state administration and the economy: industry, transport and communications, agriculture, education, administrative organs, and the people's commissariats for foreign affairs and for foreign trade.[76]

Party committees, according to the rules, were supposed to be elected, but a way around this was easily found (and is still in use today): the higher party echelons "recommend" the candidates to their subordinates. Thus candidates for the post of district secretary are "recommended" by the regional committee, and candidates for the position of regional secretary are "recommended" by the Secretariat of the Central Committee. The Secretariat of the Central Committee had to do an enormous amount of work to arrange the selection of these new governors-general. In 1922, thirty-seven secretaries of regional committees were dismissed and forty-two new ones were "recommended."[77] It is worthy of note that the Central Committee Secretariat was not content with submitting its "recommendations" to lower levels of the party, but addressed them also to the highest levels, including the Politburo of the Central Committee. Thus all appointments to the highest positions in the state were controlled by the Central Committee Secretariat under Stalin.

The feverish activity of this Secretariat and the Uchraspred created new conditions inside the party apparatus. In a letter to the Central Committee dated October 18, 1923, and in his book *The New Course*, published in December 1923, Trotsky mentioned that even when the civil war was at its height the number of party appointments (instead of elections) did not reach 10 percent of those reached in 1923. He pointed out that this method of appointing secretaries was carried out regardless of the personal views of local party organizations and that the officials of the apparatus no longer had any personal views, or at any rate never expressed them, but merely agreed with the "secretariat hierarchy." He added that the only information about the decisions of this hierarchy communicated to the great mass of party members came to it in the form of orders.[78]

Trotsky called this process the bureaucratization of the party. That was a very weak phrase for it, but it could not be otherwise, for in 1923 he was still a member of the Politburo.

In fact much more than that was happening. Social groups were moving in opposite directions. One of them—that of the secretaries of the party committees and their apparatus—was rising and beginning to give orders while the other—that of the ordinary party militants—was falling and finding itself, like nonmembers of the party, in the position of having to carry out orders without complaining or questioning them. "The party is living at two levels," Trotsky wrote. "At the top, decisions are made; at the bottom, information about those decisions is received."[79] Trotsky's letter is a kind of contemporary snapshot of the formation of classes in the new Soviet society, its division into two social strata: the controllers and the controlled.

Meanwhile the breach made by the mounting wave of power-hungry careerists continued to grow. After Lenin's death it was announced that 240,000 new members had been admitted to the party. Between May 1923 (the Twelfth Congress) and May 1924 (the Thirteenth Congress) the strength of the party increased from 336,000 to 736,000. Thus half the party consisted of new members admitted under the "Lenin enrollment." The Bolshevik old guard, who had lived for so long in exile or deportation, were alien to them. The new members had no links with these former victims of persecution; they were about to become persecutors themselves. They wanted no more revolution, but the good positions that the now well-established regime had to offer. In a word, they were potential Stalinists. Let us note in passing that *The Foundations of Leninism*, in which Stalin claims to be Lenin's political and spiritual heir, is ostentatiously dedicated to "the Lenin enrollment." As a matter of fact, this was a Stalin enrollment.

Meanwhile the Central Committee Secretariat continued with the work of building up the nomenklatura. Figures are available for 1924; the Secretariat was to be responsible for filling about 3,500 positions and Uchraspred for 1,500.[80] The nomenklatura of the regional, district, and other committees of the party was similarly considerably enlarged. In 1925 there were 25,000 employees of the main party apparatus, 767 on the Central Committee apparatus alone.[81]

In 1924, Uchraspred merged with the Central Committee's Organizational Department. The new agency was given the name of Orgraspred. It became one of the most important departments of the Central

Committee. Orgraspred, headed by Stalin's intimate L. M. Kaganovich, supervised the nomenklatura of the party as well as that of the state. It can be taken for granted that every appointment to a leading position in the state apparatus was carefully vetted. From the end of 1925 (the Fourteenth Congress) to 1927 (the Fifteenth), Orgraspred made 8,761 appointments, 1,222 of them to the party apparatus.

In 1930, Orgraspred was divided into two separate departments, one of them charged with appointments to and transfers in the party apparatus and the other with appointments to the various sectors of the state apparatus (heavy industry, transport, agriculture, the soviets, personnel on missions to foreign countries, etc.).[82]

At the plenary meeting of the Central Committee in 1937, Stalin described the party in military terms: the "higher command" consisted of between 3,000 and 4,000 "generals" (top-grade leaders), followed by between 30,000 and 40,000 "officers" (middle-grade leaders) and between 100,000 and 150,000 "noncommissioned officers" (junior leaders).[83] This military terminology clearly demonstrates the hierarchical ideas that presided over the creation of the nomenklatura.

Relations between the nomenklatura hierarchy and Stalin were not limited to demonstrations of devotion to their benefactor by the apparatchiks. Things were much more symbiotic.

Stalin's protégés were his creatures. But the converse was also true; he was their creature, for they were the social base of his dictatorship, and they certainly hoped he would ensure them collective dictatorship over the country. In servilely carrying out his orders, they counted on the fact that these were given in their interests. Stalin could of course at any moment liquidate any one of them (as he often did), but in no circumstances could he liquidate the nomenklaturist class as a whole. He showed zealous concern for his protégés' interests and the reinforcement of their power, authority, and privileges. He was the creature of his creatures, and he knew that they would scrupulously respect his wishes only so long as he respected theirs.

Their dearest wish was that their power over the country should endure and be shared with no one else. They had no use for Trotsky's theory of "permanent revolution." They had no desire to be dependent on an uncertain "world revolution." They wanted to rule.

Stalin hastened to carry out their wishes by launching the slogan of "socialism in a single country." From the Marxist point of view, that slogan was absurd. To Marx and Engels it was obvious that a classless society could not exist like an island in a capitalist ocean. But the Stalinists were delighted with this new formula, which gave socialist sanction to their authority. The fact that the victory of socialism in a single country was "total but not definitive," as Stalin said, did not trouble them. The idea was not intended to raise the hopes of Soviet citizens. On the contrary, the danger of a possible capitalist restoration was used to justify the whole of Stalin's domestic, military, and foreign policy. At the same time, the assurance that the final victory of socialism in the Soviet Union was close at hand justified the necessity of the stability and continuity of the regime.

The celebrated phrase "construction of socialism in a single country" became the theoretical foundation, not for the creation of an abstract Marxist socialism, but of what has come to be known as real socialism.

"The construction of socialism has been achieved in broad outline," Stalin announced in proclaiming the new constitution in 1936—between the first and second Moscow trials and just before the Great Purge, known in the U.S.S.R. under the name *yezhovchina.**

12. DOWNFALL OF THE OLD GUARD

While the madness of the terrible spring of 1938 was at its height and the newspapers were denouncing Fascist spies and the renegades Trotsky, Bukharin, and their cliques, I heard for the first time an analysis of events that conflicted sharply with the current hysteria. It came from a former schoolfellow of mine, Rafka Vannikov, son of the Deputy People's Commissar for the Soviet Defense Industry, Boris Lvovovich Vannikov, who later became head of the top-secret agency responsible for the development of Soviet atomic weapons.

"Have you noticed that in the past eighteen months nearly the whole of the ruling apparatus of the country has been changed?" Rafka suddenly said to me one day. He was a charming lad, but political analysis was certainly not his forte. What he had just told me must certainly have come from his father, from the Kremlin spheres.

A change in the governing apparatus had been coldly decided on in

* After Yezhov, People's Commissar of Internal Affairs (NKVD)

the Kremlin and was presented to the world as a huge unmasking of "Fascist spies."

The *yezhovchina*, which exterminated millions of people and plunged innumerable families into misery, was a complex social and political phenomenon. It was a bloodthirsty change of direction inside the new ruling class.

In 1937, twenty years after the revolution, the Bolshevik old guard was no longer young, but it could still look forward to, say, another fifteen years of life. The newcomers to the nomenklatura were unwilling to grant them this, for they coveted the leading positions occupied by these old revolutionaries. The nomenklatura, the "new aristocracy" foreseen by Shulgin, had arrived; it had passed through a hard school and had learned how to rule; the only remaining hurdle was the liquidation of the old guard.

Nevertheless a question arises. As the Secretariat of the Central Committee "recommended" candidates for election in the provinces and many other leading positions, why did the nomenklatura need Yezhov's terror?

It needed it because the elite of the party leadership at that time consisted of individuals of two kinds: Leninists and Stalinists. The latter were the Secretary-General's protégés, having been chosen for their political reliability. The Leninist old guard owed their appointments to their former membership in the organization of professional revolutionaries. Individual Leninists could be dismissed, but there was no ordinary procedure by which they could all be eliminated at a stroke. That was why in 1930, in spite of new appointments and transfers, 69 percent of the regional secretaries and secretaries of the Central Committee were still old Bolsheviks.[84] Fully 80 percent of the delegates to the Seventeenth Congress, in 1934, had joined the party before 1920, i.e., before the end of the civil war.

On what did the invulnerability of Lenin's aging comrades-in-arms depend? Their strength, as Lenin rightly saw, lay in the moral authority acquired in the course of many years in the party. It was only later that we grew accustomed to the fact that any party official could be easily arrested and liquidated as a Fascist spy—and that with the bored approval of the public. That state of mind was still unknown. Let us recall that in 1929 Stalin had been able only to expel the detested Trotsky from the country, and had not even been able to prevent him from taking his private papers with him. Membership in various opposition groups was not yet considered sufficient reason to discredit old Bolsheviks and remove them from their leading positions.

The only way of wiping out the old guard was to destroy its moral authority and turn its long years of service to the revolution into a crime. Here we come across a characteristic feature of Stalin's mentality; in his opinion, a tried and tested revolutionary might well have been playing a double game and might really be a traitor.

Stalin was well aware of the envious glances the nomenklaturists cast at the Leninists. Those old men who still preserved some loyalty to the revolution in spite of their good jobs, their prestige, and the good life they led were alien and antipathetic to the newcomers. The latter needed only a signal to fling themselves like a pack of wolves on the enfeebled old fogies who were keeping them out of good positions.

The signal was given by the murder of Kirov, the party First Secretary in Leningrad, a Politburo member. That he was killed by Stalin's orders is beyond doubt. Books published in the West have correctly analyzed Stalin's reasons for wanting to get rid of him. A number of preliminary steps taken by the dictator against the energetic Leningrad secretary have been chronicled: at the Twentieth and Twenty-second party congresses Khrushchev quoted a number of facts connected with the murder, and it is clear that in his eyes Stalin was the guilty man.

That seems reasonable enough. Stalin had already staged more than one killing. For instance, it was at his instigation that Mikhoels, the totally innocuous director of the Yiddish Theater, was murdered later: Svetlana Alliluyeva describes how her father gave the order on the telephone. His way of attributing responsibility for a murder to the other party was not new either. Let us recall Lenin's skillful staging of the hangings in Poland, when he caused the "greens" to be suspected —just as, later, the liquidation of the Ukrainian *émigré*'s leader Bandera by the KGB was attributed by the Soviet propaganda to the West German intelligence service BND. Stalin of course always denied his responsibility for these crimes, even in cases as clear as that of Trotsky's murder.

In short, the question of who killed Kirov is not a matter of dispute. The special feature of the case was that it was not an isolated crime, but the signal for mass extermination, primarily of the Bolshevik old guard. The present "controllers" of the U.S.S.R. are well aware of that, and draw their own conclusions.

That is why the inquiry into the murder instigated by Khrushchev has never been able to reach any conclusion. The old Bolsheviks who were members of the commission of inquiry appointed by the Central Committee described in private how at every step they came up against stubborn obstruction by the party apparatus and the KGB, how documents they called for were found to have disappeared, how witnesses simply became untraceable. The Stalinists' efforts in this respect were devoted not so much to concealing this particular crime as to covering the tracks that might have led back to them and revealed the part they played in the events of 1934–38.

It was a vital part. It is wrong to regard the *yezhovchina* as the work of Stalin alone, and it is still more wrong to regard Yezhov as the only guilty man.

In giving the green light for the extermination of the Leninist old guard, Stalin fulfilled the wishes of his creatures. It was not a heroic campaign. One may have an unfavorable opinion of its victims, the Leninist professional revolutionaries, but the settling of accounts with them was appalling.

It was the subtle methods of moral and physical destruction which were used that made the Moscow trials so notorious. In the "Trotsky-Zinoviev terrorist center" (August 1936), the "parallel anti-Soviet Trotskyist center" (January 1937), and the "anti-Soviet bloc of the Trotsky-ist rightists" (March 1938) trials Zinoviev, Kamenev, Rykov, Bukharin, Krestinsky, Pyatakov, Radek, and other comrades-in-arms of Lenin confessed to having been agents of Hitler and Trotsky, spies, saboteurs, and terrorists, and to having wanted the restoration of capitalism. After their confessions, the public prosecutor, a former Menshevik, Andrei Vyshinsky, declared that "these mad dogs must be shot," and he was given the verdict for which he asked. Some of the fifty-four accused were sentenced to long terms of imprisonment, but none survived. Trials of the same type took place throughout the Soviet Union in 1937 and 1938, with similar results.

Left-wing intellectuals in the West who had a touching faith in anything that came from Moscow engaged in wild conjectures about the reasons for the moral degeneration of the Leninist old guard. Bourgeois journalists noted a number of factual impossibilities in their confessions and suggested that the Leninist veterans had admitted guilt to serve the party cause. The right-wing press took the view that the accused had been subjected to a complicated process of brainwashing that gave them a new ego loaded with a heavy guilt complex in relation to the party.

There was a little story that Svetlana tells us amused Stalin greatly at this time; he continually repeated it to his Politburo cronies: A professor teased a Cheka official who did not know who wrote *Eugene Onegin*. The Chekist arrested him, and later told his friends, "He confessed. He wrote it himself." Members of the Politburo appreciated at its true value this anecdote that amused their master so much. They were aware of the truth about the Moscow trials, which was simpler and more cynical than Westerners imagined.

The secret was well kept, but it came to light indirectly through Czechoslovakia (Soviet experience was exported to the popular democracies by KGB advisers). The accused were subjected to the so-called "conveyor": an interrogation that lasted continuously for several days and nights. The interrogators worked in three 8-hour shifts, the accused were not allowed to sleep, and they were beaten and given nothing to drink. After a few days of this treatment they were ready to sign anything. The interrogators knew that this was only the first round. After being allowed to sleep the prisoner retracted, whereupon the whole thing began again; and it was repeated as many times as were necessary until the prisoner's only wish was to be done with it and be sentenced, even if it were to death.

Khrushchev calmly told the Twenty-second Party Congress, "Even when prisoners were told that the accusation of spying had been withdrawn, they kept to their previous statements. They preferred to confirm their false confessions in order to bring their torture to an end and be killed more quickly."[85]

That was the accused's state of mind when he was brought to trial. The stage was set with the greatest possible care. The accused learned his part by heart, like an actor. Ulrikh, the president of the court, and Vyshinsky, the public prosecutor, each had a copy of the text in front of him. The accused's reward for playing his part was that until the time came for his execution he was allowed to sleep and was not beaten again; that was worth more to him than a king's ransom. That was the simple method used in all the trials that took place in the socialist countries between 1936 and 1953, the "mystery" of which so baffled the Western world.

When a public confession was not necessary and only a written confession was required, the methods used were of course simpler. The chief interrogator and a number of young thugs, generally pupils at the NKVD school, beat their victim at nighttime interrogation sessions, burned them with cigarettes, or thought up other brilliant ideas of the same kind. That is how old Bolsheviks were made to confess to the most atrocious crimes.

Each confession produced more names and led to more arrests. Kaganovich was said to have described the process as "getting rid of these people in shifts." It led to the now familiar result: the accusers at the beginning of a chain of arrests were sometimes among those sentenced to death at the end of it.

One of these was Yagoda, head of the NKVD, who organized the first Moscow trial and was sentenced to death at the third. This professional Chekist and colleague of Dzerzhinski's had joined the party in 1907, and he was succeeded as head of the NKVD by Yezhov, who was secretary of the Central Committee and had joined the party in 1917, after the October Revolution. Soon after his new appointment, he had Yagoda arrested and nearly all the old Chekists dismissed. He had them replaced by members of the party apparatus. Shkiriatov, his deputy, became president of the Party Control Commission at the Central Committee. It was these newly appointed apparatchiks who carried out the tragedy.

The sycophantic press called Yezhov "Stalin's People's Commissar," and Suleiman Stalsky, the "people's artist," servilely sung the praises of the "noble hero Yezhov." The puny, hollow-cheeked little man was actually no more a monster than he was a hero. People who worked with him before 1936 on the Central Committee Department for Industry say with retrospective surprise that he showed no sign whatever of any particular sadism or of being a potential murderer. They say that the only thing that distinguished him from other bureaucrats was the particular zeal with which he carried out the orders of his chiefs. He was neither a Macbeth nor a Mephistopheles, but a keen little nomenklaturist who became one of the most sinister killers of the twentieth century.

Like all his colleagues in the party apparatus, when he was given his orders he carried them out promptly and conscientiously. At the Department for Industry his task was to organize the building of factories, so he organized the building of factories. At the NKVD he was ordered to torture and kill, so he tortured and killed.

His instructions were specific, such as this one, for instance, which was handwritten on a "confession" obtained by NKVD interrogators: "To Gen. Yezhov. The persons whom I have marked with the letters "Ar." are to be arrested—if they have not been already. J. Stalin." A list of persons to be checked with a view to possible arrest came back with the following words in the same handwriting: "Not to be checked, to be arrested."[86]

Equally definite instructions were given about what was to happen after arrest. Molotov, who was head of the government of the Soviet Union at the time, noted on the report of a Leninist's confession: "Beat, beat, beat. Torture during interrogation." These instructions, too, were conscientiously carried out.

The logical conclusion of this process was similarly in accordance with orders. At the Twenty-second Party Congress, the speaker quoted a request by Yezhov for authorization to carry out "sentence of the first category" on the persons on the accompanying list. This was graciously granted, and prisoners in the Lefortovo prison were duly dragged to the place of execution.

My discussion of the Yezhov terror is limited to its role in the origin of the nomenklatura, and therefore I have dwelt only on the question of the extermination of the Leninist old guard. But of course the real extent of the Yezhov terror was far greater. The liquidation of the Leninists was accompanied by a vast operation to intimidate the entire population by mass arrests and the exile of millions of ordinary citizens to terrible "exterminating-labor camps," to use Solzhenitsyn's apt expression. The extent of the operation can be seen by comparing figures from the all-Union censuses of 1926 and 1939. During these thirteen years the number of inhabitants of the Soviet Far East grew by 329 percent, of Eastern Siberia by 384 percent, of the North of the European part of the country by 558 percent. What had happened? Had a lascivious population multiplied immorally? No. A triumphant nomenklatura had created a gigantic army of free workers, of state slaves—the "zeks"—and at the same time transfixed all Soviet citizens with the icy fear of ending up among them.

Yezhov was merely a cat's-paw. In his place any nomenklaturist would have done the same, though that does not mean that Yezhov was not the bloodiest killer in Russian history. It merely means that any protégé of Stalin was a potential mass killer. Yezhov was not a product of hell, he was a product of the nomenklatura.

13. AFTER THE VICTORY

With the wiping out of the Bolshevik old guard, the Stalinist victory was complete. Yezhov had fulfilled his task, so he was discreetly gotten rid of. First of all, Beria was made his deputy, then Yezhov was given a second job: he was appointed Commissar for Inland Waterways, where he even made a splash by application of "Stakhanovite methods." In December 1938 he was relieved of his post of Commissar for Internal Affairs and subsequently also of his responsibilities for inland waterways. After that, all trace of him disappears. A rumor circulated in NKVD circles that he had gone mad and was in chains in a cell at a mental hospital. Secrecy about his fate has been well kept. A History of the CPSU published in Khrushchev's time says merely that he received the punishment that he deserved.

It is quite probable that this mere carrier-out of orders was really executed, but the fact remains that he was disposed of with a clemency to which one was no longer accustomed. There was no press campaign against him, there was no confession and no trial, he was not accused of having wanted to restore capitalism in the Soviet Union, there were none of the usual diatribes about the guilty man having at last received his just deserts. The penalization of his relatives that invariably accompanied the arrest of every Soviet citizen did not take place in his case, his family has never lost the right to live in Moscow. Moreover, in the spring of 1944 I was extremely surprised to see the name "A. I. Yezhov" on a door at the People's Commissariat for Education and to learn that one of the directors of that commissariat was actually the killer's brother! He had not even been struck off the nomenklatura.

Also, nothing disagreeable happened to his acolytes, some of whom were actually promoted. His deputy Shkiriatov was elected to the Central Committee and was appointed to the highly important post of president of the Party Control Commission. Vyshinsky was loaded with honors; he became a member of the Central Committee, vice-president of the Council of People's Commissars, Soviet Foreign Minister, and a member of the Academy of Sciences. Khrushchev had to overcome the stubborn resistance of the party apparatus before succeeding in expelling Molotov, though his appalling role during the *yezhovchina* was well known. But Molotov continued to enjoy all the privileges in spite of his expulsion from the party. He lives in a huge apartment in the block in Granovskogo Street, in Moscow, in which the party leaders lived, and he regularly takes rest periods at Lesnye Dali, the rest home of the Council of Ministers. How often have I seen him in the Lenin Library, in reading room No. 1, which is reserved for academicians, professors, and foreign scholars, though he is neither a scholar nor a foreigner.

The kid-glove treatment of those who supervised the extermination of the Bolshevik old guard contrasts with the severity still shown to the victims. The phony verdicts of 1936–38 still stand, and this puts Soviet historians in an awkward position; they still don't know whether or not the victims and their alleged accomplices were Fascist spies.

In the Soviet Union at the present day, those trials and the horrible repression that accompanied them are never referred to. The *History of the Communist Party of the Soviet Union,* published in several volumes, does not mention them, and Yezhov is mentioned only in a single sentence, which deserves to be quoted. It says that in the course of a check of party documents that was carried out after Kirov's death, "a number of loyal Communists were expelled from the party. The activity of Yezhov, who was responsible for that check and incited the organisations of the party to excessive mistrust was not unconnected with those expulsions."[87] That is all.

At the same time, very aggressive books and pamphlets are still published about the party's struggle against Trotskyism. Vsevolod Kochetov published his novel *Angle of Descent,* describing Trotsky's and Zinoviev's "treachery" during the civil war. By order of the Science Department of the Central Committee, historical journals published reviews demolishing an article by Bukharin's daughter Svetlana Gurvich, who tried to clear her father's memory. The purpose of all this is evident: to show that the victims of the 1936–38 trials largely deserved their punishment, even though the trials might have been phony.

Why should the apparatchiks of the present day be so anxious to show solidarity with the events of 1936–38 in spite of the end of the Stalin cult and all the official statements about the "unjustified repression" of that time? Because they are well aware that it was then that their rapid climb to control of the commanding levers of the state was crowned with success.

Here are some figures that illustrate that rapid climb. In 1930, 69 percent of the regional and district secretaries and secretaries of the central committees of the Union's constituent republics had joined the party before the revolution. In 1939, 80.5 percent had joined the party only after 1924, i.e., after Lenin's death. Of the 1939 secretaries, 91 percent were under forty; in other words, they were adolescents at the time of the revolution. The figures for the secretaries of regions and towns are similar. In 1939, 93.5 percent had joined the party only after 1924, and 92 percent were under forty.[88]

Comparison of the figures given at the Seventeenth Congress, held in 1934 and called the "victors' " congress, with those given the Eighteenth is just as instructive: 80 percent of the delegates to the former had joined the party before 1920; at the Eighteenth Congress, five years later, half the delegates were under thirty-five; i.e., they were still in school in 1920.[89] Of the seventy-one individuals elected to the Central Committee by the Seventeenth Congress, only ten were newly elected, and most of these had joined the party before the revolution. Of the seventy-one elected to the Central Committee at the Eighteenth Congress, forty-six, or nearly two thirds, were elected for the first time. Only two of those elected to the Central Committee had joined the party before the revolution (one of them was Shkiriatov, Yezhov's former deputy).[90] The Seventeenth Congress was not that of the victors, but that of the damned. The real victors' congress was the Eighteenth.

Of course, work continued on the refinement of the procedures for the replenishment of the nomenklatura and for moving around within the system. The task was set about immediately after the war. "In 1946 the nomenklatura of positions was developed and approved by the Central Committee," the many-volumed *History of the CPSU* states laconically. "Careful planning and the systematic study and verification of political and working qualities were introduced into the system for developing the leading cadres, and the creation of a reserve for promotion and strict order in the appointment and dismissal of nomenklatura workers was ensured. The nomenklatura of positions in the central committees of the Union republics and in the regional, city, and local committees was expanded."[91] After the Nineteenth Party Congress—the last to be held under Stalin—"the nomenklatura of positions was further refined and approved by the CPSU Central Committee and the Party central committees of the Union republics and of the regions and districts."[92]

But all this was simply dotting the i's and elaborating the details. The birth process of the ruling class was complete. The nomenklatura had taken power over society firmly in its hands.

The figures quoted above provide only a partial view of the irresistible advance of the Stalinist nomenklatura to victory. To complete it, one would have to add the millions of years of imprisonment imposed by military and administrative courts, the millions who died in camps and prison cells, who were tortured to death during interrogation or killed by a pistol shot at the base of the skull.

Actual figures are now safely locked up in safes and strongboxes guarded by the KGB. But the world knows that they exist, and one day the public will see them.

14. THREE-STAGE PROCESS

The birth of the new ruling class took place in three stages: first, with the formation of the organization of professional revolutionaries, the embryo of the new class; second, beginning with the seizure of power by that organization in November 1917 (and continued by establishing a two-level leadership, the Leninist old guard and the Stalinist nomenklatura); and third, with the liquidation of the Leninist old guard by the nomenklatura.

Each stage had its own sociopsychological foundations. The Bolsheviks were no quixotic idealists; they did not dash to their own destruction in the name of a vague ideal, as the populists had done. They struggled and faced danger and privation because the social structure that they fought offered them no future. They did not share the populists' romantic love of the "people," and their "sympathy" with the proletariat was pretty selfish, being dictated by the fact that only the proletariat could help them overthrow the existing regime. They had no scruples about deceiving the workers; they promised them a dictatorship of the proletariat having only their own dictatorship in mind. They were pitiless in the struggle for power, and shrank from nothing, even compromising with their own conscience in striking blows at their enemy. But they believed Marxism to be the only doctrine capable of bringing about a dictatorship of the proletariat, and they genuinely wanted to create the classless society prophesied by Marx. Lenin was not only their guide, he was the embodiment of their ambitions.

Stalin was the guide and embodiment of his nomenklatura. If he was not the exact opposite of Lenin but, rather, his continuer, the same applies to the nomenklatura; it was the heir of the Leninists in more than one respect. It was pitiless in the struggle for power, even toward members of the party, and no holds were barred in destroying whatever stood in its way—Leninists included. Compromising with their conscience was easier for its members for the simple reason that they had none. They deceived the proletariat, the peasantry, and others with a quiet mind but, in contrast to the professional revolutionaries, they never duped themselves. They have never wanted the well-being of the workers, even if they make big speeches on the subject; they have always been aware that all they are interested in is their own welfare.

Stalin, the creator of the nomenklatura, did not take risks. When he joined the party he wanted, at all costs, to make a career, whether the revolution succeeded or not. His creatures in the nomenklatura had exactly the same lust for power, never mind what it was to be used for. Yevtushenko has expressed this state of mind very well: "It does not matter to him that the power is that of the soviets, what matters to him is power." Whether Marxist theory is correct or not is a matter of complete indifference to the nomenklaturist, since belief in it has been replaced by its terminology and quotations from it. Stalinist careerists loudly declared that communism represented the radiant future of mankind, but in reality nothing interested them less than a society in which everyone would give according to his capacity and receive according to his needs. If they had ever been faced with the prospect of such a thing, the world would have been able to enjoy the fascinating spectacle of seeing the communist leaders manning the barricades to fight communism or seeking refuge from the danger of it in Switzerland.

What is the historical meaning of the bloody victory of the Stalinist nomenklatura over the Bolshevik old guard? It is that *convinced communist leaders were replaced by leaders who called themselves communists.*

There were objective reasons for this historical phenomenon. The formation of a new ruling class was in complete conflict with the communist aim of forming a classless society. When the Leninists set out on that path, they of course departed from communism, and their actions no longer corresponded with their principles, but that was not deliberate. On the contrary, the actions of Stalin's nomenklatura corresponded with its principles. Its object was indeed to establish and consolidate a new ruling class. Only, its speeches no longer corresponded with its actions.

The difference must not be overlooked. It was this and not age or the date of joining the party that distinguished the exterminators from the exterminated in 1936–38. Molotov, Mikoyan, Kaganovich, Shkiriatov, Pospelov, and others were members of the party before the revolution, but they found their way to the killers' camp; they dropped their Marxist principles in good time and merely retained the terminology. Their only aim was to assure their ascent in the new ruling class.

All that was—and still is—camouflaged by innumerable speeches about the "leading role of the working class." The 1971 history of the U.S.S.R. tells us cheerfully that "at that time [during the *yezhovchina*] the working class not only maintained its leading role but also became the ruling class in the U.S.S.R. This is confirmed by the fact that the Communist Party—the party of the working class—further reinforced its position in the state apparatus."[93]

Let us now try to sum up. In the struggle for power that took place in the Stalinist socialism, the only beneficiaries were those who sought to attain their aim (i.e., power) by the shortest possible route. Those who made the mistake of genuinely believing in Marxism and the construction of a true socialist society were wiped out. That belief brought with it a fatal weakness in the struggle for positions in the new class. The mistake, though fatal, was comprehensible. Men who believed they were establishing a classless society could not successfully establish class rule. Try to have successful family planning believing that it's the stork who brings the children!

This three-stage process is not peculiar to the Soviet Union, for it takes place wherever this type of regime is established. The Communist Party apparatus contains the new ruling class in embryo; after gaining power, it produces the new administrators and develops rapidly into a new class. Successive purges cause the early members to be quickly replaced by careerists. This development takes place everywhere and shows that a historical law is at work.

That should give Western Communists and their sympathizers serious cause for thought. Those who naively believe that honor and power await them after the revolution are deceiving themselves; for many of them it will be the concentration camp or summary execution in a prison basement; at best it will be expulsion from the party and relegation to some subordinate post. Only a small minority that quickly discards its Marxist principles and concentrates on securing the best jobs will have the prospect of becoming the executioners of the genuine Communists. Honor and power will be reserved for those now regarded as petit-bourgeois elements.

All Communists in capitalist countries ought to think about this, particularly those genuinely concerned with the welfare of the workers. I have met men of that type. They are worthy of the highest esteem, and I hope they will read the rest of this book.

The lines from the Soviet anthem I quoted at the head of this chapter have not been sung in that form since 1977. That is a pity, because when one is able to appreciate the special character of the exploits that Stalin required of his creatures, its appropriateness is striking. The first couplet should be sung in the quavering tones of the veterans of the Leninist old guard, the second in the majestic bass of the nomenklatura bureaucrats.

NOTES

1. The House of the Veterans of the Revolution was closed at the end of the thirties by Stalin's orders. It is now the Ministry of Social Affairs of the R.S.F.S.R.

2. Marx and Engels, *Werke*, Berlin, 1961–68 (henceforth referred to as MEW), Vol. 38, pp. 64–65.
3. Marx, Karl, and Engels, Frederick, *Collected Works*, London, 1975– , Vol. 6, p. 349.
4. Ibid., p. 343.
5. Ibid., p. 352.
6. Lenin, *Collected Works*, Vol. 33, p. 472.
7. Ibid., Vol. 4, p. 212.
8. Ibid., Vol. 5, p. 375.
9. Ibid.
10. Ibid., Vol. 4, p. 217.
11. Karl Marx and Frederick Engels, *Selected Works*, Moscow, 1949–51, Vol. 1, p. 329.
12. Lenin, *Collected Works*, Vol. 5, p. 438.
13. Ibid., Vol. 19, p. 139.
14. Ibid., Vol 5, p. 467.
15. Ibid., Vol. 33, p. 287.
16. Ibid., Vol. 5, p. 452.
17. Ibid., p. 472.
18. Ibid., p. 480.
19. Ibid., p. 515.
20. Ibid., p. 355.
21. Ibid., p. 13.
22. Ibid., p. 474.
23. Ibid.
24. Stalin, *Works*, Vol. 6, p. 80.
25. Marx and Engels, *Selected Works*, Vol. 1, p. 409.
26. Lenin, *Collected Works*, Vol. 17, p. 79.
27. Ibid., Vol. 35, p. 294.
28. Ibid., Vol. 43, p. 615.
29. Ibid., Vol. 37, p. 530.
30. Ibid., p. 533.
31. Ibid., Vol. 35, p. 279.
32. Ibid., p. 297.
33. Ibid.
34. Ibid.
35. Ibid., Vol. 23, p. 253.
36. Ibid., Vol. 27, p. 87.
37. Ibid., Vol. 26, pp. 234, 235.
38. Ibid., p. 239.
39. Cf. *Istorija SSSR*, 1973, No. 1, pp. 211–18.
40. Lenin, *Collected Works*, Vol. 29, p. 203.
41. Ibid., p. 210.
42. Ibid., Vol. 26, p. 313.
43. Ibid., Vol. 24, p. 44.
44. Ibid., Vol. 25, p. 366.
45. Marx and Engels, *Selected Works*, Vol. 2, p. 410.
46. Ibid., p. 30.
47. MEW, Vol. 25, p. 379.
48. Lenin, *Collected Works*, Vol. 29, p. 420.
49. *Političeskaja ekonomija*. Učebnik. Moscow, 1955, p. 378.

50. Lenin, *Collected Works*, Vol. 36, p. 521.
51. *Istorija SSSR*, 1972, No. 3, pp. 162–63.
52. S. A. Lozovskij, 'Praktik revolucii', *Kormčij Oktjabrja*, (O V Lenine v oktjabr'skie dni), Moscow, 1925, p. 84.
53. Lenin, *Collected Works*, Vol. 28, p. 139.
54. Ibid., Vol. 25, p. 473.
55. Ibid., Vol. 30, p. 98.
56. Ibid., Vol. 28, p. 97.
57. Ibid., Vol. 29, p. 423.
58. Ibid., Vol. 26, pp. 364–65.
59. Ibid., p. 415.
60. Lenin, *Polnoe sobranie socinenij*, Vol. 40, p. 222.
61. Lenin, *Collected Works*, Vol. 33, p. 483.
62. Ibid., Vol. 36, p. 606.
63. Ibid., p. 507.
64. Ibid., Vol. 33, p. 225.
65. Ibid., pp. 494, 495.
66. Ibid., p. 229.
67. Ibid., p. 257.
68. V. Šulgin, *Tri stolicy. Putešestvie v krasnuju Rossiju*, Berlin, undated, pp. 135–37.
69. Stalin, *Works*, Vol. 5, p. 213.
70. *Spravočnikpartijnogo rabotnika*, vyp. 2, Moscow, 1922, p. 70.
71. VKP (b) v rezoljucijach 1, p. 729.
72. Stalin, *Works*, Vol. 5, pp. 213–15.
73. KPSS v rezoljucijach 1, p. 729.
74. Stalin, *Works*, Vol. 5, p. 213.
75. M. Fainsod, *How Russia Is Ruled*, Cambridge, 1953, p. 158.
76. *Sovetskaja intelligencija*, Moscow, 1968, pp. 136–37.
77. VKP (b) v rezoljucija 1, p. 561.
78. M. Fainsod, op. cit., pp. 158–59.
79. L. Trockij, *Novy kurs*, Moscow, 1923, p. 12.
80. *Sovetskaja intelligencija*, p. 139.
81. M. Fainsod, op. cit., 2nd ed., p. 190.
82. Ibid., pp. 191–94.
83. Stalin, *Werke*, Vol. 14, p. 141. (Only 13 vols. of Stalin's *Works* have been published in English.)
84. XVI s'ezj VKP (b). Stenogr. otčet. Moscow-Leningrad, 1931, p. 52.
85. XXII s'ezd KPSS Stenografičeskij otčet. Moscow, 1962, T. 2, S. 586.
86. Voprosy istorii KPSS, 1964, No. 2, p. 19.
87. *Istorija KPSS*, Vol. 4, kn. 2, Moscow, 1971, p. 285.
88. M. Fainsod, op. cit., 2nd ed., p. 196.
89. XVIII s'ezd VKP (b). Stenogr. otčet. Moscow, 1939, p. 149.
90. Compiled from data in *Sovetskaja istoričeskaja enciklopedija*, Vol. 7, pp. 706–7.
91. Ibid., p. 396.
92. *Istorija KPSS*, Vol. 5, book 2, Moscow, 1980, p. 225.
93. I. B. Berchin, *Geschichte der UdSSR 1917–1970*, Berlin, 1971, p. 464.

3

Nomenklatura in the Driver's Seat

Contemporary communism is not only a party of a certain type, or a
bureaucracy which has sprung from monopolistic ownership and excessive state interference in the economy. More than anything else,
the essential aspect of contemporary communism is the new class of
owners and exploiters.

Milovan Djilas, *The New Class*, London, 1957

On the afternoon of October 15, 1964, I left the Central Committee
building and drove through the center of Moscow. The meeting had
just ended and the Central Committee apparatus and the socialist-bloc
governments had been informed of Khrushchev's resignation. A brief
announcement was to be broadcast that evening. The journalist Victor
Louis had been authorized to file a dispatch to his London newspaper
to prepare the Western press for the official announcement and at the
same time enhance the trust that that useful journalist enjoyed in the
West. I had been given the task of discreetly informing Western diplomatic circles in Moscow through Alfred Reinelt, the West German
press attaché.

The man in the street still knew nothing of what had happened, and
life was going on as usual. Everyone was awaiting the return of the
Voskhod I cosmonauts, which was imminent. Anyone who had suggested that Khrushchev had been pensioned off two days before would
have been regarded as a lunatic.

Stalin had died in bed, Beria had been liquidated by Malenkov, and
Malenkov in his turn had been sent packing by Khrushchev. Who
could have thrown out Khrushchev? I wondered. Certainly not
Brezhnev or Kosygin, who had replaced him merely by virtue of their

positions as his first deputies. Could it have been a majority of the Presidium of the Central Committee? That would not have been enough; its efforts to get rid of him in June 1957 had resulted in its being routed itself. What could it have been, then?

The next day, I was struck by the expression on the faces in the subway. Twenty-four hours earlier everyone had seemed quite calm; now they looked anxious. Just as in the worst days of Stalinism, they were nervous and insecure. What were they afraid of? Certainly not of Brezhnev or Kosygin, whom hardly anyone had an idea about. One thing was obvious: People who yesterday had practically given up mistrusting a garrulous dictator were today gripped by fear of an obscure, anonymous power of whom no good was to be expected.

Those unforgettable days caused me to consider seriously the question of who embodied that power and who were the rulers of the U.S.S.R.

1. THE CONTROLLERS ARE THE NOMENKLATURA

Answering the question is much more difficult than one might suppose, for the managers are carefully camouflaged.

History shows that the power of every ruling class is always exercised by a small minority over an enormous majority. Ensuring the permanence of such a system necessitates the use of various methods: the direct use of force against malcontents, threats to use it against all potential enemies, economic pressure and economic promises, an ideological arsenal, and finally a camouflage of the real social relations. It has always been like that. Feudal power hid behind the sacred nature of the royal power, and the power of the capitalists hides behind the prosperity that the capitalist state claims to offer everyone. In both cases the ruling class tries to dissimulate the reality of its rule.

The new class goes further: it denies its own existence. Both in theory and in practice, the controlling class tries to pass itself off as part of an administrative machine such as exists in every country in the world.

They, too, arrive at nine o'clock every morning, sit at their desks, spend hours talking, wear no uniform or sign of rank. How are they to be spotted and identified? Djilas asks that question several times without answering it.

It is not an easy question to answer. An infinite variety of details blurs the borderline between various social groups, and on top of that there is the conscious desire of the "new class" to merge into and disappear in the mass. That is why it is so difficult to discern its limits.

There is, however, an important detail that will help us. For purely practical reasons, the "new class" has to be able to mark itself off from others and know where its boundaries lie. The controller class must know who its members are. That is the reason for the existence of the nomenklatura.

The nomenklatura is the "group of intellectuals" whose "profession — is leadership" and who "by reason of that fact finds itself in certain respects in a special position in regard to those who are entrusted with doing the work." Stalin established this "new aristocracy" and taught it to govern. The governing class in the U.S.S.R., the controllers, the new class, is the nomenklatura.

It knows that, and that is why it hides behind a thick wall of secrecy. All information about positions in the nomenklatura is top secret. Nomenklatura lists are top-secret documents. Only a very restricted group of individuals is entitled to receive the "lists of leading officials" published in little looseleaf supplements. One wonders what it is about such lists that makes them so secret.

This secrecy is not without effect. Western sovietologists of great distinction either never mention it or say things such as: "In Communist personnel policy the nomenklatura forms only a small part of the system."[1] That small part is the ruling class of the Soviet Union.

2. POWER, A CHERISHED JOY OF THE NOMENKLATURA

In contrast to the bourgeoisie, the essential characteristic of the nomenklatura is not the possession of private property. As the heir of the professional revolutionaries, it is a class not of owners but of administrators. The two essential functions of the nomenklatura are administration and the exercise of power.

In Marx's view, ruling classes always perform that administrative role. But it would be a mistake to overlook the vital difference between the bourgeoisie and the nomenklatura.

The bourgeoisie exercises its control of social production primarily in the economic field: the production of material goods. That is the base on which its political importance rests. The history of the bourgeoisie is that of the advance from the artisan to the merchant, from the Third Estate's lack of rights to the conquest of power.

The history of the nomenklatura followed a totally different path, from the seizure of state power to the seizure of economic power. The nomenklatura is primarily an embodiment of the political leadership of the society. It is only secondarily, as a consequence of that leadership, that it exercises economic power. Political leadership is its main task. The whole power of the socialist state is concentrated in its hands. It alone makes political decisions, and this makes necessary a clear dividing line between its political and its purely administrative work.

This dividing line exists, and the rules of this division of labor are scrupulously respected. Only an outside observer could suppose all power in the Soviet Union to be in the hands of the Politburo or, more naively still, in those of the Central Committee of the CPSU as a whole. In fact the Politburo, though immensely powerful, has only a limited field of action. This limitation of its power has nothing to do with democracy and everything to do with the division of labor inside the nomenklatura class.

Thus the Politburo could of course appoint (or "recommend," as it is called) a president of a kolkhoz, but it would be a grave breach of the rules, and the rest of the nomenklatura would react with silent astonishment. A repetition of the offense would quickly transform astonishment into intense but still silent disapproval. Hence the apparently omnipotent Politburo prefers not to indulge in that kind of experiment, and the routine of having kolkhoz presidents "recommended" by party district committees survives unchanged.

The separation between political and administrative work is reflected in nomenklatura jargon; it is usual to say that a higher-grade official must not usurp *(ne podmenyat)* the functions of those below.

Every nomenklaturist has a strictly defined area of power. There is a resemblance here with the feudal system. The nomenklatura is a bastard kind of feudalism; every nomenklaturist is granted a fief, just as every vassal was granted a fief by the crown. The medieval fief did not consist only of territory; it also included the right of raising tribute from the inhabitants. Marx himself spoke of "vassaldom without a fief, or with a fief consisting of tribute." The nomenklatura fief is power.

In feudal Russia it used to be said that a vassal was "invested" with a town or region by his sovereign. Nowadays they say in the nomenklatura that Comrade X or Y has been "invested" with a ministry or a region.

What matters to the nomenklatura is not property, but power. The bourgeoisie is a class of property owners and is the ruling class as a consequence of that. With the nomenklatura it is the other way around; it is the ruling class, and that makes it the property-owning class. Capitalist magnates share their wealth with no one, but gladly share power with professional politicians. Nomenklaturists take care not to share the slightest degree of political power with anyone. The head of a department in the Central Committee apparatus never objects to an academician's or a writer's having more money or worldly goods than he, but he will never allow either to disobey his orders.

The "Leningrad program" expresses this very well: "In the nomenklatura you breathe a special atmosphere—the atmosphere of power."[2] I do not know whether the author of that program moved very much in nomenklatura circles, but he conveys the atmosphere precisely.

You walk down the meticulously clean corridors of the Central Committee building. The parquet flooring is new, such as is to be found only there and in the Kremlin, there are even small, thin-legged tables with bottles of soda water. On every door there are identical name cards (supplied by the Central Committee printers) with names and initials in capital letters, and nothing else. "Internal party democracy" ensures that the name of a member of the Politburo is printed in the same type as that of the most junior staff member.

You enter an office. On the left there is a telephone on a small square table, and near it a safe and a glass-fronted bookcase. If the office is that of the head of a desk there is additionally a small table and two armchairs for visitors. In the office of a deputy head of a department there is a long table for conferences; his secretary works in an anteroom. A Central Committee Secretary has a much bigger antechamber, presided over by a nomenklaturist who bears the title of secretary to the Secretary of the Central Committee of the CPSU. Next door is the office of the great man's assistant. Behind the huge office of a

Central Committee Secretary there is a lounge room. There are portraits of Lenin and the current Secretary-General on the walls of the office. All the furniture is of standard manufacture, ordered to take the place of the austere old furniture of the Stalin era. The risk of being too modern was avoided and a special style was created, semimodern bureaucratic.

There the nomenklaturist is, seated at his desk, wearing a good but not overfashionable suit; he is carefully shaved and groomed, and his hair style is not too modish either. There is no anarchical disorder on the one hand or bourgeois smartness on the other; everything is in the semimodern, bureaucratic style. In the old days, he (or, rather, his predecessor) affected the representative-of-the-proletariat style, ostentatiously untidy, rude and energetic. This gave way to a reticent, austere style, to behaving like a block of icy determination. Nowadays the fashion is for approachable informality. The man asks after your health and says pleasantly, "What do you think, Ivan Ivanovich, wouldn't it be better to do it this way?" The style is different, but underneath nothing has changed; it's still an order.

Giving orders in fact is his greatest joy. Everyone has to obey them. Just try doing otherwise, and he'll go for you like a bulldog, and the dressing-down you'll get will make you lose any inclination to disobedience that you may have felt.

He is a fanatic for power, which does not mean he is indifferent to everything else. By nature he is not at all ascetic. He likes drink—in large quantities and of good quality, Armenian brandy in particular. He also likes food—caviar, sturgeon, salmon, all of which are available in the Kremlin restaurant and at the Central Committee buffet. His hobby is the one that is "in" at the moment among his fellows; once upon a time it was football or hockey, recently it was fishing, now it is hunting. He orders Finnish furniture for his new apartment and buys books that are unobtainable on the market through the Central Committee book department—books that are officially accepted, of course. But his real passion is sitting at his desk, with the government telephone (the *vertushka)* within reach, vetting Central Committee draft resolutions that will become tomorrow's laws, making sovereign decisions that may affect the lives of millions, saying into the telephone, "Think it over carefully, but to me it seems advisable to do it this way," and then settling back in his chair, knowing that his "suggestion" will be carried out; or appearing at a conference organized by his subjects, well-known scientists or scholars, celebrated artists or writers. It's so pleasant to sit quietly in a corner and watch them scurrying to do his bidding.

For the sake of this supreme satisfaction he would be willing to sacrifice anything, even his Finnish furniture or Armenian brandy. After his dismissal, Khrushchev said it was possible to get tired of anything: dinners, women, even vodka—but there was one thing of which one could never have enough, and that was power. Djilas, who knew this environment very well, called power the pleasure of pleasures.

That pleasure is substantial enough at town, district, or regional level, but at the level of a country that extends from Sweden to Japan it becomes inordinate; and it is even more delightful when you can telephone friendly instructions to distant and exotic capitals such as Warsaw, Budapest, Berlin, Sofia, Prague, Kabul, Hanoi or deliciously remote Havana. In the course of an interview in his office with correspondents of the German journal *Stern*, Brezhnev could not resist showing them the telephone with a red keyboard on which he could get through directly to the first secretaries of all the countries in the socialist bloc.[3] You press a button, ask about the other party's state of health, send good wishes to his family, and then give him some "advice." Then you settle back comfortably in your chair and think with unimaginable satisfaction about the foreign capital, where they are already getting busy carrying out the "advice."

The leaders of the Soviet nomenklatura travel from capital to capital, and in each one of them they read aloud ("voice," in nomenklatura jargon) the same old inevitable speeches about peaceful coexistence, the inviolability of frontiers, and Soviet goodwill. But in his mind's eye each one of these orators sees tempting visions of fabulous countries and magnificent cities that it would be marvelous to have under one's thumb, to add more and more pretty keys to the telephone keyboard.

3. CAREER IN THE MAKING

As we have already said, the primary meaning of the word nomenklatura is (1) list of key positions, appointments to which are made by the higher authorities in the party; and (2) lists of persons appointed to those positions or held in reserve for them.

The principle in itself is relatively clear and logical. But let us see whether we have really understood the situation. According to the Soviet constitution, ministers are appointed by the Supreme Soviet or its Presidium; in any event, the appointment has to be ratified by the Supreme Soviet. Ambassadors are appointed directly by the Presidium of the Supreme Soviet. The director of an institute of the Academy of Sciences is elected by a general meeting of the Academy in accordance with its rules. Does that mean that those appointed to these positions are really chosen by the body to which they are nominally responsible? It does not.

Ministers and ambassadors belong to the nomenklatura of the Politburo; deputy ministers and directors of institutes belong to that of the Secretariat of the Central Committee. Until those organizations have made up their minds, there will be no vote by the Supreme Soviet, no decree of its Presidium, no election by a general assembly of the Academy of Sciences. But as soon as the nomenklatura has made up its mind, these things are swiftly dealt with as mere matters of routine.

In the Soviet Union, as in all the states of the Soviet bloc, appointments to responsible positions are always the work of the nomenklatura. That is an absolute rule.

This has to be borne in mind if one is not to go badly astray. Here is a small example. The Patriarch of Moscow and All Russia, elected by the assembly of the Russian Orthodox Church, is a member of the nomenklatura of the Politburo of the Central Committee. What gave rise to a system that leads to such extraordinary results? The nomenklatura originated with Lenin's organization of professional revolutionaries, admission to which was by decision of the leadership. Stalin, the creator of the nomenklatura in its present form, established the administrative procedure that took the place of the improvisation characteristic of illegal organizations. The informal cautiousness of comrades accepting new members with whom they would share the dangers of clandestinity was superseded by a vast filing system, with innumerable questionnaires, curricula vitae, photographs, certificates of morality, and reports by party committees and the KGB.

In the course of time, Lenin's ideas about the selection of leading personnel underwent a striking development. He anticipated the idea of the nomenklatura when he wrote: "To-day, the workers' and peasants' state is the 'proprietor,' and it must select the best men for economic development; it must select the best administrators and organisers on the special and general, local and national scale, doing this *publicly*, in a methodical and systematic manner and on a broad scale."[4]

Stalin undertook this selection methodically and systematically enough, but not publicly. So far from being public, it has always been completely secret. It was organized not by the state but by the leadership of the nomenklatura. The "proprietor" was the nomenklatura, not the workers' and peasants' state.

Recruitment for political reliability became the rule. Lenin had written that selection should depend on: (1) reliability, (2) political attitude, (3) qualifications for the job, (4) administrative ability.[5] Thus he put qualifications for the job in third place, behind politics. Stalin put this into practice—and the practice survives to the present day. The resolutions of the Twenty-fourth Congress of the CPSU contain the statement that "in the spirit of the party it is of prime importance that politically mature, competent, and capable organizers should be in the leading positions in all fields of action—in party and state, the economy, cultural, educational, and social work."[6] Political maturity is the vital factor.

A candidate for a leading position must show real ambition and goodwill. To be worthy of climbing in the social scale he must show willingness to do anything. The rules of the party declare that careerists must be ruthlessly eliminated from its ranks, but everyone knows that careerism is the chief distinguishing mark of the nomenklatura; in fact it is the secret shibboleth for admission to its ranks. This attitude has now found its way into official documents, as is shown by the following extract: "To ensure the efficiency of the administrative system, well-timed promotion to a leading position is a step not to be despised. Noticing at an early stage if a technician is interested in managerial functions and has a talent for organization and reinforcing his ambition at the right moment is one of his superior's principal tasks." The writer adds that there is reason to be highly satisfied with the practice of forming reserve pools of individuals who are "suitable for work at a higher level and deserve to be encouraged for that reason."[7]

The nomenklatura uses the military-sounding term *oboyma* (cartridge magazine) to designate these pools of careerists destined for advancement. It is from such a "cartridge clip" that entry into the nomenklatura is made. How is it done? Let us follow the career of an ambitious young man whom we shall call Ivan Ivanovich Ivanov. How does he set about things?

At the bottom of his heart, Ivanov is a kind of Rastignac; he is ready for anything if it leads to success. If the occasion arose, he would willingly follow in the footsteps of Bel-Ami. Later we will name some successful followers.

But our Ivanov knows that marriage to a daughter of a political leader or a happy idyll with a lady of the nomenklatura is not the surest way to success, but a gamble. So he arms himself with patience and gets seriously to work. It is hardly necessary to mention that he seizes the first opportunity that presents itself of joining the party, which is a *sine qua non* of success; the few exceptions merely confirm the rule. A Soviet proverb teaches: "To live well and free, pay the party fee."

So Comrade Ivanov starts at the bottom of the ladder. He begins by working as an election agent in a district election, and then as an organizer of election agents; he becomes a member of a party committee and then its deputy secretary. During all this time on the lowest rung of the ladder he shows himself to be modest, conscientious, and industrious. He tries to acquire the reputation of being a man of principle, though a kindly and understanding one. He carefully conceals from his colleagues his obsequiousness to his superiors. But he starts being selective in his friendships, and associates only with useful people, people with prospects, people who belong to the "cartridge clip." He knows that a loner does not get ahead in the party; one must belong to a clique in which everyone supports everyone else, and one must try to become its leader, for the latter will get the best job going. In short, he spares no effort and demonstrates a great deal of calculation and persistence as well as a certain amount of histrionic ability, all for the sake of qualifying for a place in the nomenklatura.

The best springboard for this is the secretaryship of a party committee. Appointments to that position have to be confirmed by the bureau of the district committee. The appointee becomes a member of the district-committee nomenklatura, but not permanently, for a party committee secretary is elected annually. So the first year is a kind of probationary period. If he is not reelected for a second term he can consider himself a failure. The normal period of office of a committee secretary is two years—or three if he is very good. So when he has secured the job, Comrade Ivanov will use his first year to make sure of reelection. During the second and third years he will try to secure a permanent nomenklatura position to make sure of a "good exit" *(vykhod)*, as it is called in nomenklatura jargon.

Ivanov's success depends on his superiors and not on his colleagues, so his relations with the latter change. His behavior becomes more and more official, and he is soon admitted to the "boss" group, who are above the common herd. Ivanov is always charming, friendly, and polite to these people and manages to appear completely trustworthy and dependable to them.

He shows a special, doglike devotion to the chief of the group—let us call him Piotr Petrovich Petrov—whose position gives him the power to propose new members of the nomenklatura. Petrov, now used to power and therefore distinctly more stupid than he used to be, takes a liking to young Ivanov, who flatters him splendidly and is always prepared to commit some mean action on his behalf at the merest hint. His heart, which has hardened behind his party card and his pass to the Kremlin canteen, is melted, and as soon as a vacancy occurs he will order the Ivanov file to be prepared.

Before this, however, he will have a word with the appropriate apparatchik—let us call him S. S. Sidorov. He will begin by talking about last weekend's shooting or fishing, and he will say casually, 'Sidor Sidorovich, there's something I want to ask you. I've found a very promising young man for the position of head of X. He's not yet in the nomenklatura, but he has a future, he doesn't drink or womanize, and he knows his job. I'm thinking of suggesting him to you, Sidor Sidorovich, and I'd like you to see him. If you like him, back him." Sidorov's fat face assumes an impenetrable expression and he says condescendingly, "Send me the file and we'll see."

A few days later, the Ivanov file lands on Sidorov's assistant's desk. The latter begins by cautiously finding out how the land lies; he docs nothing until he has seen how his chief reacts when Ivanov's name is mentioned ("Sidor Sidorovich, Petrov has sent in a file about a man named Ivanov"). Once assured that his chief has no objection ("Yes, I know; Petrov mentioned him to me"), he writes out a request to the KGB to make inquiries about any possible objections there might be to Ivanov's appointment. It takes a month or six weeks for the KGB to reply. Meanwhile Sidorov's assistant makes his own inquiries; he telephones the secretary of the party committee of the department to which Ivanov is to be appointed, to find out what his attitude is to this candidate; and he talks to the head of the district committee and to the head of the appropriate department of that committee, as well as to Ivanov's colleagues.

The essential object of all this is to share the responsibility as widely as possible in case Ivanov should turn out not to be up to the level of his reputation. All the information gathered about him serves the same purpose. The various appreciations follow the same pattern, and it is impossible to differentiate between them; the writer of every one of them deliberately adopts a "neutral" style. What matters is that the appreciation be "positive" and signed by the "triangle" (the director of the appropriate administration, the secretary of the party committee, and the president of the appropriate trade-union committee). The job for which Ivanov is intended must appear plainly on each appreciation. If Comrade Sidorov, dazzled by the brilliance of the qualifications attributed to Comrade Ivanov, decided to nominate him for a more important post, it would be necessary to start all over again, for Ivanov's qualifications would no longer apply. In the mistrustful eyes of the nomenklatura, an individual cannot be of high moral tone in general; he must be of high moral tone in relation to a particular job.

In short, what is called "the preparation of the candidature" is based on a reinsurance principle that spreads the risks. It is typical that the expression "reinsurance" has found a place in nomenklatura jargon. Though used as a negative notion, it well illustrates the state of mind.

When this process has been completed, Sidorov's office produces a draft decision; a copy is made, and it is sent on its way through the usual channels. First of all, it has to be signed by the responsible apparatchik, after which it is voted on by the party organization to which the nomenklatura that Ivanov is going to join is subordinate. At the lowest level, this is the town or district committee; at the intermediate level, it is the bureau of the district or regional committee or the secretariat or bureau of the central committee of a Soviet republic; at the highest level, it is the Secretariat or the Politburo of the Central Committee of the CPSU.

At the lowest level, the decision is made by vote at a meeting. At the highest level, there is no public vote; proposed appointments are signed individually by each member of the higher authority. Here, too, the reinsurance principle prevails; the copy of the draft resolution has to be initialed by all those responsible for the "preparation of the candidature." Curiously enough, at higher levels a majority is not necessary; at the Secretariat of the Central Committee of the CPSU the signature of five secretaries out of twelve is sufficient to confirm a decision. This of course applies to strictly routine matters that are not likely to lead to any problems.

When all this has been settled (when the resolution has been "passed," as the nomenklatura jargon puts it), a fair copy is made of a form headed "Communist Party of the Soviet Union. Central Committee [or other committee as the case may be]." This is printed in black at the top with room for the date to be filled in, and it is marked "top secret." Underneath it appears the number and purpose of the resolution (e.g., "1984. Re appointment of Comrade Ivanov, I. I., to the post of head of X"). Then follows a brief recapitulation of the above: "Comrade Ivanov, Ivan Ivanovich, is appointed head of X." Underneath this there are the words "Secretary of the Central Committee" (or other committee as the case may be) and a facsimile of his signature under the party seal.

The document thus completed is then sent to the authority officially responsible for the appointment (in our case, Comrade Petrov). A KGB messenger then takes it, well concealed in a light green envelope headed "Secretariat of the Central Committee of the CPSU" (or other committee as the case may be). The messenger carefully puts it in his artificial-leather briefcase and has to hand it personally to the chief to whom it is addressed. The latter has to sign the receipt attached to the envelope. If Comrade Petrov is away from his office, the KGB messenger telephones his superior to ask permission to hand over the document to Petrov's secretary, who must sign a receipt for it.

The head of the department opens the letter himself, reads it, carefully puts it, with other confidential documents, in a file marked "Directive organs" and locks it in his safe. Once in possession of this document, Petrov writes out the official order appointing Ivanov. The decision of the party organization is not mentioned. Directives of the Central Committee apparatus dating from 1922 in fact say that any written references "to party resolutions concerning state or trade-union matters are strictly forbidden."[8]

I. I. Ivanov has now surmounted all obstacles and can enjoy the status of nomenklaturist forever after.

4. NOMENKLATURIST FOR LIFE

Can one be expelled from the nomenklatura?

Theoretically it is of course possible to be expelled. As admission to the nomenklatura is legally no more than having one's name put on a special list, it might be concluded that a transfer to a position not on the list would automatically involve loss of nomenklatura status.

That is true only in theory. In practice, a comrade once on the list can expect never to be removed from it. If there are no major upsets or purges, if he does not attract the anger of his superiors, if he remains on good terms with his influential nomenklatura colleagues and respects the written and—more important—the unwritten rules, he would have to be implicated in some terrible scandal to be removed from the list. Normally he continues to climb the ladder, for all his later appointments will be nomenklatura appointments.

The same thing applies in most countries to civil servants and officers in the armed forces. Now, the nomenklatura is certainly not part of the latter. Is it a civil service, then?

Officially there is no such thing as a civil service in the socialist countries, but the nomenklatura would very much like outside observers to take it for a civil service. It carefully camouflages itself as an administrative machine and accepts being regarded as such—the vital objective being never to let it be seen to be a class.

Actually, the nomenklatura has nothing in common with a civil service. A civil service carries out government orders, while the nomenklatura gives the orders, in the form of resolutions, recommendations, or advice by leading echelons of the party. Civil servants are privileged servants of the state; nomenklaturists are masters.

The features that at first sight seem to obtain in both turn out on examination to be completely different. In the nomenklatura there is nothing corresponding to the strict hierarchy, the division into grades and categories, that characterizes a civil service and makes it possible to compare positions in the various branches of the administration. Nothing of that kind exists in the nomenklatura, and there is also no system of regular promotion.

There can, of course, be a certain regularity of advancement in a nomenklaturist's career: from manager of a factory to head of a ministerial department, to a director in *glavk* (the main administration), to deputy minister and minister, for instance. Other (and far fewer) nomenklaturists may have another type of career, say a same-level career: from manager of a textile factory to manager of a machine-tool factory to manager of a flour-mill combine; or a varied career: from editor of a local newspaper to deputy minister of light industry in one of the Soviet republics to head of the agricultural department of a regional party committee. Jobs, offices, staff, official cars may change, but the nomenklaturist status remains unchanged.

This is explained by the method of recruitment. Every nomenklaturist belongs to the nomenklatura of a definite leading party agency. It is this agency that appointed him, and it alone can dismiss him. As no member of the party can be unemployed, instead of being dismissed he is transferred to another job, which has to be a nomenklatura job, as the party agency concerned cannot appoint him to any other. This system assures every nomenklaturist a permanent place in the ruling class even if he is notoriously incompetent; the party may angrily banish him to the wilderness, but it will be to a small position of power in the wilderness.

Does a nomenklaturist automatically lose his status on retirement, as one would expect? Nothing of the sort. The only change is in terminology. He is no longer called a nomenklaturist but becomes a pensioner of "local," "republican," or "Union importance," as the case may be. This absurd description means that he has been given his pension by the local party committee in the first case, by the central committee of the republic in the second, or by the Politburo or Secretariat of the Central Committee of the CPSU in the third. This is the nomenklatura classification with which the reader is already familiar. In other words, he receives a nomenklatura pension.

During the Stalin era, nomenklaturists—and by no means unimportant ones—were certainly dismissed, which in most cases meant that they were physically liquidated as well; one only has to recall what happened to Voznesensky, who was a member of the Politburo, or Kuznetsov, who was a secretary of the Central Committee: both were shot as a result of the so-called "Leningrad affair."* Molotov had the official title of "Stalin's closest friend and comrade-in-arms" while his wife, Polina Semenovna Zhemchuzhina, was languishing in a camp. At the Twentieth Congress of the CPSU, Khrushchev recalled the fear with which he and Bulganin—both members of the Politburo—went to see Stalin, always wondering whether they would come away alive. Nevertheless there were some who survived after being thrown out of the nomenklatura. One of them was Mohammedzhan Abdykalykov, whom I met when he was working as secretary of the central committee in Kazakhstan, in the forties, and who became a mere reader in the Kazakhstan state publishing house after losing this high position. But this was a rare exception.

Things have changed since Stalin's death. Beria and his closest colleagues were liquidated, but some of their less compromised accomplices survived. Anatoly Marchenko mentions that at the beginning of the sixties some of Beria's men were still in the Vladimir prison; they had well-furnished cells and enjoyed privileged status.[9]

General Afanasi Petrovich Vavilov, father of a charming girl, Olga, with whom I had a youthful affair, was deputy public prosecutor of the Soviet Union for "specially important cases" during the last years of Stalinism and at the same time was first public prosecutor at the Ministry of State Security. In spite of his bloodthirsty crimes, after Stalin's death he was merely downgraded and transferred to the post of public prosecutor of a district in Siberia. Yelena Modrzhinskaya, a lieutenant colonel in the KGB, who was one of Beria's secretaries, is now a professor of philosophy (!) at the Academy of Sciences of the U.S.S.R., where she vigorously denounces bourgeois ideology.

A new factor, completely unknown in Stalin's time, is beginning to

* The "Leningrad affair" was a bloody intrigue organized by Beria and Malenkov in order to get rid of Zhdanov's protégés Voznesensky, Kuznetsov, and others. After Zhdanov's sudden death, in 1948, they persuaded Stalin that there was a plot with the aim of separating the Russian Soviet Federated Socialist Republic (RSFSR) from the Soviet Union and that for this purpose Voznesensky and Kuznetsov wished to proclaim Leningrad the capital of the RSFSR.

emerge; the fallen angels of the nomenklatura are managing to preserve some of the prestige of their noble origins. For instance, I met the likable and intelligent Alexander A. Lavrishchev, one of Stalin's minor favorites, who was given the difficult post of Soviet ambassador to Bulgaria when that country was Hitler's ally during the Second World War. In 1956 he was recalled from his post as ambassador to North Vietnam, dismissed from the Foreign Ministry, and transferred to a post in the scientific field, for which he was totally unqualified. That did not prevent him from being appointed head of a department at the Institute of World Economy and International Relations, at the Academy of Sciences of the U.S.S.R.; then he became secretary of the party committee at that institute. Valkov, after being recalled from the post of ambassador to Yugoslavia, was at the same institute. Kolomiitsev, a senior staff member of the International Department of the Central Committee, who was concerned with relations with the Spanish Communist Party, was held one day by the militia in a state of advanced drunkenness. At the militia station he made a great fuss and brandished his Central Committee pass under the noses of the militiamen. The sadists who work in the militia and are in the habit of beating up the helpless drunks whom they pick up every night did not of course dare lay their hands on a nomenklaturist. There was a discreet telephone call to the Central Committee, and the outcome was that Kolomiitsev, too, was transferred to an academic post. He soon became deputy director of the Latin American Institute of the Academy of Sciences.

A nomenklaturist's position is so secure that—up to a point, of course—even political indiscretions are overlooked. P. V. Poliakov, who was responsible for East German affairs in the Central Committee International Department, was once given the task of accompanying Ulbricht during a visit the latter paid to the Soviet Union. Poliakov, who happened to have had a little too much Armenian brandy, started making inopportune remarks to this important visitor. All Germans, including East Germans, were Fascists, he declared. The shocked Ulbricht immediately told him to get out of the car, and complained to the Central Committee. Poliakov was not expelled from the party; instead he, too, was transferred to the Academy of Sciences, to the position of scientific secretary of the Historical Institute, and was the only one of its more than two hundred members who received a "personal salary"—that is, a high one.

In the states of the socialist bloc belonging to a group that loses out in a struggle for leading positions is a grave political crime, but it does not nowadays result in a nomenklaturist's losing his envied halo. Pavel Reshetov, the president of the Committee of Youth Organizations of the U.S.S.R., who was a member of the Shelepin group, was deputy head of the Information Department of the Central Committee. That cost him dearly when Shelepin fell from power. When the Information Department was dissolved, he was appointed chief editor of the readerless journal *The Twentieth Century and Peace.* This organ of the Soviet Peace Committee was really an appendage of *Moscow News*, a foreign-language journal for tourists to the Soviet Union. Though Reshetov now had a staff of only three, he remained a member of the Central Committee nomenklatura—as a chief editor.

I have mentioned only a few instances of persons whom I knew personally, and they could of course be multiplied. Complaints in the Soviet press about transfers to other posts of nomenklaturists who have shown themselves to be incompetent in their previous jobs are not uncommon. Such complaints have been appearing for years and still continue—a sure sign that they are printed solely for the purpose of reassuring the reader. In the rare cases of dismissal, former nomenklaturists remain in a privileged position in comparison with ordinary mortals and to the end of their days retain the prestige of their former status.

"*The nomenklatura is inalienable*—just as capital is inalienable in bourgeois society," according to the Leningrad Program, drawn up by the Democratic Movement of the U.S.S.R. "It provides the legal foundation of our society, similar to the rights of private property under capitalism."[10] Marx said, "It is not because he is a leader of industry that a man is a capitalist; on the contrary, he is a leader of industry because he is a capitalist."[11] We are confronted with the same phenomenon. The nomenklatura is not inalienable by reason of its functions; it is inalienable by reason of its class character.

As we have seen, this inalienability was not born overnight. Stalin obviously had no interest in granting his creatures that kind of privilege. When he carried out the wishes of the nomenklatura by wiping out the Bolshevik old guard, he reserved himself the right to get rid of anyone, whether he was a member of the nomenklatura or not.

I heard a very good description of this state of affairs from Dimitry

Petrovich Shevlyagin, who at the height of his career was head of the Central Committee Information Department and died later as Soviet ambassador to Algeria. In 1952 he was still head of the Italian desk of the Central Committee Foreign Policy Commission (the present International Department). One evening, when we were talking in the premises of the Central Committee, we were interrupted by a call on the government telephone (the *vertushka)*. A high official in the Foreign Ministry wanted to know what was likely to happen to a couple who were under arrest—an Italian man and a Russian woman. "What is likely to happen?" Shevlyagin responded in his usual slow, deliberate fashion. "The matter is in the hands of serious agencies. The Italian may be expelled, but she—she's a Soviet citizen; her fate is entirely in the hands of the organs concerned."

The fate of the ordinary Soviet citizen and of every nomenklaturist was completely in the cruel hands of Beria's state security agencies. This caused silent but nevertheless deep resentment in the nomenklatura. After Stalin's death it was expressed openly in a formula launched by Krushchev; it was said that "Stalin and Beria had placed the state security agencies above the party and the state."

Stalin's unwillingness to guarantee the inalienability of the nomenklatura was practically the only point on which the nomenklaturists did not see eye to eye with him. This was made clear at the Twentieth Congress of the CPSU. Khrushchev's secret report, published in the West, is concerned only with Stalinist repression of the nomenklatura. The fate of millions of ordinary citizens liquidated under Stalin obviously did not interest the delegates.

The nomenklatura stated its objections to Stalin with its usual precision in political matters. It complained neither of the mass nature of the repression nor of its ferocity; all it objected to was *unjustified* repression. Apart from belatedly deploring the extermination of the old Bolsheviks, the only kind of repression that came into the unjust category was that to which the nomenklatura were subjected. In other cases it was apparently justified. At all events, there was no reason to feel sorry for the victims, who, after all, were only ordinary citizens whose fate was completely in the hands of the state security agencies.

After Stalin's death, the party leadership undertook a purge of those agencies. This took place in several stages: in 1953, after the victims in the notorious "doctors' plot" had been rehabilitated; in 1953–54, after the Beria case had been settled; there were further purges in 1955, after Malenkov's downfall, and in 1956, after the Twentieth Congress. The party apparatus secured the submission of the state security agencies and deprived them of their freedom of action against the nomenklatura. From being a mysterious monster of which everyone was terrified, the KGB turned into what it is today, a secret political police force closely linked with and subordinate to the party apparatus. The senior officials of the KGB have to report to the middle echelons of the party (inspectors, instructors, advisers).

Supervision of the KGB is in the hands of a desk of the Administrative Agencies Department of the Central Committee. This is the only desk whose head's name does not appear in the Central Committee telephone directory; he is entered only as "head of desk," without disclosing his identity.

It is not, of course, this mysterious individual who carries the real responsibility for that influential agency; this is in the hands of the head of the Administrative Agencies Department himself. His has not always been a wholly agreeable task. At all events, that was the opinion expressed in Moscow after an air disaster that took place near Belgrade a few days after Khrushchev was deposed. For reasons that have never been cleared up, an aircraft carrying a Soviet government delegation left the usual flight path and crashed into a mountainside. The most important member of the delegation was Nikolai Mironov, the head of the Central Committee Administrative Agencies Department, who had been appointed by Khrushchev and was said to have incurred the hostility of his former subordinates Alexander Shelepin and Vladimir Semichastny, the former president of the KGB and his successor, who had taken an active part in bringing about Khrushchev's downfall.

The delicate nature of the position is shown by the difficulty the collective leadership that took over from Khrushchev had in agreeing on a successor. Nikolai Savinkin, the present head, was appointed only when the KGB's activities were expanded and it was subjected to higher control. This was exercised by Ivan Vasilievich Kapitonov, who had long experience of relations between the party and the state security agencies. When I met him, forty years previously, this severe, round-faced, military-looking man was personnel secretary of the party committee of the Krasnaya Presnaya district, in Moscow.

The post of the anonymous head of desk became rather unimportant after the appointment of Yuri Andropov to the post of head of KGB and his election to the Politburo. Andropov, when Secretary General of the Central Committee, continued to supervise this agency. Thus the higher echelons of the nomenklatura continue to ensure that the state security agencies do not evade their control.

The taming of the KGB was the most important step taken by the nomenklatura on the way to securing its inalienability. The system of dismissal, transfer, and reappointment that we described above greatly facilitated the operation.

Soviet propaganda lays stress on the country's socialist achievement: free medical treatment for all, free education, and low rents. But it never mentions the social gains of the "new class," particularly its inalienability. Nevertheless, it is that gain which has made the deepest mark on Soviet society.

5.   CLASS OF THE CLASSLESS

The importance ascribed to Aryan origin in the Third Reich is paralleled by the high value attributed to proletarian origin in the Soviet Union. Soviet propagandists tried hard to find evidence of the non-Aryan origin of Nazi leaders, but without success; they tried even harder to discover evidence of the proletarian origin of the Soviet leaders, and with no greater success; for all the leaders' efforts to present themselves as ex-proletarians, most of them have never done manual work in their lives.

There is nothing surprising about this; as we have seen, Lenin had no intention of founding his organization of professional revolutionaries on a working-class base. Similarly, the careerists of the Stalinist nomenklatura were not exactly former workers either.

But the Party called itself the "vanguard of the working class," "the organized detachment of the working class," and the "highest form of class organization of the proletariat."[12]

But one myth leads to another, and it was claimed later that the leadership of the party and its apparatus represented the working class as a whole. When apparatchiks with manicured hands who had never set foot in a factory filled in questionnaires, they invariably described their "social status" as that of "worker." This was so flagrantly absurd that a sigh of relief went around the nomenklatura when the phrase "party of the working class" was dropped and the CPSU became the "party of the people."

A nomenklaturist may still sometimes be heard boasting that he started life as a worker, the object being to show that the working class is represented in the administration of the state. But the fact that an old professional secretary of a regional committee forty years ago spent one year in a factory is not conclusive evidence that he is a representative of the working class. During the war, university students were employed in agriculture, with the result that I began my working life as a worker in a sovkhoz. But that does not make me a proletarian. The fact that a "former worker" of that kind is secretary of a party regional committee does not show that the working class runs the country. There is no lack of aged American millionaires who started life as peddlers or newsboys, but that does not show that peddlers and newsboys are the ruling class in today's America.

The real part played by a class in a society is shown by what happens to those who remain in that class, not by those who leave it. When Soviet propaganda emphasizes the working-class origin of some of its leading figures, all it shows is that it is possible to rise to power in the Soviet Union only by leaving the working class. On the contrary, leading officials never leave the nomenklatura; they stay in it and live happily ever after.

From what social grades does the nomenklatura draw its recruits?

In 1971, *Kommunist*, the journal of the Central Committee, announced that 80 percent of the secretaries of the central committees of the republics and of the regional committees and about 70 percent of all ministers and presidents of the state committees of the U.S.S.R. came from the peasantry and the proletariat.[13]

The figure of 70 to 80 percent coincides exactly with the proportion of workers and peasants to the total population of the country. So what is the special feature of this "vanguard of the working class"?

Let us look carefully at the figures. Why are we given an overall figure of workers and peasants combined? What interests us is the representation of the working class in the personnel of the party. But obituaries of nomenklatura officials in the Soviet press suggest that the enormous majority of first-generation nomenklaturists were of peasant origin. Representative conclusions about the relative proportion of workers and peasants in the nomenklatura can be drawn from the fact that in 1946 there were 855 leading officials in the Minsk region alone, of whom 709 (or over 80 percent) were of peasant origin, while 58 were of worker origin.[14]

Those figures fail to corroborate the working-class origin of the nomenklatura, but they faithfully reflect the social composition of the Minsk region at the time; when the nomenklaturists began their careers, the peasantry constituted 80 percent of the population of that region, while workers were only a small minority. Once more we come to the same conclusion: the social origin of the nomenklatura simply reflects that of the population as a whole. It is not recruited from the proletariat, but from all sectors of the population.

If the nomenklatura cannot demonstrate its proletarian origins, can it at least demonstrate its democratic nature? Does it represent the people as a whole? Quite simply, no. All the Ivan Ivanovich Ivanovs who performed acrobatic feats to reach the lowest rungs of the nomenklatura ladder did not do so as representatives of their class of origin. Even a mildly confidential conversation with a nomenklaturist will make you realize that he has nothing but scorn and distaste for the class from which he sprang, though traces of it still cling to the soles of his expensive imported shoes. Mikhail Kotov, secretary-general of the Soviet Peace Committee, who is so typical of the Russian peasant in his appearance and speech, always amazed us by his profound contempt for anything that reminded him of the country and country ways.

These people's hostility toward their original environment is revealed not only by their contemptuous references to it but also by their destructive actions. It was those ornaments of the intelligentsia, the Leninists, who oppressed Russian intellectuals by every means in their power. The now aging Stalinist nomenklaturists were mostly of peasant origin, and it was they who persecuted the peasantry for year after year and in every conceivable way. We shall have occasion to speak later of nomenklatura behavior toward workers—not in words but in deeds.

The nomenklatura rightly considers itself to be a new social community; not one among others, but a group apart, having the right to look down on the rest. This idea is justified not by any exceptional virtues it possesses but by the fact that it is the ruling class.

It consists not of representatives of all social classes but of men who have become classless.

The social type of the nomenklaturist had crystallized out so distinctly that immediately after Stalin's death it found its way into literature. It is already to be seen in Ehrenburg's novel *The Thaw* in the guise of the factory manager Zhuravlev. It was a cautious first appearance, conveyed by hints and references intelligible only to the Soviet reader. Zhuravlev was followed by Loktev, an instructor on a regional committee in Granin's *Personal Opinion*. Then there was the nomenklaturist Drozdov in Dudintsev's remarkable novel *Man Does Not Live by Bread Alone*. The sensitive and intelligent official played up by socialist realism is here displaced by the entry into literature of the crude reality. That excellent writer Konstantin Paustovsky uses the name of Drozdov as a generic term for nomenklaturists in his story about a trip to Europe by a party of Soviet tourists: "Workers, engineers, and artists traveled second and third class; the Drozdovs traveled first. There is no need for me to say that they had and could have no contact with the second and third classes; they were ill disposed to everything except their own situation. Their ignorance was terrifying. Their idea of what constitutes the honor and glory of our country was quite different from ours. In front of a painting of the Last Judgment one Drozdov said, 'Is that the trial of Mussolini?' And on seeing the Acropolis another remarked, 'How could the proletariat permit a thing like that to be built?' Another, who overheard someone admiring the blue of the Mediterranean, exclaimed rudely, 'Isn't our seawater as good as that?' Those wild beasts, those exploiters, those cynical obscurantists made openly anti-Semitic remarks of which real Nazis would not have been ashamed. They have learned to regard the people as nothing but dung with which to fertilize their own careers; their weapons are intrigue, calumny, and murder . . . The Drozdovs hide behind slogans, make blasphemous speeches in which they claim to be acting for the people's good." And Paustovsky asks: "Where do these bootlickers and traitors come from who claim the right to speak in the people's name? Where do they come from?"[15]

They come from the class of the classless. They climb the nomenklatura ladder and reach the highest levels of Soviet society as lacking in roots and social attachments as the men in the doss house described by Gorky.

6. STRENGTH OF THE NOMENKLATURA

How many of them are there?

The fact that no information about the nomenklatura is published in the U.S.S.R. and that documents about them are top secret makes even an approximate estimate impossible. Nevertheless, published figures will enable us to form an opinion about the order of magnitude involved.

Sources on which we can draw are the 1959 and 1970 censuses and statistics printed in propaganda about the Soviet Communist Party. The figures in these publications include subordinates as well as the nomenklatura itself, so we must separate the various categories.

Let us first examine the top category, the "leaders of the party, the Komsomol, the trade unions, and other social organizations and their subdivisions."

Who belong to this category? The first and all other secretaries and heads of departments and divisions of party and Komsomol agencies, as well as heads and secretaries of trade-union organizations. They all belong to the nomenklatura, with the exception of secretaries of the lowest-level organizations of the party. But a substantial proportion of the inner nomenklatura, i.e., most members of the party apparatus and officials who are not heads of departments or divisions, are not included with them, and this is certainly deliberate.

The following figures are given: At the all-union level (i.e., that of the Central Committee of the CPSU and of the Komsomol, the central council and central committees of the trade unions, and central social organizations), at the level of the republics (the central committees of the Communist parties of the Union's republics and the Komsomol and the councils and central committees of the trade unions of the republics), and of the territories and regions (the territorial and regional committees of the party, the Komsomol, and the trade unions), 25,912 persons were employed in all the positions concerned in 1959, and in 1970 their number exceeded 24,571. The figure for districts and towns were 61,728 in 1959 and 74,934 in 1970.

According to the introduction of these censuses, the second category includes heads of the state administration and their deputies. Those who belong to it are the members of the nomenklatura who are active, not in the party, but in the state apparatus, i.e., the presidents of the councils of ministers of the Soviet Union and of the national republics, ministers and presidents of state committees, presidents of executive committees (of territories, regions, districts, and towns), heads of the principal administrations and departments of councils of ministers, ministries and state committees, as well as the deputies of all these officials. It can be assumed that the nomenklatura of the supreme soviets of the U.S.S.R. and of the national republics also come into this category (though, according to the constitution, they come under the heading of agencies of the state power and not of the state administration). The nomenklatura of the courts and the public prosecutor's department obviously also come into this category. As in the case of the first category, the apparatus—the KGB and the diplomatic services—are not included. It is not clear whether the nomenklatura of the armed forces is included under this heading.

The figures for the second category are as follows: At the all-union level and at that of the republics, territories, regions, and districts, 246,534 in 1959 and 210,824 in 1970; and at district and town level, 90,980 in 1959 and 70,134 in 1970.[16]

That is all that these censuses tell us about the numerical strength of these people who preside over the country's destiny. The figures certainly present problems.

The division into two categories would be meaningful if either could be identified as the central nucleus of the nomenklatura, i.e., that part of it that is active in the party organs without distinction between leadership and staff. But no figures are given about the latter. Moreover, leading officials are lumped together with those of the Komsomol, the trade unions, and other nongovernmental organizations, with the result that it is impossible to sort them out. Thus the division into two categories has no fundamental significance for the description of the nomenklatura.

The division into two levels is more interesting. The party committees of districts and towns (towns that are not subordinate to districts) are in a special position in one respect: in contrast to the higher ranks of the nomenklatura, who are in contact only with their like, the lower ranks in these cases are in direct contact with the population (though chiefly with members of the party).

So let us consider these two levels of the nomenklatura. Heads of party and state organs at the level of the central state, the national and autonomous republics, regions, districts, and big towns (of more than 500,000 inhabitants) belong to the first, and heads of the same organs at the level of districts and towns (of fewer than 500,000 inhabitants) belong to the second.

In 1959 there were 25,912 + 51,151, or 77,063, members of the first group, and in 1970 there were 24,571 + 52,276, or 76,847. Thus in the course of eleven years their number diminished. There is nothing surprising about this, for that is the tendency in every ruling class on the way up. Parkinson's law, which is about individuals and not classes, does not apply here.

But this figure of about 77,000 must on the one hand be somewhat reduced, for it includes leaders of relatively subordinate rank in the administration of the state as well as of trade unions and other nongovernmental organizations, who do not belong to the nomenklatura; on the other hand, it must be greatly increased to include the nomenklaturists of the party and state apparatus, the state security agencies, the diplomatic service, and also, apparently, the armed forces.

The numerical strength of the party apparatus is small. The Central Committee Department has a staff of about 100 to 150, and those of subordinate departments substantially fewer. The apparatus of an urban district committee has a staff of forty and that of a country district twenty. The Foreign Ministry apparatus is not as large as one may assume it to be. The building that houses it, in Smolensky Square, in Moscow, also accommodates the Ministry of Foreign Trade (six floors and the adjacent buildings). The building is irrationally designed: a large amount of space is taken up with wide corridors and elevator shafts, and the offices, even those of deputy ministers, are small; there is less room than one might imagine.

But counting the overall strength of the nomenklatura in the Party, the KGB, and the diplomatic apparatus gives us a figure that far surpasses that of the total number of positions filled by nonmembers of the nomenklatura in the categories concerned. Taking into account the required adjustments that we mentioned above, we arrive at a figure of about 100,000 nomenklaturists in the first group.

For the second group, the census figures are 61,728 + 90,890, or 152,618, in 1959 and 74,934 + 70,314, or 145,248, in 1970. The same tendency to a numerical reduction of the nomenklatura will be observed. Here, too, some adjustments must be made, with the difference that this time the number of those not belonging to the nomenklatura among the leading figures in the state and nongovernmental organizations is larger than in the first group. But, again, this is largely compensated for by the number of nomenklaturists who work in the apparatuses. Hence we shall not be far out in putting the number of lower-rank nomenklaturists at 150,000.

Thus the power of the nomenklatura in the Soviet Union is exercised by about 250,000 persons, or one thousandth of the population, who are subject neither to election nor rejection by the people, but decide its fate and lay down the people's political line.

We have not yet finished with the question of the nomenklatura's numerical strength. Many of its representatives fill key positions in the economy, in scientific and learned institutions, and in education. This part of the nomenklatura does not belong to the dominant nucleus; it does not control political affairs, but exercises its class power in its own field.

In 1959, 283,346 persons belonged to the group of heads and managers of industrial and agricultural enterprises, and in 1970 this figure had increased to 300,843. This 6 percent increase in numbers reflects the appearance of new industries. In agriculture the number of nomenklaturists has declined: in 1959 there were 8,835 managers of sovkhozes and 102,768 presidents of kolkhozes, or 111,603 altogether; in 1970 there were 25,571 + 50,518, or 76,089.[17] Research and university and high school education employ about 150,000 nomenklaturists.

Consequently, the total of this section of the nomenklatura is of the order of 450,000 to 500,000 persons, about double that of the first; therefore, the strength of the nomenklatura in the Soviet Union is about 750,000.

When one talks of a class, one thinks not only of those who take a direct part in production, but also of their families; hence we must include in our calculations the nomenklaturists' wives and children. Let us take as our basis the current statistical model of a couple with two children. In some families there will no doubt also be a mother-in-law or a brother-in-law, but in others the wife, too, will be a member of the nomenklatura, and in others again there may be no children. But we shall not be far out if we take the statistical family as a basis for our estimates.

Thus we arrive at a figure of three million. That is the rough numerical strength of the ruling class in the Soviet Union. It amounts to less than 1.5 percent of the population of the country, families included. This 1.5 percent proclaims itself to be "the leading and guiding force" in the country, "the intelligence, the honor, and the conscience of our age," "the organizer and inspirer of all the victories of the Soviet people." It is this 1.5 percent that monopolizes the footlights and, without false modesty, proclaims itself to be the spokesman of a nation of 270 million souls and even of "the whole of progressive humanity."

7. THE NOMENKLATURA AND THE PARTY

A propagandist for the Soviet Union might reply, "We do not claim that the guiding and leading force of the country is the nomenklatura alone. The guiding force, the intelligence, the honor, the conscience, the organizer and inspirer of the country is the party, which consists not of 1.5 percent but of 6 percent of the population of the country, or 17 million persons in all." So let us examine the relations between the party and the nomenklatura.

The numerical strength of the party is indeed great. One Soviet citizen in eleven is a member; in the whole country there are about 400,000 base organizations of the party, which exceeds the number of party members in October 1917, when there were 350,000.

In Lenin's time the party was small, but under Stalin it grew rapidly; in 1941 there were 2.5 million members and 1.5 million non-voting members. During the war, when applicants were accepted practically without selection, these figures increased to 4 million and 1.8 million. After the war the party continued growing to such an extent that now it numbers 17 million persons. In other words, since 1917 it has increased more than forty times, while at the same time the population has increased only 0.6 time.

What does this development conceal? As originally conceived by Lenin it was not a mass, but an elitist party, which was nevertheless overshadowed by another elite, the organization of professional revolutionaries. The party's task was to support that organization in every way possible and to act as a pool from which personnel could be drawn as required.

After the seizure of power, when the professional revolutionaries became professional rulers, the party grew bigger, but remained an auxiliary elite. As such its duties were to carry out the orders given by the ruling elite at the front in the civil war as well as in the back areas, thereby continuing to act as a reserve of personnel for those running the country. But, while the power of the nomenklatura was strength-ened and it moved further and further away from society as a whole, the link between it and the party grew weaker and weaker.

After Stalin the continuous growth of the party and the growing ossification of the nomenklatura further accentuated the difference be-tween it and its auxiliaries. The mass party, which now had millions of members, increasingly played the part of handmaiden to the nomen-klatura.

The boundary line is of course a fluctuating one. The party is still on the side of the nomenklaturist class and not on that of the people. If one may hazard a comparison with a Nazi concentration camp, its role is more like that of the kapos than that of the lower-rank SS. The kapos carried out the orders they were given, whatever they were, in the hope of getting a few extra crumbs and gaining the goodwill of their superi-ors, but they were still prisoners, and between them and the SS there was a gulf.

That is why the inflationary growth of the Soviet Communist Party reveals merely an accentuation of the breach that has been taking place for decades in Soviet society. The nomenklatura ruling class grows more and more isolated, the gulf between it and the party goes on widening, and the party increasingly becomes merely a section of the population.

It carries out nomenklatura orders with more zeal and less resent-ment than the population as a whole, but it would be a mistake to ignore the change that is taking place in its consciousness. At the beginning of the thirties, many of its members were nearly as idealistic and persuaded of the virtues of communism as are most Communists in capitalist countries today. All they believe nowadays is that the price to be paid for social advancement is repeating official lies.

The alienation felt by the nomenklatura has spread to ordinary party members and manifests itself in cynicism and continual subterranean aggressivity toward the masters of the nomenklatura, each of whose setbacks nowadays produces a strange sense of gratification in party members. This not yet openly admitted defeatism is an important element in the present state of mind of members of the CPSU. It is a direct consequence of the widening gulf between the various social strata of which Soviet society consists.

There is a rational explanation of the desire of millions of Soviet citizens to join the party and put themselves wholly in the service of the nomenklatura.

The stereotyped question put to applicants is, Why do you want to join the party? The stereotyped answer is, Because I want to take an active part in the construction of communism. It is not a good answer, because theoretically the whole of the Soviet people is already taking an active part in the construction of communism; logically, there should be no need to join the party for this purpose.

What do Soviet citizens say—not at meetings, but in private—about the reasons for joining the party? They say one thing and one thing only, and that is that you join the party if you want to have a career.

That does not of course mean an assurance of ascending to giddy heights. But if you want to be assured of not being subject to continual nagging and faultfinding by your chief, if you want some promotion, if you want to be one of the favored, rather than one of the persecuted, you join the party. While a party card is of course no guarantee of success, lack of it is a guarantee that you will not have a career of any kind. Exceptions merely confirm the rule; you come across them only in artistic and scientific circles; there are some distinguished academicians and artists who are not party members.

For example, General A. N. Tupolev, the celebrated aircraft designer, was not a member of the party; he was a stubborn and independent-minded old man who served his term in a *sharashka†* during the Stalin era. Ilya Ehrenburg was not a member of the party either. Nikolai Tikhonov, a completely conformist poet, was never a member of the party, though he was president of the Soviet Peace Committee; this offshoot of the International Department of the Central Committee is actually claimed to be a "nonparty organization," so it was considered advisable to stress this by not giving Tikhonov a party card. Another curiosity is that the obscurantist Lysenko, who liquidated the science of

† Prison in which scientific researchers had to work.

genetics in the Soviet Union, was not a party member, though he was a member of the Central Committee under Stalin.

Though there are plenty of exceptions in the intellectual field, there are no exceptions to the rule that a nonmember of the party cannot obtain a leading administrative position. If for any reason such a person is formally appointed to such a position (which in any case is possible only in the fields of science and art), no one will take it seriously, and the business of the office will in fact be conducted by an active member provided for him as a deputy. Thus academician P. L. Kapitsa, a scientist of world rank, is officially head of the Institute of Physical Problems of the Academy of Sciences, but his deputy, a party member, deals with all administrative matters. Up to the fifties it was actually a tradition in the Academy of Sciences that the president not be a member of the party, but the real head of that institution has always been a member. In the time of V. L. Komarov, the latter was the first vice-president, O. Y. Schmidt, a polar explorer and Hero of the Soviet Union, and in the time of S. I. Vavilov it was the chief scientific secretary of the Presidium and future first vice-president A. V. Topchiev, who was noted for his activism and his ignorance of science.

Thus, joining the party is not a matter of principle; to the majority the motive is the hope of promotion, and to the minority the hope of making a career.

I know the Western reader finds it hard to swallow the idea that joining the party has nothing whatever to do with political beliefs. But I should like to ask Western skeptics what political beliefs they attribute to those who join the CPSU. Is it suggested that these people really believe that the social order in their country is the most democratic in the world? That they, citizens of the Soviet Union, enjoy all liberties? That the standard of living in the Soviet Union is higher than in the West, to which, however, they are not allowed to travel? That the material prosperity of the people has steadily increased throughout the period of Soviet power, in spite of which the standard of living in the Soviet Union is the lowest of the industrialized countries? Of all the things that they have been forced to repeat in the course of the years, which are they supposed to believe? That Stalin and Beria were right when they liquidated traitors; or that the traitor Beria was carrying out Stalin's criminal orders in liquidating the innocent; or that Solzhenitsyn is a traitor because he writes about these things?

Those who join the party are required to know its program. Therefore applicants study the program adopted in 1961, which says, "In the course of the next decade [1961–70] the Soviet Union in the process of constructing the material base of communism will have surpassed the United States, the richest and most powerful capitalist country, in terms of per capita income."[18] "In the first decade an end will be put to the housing shortage"; "hard physical labor will disappear"; "the working week will be reduced to thirty-five hours in 1970 and will be still further shortened in the following decade."[19] Moreover, "by the end of the first decade there will be no more badly paid groups of workers."[20] In regard to the next decade (1971–80), the party program says things that have as much to do with reality as the Arabian Nights. When party applicants are taught such rubbish, what are they supposed to believe?

The Soviet citizen, unlike the Western reader, knows very well that when he joins the party no one expects him to believe anything at all. All that is required of him is to say nothing except what the nomenklatura orders him to say.

8. TOWARD A HEREDITARY NOMENKLATURA

The nomenklatura solved the problem of reproducing itself as a ruling class in an original manner that has never been publicized. Every holder of a nomenklatura post is given a deputy whose name is entered on a reserve list. When the post becomes vacant, the committee concerned decides whether to appoint the deputy, and if he is appointed a new name appears on the list. Where do these deputies come from? Alongside the usual way there is another procedure involved, which has not attracted attention; it is the self-reproduction of the nomenklatura, which is becoming more and more pregnant.

The chief argument of those who are not prepared to admit that the controllers in the Soviet Union are a class is that nomenklatura posts are not hereditary. That argument does not stand up. The hereditary nature of offices is not necessarily a class attribute and is therefore not included in the definition of class. Thus the working class, which made its appearance with industrialization, was and still is recruited from the peasantry; nevertheless, it constitutes a class.

But there is also something else. In the course of consolidating its position, every ruling class tries to hand on its privileges to its children, i.e., to reproduce itself and do everything possible to fend off outsiders. That is what is happening in the Soviet nomenklatura. Most high-level nomenklaturists were appointed during the Yezhov period and the war, and the present corps of officials has just had time to bring up its children, who are now of an age to become nomenklaturists themselves. They are old enough to take over nomenklatura posts in ever-increasing numbers.

Here are some examples: Leonid Brezhnev's son Yurii was appointed first deputy to the Foreign Trade Minister. So far only one of his international transactions has made the headlines: he was so carried away by the spectacle of the dancers at that expensive striptease joint the Crazy Horse, in Paris, that he tipped the waiter $100, i.e., half the monthly wage of a Soviet worker. Kosygin's daughter Ludmila, an able and serious person, has very different interests, but there was no particular interest in libraries among them. That did not stand in the way of her appointment to the nomenklatura position of manager of the state foreign-literature library in Moscow. I watched Mikoyan's son Sergo, a very nice man who was a specialist in Kashmir problems, become editor of the journal *Latin America*, thus gaining entry to the Central Committee nomenklatura. Gromyko's son Anatoly, after several years at the United States and Canada Institute of the Academy of Sciences, was suddenly appointed to the (nomenklaturist) position of Soviet minister to Washington, after which he became counselor in the Soviet embassy in East Germany. Later he became head of the African Institute of the Academy of Sciences, though he had never been a student of African affairs, but this is a position in the nomenklatura of the Central Committee Secretariat.

It did not start under Brezhnev. Grigori Morozov married Stalin's daughter, Svetlana, and made his way in the world; at the age of forty-five, twenty years after his separation from Svetlana, he tried to marry Gromyko's daughter. Morozov failed, and she married Professor Piradov, called the "professional husband." Now he is Soviet representative at UNESCO. His first wife was Ordzhonikzide's daughter, as a result of which he was withdrawn from the front line during the war and sent to the High Diplomatic School, in Moscow, which was no small advantage.

There was the young alcoholic Vasily Stalin, who became a lieutenant general before he was thirty and was air commander of the Moscow military district; and Alexei Adzhubei, Khrushchev's son-in-law, who became, thanks to this fact, chief editor of *Izvestia,* the second-most-important Soviet newspaper, and a member of the Central Committee; and Nikonov, who, because he was Molotov's son-in-law, was promoted from the modest position of university assistant professor to that of head of a department at *Kommunist* (at that time *Bolshevik),* the political and theoretical organ of the Central Committee.

Further examples are not necessary, for the phenomenon we are referring to is not the exception, but the rule. The children of party regional secretaries become workers only in the pious novels of "socialist realism"; in real socialism they automatically enter the party apparatus or the diplomatic corps. Anyone who doubted this would find it difficult to quote examples of children of nomenklatura families not appointed to nomenklatura positions or married to nomenklaturists.

It is becoming more and more obvious that the ruling class in the Soviet Union is reproducing itself. True, the posts are not in themselves hereditary, but membership of the nomenklatura class has in practice become hereditary.

In following the footsteps of an ordinary careerist, we described the narrow path that may lead to the nomenklatura by way of the party organizations. But the chances of entering it by that route are becoming more and more restricted, while the royal road of birth is more and more frequently used.

9. A CONE WITHIN A CONE

A model illustrating the social structure of the nomenklatura would consist of a cone within a cone. On the outside surface, a number of concentric rings would represent the boundaries between the various nomenklaturas, with those of the district committees at the bottom, all the way up to that of the Central Committee at the top. Similar concentric rings on the inside cone would represent the committees that are the controlling agencies of the nomenklatura, from the district committees at the bottom to the Politburo at the top. The tip of the outer cone would stand for the Secretary-General of the Central Committee. The interior cone, the core of the nomenklatura class, would consist of a hard substance that differed from the relatively soft outer cone, which would be attached to the central nucleus as by a stalk. Thus it would not be by cutting through the whole structure (the committees and their nomenklaturas), but by separating the two cones, that one would obtain two different uniform substances.

But let us go from geometry back to politics. It would be a mistake to suppose that the Central Committee nomenklatura regards district committees with contempt. It reserves its contempt for that part of the nomenklatura that is immediately subordinate to it. Its attitude to the heads of district committees is friendly and obliging; it regards them as its trusty lieges, though the feudal relationship is not direct.

Are there objective reasons for this? Why should a minister, a member of the Soviet Government and of the Politburo nomenklatura, bother about what the secretary of a remote regional or district committee thinks of him? Nothing would be easier in case of need than to give him a dressing-down on the government telephone (a thing that ministers are so good at), as he is so used to doing with his departmental heads.

But that is something a minister never does. On the contrary, he uses the friendly, almost wheedling tones on the telephone that the ministry staff never hear except at receptions for foreign visitors. (His staff never hears his servile stammerings when he is on the *vertushka* line reporting to the higher authorities, for everyone is banished from the office and the red light is on in the antechamber on these occasions, indicating that no one may come in.) For he knows that without the consent of the secretary of the district committee he can neither appoint nor dismiss the manager of a factory in that district; without the agreement of the district committee he cannot even send him on a trip to a socialist, let alone a capitalist, country. If these secretaries have a grudge against the minister, it is easy for them to make life hell for his protégés in the area; and he cannot get his own back, for the higher authorities will not sack a secretary to please him. On the contrary, the secretaries' thirst for vengeance and their skill at intrigue can cause him grave difficulties.

It would be a mistake to regard this as a sign of internal democracy, even of a very special type. It has nothing to do with democracy, but with encouraging feudal lords of the nomenklatura to behave like dictators. But where are these feudal lords? Their decisions are made in the bureaus and secretariats of party committees, and only some of them are discussed at the plenary meeting, and that for form's sake, acceptance of them being assured in advance. Thus it is not the committees of the CPSU that are the lords of the new class, but their secretaries and bureau members. It is the sum total of these that form the nucleus of the nomenklatura.

This nucleus also includes another element, the Communist Party apparatus, i.e., staff members (the word *apparatchiks* is a '20s expression no longer used in the Soviet Union). The apparatus of the CPSU is no team of technical assistants—it is a substantial political force.

That is accounted for by the monopoly of decision making exercised by the nomenklatura on all important (and many unimportant) questions throughout the country.

Let us suppose, for example, that an academician reaches the age of sixty, an occasion on which it is usual to grant him an honor—generally the Red Banner of Labor. The clumsy machinery of the Academy of Sciences is set in motion to study in depth this very unimportant matter of routine. It drafts a resolution supported by documentary evidence showing why the distinction should be awarded and does everything in its power to make it clear that the candidate is not a Sakharov, but an honest member of the Soviet Academy, perhaps one who was enriching himself, rather than science, but at all events will show the gratitude that is expected of him and will remain loyally subservient to the party. Nevertheless the Presidium of the Supreme Soviet of the U.S.S.R. will not grant this honorable man his just reward until it has received from the Secretariat of the Central Committee a formal three-line resolution such as the following: "1001. To recommend the Presidium of the Supreme Soviet of the U.S.S.R. to grant the Order of the Red Banner to Academician Servily Narcissovich Ignorantov for his services to the development of Soviet science on the occasion of his sixtieth birthday."

The Soviet Government, the Council of Ministers, is in the same position of taking orders; it, too, cannot promote even the most brilliant general until it has received an extract such as the following from the proceedings of the Secretariat of the Central Committee: "666. To recommend the Council of Ministers of the U.S.S.R. to grant Major General Alexander Philipovich Macedonian the rank of lieutenant general."

The principal agencies of the nomenklatura cling like limpets to their monopoly of decision. This results in the necessity of passing an infinite number of questions on which decisions are required through the narrow bottleneck of bureaus and secretariats. These are transformed into decision-making machines or, rather, into machines for rubber-stamping decisions that have already been prepared. There is no alternative when a lot of decisions have to be made at a single meeting. And such practice is by no means new. After his departure to the West, at the end of the '20s, Bazhanov, the secretary of the Politburo, told there were meetings at which eighty, a hundred, and sometimes as many as a hundred fifty questions were on the Politburo agenda.[21]

It would, of course, be possible to have longer or more frequent meetings, but there are other things that have to be attended to, such as conferences, intrigues, receptions and banquets, hunting and fishing parties, wives and young ballerinas. So the only solution is to rubber-stamp the draft resolutions drawn up at leisure by the apparatus.

The unexpected result of the monopoly of decision enjoyed by party bureau and secretariats is that generally decisions are made not by them but by the apparatus that share the pleasures of power with their chiefs.

What is this sharing like in practice? The situation is not of course that the secretary of a regional party committee considers an instructor or a head of a department in his apparatus as an equal partner. The distance between a secretary and his staff is great; although his orders cannot be questioned, he admits that the work cannot depend on his moods only, which is why the apparatus must "prepare" resolutions.

The term "apparatus" fits this section of the dominant class very well. Every question submitted to it is steamrollered, shaken up, and reshaped, and finally the machine delivers a resolution drafted in the insipid, wooden language of the apparatus in strict accordance with the line of the moment and phrased with the greatest caution in order to avoid criticism from any quarter whatsoever. At the same time, it has to state all the necessary facts, so that it has every chance of being accepted immediately by the bureau members or secretaries.

The first secretary changes some draft resolutions for reasons of prestige, but the great majority go through unamended.

There is a phrase for this in nomenklatura jargon: "The matter has not been decided, but predecided." This means that the resolution has been drafted and only the formality of the bureau or secretariat stamp is still outstanding.

The part played by the party apparatus goes beyond the preparation of drafts; many things are considered not important enough for the offices and secretariats to be troubled with them. The power of decision in certain cases is restricted to a very small group of persons belonging to the party apparatus.

These are the "responsible staff," which means that the librarian, the typist, or the canteen manager cannot deal with them, but even a junior member of the political staff is able to give instructions that have to be followed, in spite of the apparent modesty of his rank, say as a technical secretary or a translator. Of course, officials of the party apparatus behave with extreme prudence and make decisions only in routine matters on which it is virtually certain that whatever action they take will not be repudiated by their superiors.

At this point we can make some additions to our model of the nomenklatura. The nucleus turns out to consist of two strata: the organs of decision (bureaus and secretariats) inside, and that of the party apparatus responsible for predecision on the outside.

The model requires completing in another respect also. There is a widespread view in Western literature on the subject that there are three controlling forces in the Soviet Union: the party, the police, and the army. This view is based on an analogy with the power structure of Nazi Germany. What is meant by party in this case obviously does not refer to the millions of members of the Soviet Communist Party, but to the committees and the apparatus, i.e., the central part of our model. As we have seen, this social group is not just part of the ruling class; it indisputably exercises power.

In the case of the police the situation is different. The police in the Soviet Union are no more a homogeneous body than they were in the Third Reich: there are the secret police (KGB) and the agencies controlled by the Ministry of Internal Affairs (MVD) which is responsible for the supervision of the camps; there is the militia, which is responsible for the detection of crime and for traffic control; and there is also the authority responsible for issuing passports, well known abroad: the "Visa and Registration Department" (OVIR), which hands out—or does not hand out—passports to Soviet citizens who want to emigrate or to make private visits to other countries.

The apparatus of the KGB belongs completely to the nomenklatura (as does that of the diplomatic services) and is thus part of the governing class. In the MVD, as in other ministries, there are nomenklatura posts side by side with others. The MVD agencies are supervised by the KGB under the direction of the Central Committee Department of Administrative Organs or of the corresponding departments of party committees lower in the hierarchy.

The armed forces under the Ministry of Defense constitute an authority on a par with the Ministry of Internal Affairs and other ministries. Its leaders—marshals, generals, and admirals—are all members of the nomenklatura, and there is the same type of hierarchy as in the civilian nomenklatura.

The power of the military in Soviet society could be immense; they employ vast numbers of people and have a huge budget. But the nomenklatura class takes appropriate steps to counter any potential threats to its authority from that source.

The first of these is purely military. Special divisions of home-service and frontier troops are completely separate from the rest of the army and are controlled by the KGB or the MVD. They are fully equipped and highly trained and are a serious force capable of crushing a revolt by any army unit. To deprive such a revolt of any chance of success, the authorities have taken a step unparalleled in any other country: all stores of arms and ammunition are under the control not of the army, but of the home-service force.

The second group of measures is perhaps even more important; steps are taken to satisfy the military authorities completely on the material plane. The army nomenklaturists enjoy special privileges that give them no excuse whatever for envying party officials. Marshals and generals are able to indulge to the full their passion for giving orders and their taste for parading in handsome uniforms; and their material situation is such as to remove any temptation to risk their lives by undertaking a *coup d'état,* which, if it succeeded, would merely enable them to occupy chairs left vacant by the apparatchiks, whereupon they would have to assume the ungrateful task of managing Soviet agriculture, for instance, themselves. The nomenklaturists of the army realize that the way to a successful career is not to attempt an armed *putsch*, but to obey authority and intrigue against one's rivals.

As an additional precaution, there is an unwritten rule that the army nomenklatura must consist only of persons uninterested in politics. Nomenklaturists who work in the political agencies are an exception to this, but they are the eyes of the party apparatus. That is their real as well as their official function: the main political administration of the armed forces is officially considered to be a military department of the Central Committee, whose Moscow office was merely moved from Old Square to Gogol Boulevard. The nomenklaturists of the Central Committee who work there have been given high military rank to prevent them from being regarded by the army as *shpak* (a contemptuous military term for civilians). The political officials attached to the troops also belong to the party apparatus and thus to the nomenklatura.

The latter is also represented in the armed forces by the special sections. In this also the army resembles every other branch of the Soviet administration, each one of which has a "special department" (also called "first department") manned by the KGB. In the course of the past twenty-five years, foreign departments have also been established in all administrations and services that have contacts with foreign countries. These are foreign branches of the KGB, or in some cases the GRU (military secret service).

The subordinate role of the army and the MVD is completely legal, and the subordination is to the reigning nomenklatura. Probably there was no three-way division of power in Nazi Germany, either; there, too, the party bosses and secret police ruled the roost; the generals played only a restricted role and were cruelly punished after the *putsch* of July 20, 1944.

Though there is no three-way division of power, the idea is based on a correct observation. The KGB and the military nomenklatura have a special place in the nomenklatura; they are the pillars of its class power. That is a phenomenon that must be represented in our model. The nomenklatura of the armaments industry—the Ministry of Medium Machinery Construction (an incomprehensible phrase that conceals the huge nuclear armaments industry), as well as other ministries and departments—must also be included in the military nomenklatura.

The situation can best be illustrated by representing the police and army nomenklatura by two rows of points starting from the base of the cone, from the central nucleus of the party apparatus. A third row, of smaller points of the same type, can stand for the nomenklatura of the propaganda agencies (press, radio, television, so-called creative associations—unions of writers, of composers, of journalists and so on, the *znanie‡* society, etc.). A fourth row of points of similar size can stand for the nomenklatura of the foreign service to which the Foreign Ministry apparatus belongs, as well as that of the Soviet friendship societies, the various committees for defense of peace, for solidarity with the peoples of Asia and Africa, the youth organizations, the Soviet women, the veterans, etc., as well as foreign-policy research institutions.

The most important supports of nomenklatura class rule are police terror and military strength. But propaganda and the foreign service also play their part.

Thus the cone of the model we have completed looks like a rocket with four vanes, two of them long and two shorter. This rocket does not travel in empty space; on the contrary, the nomenklatura organism is surrounded by the nourishing soil that the great mass of party members constitute. This mass continually tries to rise above the level of ordinary people and secretly dreams of joining the nomenklatura. Internally it is in a state of continual motion. Individuals as well as whole groups try to draw nearer to the fascinating center of the cone, while others are thrown out and the remainder are afraid of being thrown out and put up with being where they are. The successful get as close as they can to the central core and try to find a way in; these people are the secretaries of the party organizations and the members of the party committees; they are the deputies and closest colleagues of nomenklatura officials. They constitute a superior level of party members that could be described as a prenomenklatura level. That is the level from which a takeoff is possible such as we were able to follow in the case of Comrade Ivanov.

Raymond Aron sees three elements in every class society: (1) the elite, (2) the ruling class, and (3) the political class. Not only the ruling class, but also all those who have distinguished themselves at the national level and have earned the gratitude of the ruling class belong to the elite. The political class is that part of the ruling class that actually

‡ Agency organizing public lectures.

4

Exploiting Class

Capitalism is the exploitation of man by man. And what is socialism?
they ask. Socialism is the opposite, we reply.

Radio Armenia *

History shows that every ruling class has always been an exploiting
class. Engels says with good reason that "once in the saddle," that class
"has never failed to consolidate its rule at the expense of the working
class and to transform social leadership into exploitation."[1]

Does this apply to the nomenklatura?

To find the answer we must consider some real problems of the
political economy of "real socialism."

1. SOCIALIST PROPERTY IS THE COLLECTIVE PROPERTY OF THE NOMENKLATURA

Clause 10 of the Soviet constitution proclaims that the economic
system of the U.S.S.R. is based on socialist ownership of the means of
production in the form of state (all peoples) and collective farms of
cooperative ownership. Property of trade unions and other social organizations, necessary for the realization of their statutory functions, is
also "socialist property."[2]

What does that mean?

Ownership implies the owner's unrestricted right to do what he likes
with his property, including the right to transfer it to another owner or
to destroy it. From the Marxist point of view, a ruling class is a class

---

* This is one of a series of Soviet political jokes in the form of questions to and responses
of the Armenian radio station.

that owns the means of production. Does that apply to the nomenklatura?

Soviet propagandists challenge the "anti-Communist lackeys of world imperialism" who talk of a "new class" in the Soviet Union to show where in the Soviet Union there are factories, workshops, or farms that belong to private owners. In the Soviet Union, they say, the means of production are the property of the state and therefore of the working people. The principle that there can be no exploiting class if the means of production are in the hands not of private owners but of the state is considered to be a Marxist principle. In fact it is not.

Marx considered the basic contradiction of capitalism to be between the social nature of production and its private ownership. But, to Marx, private property is not the appropriation of the products of labor by individual capitalists: if that were the case, to get rid of the contradiction it would be sufficient for capitalists to organize themselves into companies (limited companies, for instance) to get rid of the contradiction. By capitalist appropriation of the means of production and the products of labor, Marx means appropriation by capitalists as a whole, i.e., the capitalist class. Can capitalist property take the form of group property from the Marxist point of view? It certainly can. That is what takes place in capitalist combines, trusts, etc.

From the Marxist standpoint, can the management of capitalist property be undertaken by the state? That is what happens in many capitalist countries where a big nationalized sector exists, but, again from the Marxist standpoint, that does not alter the fact that the means of production are owned by the capitalist class.

That is because, for Marx, the state is not above classes. The state is an apparatus of the governing class. The latter can manage its property indirectly through that apparatus without altering the class nature of the property; that is the theory on which the idea of state monopoly capitalism is based.

State administration of the property of the governing class has existed in all class societies. It played an important part in slaveholding society and in the economy of early Eastern despotisms; the economy of Sparta was based on it. Under feudalism, vast areas of land were owned by the crown, which was the name then given to the state-administered property of the feudal class. Would Marx and Engels have argued that property exists only when the owner is officially and legally recognized as such? In fact they maintained the opposite, namely that property is a factual and not a legal category, that a thing "only becomes true property in intercourse and independently of the law."[3] That means that from the Marxist angle the fact that property is not credited directly to the nomenklatura is of no importance.

So far from being new, what we are saying is elementary Marxism. Only because that theory is insufficiently known in nonsocialist countries and thinking about it is banned in socialist countries, Soviet propaganda can manipulate people's consciousness by using that argument.

In the Soviet Union the nomenklatura is the *collective* owner of the "property of the state." There is nothing surprising about that. Its proclaimed dedication to the principle of collectivism forced it to adopt a collective form of ownership. That is no evidence of its progressive nature in comparison with private property in capitalist countries; the Spartans were collective owners of the helots, and in the Middle Ages the Church was the collective owner of vast wealth. That does not mean that the Spartans or the medieval Church were more progressive than modern capitalism.

Obviously there are differences between nomenklaturist and capitalist collective property. Shares in the former are neither bought nor sold; they are granted on entry into the nomenklatura class, and their relative amount depends on the position attained in the hierarchy. Exclusion from the nomenklatura entails their loss. In no circumstances can a nomenklaturist touch or handle his entitlement, but the money and material advantages that accrue to him are comparable to the dividends paid out in the capitalist world.

There are two forms of socialist property in the Soviet Union: state property on the one hand, and kolkhoz and cooperative property on the other. The former belongs to the nomenklatura. And the latter, since it is also called "socialist property," must have something in common with the former. Evidence of this is the ease with which one is transformed into the other. Once upon a time there were "machine and tractor stations" (MTS), which were considered property of the state. Khrushchev agricultural machinery was transferred to the kolkhozes, representing a shift from state ownership to collective ownership. Likewise, under Khrushchev, a number of kolkhozes were transformed into sovkhozes, involving a change of property relations in the opposite direction. None of this caused the slightest difficulty or raised any problems similar to those that occur in capitalist countries when nationalization or reprivatization takes place. In short, the two forms of ownership are obviously connected, but within the framework of the official ideology it is impossible to explain how or why.

Are there only two forms of socialist ownership of the means of production in the Soviet Union? To whom, for instance, does *Pravda*, the organ of the Central Committee, and its publishing house belong? As the party is not the state, does that mean that *Pravda* is kolkhoz, or cooperative property?

No thought was given to this question when the theory of the two kinds of socialist property was noisily promulgated. It was quite obvious that the ownership of *Pravda* was identical with that of the government organ *Izvestia*, the trade-union journal *Trud*, *Literaturnaya Gazeta* (the organ of the Soviet Writers' Association), and the *Journal of the Moscow Patriarchate*. Only later was it realized that the property of the trade unions, the so-called creative associations, the *znanie** ("knowledge" society, the sporting associations, the churches, religious groups, and others), did not come into either of the two categories. But it was too late; the proposition that there were only two forms of socialist ownership had already become a dogma, like the dictatorship of the proletariat or the "state of the whole people." It was impossible to change the figure two, which everyone had already learned by heart, so a way out worthy of Solomon was found. It was decided that, though there were only two forms of property, there was also a third, namely a newly discovered category belonging to "nongovernmental organizations." This did no harm to the reputation of socialist society, and it was introduced reluctantly only because it was discovered too late. But the incident was highly instructive, for it showed that the theory of differing forms of socialist property was pure fiction. Actually, of course, the three forms have one and the same master, the nomenklatura.

In fact the relationship between the nomenklatura and the means of production corresponds precisely to the idea of property relations. Only the nomenklatura can eliminate this or that means of production at its pleasure. When the Soviet Army was retreating during the war, it was the nomenklatura that decided to blow up the dam of the Dniepr

* Agency for organizing public lectures.

power station, that legendary construction of the thirties, as well as many other industrial enterprises; and in many cases this was done in spite of the frantic protests of the alleged owners of these Soviet enterprises, the workers who were thus condemned to unemployment and hunger.

The nomenklatura is quite openly the owner of the social organizations. Among these, the party organizations take first place, followed by organizations administered by organs of the party—generally directly but sometimes indirectly through state agencies (e.g., the Council for Religious Cults in the case of the Church).

Kolkhoz property belongs theoretically to the members of the kolkhoz. But are they its real owners? Do kolkhozes really belong to the peasants who work in them?

There is another question that must be answered first. Do the members of a kolkhoz, for instance, have the right by unanimous vote to wind it up and share out, sell, or destroy its property, the means of production, and the produce of their own labor? Any such project would inevitably lead to reprisals. Members of kolkhozes have strict instructions about the use of "their" property. Even if they are dying of hunger, they do not have the right to decide for themselves whether or not to kill their cattle. The state solemnly granted the kolkhoz land for its "free enjoyment in perpetuity," but it does not even have the right to set aside a small part of this land to be used as allotments. That is a strange form of "enjoyment."

Soviet citizens do not have to be well versed in theory to know that kolkhozes do not belong to the peasants who work on them. When townspeople are enrolled in the autumn to go and save the harvest, they are well aware that they are working not for the members of the kolkhoz but with the latter for the real owners. It is obvious to everyone that the kolkhozes have a boss. Who is he?

Anyone who has ever been to a Soviet village knows who the boss's representative is. This is the district committee of the party, whose plenipotentiary is the president of the kolkhoz; he is "elected" by a plenary meeting of members of the kolkhoz but is sent to it by the district committee. Presidents of kolkhozes belong to the nomenklatura of the district committees of the party, which in fact control the kolkhoz property. During the war, kolkhoz cattle were killed or evacuated and granaries burnt down in the face of the advancing Germans by decision of the district committees; and it was by decision of these committees that the kolkhozes were reorganized, regrouped, or divided up.

But the district committee does not own the property of the kolkhoz; it is merely a plenipotentiary acting under the orders of the regional committee.

By dividing regional committees into industrial and agricultural committees, Khrushchev tacitly admitted the existence of an owner both of industry and of agriculture. We already know who the owner of industry is, and the owner of agriculture is the same. All socialist property belongs to the nomenklatura. The state, kolkhoz, and cooperative property, as well as the property of social organizations . . . belongs to the nomenklatura. It is this common ownership that makes the transition from one to another so simple; the so-called differing forms of socialist ownership are merely differing forms of administration by the proprietorial class.

But why this variety? If there is only a single owner, would it not be simpler to have a single form of administration? That apparently logical question overlooks the way in which socialist property originated. The new class began by expropriating everything that could be expropriated. All the property seized at the time of the revolution—that of the nobility and that of the bourgeoisie—was declared to be state property, and the former owners were liquidated. For tactical reasons, the land that was seized was given to the peasants to enable them to exploit it, in accordance with the revolutionaries' slogan. The subsequent total collectivization undertaken between 1929 and 1932 was simply the expropriation of the peasants by the nomenklatura. The peasants could not be liquidated. So the expropriation was dressed up to make it appear that they had voluntarily organized themselves in cooperatives. That was how the "two forms of socialist property" came into existence. Though Stalin, and after him Khrushchev, announced that, in accordance with nomenklatura opinion, the time had come "to raise kolkhoz property to the rank of property of the people as a whole," nothing has yet come of it, for fear of a reduction in agricultural production.

As for the property of the social organizations, this was a topical question at a time when Khrushchev was trying to breathe life into the slogan of the construction of communism. However, his downfall put an end to talk of any such development.

To sum up, the process of liquidating private property and turning it into socialist property was merely a transfer of all the country's wealth to the new ruling class, the nomenklatura. The only exception was the modest maximum of personal property that the individual citizen was allowed. That is what the liquidation of private property means under real socialism. As is appropriate to every governing class, the nomenklatura holds all the means of production of the society at its proprietorial discretion. Under real socialism the nomenklatura is the collective employer.

2. THE NOMENKLATURA AND SURPLUS VALUE

The theory of surplus value is the ideological dynamite in Marx's analysis of the capitalist mode of production. Surplus, or added, value results from the difference between the value of the product and the expenses necessary to its manufacture (including wages, cost of raw materials, amortization of machinery, etc.).

Marx and Engels were inclined to suggest to their readers that surplus value was characteristic of capitalist society only. Engels wrote on the subject: "It has been proved that the appropriation of unpaid labor is the fundamental form of the capitalist mode of production and of the exploitation of the worker that results."[4] But Marx obviously realized that surplus value was created in other modes of production. In his "Wages, Prices, and Profit," he shows without explicitly saying so that in regard to surplus value there is no difference in principle between slaveholding, feudal, and capitalist societies.[5] Later, in the first volume of *Das Kapital*, he remarks briefly but unequivocally: "Capital has not invented surplus labor. Wherever a part of society professes the monopoly of the means of production the laborer, free or not free, must add to the working time necessary for his own maintenance an extra working time in order to produce the means of subsistence for the owners of the means of production."[6]

Thus surplus value appears in every society; without it no society, even a socialist society, could exist. Marx refers to this, though with many reservations, in *Das Kapital:* "The abolition of the capitalist productive process will make it possible to confine the working day to necessary labor. But in such stable conditions the field for the latter will expand. . . ."[7] Without specifically saying so, Marx and Engels feared that misuse of surplus value might arise even under socialism. That is why Marx insists, in the third volume of *Das Kapital,* that surplus labor and surplus product under socialism "should be used only on the one hand for the formation of an insurance and reserve fund and on the other for a continuous expansion of production to the extent determined by social requirements."[8]

Since the champions of ideal socialism themselves recognized the necessity of surplus labor, Lenin and Stalin, the architects of real socialism, could not ignore the role of surplus value in the system they established, however much they would have liked to. They simply sought excuses for it. Thus Lenin insisted that "in socialism the surplus product does not go into the pockets of the possessing class, but goes to all the workers, and only to them."[9] Similarly Stalin never ceased to repeat that in the Soviet Union everything belonged to the workers; for many years he preferred to say nothing about surplus product. Only in 1943 did he explain to Soviet economists that workers in the Soviet Union created surplus product; that was one of Stalin's rare contributions to economics that has any connection with the truth.

Nevertheless the revelation that the surplus value stigmatized by Marx as being synonymous with exploitation of the workers also exists with them is extremely unwelcome to the nomenklatura. After Stalin's death the Marxist idea of "necessary labor" was suddenly replaced, and surplus labor (on which the formation of surplus value is based) was rechristened "work for society." Despite this terminological masquerade, one cannot help wondering to whom the surplus product really goes. The panjandrums of scientific communism reply that it goes to the "state of the whole people," who else? Since it is the workers' own state, there can be no question of exploitation.

That was not Engels's view. At the end of his life, in 1891, he wrote: "That is the sensitive point. So long as the possessing classes remain at the rudder, all nationalization means not the abolition of but only a change in the form of exploitation."[10] In his "On the State," Lenin stresses: "It is impossible to compel the greater part of society to work systematically for the other part without a permanent apparatus of coercion."[11] The state apparatus of real socialism performs that function in an exemplary manner, and it is the nomenklaturist class that benefits from this "coercion."

According to Marxist theory, the appropriation of surplus value is exploitation no matter what it is used for, whether to satisfy the whims of the exploiters or to manage the economy. Since the nomenklatura appropriates the surplus value under real socialism, in that sense it exploits the workers. No propaganda can disguise the fact that the nomenklatura constitutes the exploiting class in Soviet society. And so long as the Soviet economy represents the collective property of the nomenklatura class and not the individual property of its members, the exploitation of the workers looks not like exploitation of man by man but like exploitation of man by the state. However, the nomenklaturists cannot conceal the fact that each one of them personally receives his share of the surplus value produced,—in the form of high salaries, town houses, dachas, and cars at their disposal, stays in Central Committee rest homes, and generous Kremlin rations.

As the surplus value first passes through the common pot of the nomenklatura state before being shared out between individuals, it is impossible to establish which member of the nomenklatura exploits which worker. But the impossibility of naming names does not alter the fact that there is exploitation.

The citizens of the country of "real socialism" are beginning to realize that exploitation of man by man does exist in the Soviet Union. Not for nothing is the joke we used as a motto at the beginning of this chapter so popular in the Soviet Union. It must be stressed that specifically from the Marxist standpoint the reality of exploitation in the country of real socialism is incontestable. That is why Soviet attempts to dispute it are so ridiculous—such attempts, for instance, as (I am quoting a Soviet author):

"State ownership means that in the socialist countries the means of production are in the hands of the whole people. . . . Can it be claimed that in these conditions the property of the state is administered by a new class of proprietors who make use of them? No, it is impossible. In socialist society working men are joint proprietors of all the means of production; they do not and cannot sell their labor, for that would mean that they were selling themselves to themselves. In those conditions it would be absurd to talk of a relationship of exploitation. The exploitation of man by man exists only when the section of the society that controls the means of production appropriates the labor of the other section, which is thus dispossessed of its means of production and so forced to work for the proprietors of the means of production. That situation does not and cannot exist in socialist society."[12] One recognizes the classic formula: It doesn't exist because it shouldn't exist. But surplus value and the exploitation of man by man exist under real socialism. That is the foundation on which its economic system rests.

3. PRIMITIVE EXPROPRIATION

According to Marxist theory, the bourgeois class began with the primitive accumulation of capital obtained by barbarous methods of exploitation. The nomenklatura class has renounced neither accumulation nor such methods of exploitation, but it began differently.

According to Marx, the socialist economic system should be the result of an irresistible stream of change reaching the point of maturation; the rotten old system of private property would collapse under the shock of progressive forces coming from the outside. Marx's celebrated words sound like a tocsin: "Capitalist monopoly becomes a fetter upon the method of production which has flourished with it and under it. The centralisation of the means of production and the socialisation of labour reach a point where they prove incompatible with their capitalist husk. This bursts asunder. The knell of capitalist private property sounds. The expropriators are expropriated."[13]

The expropriation of the previous owners indeed took place. But for some incomprehensible reason it did not look like the irruption of a historical necessity that had reached full term, but took the form of a bank robbery.

The following is not a colorful description by individuals concerned, but is taken from a Soviet publication, *The Economic History of the USSR.*[14]

On November 20, 1917, the State Bank in Petrograd was occupied by an armed party of soldiers and marines led by the deputy commissar for finance, who had been in power for a fortnight. From whom was he seizing his country's state bank? After all, the bank was not capitalist private property, but belonged to the Soviet state, and the deputy commissar for finance would have had difficulty in explaining whom he was dispossessing. This dramatic action can be explained only by the mentality of the nomenklatura class then in the state of gestation: you cannot successfully control something unless you have previously seized it by armed force.

The following week was devoted to the preparation of another operation. Lenin himself was appointed to head the government special commission for bank seizures. This strangely named agency was set up by the Soviet Provisional Government (as it was still called) just after the elections to the Constituent Assembly.

It soon became evident that to Lenin's followers those elections were a farce; the Bolsheviks intended to remain in power, not provisionally, but permanently, and in that context the seizure of private banks was intelligible. All of them were seized in the purest gangster style by armed parties acting on Lenin's orders on the night of November 26, 1917. Next day, a decree was issued declaring all the banks in the country to be a state monopoly and amalgamating them with the State Bank.

After this wholesale expropriation of the banking system, Lenin's government was faced with the problem of what to do with the securities owned by the population. A simple solution was found: In January 1918 all shareholdings were canceled, and in February all state loans were canceled too, those of the czarist and of the provisional government alike. That was how the incipient nomenklatura laid its hands on the people's savings.

A democratic gesture was subsequently made to the smaller owners of government securities; all those whose total holding did not exceed one hundred thousand rubles received from the new State Bank an amount of stock corresponding to their previous holdings; this was modest compensation, since the value of the stock was quickly reduced to zero by catastrophic inflation.

Having gotten rid of its internal debt in this brilliant fashion, the Soviet Government disposed of its external debt in a similar way. It simply repudiated it, a step it justified by an argument of principle: those debts had been contracted for imperialist purposes by the czarist government, which was an enemy of the people. But it soon turned out that it was more a matter of money than of principle. At the Genoa conference in 1922 the Soviet Government said it would be willing to recognize the proudly repudiated czarist loans on condition that Western governments gave it a larger sum as compensation for the damage Russia had suffered as a result of foreign intervention in 1918–20. As the West had no intention of providing camouflaged support for the Soviet Government in this way, the outcome was the expropriation of foreign subscribers to Russian loans.

All state enterprises passed into the hands of the new government, and only the nationalization of private firms presented a problem. Here, as with banks, a start was made with vague references to sabotage, or the danger of sabotage, and in December 1917 Lenin's government nationalized a whole series of big private enterprises (the Putilov works, the Sestroretsk combine, and a number of factories in the Donetz basin and the Urals). Then came the merchant fleet, in January 1918. Attempts by owners to sell their property abroad were nipped in the bud; selling businesses was forbidden.

The time had now come for a major *coup*. On January 28, 1918, a decree was published transferring heavy industry and the privately owned railways to the Soviet state without compensation. This operation was carried out almost as quickly as the seizure of the banks and the people's savings, and by October 1918 it was over. All that remained in private hands were small and some medium-sized firms. But even this was not tolerated for long; a decree of November 20, 1918, dispossessed the owners of all firms employing more than ten workers, or five in the case of a mechanized workshop. Thus only home industries escaped nationalization.

A breakthrough of a historical necessity? Not quite, because the necessity proved to be very different from total nationalization. In the spring of 1921 the adoption of the NEP (New Economic Policy) resulted in the reprivatization of many firms.[15]

Nationalization was of course completed later—by Stalin. Some of the NEP people were shot, and the rest disappeared into camps. As we know, this did not improve the Soviet economy.

No, the establishment of the economic system of real socialism was not the result of a historical necessity that had reached full term. On the contrary, the nomenklatura seized by force the whole property of the country in three successive assaults (the nationalization measures of 1917–20, the NEP retreat, and then collectivization).

The beginning of the economic activity of the nomenklatura took place under the aegis not of primitive accumulation but of *primitive expropriation*.

4. THE FUNDAMENTAL LAW OF REAL SOCIALISM

Stalin's definition of the "fundamental economic law of socialism" pretends that it is the "maximum satisfaction of the ever-growing material and cultural needs of the whole population by the uninterrupted growth and constant perfecting of socialist production on the basis of the most advanced technology."[16]

Now, everyone knows that, wherever real socialism has triumphed, the satisfaction of needs has declined, and the more complete the victory the more precipitous the fall. The satisfaction of the needs of society is obviously not the fundamental economic law of real socialism.

What is it, then? Maybe the "maximum profit" proclaimed by Stalin as the fundamental economic law of capitalism?

No. Production under real socialism differs strikingly from capitalist production—not only does it tolerate the nonprofitability of factories or whole branches of industry, it actually permits them to work at a loss over long periods, which is an impossibility for a private concern in a capitalist country.

What is it, then, that is more important to the nomenklatura class than maximum profit? The profitability of production is coolly sacrificed whenever it is necessary to reinforce the nomenklatura's power. Here, it seems, we come across the real economic law of real socialism.

Djilas says that the "new class" is fanatical for industrialization, which it pursues by every possible means without troubling about demand. Kurón and Modzelewski claim that this class worships industrial production and that the objective of the "central political bureaucracy" is production for production's sake.[17]

That is not convincing. The nomenklatura is not interested in producing goods for popular consumption or setting up industries at random. Nomenklaturists are fanatics, not of industrialization or even of profit, but of power. Their chief interest in the economic field is to use it for the consolidation and maximum extension of their power, and they concentrate on the production of what is necessary for that purpose.

The nomenklatura's main objectives are the production of arms and the latest technical equipment for the police.

The fundamental economic law of real socialism is that the nomenklatura ruling class endeavors by economic means to assure the security and maximum extension of its own power. That, not any kind of blind fanaticism, let alone a disinterested desire to satisfy the needs of the working population, is the basic law of the real Soviet economy.

And what is the guiding principle of the working population in the process of production? Does it seek to perpetuate the power of the nomenklatura? Its simple and comprehensible aim is to produce goods for consumption by itself, not by the nomenklatura. It wants a supply of goods not restricted to the special shops of the privileged class; it wants homes with enough room to live in, not barracks and state dachas; it wants cars for ordinary mortals, rather than tanks and government limousines; it wants butter instead of guns.

The contradiction between those two kinds of objectives sheds a clear light on the antagonism existing in real socialist society, an antagonism well expressed by Stalin himself. In one of his last writings, his letter "On the mistakes of Comrade L. D. Yaroshenko," he wrote: "Comrade Yaroshenko forgets that men do not work for the sake of production as such, but to satisfy their needs. He forgets that production not aimed at the satisfaction of the needs of society fades away and dies."[18] That is what is happening under real socialism.

5. THE PLANNED ECONOMY AND ULTRAMONOPOLY

My early school years corresponded with the period of the first Five-Year Plan. We studied it with the aid of Ilyin's book *The Story of the Great Plan,*[19] which begins with a description of the alleged anarchy of capitalist production.

An American entrepreneur suddenly discovers there is a big demand for men's hats, which he sets about producing at a tremendous rate.

Other capitalists follow his example. All available capital is invested in the production of men's hats, which accumulate in huge quantities in shops and warehouses. But there is no need for all these hats for which there are no customers, and soon businesses collapse, banks fail, the unemployed vegetate in the employment exchanges, and economic crisis works havoc. Now another capitalist has the brilliant idea of producing cigarette lighters. The whole tribe of capitalists immediately plunge into the business of producing lighters—and once more there is a huge accumulation of unsalable stock, businesses collapse, banks fail, etc. Under a planned economy, in which everything is worked out in advance and production does not exceed what is required for the satisfaction of the continually growing needs of the Soviet citizen, things are quite different.

We liked Ilyin's book. It was printed on good paper such as was to be seen nowhere else and it was illustrated with photographs of well-made hats and elegant lighters that the planned economy did not produce. It was not until many years later in Vienna that I first met a Western entrepreneur, a small Swiss manufacturer. He laughed heartily at the ideas that I owed to Ilyin and explained to me that every capitalist had to plan his production very carefully, if only because, unlike the architects of the Five-Year Plan, it was his own money that he was investing and not the state's.

Meanwhile theoretical analysis of the planned economy in the U.S.S.R. has not yet advanced beyond the Ilyin level of argument. Actually it has been enriched only by Stalin's declaration that planning is a law of the socialist economy.

With that one can only agree. It is an organic and not a fortuitous feature of real socialism.

Like the factory belonging to the Swiss manufacturer, the whole Soviet economy is a single enterprise belonging to a single owner, the nomenklatura, which exercises complete control over what can be more accurately described as the huge syndicate of which the Soviet economy consists. The word syndicate is Lenin's. In his *The State and Revolution* he describes as follows the path that leads to the setting up of the socialist economy: "The expropriation of the capitalists, the conversion of *all* citizens into workers and other employees of *one* huge "syndicate"—the whole state—and the complete subordination of the entire work of this syndicate to a genuinely democratic state, *the state of the Soviets of workers' and soldiers' deputies.*"[20]

That program was successfully carried out—with the difference that the state that controls the syndicate of the Soviet economy is not a democratic but a nomenklatura state, and that its managers are not representatives of soldiers and workers but members of the nomenklatura governing class, who represent no one.

Let us call this syndicate an ultramonopoly. This, too, is a Soviet-born idea. A collective study by Soviet authors states: "However big capitalist monopolies may be, however concentrated property may be in the hands of state monopoly capitalism (in some countries as much as 40 percent), nevertheless it is under socialism that the greatest concentration of property is attained by means of the general national concentration of all the major means of production."[21] That is ultramonopoly.

The sole owner is the nomenklatura class. Of course it has to plan the work of the ultramonopoly through the agency of the state, just as the Swiss small manufacturer has to plan at his modest level. So it is not surprising that there is planning in the Soviet Union. What is surprising is that the planning is so obviously unrealistic, as the results never correspond with the forecasts.

What is just as surprising is that, contrary to the belief of some people in the West, planning never ensures the necessary balance between various branches of production that is proclaimed in *The Political Economy of Socialism.* Evidence that this requirement is not taken seriously is provided by the continual encouragement that is given to exceed the targets laid down in the plan. A branch of industry or an enterprise may manufacture things that are completely useless from the point of view of the plan, but the more they produce the more they are congratulated. In their economic thinking the masters of the nomenklatura give absolute priority to getting maximum production from the workers for the same wage. Though the production of useless goods often involves loss, the nomenklatura class is incapable of dropping the seductive idea of producing huge quantities of things that, though useless, create the impression of costing nothing. In a productive system that allegedly aims at production in optimal quantities, the nomenklatura encourages imbalance.

The nomenklatura class exercises unlimited sway over the huge syndicate of which the Soviet economy consists. That is the principal feature of the country's economic organization. Nevertheless the outside world goes on believing that its chief characteristic is economic planning.

There is nothing surprising in the fact that the nomenklatura has nothing but scorn for the hesitant efforts of Western capitalist countries to introduce elements of economic planning. For it is in fact possible to plan only when the whole economy of a country has been turned into a single syndicate belonging to the ruling class. Otherwise a plan can be no more than a set of recommendations that may or may not be followed, rather like the recommendations of a business research institution. The nomenklatura, which controls everything, obviously has nothing but contempt for planning of that kind.

It was in fact real socialism that introduced the idea of planning into economics; that is its chief contribution to the development of the world economy, but that positive aspect should not be confused with the question of the actual results of planning by the nomenklatura syndicate.

It has been customary since Marx's time to describe the regulatory mechanisms of the market as primitive and anarchical, and there is some truth in the description. The capitalist market is anarchical in the sense that it lacks a controlling authority. It is primitive in the sense that its reactions are not the result of considered analysis of the overall market situation or logical deductions from such analysis. But these two points are a sign not of the weakness but of the strength of the market mechanism.

Let us recall the fable of the millipede that when it tried to move its legs consciously could not move at all. Or let us consider the human organism, which has millions of cells, each one of which works. If you tried consciously to give orders to each one of them, none of them would work, and you would quickly find yourself in a mental hospital. In devising the nervous system, nature gave consciousness a protective mechanism that frees it from tasks that can be done without it. The same can be said of society and the mechanism of consciousness. The fact that Marx, who was an admirer of Darwin, did not take account of this phenomenon is a direct result of eighteenth-century rationalism.

The regulatory mechanism of society in the economic field is the market. It is incomparably more sensitive, more flexible, and quicker to react than the most efficient bureaucracy, let alone a bureaucracy selected on political grounds. Moreover, when bureaucratic orders are given several years in advance and constitute a rigid norm for a five-year period, no flexibility in economic reactions is possible. The planning agencies can be expanded and the figures inflated, but the result is no substitute for the self-regulatory mechanisms of the market.

The market has a self-regulatory ability, but it is neither social nor human; hence crises of overproduction, unemployment, and bankruptcies. The market mechanism does a great deal, but it cannot do everything.

We have already mentioned the need of rational planning. It is useful to introduce an element of consciousness into the market. It is useful to have a plan drawn up by experts in a purely advisory capacity. Planning of that kind is certainly not to the taste of the nomenklatura, but it could certainly be very effective. On the contrary, a plan that is laid down by a bureaucracy in the form of law and is accompanied by the destruction of the self-regulatory mechanism of the market paralyzes development. It does not of course completely halt the process of production (which would mean the liquidation of human society), but it stifles the market by ultramonopoly, and the consequences are serious.

6. THROTTLING TECHNICAL DEVELOPMENT

In his *Imperialism, the Highest Stage of Capitalism,* Lenin writes: "As we have seen, the deepest economic foundation of imperialism is monopoly. This is capitalist monopoly, i.e., monopoly which has grown out of capitalism and which exists in the general environment of capitalism, commodity production and competition, in permanent and insoluble contradiction to this general environment. Nevertheless, like all monopoly, it inevitably engenders a tendency to stagnation and decay. Since monopoly prices are established, even temporarily, the motive cause of technical and, consequently, of all other progress disappears to a certain extent and, further, the *economic* possibility arises of deliberately retarding technical progress." And Lenin continues: "Certainly, monopoly under capitalism can never completely, and for a very long period of time, eliminate competition in the world market (and this, by the way, is one of the reasons why the theory of ultra-imperialism is so absurd). Certainly, the possibility of reducing the cost of production and increasing profits by introducing technical improvements operates in the direction of change. But the *tendency* to stagnation and decay, which is characteristic of monopoly, continues to operate, and in some branches of industry, in some countries, for certain periods of time, it gains the upper hand."[22]

Lenin was writing about capitalist countries, but, as he insists, what he says applies to *all* monopolies. A monopoly is in permanent contradiction to its capitalist environment, which explains why it cannot develop to its logical conclusion, which Kautsky called ultraimperialism. Thus the big Western combines described as monopolies in Marxist propaganda are not monopolies in the economic meaning of the term, for none of them is able completely to monopolize production in its field. But to the extent that they succeed in fixing prices like a monopoly and in eliminating competition, the tendency to stagnation and decay mentioned by Lenin duly makes its appearance. Lenin quotes an example: "In America, a certain Owens invented a machine which revolutionised the manufacture of bottles. The German bottle-manufacturing cartel purchased Owens's patent, but pigeon-holed it, refrained from utilising it."[23]

It would be manifestly absurd to suggest that nowadays bottles are not made by machinery; the market and the pursuit of maximum profit made this inevitable.

But what is the situation under real socialism, in which the capitalist environment has been destroyed and the ultramonopoly of the ruling class has been put in its place?

Suppose yourself to be a Soviet citizen. Speeches, broadcasts, bills, and placards are aimed at "awakening a feeling of ownership" in you— in other words, making you work tirelessly for the enrichment of the Soviet state. But you weren't born yesterday, and you have realized since childhood that the owner isn't you, that the author of these appeals doesn't believe his own words, and that he writes them only to earn his living and pursue his career. He has his interests, and you have yours. And yours, as you are very well aware, are to do as little work as possible for the maximum possible pay.

The production norm of course imposes certain limitations on you in this respect. But what happens if you do not respect the norm? Nothing very dreadful; there is no unemployment, people are needed, you will not be fired, and even if you are, the factory next door will give you a job immediately. Your superiors are well aware of that, and they will not impose norms on you that you are unable to fulfill.

Now, suppose you are head of a department, a manager or chief engineer. What are your interests in that capacity? At party meetings you will obviously say how passionately you care about the growth and development of your enterprise. But do you really care? Your interests are to be rewarded and praised for slightly overfulfilling the norm and climbing the promotion ladder. You have no sympathy with the workers, and you would be perfectly willing to drive the lazy fellows to work harder to help you in your ambitions. On the other hand, you know what they think, and you know that if you put too much pressure on them it will create difficulties that will inevitably bring down on you the anger of your superiors. So what are you to do? A manager is not expected to produce maximum profit (in the absence of free competition it is hardly possible to establish what that would be), but simply to reach the targets laid down in the plan. You need exceed them only slightly to be assured of congratulation and reward. An excessive and unexpected overfulfillment of the norm would result in nothing but trouble; you would be unpopular with your staff and with other managers, and the authorities would suspect you of having hitherto dragged your feet or accumulated secret reserves. Your norms would be increased, and the whole thing could only have an adverse effect on your career.

That is why your interest is to take the easier course, that is, to fulfill a minimal plan. You will do everything in your power to persuade the authorities that your enterprise has reached the limits of its potential. In any case, it is generally you who fix what is required, for neither the higher administration nor the ministry, to say nothing of the State Planning Commission, has any idea of the real situation, so all they can do is rubber-stamp the proposals you put to them.

To ensure that all goes smoothly, you need only add a small percentage increase to the production figures of the previous period. But you must emphasize that fulfillment of this new plan will require the utmost effort on the part of all your forces and the mobilization of all your available reserves.

Now, why do the administration and the ministry accept such proposals?

Imagine yourself a high official in the administration, or even the minister. How do your interests differ from those of a manager? In no way whatever. You, too, want to keep your job, you want a decoration, you want to be considered a highly efficient administrator by the Central Committee. You do not of course have the slightest interest in the workers and departmental chiefs, whom you see only on your tours of inspection, when they display enormous personal respect for you. You would cheerfully sacrifice them all if your career required it. But your career requires something else of you. To set an example, you may, perhaps, punish a departmental head who makes a nuisance of himself or a manager who cannot count on the support of the regional party committee, thus impressing your superiors with your vigilance. But it is still more important that your superiors should see something else, namely that the enterprises that report to the main administration or the ministry regularly achieve their norms, are in the van of proficiency, and are awarded red banners for doing more than was required of them. So you will not impose on them a plan impossible to fulfill; you will take the easier course of gravely putting your signature to the plans submitted to you. Nor will you undertake the painful task of checking the accuracy of the accounts submitted to you. All that matters is that the plans should be correctly drawn up, so that the supervisory commission will find nothing to criticize in them. You will of course make long speeches at congresses, conferences, and party meetings about the necessity of putting one's shoulder to the wheel and harnessing all energies for the formidable tasks ahead. But your interest is that all the enterprises reporting to you produce evidence to show that your plans have been fulfilled and even exceeded, and that plans just as easy to fulfill, that is to say minimal plans, are prepared for the future.

The plans are next submitted by the ministry to Gosplan, the State Planning Commission. Now imagine yourself in the position of one of the higher-ups of Gosplan, or suppose you are actually its chief, a deputy prime minister. You are presented with a succession of secret files signed by ministers and stuffed full of plans. You know that no minister will have signed plans for which his ministry bears responsibility without the agreement of the appropriate department of the Central Committee of the party. You have no interest in finding out whether these departments have really carried out a detailed check of this terrifying mass of figures, or whether the minister has simply agreed to them with the head of the department in the course of a shooting party or over a bottle of imported brandy. The head of the department has taken responsibility for them, and he is not your subordinate; who knows? one day, perhaps, he might become a secretary of the Central Committee. You have no intention of attracting the hostility of an influential man for the sake of some stupid figures. Moreover, your staff assures you that the figures are correct, for they represent an increase in comparison with last year. So you are covered, and you sign a huge quantity of plans that will get lost in an ocean of statistics that no one, and certainly no member of the Politburo, is capable of checking.

But even while signing the plans you know that that is not the end of the story. Soon you will be receiving the first proposed modification of the plans, a process that will go on to the end of the first quarter of the period concerned. Your role is neither to insist on strict fulfillment of every detail of the plans nor to punish every one of those who fall short of such fulfillment. What happens to the latter is obviously a matter of complete indifference to you, but, if a large number of plans turn out to be unsatisfactory, you run the risk of being held responsible, for you will have approved plans that turn out to be unsound. So to demonstrate your firmness and show the famous "Bolshevik intolerance" of all shortcomings, you will sacrifice a few of those who have failed. But in the vast majority of cases you will introduce modifications throughout the period of the plan the only purpose of which is to reduce the original figures.

Only naïve foreign observers are taken in by solemn statements to the effect that the plan is law and must be fulfilled at all costs. Officials in the Soviet economy know that plans are generally revised and that the final results are very much lower than the original targets.

Now put yourself in the position of a member of the Politburo, or even the Secretary-General himself. Do you suppose you will shout at the people concerned and tell them to change their plans completely? Even though you have no sympathy whatever for all these departmental chiefs, factory managers, heads of central administrations, and members of the Gosplan, who are just a swarm of ants as seen from your height, you will do nothing of the sort. You, too, have your interests, which are in broad agreement with those of the nomenklatura class. Of course it would be desirable to get greater benefit from the toil of all those ants, but the vital thing is to authorize nothing that could in the slightest degree threaten your own unlimited power and that of the nomenklatura. That is the overriding need. It would of course be possible to eliminate some of the idlers who have not fulfilled their norms and give them no more work, or increase their norms. But then you would be faced with the problem of what to do with the unemployed. You can't follow the example of the Yugoslav revisionists, who allow their unemployed to work abroad, for when they come home again they are dangerous and are not to be trusted. Should one allow them to vegetate in poverty? But that might be dangerous too. Should they all be sent to camps? But times have changed.

Thus, though you are Secretary-General of the Central Committee, you have no choice. Your interests require that nothing should change. You can insist, give orders, issue slogans, you can even announce economic reforms, but actually there must be no change.

Thus the circle is closed. A bureaucratic plan conceived in the ultramonopoly of real socialism leads to the inevitable result: a field of force that acts on the whole hierarchy from apprentice to Secretary-General and works steadily and persistently in the direction of minimizing the plan. It is not the result of a conspiracy; on the contrary, the fate of each individual is a matter of total indifference to all the others. It rests on an extremely solid foundation, the common interests of everyone concerned.

As this field of force automatically appears in every enterprise, every kolkhoz, every sovkhoz, it is irresistible. Ministries have been set up, split up, abolished, replaced by sovnarkhozest† and state committees, and then new ministries have been established; there have been workers' and peasants' inspection, then state control commissions, and later a people's one. But no reorganization, and of course no propaganda has been able to break the lines of force and overcome the negative dynamism peculiar to the economic system of real socialism.

Marx did not foresee this dynamism, but Lenin glimpsed something of the sort, for big combines already existed in his time. He rightly insisted that the danger was not of absolute stagnation, but only of a

---

† "Councils of people's economy": regional economy-management agencies created by Khrushchev with the aim of decentralizing the Soviet national economy.

tendency to it; the growth of production continues, but on a scale abnormally small in comparison with the potentialities.

This tendency is manifestly greater under real socialism than it is under capitalism, since even where big combines exist, the free market works against it. Meanwhile the economic system of real socialism has led to a total indifference to the objective results of their work on the part of all those involved in production at all levels of the social scale.

To stick to Marxist terminology, it is correct, in regard to this matter of stagnation, to talk of a tendency to the reduction of the development of the productive forces.

This process is illustrated in a nutshell by the problem of introduction *(vnedreniye)*. This term refers to the introduction into production of new scientific or technical advances. We have here a phenomenon of the type that Lenin was referring to with his bottle-manufacturing example—with the difference that under real socialism the problem is especially acute. The Soviet press, incidentally, makes frequent references to the problem of "introduction," and the subject is perpetually on the agenda of the Academy of Sciences and other scientific institutions. The State Committee for Science and Technology, which is chaired by a deputy prime minister, was set up to tackle the problem.

How do some of these conflicts manifest themselves in Soviet industry? Let us look, for example, at Vladimir Dudintsev's *Man Does Not Live by Bread Alone*.

From the Western point of view, the plot of the novel sounds like a farce: the nomenklaturist Drozdov, a factory manager, engages in vigorous intrigue to prevent the introduction of new machinery that will increase his output. Under real socialism a conflict of this sort is not paradoxical and comes as no surprise to anyone in the Eastern bloc. As we mentioned above, a manager is expected to exceed his norm only by the small amount that will assure him of a reward. Hence the introduction of new machinery can lead to nothing but trouble, for a substantial change in his output figures can cause him to lose his reward and can threaten his future, as his norms under the plan will take the new technical possibilities into account and will be increased. So a sensible manager will do everything he can to prevent the introduction of new technology, particularly as his workers have no interest in such innovations either, because it is their norms of production and not their wages that will be increased as a result.

The bureaucratic planned economy is basically hostile to technical progress. This applies not only to the introduction of new machinery, but also to the techniques of office efficiency, in which the Soviet Union is so backward that average Western offices, to say nothing of banks or big business firms, are noticeably better equipped than the administrative offices of the Central Committee.

In practice, though not in speeches, the attitude to technical progress is exactly the reverse of that under capitalism. The latter, when a scientific advance has been made, is faced with the problem of industrial espionage, while real socialism is up against that of "introduction." There are also other signs of the tendency to the reduction of development of the productive forces: the poor quality of the output of socialist enterprises, for instance. In the West there is a widespread belief that in spite of their mediocre appearance, Soviet products are characterized by solidity and good quality. Citizens of the Soviet Union know that their quality is on a par with their appearance.

The basic reason for this is that planned production aims at quantity, expressed either in units or in value. Those are the terms in which the plan has to be fulfilled, and quality is secondary. The impression given is that output has to reach state standards of quality (GOST), but checks are very superficial. They are carried out by the technical supervisory section (OTK) that exists in every factory. But the checkers are very subordinate people, and all they can do is occasionally trip up an unpopular superior, at the very most the head of a department. They will never run the risk of compromising the plan, fufillment of which is essential to them if they are to be rewarded.

The nomenklatura is well aware of this, as it tacitly implies by submitting the armaments industry, in which it has a vital interest, to checking by representatives of the Defense Ministry (the Voyenpred), who are not subordinate either to the factory managers or even to the armaments ministries. Products for the KGB are also subjected to extremely strict quality control.

The poor quality of output is one of the ways in which fulfillment of plans is facilitated. It is tolerated by the nomenklatura; and in this respect the restriction of progress and development is even more obvious than it is in the quantitative respect; the quantity of goods increases, but in many cases the quality declines.

Another manifestation of this restriction, less immediately obvious but familiar to Soviet consumers, is the following: When the plan lays down objectives not quantitatively but in terms of value, a factory will try to produce expensive variations of the same product, which enables it to manufacture less while still fulfilling the plan. If you happen to see in a shop an article that is pretentious and for that reason is offered at an exaggerated price, you can be certain that the factory manager has chosen that method of fulfilling his plan. He is totally indifferent to whether or not it finds a buyer.

The tendency to the reduction of the productive forces has of course not escaped the notice of the nomenklatura. But as a class it refuses to admit it, and it conceals the effects as well as it can. Thus the practice of *pripiski* ("writing in"), which is pure and simple fraud, has developed; imaginary amounts are knowingly entered in the accounts for goods that have not been manufactured. This practice is based on clear recognition of the completely theoretical and bureaucratic nature both of the planning and of the accounting; ministries and Gosplan offices issue theoretical instructions without knowing the real state of affairs, and the response is similarly unrelated to actual output.

Sometimes the perpetrators are discovered, but it is obvious in most cases that those who have resorted to these practices have been doing so for many years, so evidently there is no difficulty in doing so under real socialism. Since economic planning is controlled by people in the highest places, it is the pillars of society and not petty crooks who are responsible for these falsifications.

One of them was A. E. Larionov, the first secretary of the Riazan regional committee, who solemnly undertook to increase meat production in his area by 280 percent in the year ending in 1959 and was congratulated by Khrushchev on achieving this. A year later his claims turned out to be completely phony. In fact he had had the meat bought in the state shops of Riazan and the surrounding area, and then "delivered it to the state." Tursunbay Uldzhabaev, the first secretary of the central committee of the Communist Party of Tadzhikistan, was an even more highly placed humbug. He insisted for several years that his republic was going to have the highest production of cotton in the world. High-sounding words were written and spoken both in the Soviet Union and abroad to the effect that socialism had enabled backward Tadzhikistan to exceed world standards of cotton production. But in April 1961 a less triumphant plenary meeting of the Tadzhikistan central committee announced that the planned cotton output had not been reached for a long time and that the accounts submitted by the first secretary were false. The fraud was on such a scale that the expression *pripiski,* "writing in," no longer applied.

During the seventies, the Politburo at last decided to denounce the Georgian scandal, which every one had known about for a long time. It had begun many years before, under Stalin.

It seems that the latter thought it useful to have a republic that was totally devoted to him; it was there that he spent most of his holidays, and it provided Beria with many of his staff in the state security agencies.

The unusual size of the individual plots of land at the disposal of kolkhoz peasants in Georgia and the elegance of the crowds strolling in the streets were obvious to everyone, and there was general surprise that Georgians had much more money to spend than Soviet citizens generally have. Everyone knew that nowhere else in the Soviet Union was there so much corruption, and that there was nothing that could not be bought there, including a place at the university, a university degree, or even a certificate to the effect that the holder was a Hero of the Soviet Union. The Stalin cult was officially continued in Georgia after the dictator's death, and corruption continued too. Many Georgians considered their republic a region apart; newcomers who expressed surprise at the unusual ways that prevailed there were told that if they didn't like them they could go back to the Soviet Union.

To state the situation in Marxist terms, the rate of exploitation in Georgia was lower than elsewhere in the U.S.S.R. Nevertheless the rates of growth foreseen in the plans were identical with those in the rest of the country. Vassily Mzhavanadze, the first secretary of the central committee of the Georgian party, a nonvoting member of the Politburo, proudly published reports stating that the plans were fulfilled and even exceeded, but these reports were all phony. Thus with Mzhavanadze the frauds reached right up to the Politburo.

In the end Mzhavanadze was retired, but his methods were perpetuated at the highest level of the nomenklatura. As a matter of fact they had prevailed there even before Mzhavanadze, with the difference that while on the lower levels the object had been to throw dust in the eyes of the Moscow leadership by publishing phony statistics; the latter, having no hierarchical superior, sought to deceive the rest of the world by the same means.

The question of the falsification of Soviet statistics has been examined at length in the West. The American sovietologist Naum Jasny has analyzed the statistical data published in the U.S.S.R. and has revealed many falsifications. Let us mention just two examples published by the Soviet Central Statistical Office concerning the results of the 1948 plan. Kolkhoz sales in 1948 were stated to have exceeded by 22 percent those of 1940, before the Soviet Union was involved in the war. The Twentieth Party Congress revealed that the Statistical Office had "recalculated" the figures for 1940 and reduced those published at the time from 41,200 to 29,100 million rubles. It was only thanks to this juggling that the 1948 figures (35,000 million rubles in 1940 prices) were made to look better than those of 1940. The same publication claimed that the real wages of a Soviet worker in 1948 had more than doubled since the previous year. Naum Jasny showed that when the currency reform of December 15, 1947, was taken into account these wages had actually fallen.[24]

But the nomenklatura leaders continually shelter themselves behind false statistics, masking the effects of the economic stagnation that they of course cannot admit. The nomenklatura class has good reasons to conceal this trend, the historical dimension of which is especially dangerous to real socialism, because when productive relations hamper the development of the productive forces, the social order goes inexorably into decline. According to historical materialism, the conflict between restrictive productive relations and productive forces that are expanding leads to a social explosion that results in the establishment of a new social order; that explosion is what Marxism calls social revolution. Whether it takes place by violence or by the nonviolent transfer of power to a new class, its essence is always the conflict we have just described, the explosion of productive relations that have become too restricting. Can it be claimed that real socialism is heading for a social revolution that will result in the nomenklatura's loss of power? The nomenklatura obviously does everything it can to prevent such an idea from germinating.

7. THE CONTINUAL CRISIS OF UNDERPRODUCTION AND
THE PRIMACY OF HEAVY INDUSTRY

In the second volume of *Das Kapital,* Marx foresees "continual relative overproduction" during the period of socialism and communism.[25] Real socialism has not confirmed that prediction.

Overproduction is a characteristic feature of the capitalist and not of the socialist economy. Capitalism periodically suffers from crises of overproduction due, as we have seen, to the distribution mechanism of the market. The overproduction is relative; it exceeds not the needs of consumers but merely the effective demand. That is why it is not the market mechanisms alone that lead to such crises; they are always connected with a high level of prices.

Communist propaganda proudly claims that the countries of real socialism are not subject to crisis. That is false. They suffer not from periodical crises of overproduction but from a permanent crisis of underproduction. Let us insist on that point: crisis is not periodic, but chronic; it has become the everyday reality of economic life under real socialism. The Soviet citizen has long been used to everything being in short supply. Sometimes he is lucky and comes across a shop to which a quantity of goods have been "assigned," as the saying is; the result is that he is in the habit of going about with what is called optimistically an *avoska,* a "perhaps" shopping bag. But it is not only individual consumers who take advantage of their luck when they find something to buy; factory managers do the same when they have the chance to stock up with tools and raw materials; the newspapers, with simulated naïveté, then criticize them for this.

The permanent crisis of underproduction affects the whole economic behavior and style of life of the Soviet people. Western observers, however, have the impression that the armaments industry does not suffer from it.

It would be wrong to conclude that the tendency to the reduction of the development of productive forces acts selectively. The managers and engineers of the Soviet armaments industry complain of the same difficulties as their colleagues in other industries. It could not be otherwise, as the planning is done in the same way; there is the same tacit complicity among the producers and the same systematic whittling down of forecasts to facilitate the procuring of rewards and decorations;

as everywhere in real socialism, what counts is not the actual results, but reports of successes that will bring increases in salary and other benefits.

The basic need of the nomenklatura as a ruling class is the consolidation and expansion of its power. It undertakes this by the manufacture of the latest types of weapons and equipment for its armed forces and by the creation of special devices for the state security agencies. It concentrates on the development of the heavy industry and technology that provide the foundation of military strength, and constructs fortifications, military strongholds, and impenetrable frontier defenses. Propaganda and indoctrination machines continue the task, as do espionage and financing Communist parties in capitalist countries.

Heavy industry satisfies the nomenklatura's armament needs. That is the explanation of the emphasis placed in the U.S.S.R. on its development, which has nothing to do with the mystical fanaticism for industrialization that Djilas attributes to the "new class."

It is well known that Lenin did not lay particular stress on development of the heavy industry that Stalinist historiography retrospectively attributed to him. In his last speech, on November 13, 1922, Lenin indicated a different order of priorities: "The salvation of Russia lies not only in a good harvest on the peasant farms, that is not enough; and not only in the good condition of light industry, which provides the peasantry with consumer goods—this too is not enough; we also need heavy industry."[26] Thus heavy industry was allotted only a complementary role.

Nevertheless the idea made headway in Lenin's mind that heavy industry was more than a mere supplement to agriculture that made it possible for peasants to sit in tractors, as he put it. In his speech to the third congress of the Comintern he said that "a large-scale machine industry capable of organising agriculture is the only material basis that is possible for socialism."[27] And this not only for agricultural development.

The chief objective was clearly laid down in Lenin's *The Impending Catastrophe and How to Combat It*: "The war is inexorable," he wrote. "It puts the alternative with ruthless severity: either perish or overtake and outstrip the advanced countries *economically as well.* . . . Perish or forge full steam ahead. That is the alternative put by history."[28] Stalin's frequently quoted statement that in the past Russia had been beaten over and over again because of her backwardness, and that an end must be put to her military backwardness "or we shall go under,"[29] was merely a paraphrase of Lenin's words.

So the purpose of the industrialization announced by the two fathers of the nomenklatura class was the creation of military power, a purpose that it now tries to conceal.

Stalin invented the principle of "favoring the development of the means of production," implying the primacy of heavy industry, the essential purpose of which is the equipment of the nomenklatura's military and police machine. In Soviet statistics, "Group A" refers to the production of means of production and "Group B" to the production of consumer goods. (These categories should not be confused with Marx's categories of heavy and light industries; included in the former are consumer goods such as refrigerators and television sets, for instance, and in the latter producer goods such as transmission belts.) Stalin's principle has been interpreted as meaning that to ensure the production of consumer goods, Group A (producer goods) must be provided first.

Group A has been developing at an accelerating pace for more than half a century, or more specifically since 1927. The emphasis on the development of heavy industry (and primarily of armaments) at the expense of consumer goods can be followed from one five-year plan to the next.[30] We restrict ourselves to Soviet sources.

First Five-Year Plan (1928–32). Preparation of this plan took five years, beginning in 1923; it was fulfilled in four years and three months. But how? Heavy industry fulfilled the plan by 109 percent, and the subgroup 1 share in it increased from 39.5 to 53.4 percent; but the consumer goods industry, "in connection with the transfer of various enterprises to the production of armaments that took place at the end of the five-year period," did not fulfill the plan.[31] It struck no one at the time that the fulfillment of the plan by Group A did not mean that the plan as a whole had been fulfilled and that it therefore should not have been ended prematurely. That illustrated the attitude of the nomenklatura to the production of consumer goods.

Second Five-Year Plan (1933–37). This again was proudly claimed to have been fulfilled in four years and three months. The heavy-industry sector more than doubled. The report on this plan was followed by the comment that "because of war threats heavy expenditure had to be made on the production of war material. That was why light industry did not fulfill its program."[32] A number of factories for the production of consumer goods that were proposed under the plan were not even built.[33] Nevertheless the plan as a whole was regarded as having been overfulfilled.

The *Third Five-Year Plan* (1938–42), covering the years that saw the outbreak of war and the German invasion of Russia, was, naturally enough, "based on the necessity of securing a big increase in military potential and defensive ability. The enforced expansion of the armaments industry, the setting up of big state reserves of fuel and electrical power in particular, and the production of other products necessary for war were foreseen."[34]

Between 1943 and 1945 there was no plan.

In accordance with the Stalin tradition, the *Fourth Five-Year Plan* (1946–50) was fulfilled in four years and three months. The level of industrial production in 1950 exceeded that of 1940 by 73 percent, "but the production of goods to meet the needs of the masses did not yet reach the prewar level."[35]

Fifth Five-Year Plan (1951–55). Stalin died during this period, but no radical change was made; the plan was fulfilled in four years and four months. At the end, Group A predominated to the extent of 70.5 percent,[36] but agriculture had developed less quickly than forecast. The growth of agricultural production did not reach the planned level. Crops were small and the production of livestock by the kolkhozes did not reach expectations.[37]

The *Sixth Five-Year Plan* (1956–60) was adopted by the Twentieth, or "destalinization," Congress of the Party. It foresaw a 70 percent growth of Group A and a 60 percent growth of Group B.[38] These objectives were not attained, as Khrushchev's five-year plan was changed in mid-career into a seven-year plan.

The *Seven-Year Plan* (1959–65) preserved the emphasis on production of the means of production.[39] The plan was not clearly fulfilled for agriculture; in six years, production increased by only 5,000 million rubles instead of the 34,000 million rubles (in 1958 prices) laid down in the plan; the rate of increase in cattle production, in contrast to the preceding plan, declined by half, and there was an absolute decrease in the production of pigs, sheep, and poultry.[40] "Also light industry and the food industry produced less than the plan foresaw, chiefly because of the shortage of agricultural raw materials."[41]

That alarming statement was the result not of an agricultural disaster but of drawing up a balance sheet that was rather more objective than usual. After Khrushchev was sent packing, in October 1964, the new leaders had no reason to conceal the real results of the plan. Hence also the curious fact that only the years up to the end of 1964, that is, the first six years of the seven-year plan, are referred to, the point being that 1965 belonged to the Brezhnev era, in which everything was bound to go well.

Eighth Five-Year Plan (1966–70). It was announced that in the course of this plan the rates of growth of Groups A and B were to be assimilated to each other. The results were as follows: In 1970 the share of Group A in industrial production as a whole was 74 percent, while that of Group B was 26 percent. These figures were so revealing that at the last moment they were removed from Brezhnev's report to the Twenty-fourth Congress.[42] These facts conflict with a view that is widespread in the West and even in the Soviet Union, but in 1970 it was still possible to deduce them from incautiously published statistics. Within Group A, the proportionate output of means of production intended solely for the manufacture of producer goods (Group A1), so far from having diminished since Stalin's time, had actually increased in comparison with Group A2 (output of means of production of consumer goods). It reached 72 percent during the Stalin era (in 1950) and 78 percent under Khrushchev (in 1960), and under Brezhnev and Kosygin (1965–66) it amounted to 82 percent.[43] Thus it is clear that the main lines of Soviet economic policy are fixed not by secretaries-general, but by the ruling nomenklatura class. Secretaries-general come and go, but the policy remains.

It is noteworthy that the Eighth Five-Year Plan was the only one in which the forecasts for Group B were fulfilled and actually exceeded.[44] The causes of this were the events of 1968 in Czechoslovakia and those of 1970 in Poland.

Those events soon belonged to the past and life returned to its usual channels, as was plainly shown by the *Ninth Five-Year Plan* (1971–75). As this was an ordinary plan, there was no question of the rate of growth of Group A being overtaken by that of Group B. The figures for Group A were cautiously left unpublished, but the results were discernible from the statement that "industrial production increased by 43 percent," while "production of consumer goods increased by 37 percent."[45] As for Group B, the plan was unfulfilled for the eighth time out of nine. At the Twenty-fifth Congress, Brezhnev announced that the planned figures had not been reached in the food or consumer-goods industries, and he concluded that they had not yet learned how to accelerate the rates both in Group B and in the service industries while encouraging the growth of heavy industry. "Many people bear the responsibility for this."[46]

The many people who indeed bore the responsibility for this were the nomenklaturists. In sixty years of government and fifty years of economic planning, they had not yet managed to give the people the consumer goods they wanted.

In the *Tenth Five-Year Plan* (1976–80) the nomenklatura forecast that the difference in value between the output of producer and consumer goods respectively, which was 237,000 million rubles in favor of the former, would reach 361,000 million rubles in 1980. The total output of consumer goods was expected to be only between 186,000 and 189,000 million rubles.[47] That means that in terms of money the output of heavy industry was to be nearly double that of consumer goods.

In fact the discrepancy is greater than that, as Soviet statistics quote the (low) manufacturers' prices that hardly exceed the cost of production and are used by state enterprises in their balance sheets for Group A, while for Group B they quote retail prices, which sometimes (in the case of private cars in particular) exceed the cost of production by from 800 to 900 percent.

Our study of 10 five-year plans leads to an interesting conclusion. The preference given to the development of producer goods means not only that the nomenklatura systematically favors Group A at the expense of popular consumption; it also means that the nomenklatura's purpose is to fulfill the objectives it lays down for Group A and deliberately to sabotage its forecasts for Group B. In so doing, the nomenklatura thus reduces the production of consumer goods to a pitiful minimum, something it has been doing for half a century.

Thus this "preferential development of producer goods" is a hypocritical euphemism concealing a policy exclusively devoted to the class interests of the nomenklatura, whose aim is to reinforce their power at the expense of the basic needs of the population.

8. MARXIST EXPLOITATION

We have now made the acquaintance in broad outline of the structure and working of real socialism, the system that enables the nomenklatura to skim off the surplus value. Let us now take a closer look at how they do it.

The capitalist process of appropriation of surplus value described by Marx in *Das Kapital* was rapidly taken over by the nomenklatura. Lenin is said one day to have called Stalin "a Genghis Khan who had read *Das Kapital*." This applies to the nomenklatura as a whole.

Though to Marxist ears it may sound blasphemous, the fact remains that the nomenklatura has knowingly organized "socialist production" on the basis of a capitalist-type exploitation of the workers such as was analyzed by Marx.

The nomenklaturists have studied Marxist economics and they know that there are two main ways of increasing surplus value: (1) by lengthening working hours ("absolute surplus value") and (2) by reducing the working hours necessary for a given amount of production ("relative surplus value"). The nomenklatura uses both methods.

9. LENGTHENING WORKING HOURS

After the October Revolution, working hours were first reduced and then lengthened again. I remember Komsomol leaders having to correct us in our early days at school when we repeated what we had been taught, namely that working hours in our country were the shortest in the world, which was no longer true. Working hours were increased. The five-day week (of four working days) gave way to a six-day week (of five working days) and in 1940 to a seven-day (forty-eight hour) week. The month's vacation promised after the revolution was reduced to twelve days, and the number of holidays during the year was reduced. First of all, the religious holidays of Easter and Christmas were abolished, and a number of revolutionary holidays suffered the same fate: January 22, the anniversary of the "bloody Sunday" of 1905 (which was combined with January 21, the anniversary of Lenin's death); March 18, the anniversary of the Paris Commune; the anniversary of the February revolution; and International Youth Day (August 31). Moreover, innumerable *subbotniks* and *voskresniks*—working Saturdays and Sundays—were introduced.

Lenin had been a pioneer in imposing strict work discipline to ensure that the lengthening of working hours would produce the expected increase in surplus value, and he launched a campaign against "groups and sections of workers who . . . work as little and as badly as they can and grab as much money as possible from the state."[48]

Stalin progressively introduced labor legislation of a kind that Europe had not known for a long time. A decree of the Presidium of the Supreme Soviet of the U.S.S.R. dated June 26, 1940, made absenteeism or being twenty minutes late for work (which counted as absenteeism) a criminal offense punishable by forced labor. A strict system of checks was introduced to ensure that medical certificates were not given except in cases of serious illness. As in the labor camps, hospital doctors were given an upper limit for the issue of medical certificates.

Work books and reports on employees also had a strictly disciplinary function. Every wage earner in the Soviet Union has to have a work book, in which every change in his working life is recorded. Without it a Soviet citizen cannot get work or a pension. For a long time, signed reports by the members of the "triangle" (manager, party secretary, trade-union committee president) were required before an individual could be employed. This was later abolished, for making semiofficial inquiries about the individual's behavior in his previous employment was found to be preferable. But reports of this type are still effectively used to the present day.

10. MAKING THEM WORK HARD

Marx believed that after the proletarian revolution the problem of motivating workers would no longer arise; since they were working for themselves, they would work with a will. That is not what happened after the victory of real socialism. The nomenklatura has long since given up pretending that labor productivity is not still a major problem.

It is interesting to note that Lenin himself clearly expressed this idea on the eve of the October Revolution, when he was considering what was to happen after the seizure of power. In his *The State and Revolution*, he was not satisfied with announcing that in the Soviet state the workers would not be able to "dispense with subordination, control and 'foremen and accountants.' "[49] He coldly remarked that "escape from the popular accounting and control will inevitably become so incredibly difficult, such a rare exception, and will probably be accompanied by such swift and severe punishment (for the armed workers are practical men and not sentimental intellectuals, and they will scarcely allow anyone to trifle with them), that the *necessity* of observing the simple, fundamental rules of the community will very soon become a *habit.*"[50]

In referring to the simple, fundamental rules of the community, Lenin had labor discipline in mind, not behavior in public places; by "armed workers" he meant the punitive agencies of the state (the real workers were other, unarmed workers, who were subject to supervision and control by accountants and had to expect "swift and severe punishment" if they were found wanting). Lenin's ideas on the subject were very clear: strict control and severe punishments were to result in greater productivity in the service of the Soviet state.

In czarist Russia before the First World War a great deal of interest was taken in systems of industrial management worked out in the West, Taylorism in particular. Taylor's principal works were translated into Russian, and Russian authors such as Levenstern, Poliakov, Pankin, etc., advocated the introduction of Taylorism into Russian factories.

As was only to be expected, Lenin severely criticized "this 'scientific' system of extracting sweat," as he called it before the revolution. But in 1914, still before the revolution, he remarked mysteriously that "without its originators knowing or wishing it," the Taylor system "is preparing the time when the proletariat will take over all social production."[51]

As soon as that time came, after the Bolshevik victory, Lenin discovered many virtues in Taylorism, which was hastily introduced into the Soviet economy and called "scientific organization of labor" (NOT).

"Hastily" is no mere phrase. The civil war in western Russia ended at the end of 1920. In August of that year a Central Institute of Labor was opened in Moscow at the instigation of the Central Council of Trade Unions. Anticipating Stalin's remark that workers were "screws," the organizers of the institute explained that they wanted to "handle men as one handles nuts and bolts, machines."

The "first all-Russian conference on questions of NOT" met in January 1921. The problem that faced it was to find out how "to obtain optimal output in socialist society with the maximum of joy in labor."[52]

Meanwhile the institute had already chalked up some scientific successes. All workers' movements were described as consisting of the application of either shock or pressure, and the "biomechanics of shock and pressure" were worked out on that basis.

Neo-Taylorism was extended to the whole of the Soviet Union. In 1925 there were altogether about sixty NOT institutions, and a "Central Council for the Scientific Organization of Labor" (SOVNOT) was founded to coordinate their activities. All these institutions devoted themselves to time-and-motion study with a view to enabling the worker to use his working time as productively as possible. The NOT theorists claimed that activist workers wanted less leisure and a longer working day, and that the conveyor belt came closer than anything else to Marx's ideas about the progressive organization of production.

Lenin himself had said that the key to the victory of socialism over capitalism was increased productivity, and increasing it, no matter how, was an absolute necessity to the nomenklatura. Under Brezhnev, a new principle was introduced according to which increased labor productivity under socialism had to be greater than the increase in wages.

The nomenklatura imposes strict labor discipline in order to get as much work done as possible. In spite of the claim that this labor discipline is freely and spontaneously agreed to by the workers, it is in fact based on fear of punishment. As early as April 20, 1920, Lenin signed a decree on "the struggle against work dodging," introducing the principle of supplementary work to make up for lost time, whether after ordinary working hours or on free days. This first step to legislation contrary to the workers' interests was followed by many others, to which we have already referred.

But all that is history. What about the situation at the present day? Let us quote the party journal *Kommunist:* "Socialist labor discipline involves . . . an obligation on the part of management to organize labor rationally and . . . an obligation on the part of the workers and staff to devote all their strength to their work." That is all that is required of the workers: merely to sacrifice all their strength to it.

And what is expected of management? What does the obligation to organize labor rationally imply? *Kommunist* tells us that "skill in organizing labor requires maximum use of working hours, the creation of an atmosphere propitious for work, accountability, and control."[53]

All that this discipline and socialist organization of labor means to the nomenklatura is the maximization of surplus value.

The nomenklatura considers that its essential mission is the maximization of the norms of production, and from its point of view it is quite right.

And what of the nomenklatura? In spite of its long tirades in the press about the Soviet people's tireless enthusiasm for work, at the bottom of its heart it believes that workers are idlers who do half a day's work for a full day's pay and stubbornly refuse to give their all to the state, and that this permanent go-slow must be broken.

In its search for strikebreakers, the nomenklatura hit on the Marxist idea according to which the bourgeoisie in its efforts to divide the working class established a labor aristocracy which it fed with crumbs from the table of its profits.[54] It promptly set about creating such an aristocracy in the U.S.S.R.

Again it was Lenin who, in December 1917, just after the October Revolution, proposed to the party leadership the introduction of "socialist competition."[55] In the following April there took place the "great initiative"[56] so much praised by Lenin, the first "Communist *subbotnik,*" or working Saturday, conducted by the party cell of the right-of-way inspectors of the Moscow freight yard. Such initiatives multiplied, and Lenin had himself photographed during a *subbotnik* at the Kremlin shouldering a load of wood that had been discreetly brought to the spot by his bodyguard. As this new kind of competition had of course to be presented as a spontaneous popular revolutionary initiative, Lenin's essay under a frank title, *How to organize competition,* was published only ten years after his *A Great Beginning.*[57]

On the basis of this ordered competition, the nomenklatura first organized the shock-workers *(udarniki)* movement, which was followed by the Stakhanovite movement and the Communist labor brigades. The methods used were given great publicity in the press and were

approved by the Central Committee and the regional party committees. The object of all this hullabaloo was and still is to secure acceptance by the workers of higher norms that would be regarded not as
products of the bureaucratic imagination, but as real norms capable of
being fulfilled and even exceeded by the best workers.

The Stakhanovite movement well illustrates the devices to which the
nomenklatura resorts. As is stated in all the Soviet history books, it
began on the night of August 31, 1935, when Alexei Stakhanov, a
miner at Centralnaya-Irmino, in the Donetz basin, was said to have
exceeded his norm by fourteen times during his regular shift. A miner
at the same pit later told me that Stakhanov did not stand out in any
way and was fond of drink, docile by nature, and good-looking. It was
obviously his photogenic appearance that enabled him to become a
hero.

Records in the coal mines were broken so frequently after this that
things became utterly absurd. Nikita Isotov, for instance, was stated to
have dug 240 tons of coal, or thirty-three times the norm, in the course
of his shift.[58]

Can a single man without special technical aids do the work of
thirty-three miners? Either the thirty-three miners are shockingly lazy,
or it is a lie. As neither of these alternatives suited the nomenklatura,
later records were kept within more suitable bounds. Norms were no
longer expected to be exceeded 1000 percent, but they were substantially increased all the same.

The efforts of the nomenklatura to create a Stakhanovite movement
among the kolkhoz peasantry by using the same demagogic methods
failed to produce the desired results. These peasants had long since lost
confidence in the party leaders and refused to break records in return
for a vague promise of favors from the nomenklatura. The result was
that a list of awards unprecedented in the history of honors and decorations had to be introduced for their special benefit. Fulfilling the prear-
ranged norm for the harvest earned an appropriate decoration, and
exceeding it was a qualification for the title of Hero of Soviet Labor. It
was only by this system that any results were obtained.

Not content with trying to exploit human vanity, the nomenklatura
exploited the inexperience of youth. Youth brigades were formed, and
teams of building workers were set up in the komsomols. Results were
not always up to expectations; the city of Komsomolsk, on the River

Amur, allegedly constructed by the Komsomols, in reality had to be built by labor-camp inmates. Efforts were actually made to rouse enthusiasm even among the latter, as Solzhenitsyn has well described in his uncensored *The Gulag Archipelago*. In his censored *A Day in the Life of Ivan Denisovich*, he was forced to celebrate this pseudo enthusiasm. The single aim of all these methods was to maximize labor output.

11. LOW WAGES

The relation between a worker's wages and his exploitation by the possessing class has long been a basic idea in economics. Thus David Ricardo (1772–1823) stated the following economic law: The higher a worker's wages, the lower the master's profit, and *vice versa*.[59] A low level of wages and a high level of profit is a distinguishing mark of all the countries of real socialism, the high level of profit being manifested in particular by the high rate of accumulation, which in the Soviet Union is 25 percent of total revenue.[60]

Economics has familiarized us with the idea of the statistically average family consisting of husband, wife, and two children. The minimum standard of living is calculated with reference to such a family; it is reached when the head of the family can support the four persons concerned.

Soviet statistics ignore the idea of a minimum standard of living. The Soviet citizen hears of it only when he reads in the newspapers that in some capitalist country a certain percentage of families are living below that minimum. He then wonders why they have not died of hunger. He is unaware of the fact that he himself, everyone in his environment, and everyone he meets in the street—except the passengers in the limousines who pass without seeing him—all earn less than the statistical minimum wage, for no average Soviet citizen can keep a family of four on his wage.

Let us quote official figures: In 1983 the average wage of factory and office workers was 181 rubles a month (i.e., 229 U.S. dollars‡), of kolkhoz peasants 138 rubles (i.e., 165 U.S. dollars). Such sums are

‡ 100 U.S. dollars = 79.10 rubles (January 1, 1984).

sufficient for a single man to live on, but only with difficulty. (We will go into more depth on "average wages" in the following chapter.)

It should be noted that the figure for "factory and office workers" (above) refers to ministers and marshals; kolkhoz peasants, pensioners, and students are not included. In reality, 181 rubles a month is not the mean wage, but a good one. The true mean wage hardly exceeds 120 rubles. A more accurate figure cannot be given, for in the Soviet Union statistics about pay are kept secret.

What about increases? The nomenklatura claims that increased pay must be preceded by increased productivity because more must be produced before more money can be distributed.

That seems a rational argument, the only surprise being that the Bolsheviks did not accept it. At the Twelfth Party Congress, in 1923, for instance, it was claimed that increased pay led to increased productivity, and not the reverse.[61] At the fifteenth plenary conference of the party, in 1926, there was a conflict on the subject between the nomenklaturists who followed Stalin and the opposition, who claimed that "the problem of wages and salaries must not be tackled on the basis that the workers must produce more before earning higher pay; the system must work the other way about: higher pay . . . must be the basis for higher productivity of labor."[62]

The nomenklatura argument that sounds so convincing is obviously less so in practice. In fact, it is simply false.

Put yourself in the position of a construction worker building a factory. Would you be prepared to wait for the factory to be completed and for the money for the first goods it manufactures and sells to come in before getting your pay envelope? In that case you would die of hunger before the building was finished. In practice you get your pay regularly; in other words, you receive payment in advance; and the question is not where the money comes from (it comes from the State Bank printing works, from which the Soviet state gets money for all its purposes). No, the question is a different one. The state is able to pay you because the country's production does not begin with that factory. Production is going full steam ahead; an enormous amount of surplus value has been accumulated and is continually increasing. The real stumbling block is not that the nomenklatura has to sell the goods your factory is going to produce before being able to pay you, but surplus value. The nomenklatura has accumulated sufficient surplus value to be able to pay higher wages, but in no circumstances is it willing to renounce the smallest part of the surplus value it has extorted. It wants to avoid having to do so even if increased productivity might be the result, for it is well aware of the acuteness of the conflict between it and the workers, and it does not believe the latter are willing to show gratitude for a derisory increase in their scandalously low pay by increasing productivity.

The nomenklatura prefers coercion to offering incentives; it prefers the stick of propaganda and organization to the carrot of higher wages. In this respect it marks itself off from capitalism and puts itself on the same level as feudal lords and slave owners. That does not mean that the nomenklaturist class does not also practice capitalist methods of exploitation. In considering capitalism, Marxist economics distinguishes payment by time (according to Marx, a fairer form of remuneration) from piecework (which makes it possible to extort a maximum of surplus value).

The Soviet economics manual that we quoted earlier states: "Piecework in the capitalist system leads to a continual increase in the work rate. At the same time, it facilitates the employer's task of supervising the workers. The rate of work is controlled by the quantity and quality of products that the worker has to produce to make a living. He is forced to produce more, to work harder. As soon as a larger or smaller number of workers reach a higher level of productivity, the capitalist reduces wages . . . the worker tries to keep up his level of pay by more work, either putting in more hours or producing more in an hour. . . . The result is that the more he works the less he earns (K. Marx, *Labour, Wages, and Profit*). That is the essential feature of piecework under capitalism."[63]

In 1975, according to the Central Statistical Office of the U.S.S.R., 56.2 percent of industrial and building workers were paid piece rates and only 43.8 percent by the hour.[64] Piecework is nowadays said to be a "progressive form of payment." The nomenklatura solves this conflict with dogma by calmly explaining that under the socialist system workers produce for themselves.

In insisting on higher productivity without higher pay, the nomenklatura obviously assumes that no one in the Soviet Union reads *Das Kapital*. The nomenklatura argument, translated into Marxist terms, is that under socialism the value produced by the workers, including the surplus value, must increase in comparison with wages. Now, the ratio between surplus value and wages expressed as a percentage is what Marx calls the workers' exploitation rate, and that is the rate the nomenklatura is set on increasing.

12. WOMEN'S AND CHILDREN'S LABOR

How does the average Soviet family live on a wage that is 40 percent of the unemployment pay of an American worker? It manages to do so only because the wife and in many cases the children work too.

Propaganda of course presents this phenomenon as a "socialist achievement." In fact, as Marx pointed out, it is merely an additional means of exploitation. According to the Soviet economics manual, ". . . the value of the labor force is determined by the value of the means of existence that the worker needs for himself and his family. Hence, if his wife and children are drawn into the productive process, his wage is diminished; the whole family now receives practically the same amount as the head of the family earned alone before. Hence exploitation of the working class as a whole is still further increased."[65]

Although Soviet propaganda condemns capitalism for using child labor, it is widely employed in the U.S.S.R. Apprentice schools (FZU) were opened in the twenties, and the pupils had to work in factories. Many orphans and homeless children were thus used as cheap labor on the pretext that they were receiving an education in conformity with the principles of the educator and chekist Anton Makarenko. Under Stalin, manual-labor schools were established at which the children wore black uniforms and military discipline prevailed. Backward or undisciplined children were compulsorily sent to these schools.

But in the case of women's work, no coercion is required; economic necessity is sufficient. For the vast majority of families in the Soviet Union it is a sheer condition of survival that the women work; that is why there are practically no housewives below retirement age. All this is plainly evident from official statistics. Women represent 53.6 percent of the total population and 51.5 percent of the working population.[66] Since Stalin, the tradition has been that the wives of officers, generals, and academicians do not work, and this trend is increasing among the wives of senior nomenklaturists.

As was to be expected, this policy of the nomenklaturist class has had various consequences for Soviet society. Some are positive. As their husbands are unable to support them, women have become financially independent and emancipated. Other consequences are disquieting to the highest quarters in the land; the birthrate is insufficient and the population problem is becoming acute. Benefits granted to large families, inspired by the system of awards introduced by Stalin (the title of Heroic Mother and the Maternal Medal of Honor), have not produced the hoped-for results. In the industrial and cultural centers, large families have become rare, and the fact that there is a slow increase in the birthrate is due solely to the Asian republics.

13. CHEAP LABOR

In its quest for surplus value, the nomenklatura has ventured into territory unexplored by Marx. It has drawn novel practical consequences from Marx's theory that the reduction of working hours increases the relative surplus value. This brings us to the question of the standard of living of the Soviet people.

In every society based on exploitation, the worker creates a product for his employer and produces a certain standard of living for himself and his family. The greater the demand for the product, the higher the standard of living.

The classics of Marxism-Leninism predicted that socialism would involve a leap forward in the people's standard of living. "Socialism alone," Lenin said, "will make possible the wide expansion of social production and distribution on scientific lines and their actual subordination to the aim of easing the lives of the working people and of improving their welfare as much as possible."[67] He generously promised "full well being and free, *all-round* development for *all* members of society."[68]

All this turned out to be empty verbiage, for in the past sixty years the standard of living of the people in the real-socialist countries has been lower than that in capitalist countries.

The history of the past half century has provided us with laboratories enabling us to make comparisons. The difference, for example, in living conditions between the two Koreas or the two Germanys is so striking that nomenklatura propaganda makes no attempt to dispute it. Under the Hapsburg monarchy and in the interwar period, the standard of living in Bohemia was considered to be distinctly superior to that of Austria. When propaganda about the "blossoming" of Czechoslovak socialism faded out, during the "Prague spring," the Czechoslovak Communist leadership openly undertook the task of catching up with the Austrian standard of living. It is hardly necessary to add that this objective has not yet been attained.

What indeed has happened in North Korea, Czechoslovakia, the German Democratic Republic, and East Berlin? Natural disasters, earthquakes, epidemics? Nothing of the sort. All that happened was that the real-socialist system was introduced. Why, in spite of the predictions to the contrary of Marx, Engels, and Lenin, does that system have such disastrous consequences for the people's standard of living? The only official explanation that the nomenklatura has yet found for the obvious backwardness of the socialist countries in this respect is the Marshall plan—as if Moscow had not stigmatized it at the time as exploitation of Western Europe by American imperialism, and as if a good quarter of a century had not passed since then. Privately, any member of the nomenklatura will admit that the reason why these people are so badly off is that they work so badly. Why do they work so badly, when the idea is being continually drummed into them that they are the owners now? The answer is that they are so harshly exploited by the nomenklatura, for whom they actually work. This harshness is ineffective. The greater the efforts of the nomenklatura to exploit the workers, the less interest they show in the results of their labor.

As the productivity of Soviet workers remains low, the nomenklatura has evolved a method that assures it of relative surplus value. At first sight, the method has the advantage of seeming humane, for low prices are fixed for a number of products and services.

Is the cost of living in the U.S.S.R. really low? It is not. Foreigners who live there complain of the high cost of living and try to do their buying in the West. Western correspondents in Moscow consider that the official exchange rate overvalues the ruble in relation to Western currencies. The unofficial exchange rate in the Soviet Union is now four rubles to the dollar, nearly six times the official rate.

In the Soviet Union, labor is a cheap commodity. To maintain the labor force, the nomenklatura allocates to it a carefully defined minimum of products and services at genuinely low prices in relation to Western prices; to the average Soviet wage earner these prices are not low, but they are manageable; they are fixed in relation to the low level of wages and incomes. Thus, by adopting a modest lifestyle, the average Soviet wage earner can maintain his working strength and raise his children. Pensioners cannot manage under this system, and are thrown back on the support of their families; if they have none, they quickly end up in old people's homes, where their expectation of life is short: the nomenklatura has no more use for them.

It seems absurd that this system is capable of rousing the enthusiasm of some Western Marxists, who go into ecstasies about the low rents and the low price of bread, noodles, and streetcar tickets. Marx would hardly have shared their enthusiasm, for he did not consider a low cost of living to be a benefit to the workers; on the contrary, he regarded it as a method of increasing their exploitation.

It is true that rents are low in the U.S.S.R. But it is wrong to suppose that the average Soviet citizen may have a hundred square meters of living space at his disposal, as is quite frequently the case in the West. Actually a maximum of twelve square meters per person is authorized. Would one of our pro-Soviet enthusiasts be prepared to live with his wife and child in a mini-apartment? That is the fate of the average Soviet family.

It is true that public transport is cheap. But a private car is a luxury, and to buy one an average Soviet wage earner would have to save his wages without spending a kopek for three and a half years. It is true that in the Soviet Union bread, noodles, potatoes, milk, vegetables, maize, and other basic foodstuffs are cheap. But meat, fish, poultry, fruit, chocolate, coffee, and canned goods are dear and hard to come by. As bread, followed by noodles and potatoes for dessert, hardly makes a satisfactory meal, about 80 percent of the budget of the average family goes on food.

It is correct that medical treatment is free. But the hospitals and outpatient departments at the people's disposal are perpetually overcrowded; to see a doctor you have to line up for hours. Doctors in outpatient departments have to keep to a norm of fifteen minutes per patient, and half the time is spent in filling out and signing the patient's medical card (the doctor has to do this himself, for few nurses are available). Also, it has become usual to give presents to doctors and nurses to attract their attention, or even to pay them, so free medical attention is no longer assured. Would it not be better to make a deduction from wages to pay for health insurance, which would enable patients to choose their doctor?

All the more so as there is nothing under real socialism or any other political system that is or could be free—including "free" medical care. All material goods are produced by the workers and by them alone, while the state and the nomenklatura neither toil nor spin. The only activity of the nomenklatura consists in sharing out goods produced by others, and its sole aim is to assure itself of the lion's share, to satisfy its own class needs.

But it is true that it is possible under real socialism to obtain a hundred square meters of living space for a ridiculous rent, and a dacha besides, and that it is possible to buy a car—or even to have one for nothing, with a driver thrown in—as well as plenty of excellent and cheap food for your family, the free use of good hospitals, and a free annual vacation at a health resort. All this is possible, but on one condition: it is necessary to be a member of the nomenklatura. This is a matter with which we shall deal in the next chapter.

The nomenklatura has clearly laid down the limited needs of the primary producer: accommodation not exceeding twelve square meters per person, a simple diet, cheap public transport to take him to work, and cheap propaganda newspapers and propaganda films. For intellectuals there are modestly priced authorized books (to prevent them from having bad thoughts during their leisure hours); medical attention is provided in case of illness (to get people back to work as quickly as possible); there is a small old-age or disability pension (not higher than 164 dollars per month) and an allowance of twenty rubles (26 dollars) to help with funeral expenses.

It would be wrong to regard the compulsory standard of living laid down by the nomenklatura for the great mass of the population as a sort of safety net for the most impoverished. There is no such safety net; in the Soviet Union there is no unemployment pay; instead there is a law against "parasites" that applies to those who lose their jobs and condemns them to forced labor in a kind of banishment. This obligatory way of life, so far from being a social benefit, is a measure taken by the exploiting class for the purpose of diminishing necessary labor and thus increasing surplus labor and consequently surplus value. We are not here trying to show things in an unfavorable light. On the contrary, we should feel gratitude to a regime that is capable of putting whole classes and nations into concentration camps, as was done in Stalin's time, but does so no longer. There are countries in the world to the inhabitants of which the realities we have just described may be attractive. But for anyone living in the West to show enthusiasm for them is grotesque. The nomenklatura's attempt to hold them up as tremendous socialist achievements is merely cynical.

14. THE EFFECTIVE WAGE

The imposition of a compulsory standard of living on the exploited is not a recent invention, for it was practiced by slave owners and feudal lords. But nomenklatura ingenuity resulted in the discovery of an entirely new method of appropriating surplus value. When Marx analyzed capitalist exploitation, he was never faced with the problem of underproduction, which was unknown in that kind of society, so he failed to discover the possibility of additional exploitation that that type of crisis puts into rulers' hands.

He began his analysis by noting that in the course of the productive process commodities were produced. Living in a capitalist country, it seemed obvious to him that those commodities were intended for consumers. It was similarly obvious to him that the production of means of production ultimately served the same purpose, that of meeting the demands of consumers able to pay for them, for only a commodity that is quickly sold puts money in the capitalist's hands and at the same time creates surplus value; the capitalist needs both for the purpose of making fresh investments.

That was the foundation on which Marx based his celebrated formula money-commodity-money[1] (M-C-M[1]), in which M[1] stands for a sum of money increased by the surplus value that has been realized. It did not occur to him that that formula applies not to all kinds of production, but only to the capitalist kind.

For the nomenklatura does not need to sell the commodities produced to realize the surplus value. Unlike the capitalists, it has no need to obtain money from anyone, for it controls the state and prints as many bank notes as it wants.

As the whole product is delivered to the state, i.e., to the nomenklatura, all the surplus value is available to it and, moreover, in the form in which it wants it, according to its production plans. In these circumstances the nomenklatura state must not produce to meet customers' needs; the nomenklatura can produce to meet its own class needs directly.

These needs are not those of the ordinary consumers. The relatively small nomenklaturist class can quickly meet to the point of full satiety its demand for goods of high quality for its own use, particularly imported goods or goods intended for export. It is heavy industry, and primarily the arms industry, that fulfills the nomenklatura's needs as a class.

Being an ultramonopolist, it can decide the quantities to be produced at its own sweet will. It would be perfectly willing to use the whole of the country's productive capacity for the satisfaction of its own needs without leaving anything over for anyone else, but it cannot do that, for the population needs consumer goods. That is why it has to introduce these into its plans, though it considers them bad business, tolerable only as a concession to the masses.

It is absolutely essential that readers in nonsocialist countries grasp these vital facts, without which the chronic plight of light industry and agriculture in the U.S.S.R. is unintelligible. Not till they have done so will they cease feeling the typically Western surprise that a country able to send rockets all over the solar system has not yet managed to solve the problems of the shoe-manufacturing industry, or that the country with the largest acreage in the world, with an age-old agricultural tradition, has every year to buy cereals abroad. Only when the reader has understood that the consumer-goods industry, and to a large extent agriculture also, are considered by the nomenklatura to be a necessary evil, a concession to the labor force (with the result that expenditure on these things is reduced to a minimum), will he be able to form an accurate idea of the economic development of the Soviet Union.

In economics and statistics a distinction is made between nominal and real wages. Let us consider the latter.

According to the Soviet economics manual, ". . . the real wage is the wage manifested by the worker's means of existence; it shows what consumer goods and services are at the worker's disposal and how much he can buy with his paycheck."[69] But what happens when there are no consumer goods for the wage earner to spend his money on? That is an eventuality not foreseen by Western economists, but it is a phenomenon characteristic of real socialism as a result of the continual crisis of underproduction and the primacy of heavy industry.

Let us consider the case of a tractor mechanic in Siberia. Like all wage earners in the Soviet Union, his knowledge of his gross wage is purely theoretical, because of the various deductions. Nevertheless the net pay of an agricultural mechanic is relatively high. But all that is for sale at the shop in his rural district is black bread, macaroni, canned fish of doubtful freshness, vodka, salt, matches, candy, and cigarettes; and sometimes there are beer and sausages. What is his real wage?

Real socialism dislikes the idea of the real wage and suppresses it, for it is a bourgeois idea born of material abundance, of the existence of more goods than money. Under real socialism the opposite situation prevails: large sums of money in the people's pockets which they would like to spend on consumer goods cannot be spent on them, because they are perpetually in short supply; and that in spite of the fact that, as we have seen, wages are low and the price of many products is high.

Hence we propose to introduce a new category, that of the *effective wage*. Unlike the real wage, it refers to the actual amount of consumer goods and services desired by the wage earner that he can buy with his wages.

Consequently it is only in the best of cases, that is, when the whole of the amount received can really be spent on consumer goods and services, that the effective wage coincides with the real wage. Under real socialism this happens only to the salaries of that part of the nomenklatura that has access to special shops, restaurants, and buffets (with which we shall deal in the next chapter). When the worker's real wage becomes an effective wage, the exploitation rate increases substantially. For as soon as the nomenklatura makes available to the worker fewer consumer goods and services than he could buy with his wage, the pay of the work force is in fact diminished. Thus to the nomenklatura the difference between real and effective wages is an additional source from which surplus value is appropriated.

This appeared plainly during the war. Soon after it broke out, a strict but physiologically acceptable rationing system was introduced. Later it was announced that food would be available not on all ration cards but only in exchange for the coupons published on a list; special coupons were issued for clothing and shoes and the services. Only privileged people obtained these, with the result that nothing but bread was available on ordinary ration cards, with rare occasional extras. When the newspapers reported that the bread ration in Italy was only 150 grams a day, no one in the Soviet Union believed it; everyone knew that on such rations the Italians must long since have been dying of hunger, just as the inhabitants of Leningrad were, who also received 150 grams of bread a day. It never occurred to anyone that there could be a country in which ration cards entitled one to anything other than bread. In short, Soviet citizens know that what matters is not your entitlement, but what you actually get.

The difference between real and effective wages is also shown by the Soviet people's savings, which are substantial. This is not the evidence of prosperity that Soviet propaganda claims it to be, for if a normal supply of goods and services were available it would be impossible to save on a wage of 181 rubles a month. Those savings are explained by the difference between the real and the effective wage; and the money in nomenklatura savings accounts comes from surplus value. It is not the prosperity, but the exploitation, of Soviet workers that their high rate of savings conceals.

There is yet another field in which Marxist theory has been enriched by the practices of the nomenklaturist class. Marx differentiated between surplus value and use value and analyzed exploitation only in regard to the former. But it is evident that calculation of the amount of surplus value is not a sufficient guide to the amount of exploitation. At the abstract level of economics, the particular type of production at issue may be immaterial, but it is extremely important to the life of a society to note that if the product is guns, the degree of exploitation is not the same as if it were butter. It is correct to argue that slaves in ancient Egypt who worked on the irrigation of the fields that were necessary to ensure their food supply were less exploited than those who built the pyramids, just as the serfs who performed the hard labor of digging a well from which they would later be able to draw water for their own use were less exploited than the lace makers who embroidered the splendid robes of their lords. Similarly the engineering workers in the German Democratic Republic who make cars that one day they may be able to buy are less exploited than their comrades who manufacture automatic firing devices for shooting down would-be fugitives at the frontier.

It must be appreciated that the priority for the production of producer goods proclaimed by Stalin and stubbornly practiced by the nomenklatura ever since is not an abstract ideological principle. It conceals the perpetuation of an additional source of exploitation of the primary producers, who are forced to devote their working strength to the manufacture of goods needed only by the nomenklatura; to them, that production is either useless or actually harmful. While continuing to produce consumer goods in insufficient quantity, they are forced to cement the low level of their effective wages with their own hands. Thus the theoretical enrichment of Marxism is limited to the enrichment of the nomenklatura. That is why it keeps mum about that discovery.

15. THE DEGREE OF EXPLOITATION

What is the exact extent of the appropriation of surplus value by the nomenklatura class? That would be a suitable subject for an economic study; here we can indicate only its order of magnitude.

Kurón and Modzelewski concluded that at the beginning of the sixties an industrial worker in Poland used a third of his working time on the making of the necessary product, while the other two thirds went to the creation of surplus value.[70] That does not take into account the difference between the real and the effective wage as a factor increasing the surplus value. The Soviet Union or any other COMECON country hardly differs from Poland in this respect.

This high level of surplus value explains the familiar fact that investment in those countries takes up a larger share of the national product than in capitalist countries. Nowhere do investment funds fall from heaven, and their source is surplus value, under real socialism and under capitalism alike. The difference in the order of magnitude of investment in the two types of economy thus reflects the difference in the per capita production of surplus value; in this field the countries of real socialism are in the lead. It is well known—and the nomenklaturist states do not deny—that the productivity of labor in them is lower than it is in advanced capitalist countries. That means that the workers under real socialism, who produce less than their colleagues in the advanced industrial countries, nevertheless create more surplus value. The explanation of this paradox is the substantially higher exploitation rate.

That is not a new phenomenon; it existed in the colonies. The countries of real socialism are low-wage countries, like those of the Third World. These low wages enable the nomenklatura to use dumping methods to compete in capitalist markets. Representatives of West German textile firms talk of the difficulties created by shirts and suits imported from East Germany and sold for a few marks. In fact, in East Germany shirts are a good deal more expensive than in the Federal Republic, but the economic managers of the nomenklatura are willing to renounce their superprofits in East German marks and sell part of their wares at dumping prices in the West for the sake of obtaining hard currency.

There is another way of exploiting the low wages under real socialism that is more pleasing to Western entrepreneurs. For the sake of hard currency the nomenklatura class is prepared to share some of its surplus-value profits with Western capitalists. Strange deals are arranged under the vaunted banner of economic cooperation between countries of different economic systems. "American" cigarettes are manufactured in Bulgaria and sold in the West; men's suits made of American material and cut in American style are made in Romania for the American market. The difference in wages between East European and American workers must indeed be substantial to justify the costs (transport, insurance, packing, and the rest) and give the Americans a bigger profit than if they produced the same goods at home! And at the same time it must be big enough to assure the East European employers who fill the orders the gains foreseen in their plan.

The comparison with colonialism is tempting; we refrain from it only to the extent that we forbid ourselves the use of big words, the inflation of which in the world is even greater than that of money.

16. TAPPING SURPLUS VALUE

Thus surplus value is produced for the nomenklatura, to whom it accrues in the form of a "gain," which is merely another word for profit.

The fact that in the West the idea of profit is associated exclusively with capitalism, and more particularly with big combines and multinationals, is one of the successes of Communist propaganda. Though the chief concern of the nomenklatura, as we have seen, is the consolidation and extension of its power, it certainly does not turn up its nose at profit. The nomenklatura presents its efforts to increase productivity in a patriotic light, and whenever these result in some success there is a perceptible influx of money into its coffers.

Let us take as an example the Stakhanovite movement, of the thirties, which we mentioned earlier. Stalin expatiated at length on the roots of this movement, which, he said, had matured and caused the working masses to deliver a furious assault upon norms which for undiscoverable reasons had suddenly become out of date. The newspapers outdid themselves in praise of Stakhanovite achievements, but the gist of the matter was summed up as follows in the standard Soviet history textbook: "An important result of the Stakhanovite movement," it says, "was the increase in the profitability of heavy industry. Against a gain of 430 million rubles in 1934 there was a gain of 3.2 thousand million rubles in 1936."[71] In other words, the profit of the nomenklatura increased seven and a half times in two years. What multinational can boast of such a result of its exploitation of primary producers?

The situation has not changed. The percentage growth of nomenklatura profit is no longer so great, but its amount is still remarkable. At the Twenty-fifth Congress it was incidentally noted that during the Ninth Five-Year Plan (1971–75) the profit was 500,000 million rubles, an increase of 50 percent compared with Brezhnev's first plan (1966–70)[72]—a real profit explosion.

The profit is the surplus value produced by the workers for the benefit of the nomenklatura. But what is the mechanism by means of which it ends up in the coffers of the nomenklaturist state?

It does so by means of the tax system, the present form of which dates back to the 1930 tax reform, i.e., the period just after the beginning of the collectivization of agriculture that completed the transformation of the Soviet economy into a nomenklatura supermonopoly. The tax system is adapted to this supermonopoly. As the nomenklatura is the owner of the economy and the state is the mechanism by means of which it exercises power, there is no point in taxing the population directly; that is why less than 10 percent of the state revenue is raised by that means. About 90 percent of the Soviet budget comes "from the socialist economy," as the fine phrase puts it.

In the capitalist world the taxation of private firms means that the state recovers a percentage—often a substantial percentage—of the surplus value realized by the employers. Under real socialism, all enterprises belong to the state. So whose surplus value is confiscated when these enterprises are taxed? No one's. The socialist state merely accumulates in its banks the surplus value collected by its agents, the managers of enterprises.

This process is called paying in the profits of socialist enterprises. It consists of leaving the undertaking a previously arranged proportion of the surplus value that has been produced by the workers for future investment and other purposes foreseen in the plan and using the rest for the state budget. Under this system, taxing the people is unnecessary; the surplus value is taken directly from the undertaking and the state fixes pay and pays it out itself, so why should there be any taxes?

In Albania this has been pushed to its logical conclusion, and taxes have been abolished. In Khrushchev's time a law was made aiming at the progressive abolition of taxes in the Soviet Union. Communist propaganda expatiated on this noisily and at length in order to create the impression that taxation had been abolished. In fact the abolition applied only to those earning less than 70 rubles a month. Its extension to other categories of workers was stated to be impossible.

In any case, Khrushchev's law, since it dealt only with direct taxation, did not affect the major part of the taxation imposed by the nomenklatura, which is indirect. Before the revolution, when Lenin was busy denouncing the crimes of czarism, he sharply condemned the injustice of that form of taxation; "The richer the man, the *smaller* is the share of his income that he pays in indirect taxes. That is why indirect taxation is *the most unfair* form of taxation. Indirect taxes are taxes on the poor."[73]

But it was this kind of taxation that the nomenklatura introduced in the form of a turnover tax levied on the "socialist economy." The confused attempts of Soviet economists to explain that this is not a real tax, because it does not represent a transfer from one kind of property to another, carefully evade the question of who it is who actually pays these taxes.

The answer is obvious: The tax is included in the selling price of goods as the difference between it and the factory price. As soon as the goods are delivered to the selling organization, the factory pays the state an amount of tax proportionate to the selling price.

The rules are strict. The tax has to be paid on the third day after delivery of the goods. Small concerns are allowed to settle on the third, thirteenth, and twenty-third of each month. Only very small undertakings, whose liability to tax is less than 1,000 rubles a month, are allowed to settle on the twenty-third of each month. Thus the nomenklatura gets its surplus value promptly.

The selling organizations add the turnover tax to the retail price, and it is at this stage that the real payer of the tax, the retail customer, makes his appearance. As the turnover tax is levied predominantly on the production of consumer goods, the retail customer is in reality the whole population of the Soviet Union. It is on the latter that the nomenklatura imposes this indirect tax, which it calls "a state receipt from the socialist economy."

The amount raised by this means is of course kept secret, but it is possible to get a rough idea of the amount involved by studying the figures published in the course of the last years of the Khrushchev era, when censorship was relaxed a little. Taxation accounted for between 50 and 75 percent of the selling price of the following goods: petroleum, refined and unrefined; bicycles (for adults); cars; cameras; typewriters; fountain pens; textiles; matches; thread; etc. It accounted for between 33 and 66 percent of the selling price of needles, sewing machines, pots and pans, aluminum goods, carpets, rubber goods, electric light bulbs, electric cord, writing paper, cement; and for 50 percent in the case of flour, 55 percent in that of sugar, 70 percent in that of leather shoes, and 77 percent in that of artificial silk.[74]

What happens to the surplus value thus accumulated? It would be naïve to suppose that the nomenklatura consumes it completely. As in other social systems based on exploitation, the ruling class, however extravagant it may be, cannot possibly spend on its personal needs the surplus value resulting from the labor of many millions. But, apart from the personal needs of its members, the nomenklatura has collective class needs that consume the lion's share of the surplus value produced in the Soviet Union.

The principal elements of these class needs are on the whole correctly described by Kurón and Modzelewski,[75] but they are put in a traditional Marxist context and their significance in the system of real socialism is not brought out. The class needs of the nomenklatura arise not from any ideological system but from its class interests. It spends the money on running the party and its apparatus, the KGB, the armed forces and the armament industry, the apparatus and the troops of the MVD (Ministry of the Interior), and the camps and prisons. A small part of the expenditure goes to less vital appendages of the system, i.e., the courts and the militia.

A considerable further sum goes to the agencies responsible for the ideological formation of the population, as well as those concerned with relations with foreign countries (political, economic, or cultural, i.e., in fact political), though not nearly so much is spent on these as on the institutions that are vital to the nomenklatura's power.

What is called "socialist accumulation," i.e., economic investment, takes second place. The accumulation concerned is the collective property of the nomenklatura, which comes next in the scale of their interests.

Last of all come science, culture, education, health, sport, etc. Though the exclusive interests of the nomenklatura are always paramount, the class element is less pronounced here.

These three categories of expenditure are very differently regarded by the toiling people.

The third is the most acceptable, since it includes health, education, scientific development for peaceful purposes, and culture (to the extent that it is not completely subject to propaganda).

Similarly, there are some aspects of the second category that are acceptable to the population. The most important of these is job security as a consequence of investment in industry; this, though carried out by the nomenklatura for the sake of the surplus product, provides the workers with their livelihood. Also this investment goes to the production of consumer goods and to the building industry—in short, to satisfying workers' needs.

A careful search will lead to the discovery of some aspects beneficial to the population even in the first category: the militia and the courts (though these are loathed by a large part of the population) at least partially serve its interests.

But by far the largest part of the surplus value extorted from the working population by the first two categories is spent on aims that conflict with its interests. How else could the nomenklatura objective of assuring and expanding its power and continuing to profit from surplus value be described? Under the system of real socialism, as Kurón and Modzelewski point out, the worker produces "a minimum livelihood for himself and maintains the state power that is against him. The product of his labor confronts him like a strange, hostile power because, though he produces it, it does not belong to him."[76]

17. COMPULSORY LABOR

Marx discovered not value but surplus value. Why did that discovery have to be made?

The creation of surplus product by primary producers and its appropriation by the ruling class have been a familiar phenomenon for centuries. Eduard Bernstein pointed out correctly that in the precapitalist age no one tried to conceal it. "When slaves produced goods for barter they were pure surplus-labor machines, and serfs performed surplus labor in the manifest form of forced labor and taxes paid in kind."[77] Primary producers were thought of as working animals who were allowed to live to the extent that they brought profit to their owners.

But with the triumph of capitalism and the development of bourgeois democracy this idea began to belong to the past. Equality before the law of all men and all social classes was proclaimed for the first time; the production of surplus value continued, of course, but in more concealed form. That was why Marx's theories appeared to be a discovery.

Capitalism also resulted in a modification of exploitation. Trade unions were formed to defend workers' rights; the right to strike for the improvement of working conditions is recognized and practiced; the unemployed are no longer reduced to beggary, but receive social security payments that enable them to live; workers can freely choose their employer and even go abroad. These social advances certainly did not create an ideal society, but they led to a diminution of exploitation and a substantial improvement in the wage earner's standard of living. It must be emphasized that these things were the result not of humanity on the capitalists' part but of the working-class movement and to an important extent the ideas of Karl Marx.

And what is the position in the countries where the complete victory of these ideas has been proclaimed? Their citizens are obliged to work or, rather, are assigned to jobs unless they are minors, pensioners, or disabled; otherwise they are "parasites" and are liable to legal penalties.

This is officially justified by Communist morality. "Work in the U.S.S.R. is a question of honor, glory, courage, and heroism," Stalin proclaimed. The nomenklatura insists that work is an obligation on everyone engaged in the construction of Communist society. These fine words do not explain why those who have no desire for honor and glory should be arrested and taken to the militia station.

The truth of the matter is that Communist morality does not come into it; everyone in the Soviet Union knows that members of nomenklaturist families do not have to work and do not get into trouble for not working. As we have already mentioned, the nomenklatura, in accordance with Marxist theory, believes that every worker adds to the profit. Nonworkers therefore cause loss, besides manifesting a certain spirit of independence in relation to the state, which is intolerable. Finally, subjecting all workers to the service of the state assures the nomenklatura of much more complete control of the population.

And what about the much vaunted "achievements" of the workers in the countries of real socialism?

The trade unions in these countries do not defend the interests of the workers against the employer, who in this case is the state; instead they ensure labor discipline and the carrying out of the employers' plans. Stalin rightly called them "the party's (i.e., the nomenklatura's) transmission belts."

On the pretext that the workers are working for themselves, there is no such thing as the right to strike. One would have supposed that if the workers were really working for themselves, it was the workers' business to decide whether they wanted to strike or not. But the nomenklatura is not prepared to discuss the matter; it simply treats any downing of tools as a crime against the state.

There is no unemployment pay, on the pretext that there is no unemployment. That is another phony argument. In a country of 270 millions, it is impossible to prevent there being several tens of thousands of persons at any given moment who for various reasons are not working, are changing jobs, or have been fired (Soviet labor legislation considers dismissal to be a disciplinary measure). Not a single one of them receives unemployment pay.

Workers cannot change their employer, for the only employer is the state, and emigration is practically forbidden. For many years, workers in the Soviet Union did not have the right to change jobs; it is permitted now, but the press continually denounces these "flighty" job changers *(letuny)* and makes suggestions about getting them to change their ways. Peasants still do not have the right to leave their kolkhoz. Thus the nomenklatura has resuscitated precapitalist working conditions.

In slave and feudal societies alike, the primary producer did not work for his master because he wanted to work for his living, but because he was forced to. His labor, in Marxist terminology, was subject to extraeconomic constraint. Capitalism broke with that tradition. What it needed was free men who sold their working power to the employer. There is constraint here, too, but it is economic constraint. Whatever social class he may belong to under capitalism, he is not obliged by law to work. Under real socialism, however, work is a universal legal obligation on everyone, even those who see no point in working. But everyone is not really everyone; nomenklaturists' wives do not have to do any kind of work and are not treated as parasites. Nomenklatura children are given agreeable sinecures.

The obligation to have a job has serious consequences. Every employee regards his job as compulsory labor, even if he chose it freely, even if he can change it, even though he depends on it for his livelihood.

When (1) work is compulsory, (2) pay and conditions are laid down exclusively by those who exercise the compulsion, (3) physical force is used to prevent workers from leaving their jobs or giving up work, one is justified in speaking of forced labor. All these conditions apply under real socialism.

In the first place, everyone is compelled to have a job. The fact that the vast majority could not survive without one does not change its coercive nature. Slaves or medieval serfs could not survive without working either, but that did not alter the compulsory nature of their work.

Secondly, pay and working conditions are laid down by the nomenklatura alone. It alone fixes the pay of various categories of employees, and it does not negotiate. We have already mentioned the sad role of the trade unions and the lack of the right to strike. Even collective complaints are forbidden; the high priests of socialist collectivism dismiss such complaints with the contemptuous term *kolektivki*.

Thirdly, it is impossible to get away from the nomenklatura employer. Changing jobs merely means changing from one of its representatives to another. There is no escape from this within the frontiers of the country; for the nomenklatura state is omnipresent, and it has deliberately blocked all routes to work that is not for it—and going abroad is impossible.

What is the use of all those fine words about work as Soviet man's reason for living when in fact he has been plunged back into a system of extraeconomic compulsory labor as in the age of slavery or feudalism?

18. ALIENATION UNDER REAL SOCIALISM

When a Soviet citizen who has studied economics reaches the West and reads neo-Marxist literature, he is disconcerted by the noisy chatter about alienation and the "anthropological" ideas of the young Marx. He may at a pinch be able to reconcile himself to the idea that Marx may once have been young, though in the Soviet Union the founder of Marxism is always associated with the image of the bearded veteran portrayed in the stereotyped pictures or busts, while the word alienation suggests nothing at all, or at most a routine phrase from court reports: "alienation of the accused's property for the benefit of the state."

Nevertheless it gradually dawns on the new arrival from the Soviet Union that, yes, he has heard the term before, in his economics course, though the lecturer did not linger over it; and then he suddenly realizes why. Marx tried to give his readers the impression that alienation arose only under capitalism. At this point criticism of Marx is unavoidable; for scholarly accuracy should have made him admit just the opposite: that alienation was less marked under capitalism than in earlier social systems.

A slave was regarded as a working animal and obviously took no interest in his work. Similarly a serf performed forced labor, though he could retain something of what he produced.

Under capitalism the worker enjoys personal freedom. He works because he has to earn a living, not because he is forced to by someone who has been his master from birth. Legally he has the same rights as his employer, though economic dependence creates inequality between them. The primary producer obviously has no interest in working harder than necessary to increase his master's profits, but is prepared to do overtime to earn more for himself. There is alienation here, but much less of it than in feudal, let alone slave, society. Can it be claimed that alienation disappears under socialism, as Marx predicted? On the contrary, it increases. It is not because the victory of socialism has made it obsolete that Soviet economists skip the subject of alienation; they do so because it has become an everyday, omnipresent reality.

How could it be otherwise when it is made very plain to the citizens of the Soviet Union and its satellites that they have no right to poke their noses into nomenklatura affairs and that it is their business dutifully to carry out the instructions of the authorities while singing the praises of the beloved party? What can that lead to but alienation?

Marx said that the cause of alienation was the private ownership of the means of production. But collective ownership of the means of production by the ruling class has changed nothing in this respect. The cause of alienation in the economic field is not the form of ownership, as Marx assumed; its cause is the purpose and actual results of production.

The capitalist search for maximum profit is certainly not an objective capable of inspiring the workers; hence alienation under capitalism. But the results of capitalist production are not restricted to exploitation of the workers and profit for the owners; they also include the creation of an abundance of consumer goods and much better pay for the workers than under real socialism. This keeps alienation within bounds. In the socialist countries it is not only the aim of production, i.e., the consolidation and expansion of the power of the nomenklatura, that alienates the producers; the actual result, the reinforcement of the military and police apparatus of the state instead of the production of consumer goods, fails to rouse the worker's interest in the result of his work. After sixty-five years, nomenklatura exhortations to work with enthusiasm have worn thin and have ceased to be effective.

Hence the growing alienation, the workers' feeling that they are subject to compulsory labor. They have no free trade unions and no right to strike, and the labor laws are reminiscent of legislation against "vagabonds" in absolute monarchies. The production of surplus value and exploitation by the nomenklatura class have resulted in a strange regression to precapitalist forms.

We have not sought here to undertake a systematic exposition of the political economy of real socialism, but have merely mentioned some essential points that are indispensable to the understanding of the problems presented in this book.

A systematic and exhaustive study of the political economy of real socialism is still a task for the future, but the few observations in this chapter will perhaps have given the reader a better picture of the reality of that economy than all the volumes published on the subject by the official Soviet agencies.

NOTES

1. MEW, Vol. 20, p. 263.
2. *The Constitution of the Communist World*, William B. Simons, ed., Alphen aan den Rijn, 1980, p. 356.
3. Marx and Engels, *Collected Works*, Vol. 5, p. 91.
4. MEW, Vol. 20, p. 26.
5. Marx and Engels, *Selected Works*, Vol. 1, pp. 361–405.
6. Marx, *Capital*, p. 259.
7. Ibid.
8. MEW, Vol. 25, p. 883.
9. *Leninskij sbornik XI*, p. 382.
10. MEW, Vol. 38, p. 64.
11. Lenin, *Collected Works*, Vol. 29, p. 479.
12. S. I. Sdobnov, *Sobstvennost' i kommunizm*, Moscow, 1968, pp. 92–93.
13. Marx, *Capital*, Vol. 2, London, 1942, p. 846.
14. V. T. Cuntulov, *Ekonomičeskaja istorija SSSR*, Moscow, 1969.
15. Ibid. pp. 186–188, 190–193, 204, 234.

16. Stalin, *Werke*, Vol. 17, p. 291.
17. J. Kurón and K. Modzelewski, *Monopolsozialismus*, Hamburg, 1969, pp. 30–32, 46.
18. Stalin, *Werke*, Vol. 17, p. 325.
19. M. Iljin, *Fünf Jahre, die die Welt verändern*, Berlin, 1932.
20. Lenin, *Collected Works*, Vol. 25, p. 470.
21. *Problemy izmenenija sozial'noi struktury sovetskogo obščestva*, Moscow, 1968, p. 67.
22. Lenin, *Collected Works*, Vol. 22, p. 276.
23. Ibid., p. 276.
24. Naum Jasny, *Essays on the Soviet Economy*, Munich, 1962, pp. 270–72, 276–81.
25. MEW, Vol. 24, p. 465.
26. Lenin, *Collected Works*, Vol. 33, p. 426.
27. Ibid., Vol. 32, p. 459.
28. Ibid., Vol. 25, p. 364.
29. Stalin, *Works*, Vol. 13, pp. 40–41.
30. I. B. Berchin, *Geschichte der UdSSR 1917–70*, Berlin (East), 1971, p. 378.
31. V. T. Čuntulov, op. cit., p. 254.
32. Ibid., p. 281.
33. I. B. Berchin, op. cit., p. 410.
34. V. T. Čuntulov, op. cit., pp. 294–95.
35. I. B. Berchin, op. cit., p. 590.
36. V. T. Čuntulov, op. cit., p. 363.
37. *Istorija SSSR. Epocha socializma (1917–57)*, Moscow, 1957, pp. 699–700.
38. V. T. Čuntulov, op. cit., p. 369.
39. Ibid., p. 383.
40. Ibid., p. 395.
41. I. B. Berchin, op. cit., p. 708.
42. *Osteuropa-Wirtschaft 1971*, No. 3, p. 209.
43. *Ekonomika i organizacija promyšlennogo proizvodstva*, 1970, No. 1, p. 31.
44. I. B. Berchin, op. cit., p. 708.
45. *Hauptrichtungen der Entwicklung der Volkswirtschaft der UdSSR in den Jahren 1976–1980. Entwurf des ZK der KPdSU zum XXV. Parteitag*, Moscow, 1976, p. 34.
46. *Pravda*, Feb. 25, 1976.
47. A. N. Kossygin, *Hauptrichtlinien der Entwicklung der Volkswirtschaft der UdSSR in den Jahren 1976–1980*, Moscow, 1976, p. 34.
48. Lenin, *Collected Works*, Vol. 28, p. 97.
49. Ibid., Vol. 25, p. 425.
50. Ibid., p. 474.
51. Ibid., Vol. 20, p. 154.
52. *Autonomie*, October 1975, No. 1, p. 8.
53. *Kommunist*, 1975, No. 10, p. 46.
54. Lenin, *Collected Works*, Vol. 22, p. 194.
55. Ibid., Vol. 26, p. 404.
56. Ibid., Vol. 29, p. 411.
57. *Pravda*, Jan. 20, 1929.
58. I. B. Berchin, op. cit., p. 406.
59. *Političeskaja ekonomija*, Učebnik. Moscow, 1955, p. 307.
60. A. N. Kossygin, op. cit., p. 14.
61. *KPSS v rezoljucijach . . .* , Moscow, 1954, Vol. 1, p. 698.
62. *XV Vsesojuznaja Konferencija VKP(b). Stenografičeskij otčet*. Moscow, 1927, p. 507.

63. *Politiceskaja ekonomija,* pp. 127–128.
64. *Vestnik statistiki,* 1976, No. 1, p. 91.
65. *Politiceskaja ekonomija,* p. 132.
66. *Vestnik statistiki,* 1976, No. 1, pp. 80, 85.
67. Lenin, *Collected Works,* Vol. 27, p. 411.
68. Ibid., Vol. 6, p. 54.
69. *Politiceskaja ekonomija,* p. 130.
70. J. Kurón and K. Modzelewski, *Monopolsozialismus,* Hamburg, 1969, p. 22.
71. I. B. Berchin, op. cit., p. 408.
72. A. N. Kossygin, op. cit., p. 49.
73. Lenin, *Collected Works,* Vol. 6, pp. 402, 403.
74. A. Smirnov, *Ekonomiceskoe soderžanie naloga s oborota,* Moscow, 1963.
75. J. Kurón and K. Modzelewski, op. cit., pp. 22–25.
76. Ibid., p. 26.
77. Eduard Bernstein, *Die Vorraussetzungen des Sozialismus und die Aufgaben der Sozialdemokratie,* Stuttgart-Berlin, 1921, p. 75.

5

Privileged Class

"He is saturated to the edge
Everything is good and has good reasons:
The nomenklatura privilege,
Also the nomenklatura treasons."
Alexander Galich: Pokolenie
obrechennych Frankfurt
a.M. 1974, p. 28

The rules are the same for everyone, only the exceptions differ.
Literaturnaya Gazeta, December 28, 1977

I must make a confession; it was under the influence of the West that I decided to write this chapter.

As long as I lived in the Soviet Union I thought it natural that, in accordance with historical tradition, the ruling class should also be the privileged class. It was only after I came to the West that I started asking questions about the extent of those class privileges.

In both East and West I have had occasion to meet people of widely differing social origins, among them individuals who were at the top of the ladder, and I then made a discovery that amazed me: the privileges of the ruling classes in the West were far smaller than those in the countries of real socialism.

I realized for the first time that ministers in the West live on their pay, just like other people. They are certainly well but not excessively paid. If they want to build themselves a country house, they have to save for a long time and sometimes do without certain things. They do not always have domestic help; their wives do the cooking and housework themselves, which would be unthinkable in a socialist country.

I witnessed how a Western minister who was at the same time deputy chairman of the government party carelessly damaged his neighbor's car; the police confiscated his driver's license and he had to pay for the damage. Not so in the Soviet Union, where the militia would make inquiries to find out whether a neighbor who had had the nerve to park his car at a place where the minister passed every day had bought it in a legal way.

I have seen in a European country that the Prime Minister did not live in a luxurious mansion, that his family lived a perfectly ordinary life, and that the building in which they lived did not swarm with secret police. I have seen a head of state of one of the most influential countries in the Western world leaving his official residence on his retirement and going back to live in the apartment he had occupied when he was merely a lawyer. The ordinary people he met in the street went on showing respect and liking for their former President, but there was no question of his living in style at the taxpayers' expense to the end of his days.

To me all this was totally unexpected. But I realized that to Western readers this state of affairs was perfectly normal and that it never occurred to them that it could be otherwise. That is what led me to write this chapter.

1. WHO LIVES HAPPILY IN RUSSIA?

Every Soviet schoolchild has to learn by heart the poem *Who Lives Happily in Russia?* by N. A. Nekrasov, a nineteenth-century revolutionary democrat. It tells the story of seven peasants who set out to find a happy man in Russia. After much searching, they discover one man, the young revolutionary Grisha Dobrosklonov. Children at first fail to see exactly what his happiness consists of, since his fate is "consumption and Siberia," but they are told that, as the revolution ultimately triumphs, his cause does not perish. There is a similar quick answer to the question at the present day: Who lives happily in Russia? The nomenklatura.

Since this state of affairs can no longer be concealed from the people, that is something that every Soviet schoolchild knows. There were no reports in the Soviet press about the many cars that were presented to Brezhnev in the countries through which he passed, but everyone can see ZILs and Chaikas being driven around with party dignitaries comfortably installed in the backseats. The Soviet media do not mention the shops that accept payment only in foreign currency or the special department at the GUM stores, but in the course of their everlasting search for things to buy, Soviet customers will more than once have been advised to "keep moving" by one of the grim-looking doorkeepers who guard the entrances to those mysterious shopping places. The *dolce vita* led by the nomenklaturists can no longer be denied; all that can be concealed is the full extent of their privileges and many details about them that their troublesome fellow citizens might be curious about. So the nomenklatura tries to justify its way of life, which, not without succumbing to inconsistency, it does.

I quote: "In the Soviet Union there still exist at the present time substantial disparities in the level of salaries received by various categories of officials belonging to the state apparatus. Higher salaries are received by those in leading positions who have a wide range of authority and at the same time carry great responsibility for the tasks entrusted to them and generally have high technical and political qualifications. This category is numerically insignificant in comparison with the rest of the staff of the state apparatus."[1] The only thing the author of this passage omits is that these truths apply not only to the state apparatus but above all to the party apparatus.

An article in *Pravda* entitled "The Relationship Between Work and Consumption" tries to justify this state of affairs. "Work does not yet constitute a primary necessity for all Soviet citizens," it says. "Hence the need of material incentives."[2]

Material incentives should be needed only by those who do not consider work a primary necessity. A category of Soviet citizens that has no need of incentives already exists, if *Pravda* is to be believed. And where are they to be found if not among those who are most determinedly constructing the Communist society, i.e., the vanguard, the nomenklatura? Logically, therefore, these people should be happy to do their work without the additional encouragement of material incentives.

These remarks should not be regarded as ironic. What we have just said coincides completely with the ideas of Marx and Lenin, who claimed that top-level pay should not exceed that of a skilled worker. This was reflected in Lenin's instructions about maximum pay in the party; the pay of a party member was not to exceed the modest level that was laid down. Lenin said that "for a certain period of time"[3] higher salaries were to be paid to "bourgeois specialists" who, by reason of their venal nature, were ready for the sake of money to contribute to the construction of the communism that they hated. So how did it come about that the vanguard of the working class started demanding and getting much more than those greedy "bourgeois specialists"? *Pravda* has not answered that question.

Since the party theorists are caught in the net of their own contradictions, men of letters go zealously to their aid. They strive to inculcate into the minds of ordinary Soviet citizens the idea that the activities of their superiors are beyond the comprehension of ordinary workers, and that in any case it is improper to compare themselves with the nomenklatura.

The poet Sergei Mikhalkov, who has a reputation for particular servility to the regime, wrote a fable entitled *Hard Earned Daily Bread*, in which he compares the ordinary Soviet citizen to a draft horse "that brings the oats and takes away the dung," while the nomenklaturists are "thoroughbreds" that, as the poet modestly notes, "have all that their status calls for." In its blindness the draft horse envies them, wrongly, as it turns out, for it fails to appreciate the difficulties of the horse race. Finally, the poet draws the moral:

> That happens if one
> Who is not very bright
> Is judging how live
> All those in the limelight.[4]

In other words, the Soviet citizen must not take the liberty of passing judgment on those people's way of life, but should content himself with fetching oats for the nomenklatura horse and removing its dung.

The strumming of this lyre is accompanied by a chorus of party ideologists who argue that the draft horse's petit-bourgeois ideas are unworthy of a Communist, that the basic principle of socialism is "from each according to his capacity, to each according to his work," and that, as Marx pointed out, there is simple work and there is also complicated work. In this context the ideologists neglect to mention what Marx said about payment for work done.

The nomenklatura is well aware of the conflict with Marx's theories and Lenin's political testament. That is why it tries to hide the realities of its comfortable existence. During the Renaissance, Boccaccio exposed monkish hypocrisy. The nomenklatura still awaits its Boccaccio.

Let us now describe in some detail the privileges of the nomenklatura, taking as an example an official halfway up the hierarchical ladder—let us say the head of a Central Committee desk—and let us compare his position with that of an average Soviet citizen, relying on statistics when these are available and, when they are not, on our own, everyday experience.

2. EARNINGS OF HEAD OF A CENTRAL COMMITTEE DESK

As we mentioned in the previous chapter, an average Soviet factory or office worker earns 181 rubles a month. The pay of the head of a Central Committee desk is 450 rubles a month. This responsible individual has the right to thirty days' vacation a year, plus traveling time to and from his vacation resort. The average worker has a two-week vacation. At the beginning of his vacation period, the head of a desk receives an additional month's salary, 450 rubles, as a "rest-cure allowance." His vacation is cost-free, for he stays free of charge for a month at a Central Committee or Council of Ministers rest home. His wife stays at the same establishment for a very small fee, and his children are sent to a first-class pioneers' camp. He thus receives thirteen months' pay, but lives at his own expense for only eleven months. Thus his real monthly salary is 531 rubles, 80 kopeks.

That is not all. He is also entitled to the famous *kremliovka*, the pride and joy of every successful nomenklaturist. There exist two kremliovka categories: one hundred twenty and ninety rubles a month. These are not ordinary rubles. Kremliovka prices are calculated according to a prewar price list. Kremliovka consist of coupons allegedly entitling the holder to "medical nutrition." But the holders are not the sick, they are the high nomenklaturists. There are three coupons per day: "breakfast," "lunch," "dinner." Almost all kremliovka holders prefer to receive their meals as a food basket full of luxuries that are normally unobtainable in Moscow, let alone the provinces. These are distributed at the Kremlin canteen at No. 2 Granovsky Street and (for the second category) in the "House of the Government," at No. 2 Serafimovich Street. In his book *The Russians* the American journalist Hedrick Smith draws a very accurate picture of nomenklaturists and their wives arriving at the Kremlin canteen and quickly disappearing behind an ordinary-looking glass door surmounted by a panel with the words "Pass Office." Later they are to be seen emerging laden with big brown-paper parcels and taking their seats in the limousines that have been waiting for them.[5] Smith does not mention another category of visitors: the drivers and domestic servants who go there to fetch the multilayered aluminum Kremlin lunch containers. Helpings are so ample that a single portion is enough to feed a whole family. Many a nomenklaturist wife prefers dependence on the Kremlin canteen to relying on the talents (and honesty) of her own cook (whom of course she could not do without).

Our desk head has an allocation of ninety rubles' worth of kremliovka coupons a month.[6] Some nomenklaturists (they are infallible in such matters) have estimated that in terms of present prices these food coupons are worth three hundred rubles a month, or thirty-six hundred rubles a year spread over eleven working months.

At this stage let us draw an interim conclusion: the desk head really earns eight hundred sixty rubles a month, nearly five times as much as an average factory or office worker.

But supposing we compare his earnings not with those of a statistically "average" citizen, but with a real one, who is distinguished from the former in two ways: (1) a share in the nomenklatura income is not allotted to him, and (2) he is not only a "factory or office worker," but perhaps a kolkhoz peasant, a student, or a pensioner, categories with income much more modest than those of ordinary factory or office workers (which is why they do not appear in these statistics).

In the absence of the required figures, it is impossible to give a figure for the average income of an ordinary Soviet citizen, but everyone in the Soviet Union knows that it is hardly more than 100–120 rubles a month, from which it follows that our desk head earns nearly eight times as much as an average citizen.

Let us add that the former is entitled to an allowance equal to 10 percent of his salary "for knowledge of a foreign language and using it in the service"; for a knowledge of two languages the allowance is 20 percent, even if his knowledge is questionable and he never makes use of any foreign language in the course of his work.

But that is not all. His effective salary equals his real salary. He buys whatever he needs at the special shops or "buffets" to which he has access, while the ordinary citizen has to put up with what he manages, with a great deal of enterprise and ingenuity, to procure from the ordinary state shops, which are always inadequately stocked. It would be possible to express this difference in percentage terms if figures for the average consumption of goods by the Soviet population were available, but in the Soviet Union such figures are state secrets.

Let us assume, then, that our head of a desk earns ten times as much as an ordinary worker. That figure may be wrong but, if so, it errs on the low side. If our head of a desk earns ten times as much as an ordinary Soviet mortal he does not pay ten times as much in income tax. The maximum rate is 13 percent, which is deducted monthly at source as soon as pay reaches two hundred rubles; in other words, the principle of progressive taxation is not applied in the Soviet Union to monthly pay of two hundred rubles upward—a real triumph of egalitarianism. So our head of a desk pays 13 percent in tax, but only on his basic salary of four hundred fifty rubles a month.

Stalin devised another source of income for his nomenklatura, a completely illegal one known as the "packet." In addition to their salary, the cashier handed to officials whose names appeared on a special list in the accounts department a bundle of bank notes in an envelope. This "packet" was not necessarily very thick; I recall in particular that at the beginning of the fifties Yuri Volsky, assistant to the head of the Soviet Information Office, received a "packet" containing the ridiculous sum of fifty rubles. But it was not the cash that counted, so much as the principle. From the moment that he was granted the right to a nomenklatura "packet" he could "look to the future with confidence," as the Soviet press puts it; and not without reason, for he was subsequently appointed Soviet ambassador to Argentina and later to Mexico and to Jamaica.

The "packet" was so secret that it was forbidden to use it even to pay party membership fees. On Stalin's death this special gratification that smelled of corruption was abolished—to be replaced by others.

3. INVISIBLE EARNINGS

Like Stalin's packets, the benefits we are going to mention now come into the category, familiar to Soviet economists, of "invisible earnings." This term remained in use until the beginning of the seventies, and was then replaced by the term "social consumption fund," which covers some of the privileges I mentioned above, such as vacation homes, pioneer camps, crèches, and so forth. A share in this fund is allotted to everyone, including the average wage earner, by the Central Statistical Office, which with simulated naïveté assumes that the benefits available are shared out fairly to everyone and that the most disadvantaged in fact gain most from them. The result is that the average wage earner is statistically allotted places in convalescent homes that are reserved for the Central Committee, the Council of Ministers, or the KGB, or even living space in a state dacha, though every Soviet wage earner knows very well that he will never get anywhere near any of them. That is why the old term was dropped; the Central Committee apparatus began to look closely at the term "*invisible* earnings" and discovered some irony in it.

So far as nomenklaturists are concerned, their invisible earnings are perfectly visible. We say that without the slightest irony, so there is no point in using any other term. But we shall use it with reference not to benefits such as places in a crèche, but to subsidiary income resulting from places in the hierarchy.

Let us begin with fees from books, articles, and lectures. A Soviet author may be able to write like Tolstoy, but that is no guarantee that he will ever be published. In every editorial office there is an authors' file showing whether the individual concerned is or is not a member of the party and what his nationality, education, profession, and job are. I have myself been an editor and have filled in forms giving this information about the authors. The directives are simple: In considering work for publication, priority must be given to members of the party, Russians, if possible with a university degree (the "nationalities" are also acceptable, unlike the Jews, who are regarded as undesirable). Ideally the potential author should be the holder of a nomenklatura post. And if it is a Central Committee post or comes under some other party agency, it doesn't matter what the author writes; it can be the greatest nonsense, for it will be rewritten. The revised version will be humbly submitted for the author's signature and he will be paid at the highest rate. That is why so many nomenklaturists write articles and even books.

The party press pays best. No newspaper pays better than *Pravda,* and no periodical is more generous than *Kommunist.* Since the beginning of the fifties, payments have been declining, but the nomenklatura publications are exempt from any reductions. The payment is still three hundred rubles for twenty-four typed pages, or the equivalent of an average worker's three months' wages.

Another source of a nomenklaturist's revenue is foreign travel. The party apparatus (and the KGB if the journey is to a capitalist country) has complete discretion in the matter. Everyone knows that the many obstacles put in the way of those who wish to travel are easily surmounted only by nomenklaturists.

Because of the chronic shortage of consumer goods in the U.S.S.R. and the other countries of real socialism, foreign products are keenly sought after as status symbols, and therefore represent capital in hand, for they can be easily sold at highly advantageous prices. Thus nomenklaturists often suddenly decide that things they have bought abroad are not needed after all, or don't fit, or simply that they no longer like them. They don't actually sell them themselves, of course, but use the good offices of third parties, such as their wife's aunt's best friend, for instance.

Sometimes it is possible to manage without the disinterested intervention of one's wife's aunt's best friend. The Soviet state, yielding to the entreaties of the nomenklatura, has found a legal way of permitting the acquisition of foreign goods. In every one of the states of the socialist community there are shops in which goods can be paid for only in foreign currency.

What a brilliant idea! In no other country in the world, whether industrialized or underdeveloped, are there whole chains of shops, restaurants, and bars in which the national currency is not accepted. Unfortunates without foreign currency or special coupons purchasable with foreign currency cannot enter these establishments without being confronted with a doorkeeper of the type we mentioned above.

This system was introduced in spite of the fact that in the Soviet Union (and the other countries of real socialism) inflation is officially nonexistent and that the ruble is proclaimed "the world's most stable currency." *Izvestia,* the government organ, publishes the foreign-exchange rates regularly at the beginning of the month. The ordinary Soviet citizen, unfamiliar with the peculiarities of the international monetary system, regards this as merely an absurd tabulation generally tending to show that the fluctuations of the market are favorable to the ruble, though everyone knows that the ruble cannot be exchanged for any other currency.

But a nomenklaturist who goes abroad understands those figures and knows that rubles *can* be exchanged for other currencies, for it is on the basis of those exchange rates that he obtains foreign currency. If he can produce the necessary authorization, the Foreign Trade Bank, in Neglinnaya Street, in Moscow, will exchange rubles up to a maximum amount for him. He will invariably try to sell as many rubles as possible, for he parts with the world's most stable currency without regret. He can use the foreign currency he does not spend to buy "checks" at Soviet trade agencies abroad. Formerly they were called "certificates": the ones for hard, i.e., Western, currencies, others for the currencies of underdeveloped countries, the third for those of the real-socialist countries. The best products were sold for Western currency certificates, the worst for "socialist" certificates. Even cars or cooperative apartments can be bought in the Soviet Union with these checks or with foreign currency received while abroad, and at a price substantially lower than the owner of ordinary rubles would have to pay.

The invisible earnings of our departmental head and many other nomenklatura officials widen the gap between them and other Soviet citizens. Other, nonfinancial privileges transform the gap into a gulf.

4. THE NOMENKLATURA BAKSHEESH AND CORRUPTION

We have seen that nomenklaturists earn a good living, but that does not satisfy them. Not content with pocketing the dividends that accrue to them from surplus value, they try still further to exploit the capital that their dominant position represents. Another source of income is available to them in the form of bribes.

Corruption is not the monopoly of any country or society. Everyone remembers the scandal caused in the West by the generosity of Lockheed. But corruption thrives on fertile soil, and the most fertile is bureaucracy triumphant. The fewer the checks on bureaucratic omnipotence, the easier it is for bureaucratic bigwigs to have their palms greased. It is not surprising that it was in medieval Eastern despotic societies with an administrative apparatus of vast ramifications and a total absence of free information that corruption gradually insinuated itself into all the interstices of the social fabric. This tradition, like many others, was established in Russia under the Tatars, and it took deep and lasting root.

It is important to appreciate that the acquisition of power by the nomenklatura reinforced, rather than weakened, the tradition of corruption, for under the real-socialist system the unlimited domination of a bureaucracy has assumed unprecedented dimensions.

Nomenklaturists are of course forbidden to accept bribes, but they do so frequently and on a large scale. Punishment is rare and mild. The nomenklaturist class in fact tolerates corruption. It is especially rampant in the Soviet republics in Transcaucasia and Central Asia, which for historical reasons have been most lastingly infected with the virus.

Let us take a not very important republic, Azerbaijan. The information at our disposal can be relied on, for it comes from the secret files of the central committee of the Azerbaijan party. The documents were published by Ilya Zemtsov, who worked in the information department of the Azerbaijan central committee before he emigrated to Israel.

To throw light on the situation in Azerbaijan, let us quote some figures. The sums involved are not exceptional for the nomenklatura; they are completely within the bounds of the usual. Thus, according to the 1969 tariff, appointment to a post as district public prosecutor would cost thirty thousand rubles. That relatively modest sum would enable a party member to transform himself into a guardian of socialist legality when a vacancy occurred.

Another position as a guardian of public order, and a much more onerous one, was also for sale, that of chief of the district militia. In this case the asking price was fifty thousand rubles.

For the same sum one could be appointed president of a kolkhoz. This appointment was nominally by election, but, like all Soviet citizens, members of a kolkhoz vote for the candidate "recommended" to them. The president of the kolkhoz belongs to the nomenklatura of the district party committee.

The position of manager of a sovkhoz, similarly reserved for the nomenklatura, was more expensive, at eighty thousand rubles. This is a more profitable position, with better prospects of advancement in the nomenklatura hierarchy.

The secretaries of the district committee would formally decide to recommend the appointment after pocketing the purchase price, which would come as a welcome supplement to their nomenklaturist salary and special allowances.

To secure appointment to the post of district secretary you had to dive deep into your pocket, much deeper than if you wanted to become a district prosecutor. In 1969 it would have cost you two hundred thousand rubles to be appointed first secretary of a party district committee in Azerbaijan, but only one hundred thousand rubles to be appointed second secretary. In these instances payment had to be made to the secretaries of the central committee in Baku, as the jobs in question were this committee's nomenklatura jobs.

Secretaries of district committees are in a very lucrative situation; they have wide powers and, as we have just seen, are in a splendid position to secure illicit handouts. Hence the high price. Cheaper posts were also on offer in the Azerbaijan nomenklatura. Thus, becoming a theater manager cost between ten thousand and thirty thousand rubles, and director of a research institute forty thousand rubles, while the title of member of the Academy of Sciences of the Soviet Socialist Republic of Azerbaijan was reasonably priced at fifty thousand rubles.

Becoming head of an institution of higher education was much more expensive than becoming an Azerbaijan "immortal"; the figure, which varied according to the institution,[7] might be as high as two hundred thousand rubles, which is intelligible enough if it is borne in mind that this dignitary illegally charged would-be students fees for admitting them. Here, too, the amount varied from establishment to establishment. At the time, it cost ten thousand rubles to be admitted to the foreign-language institute, between twenty thousand and twenty-five thousand rubles to be admitted to the University of Baku, thirty thousand rubles to be admitted to the medical school, and no less than thirty-five thousand rubles to secure entry to the institute of agricultural studies.[8]

There was a realistic tariff not only for important positions at district level but also for some scientific and cultural appointments and even for posts in the government of the Azerbaijan Republic. The position of minister for social security was cheap at one hundred twenty thousand rubles, for extracting additional profit from the costs of extremely inadequate pensions was hardly possible. The almost equally unpromising post of minister of communal economy was available at one hundred fifty thousand rubles. But it would have cost you two hundred fifty thousand rubles to become trade minister, though the functions of that office were theoretically on a par with the others:[9] the chronic shortage of goods held out the prospect of enormous profits.

These figures are taken from a secret report by G. Aliev, first secretary of the central committee of the Azerbaijan party, who is now a member of the Politburo of the CPSU Central Committee and first vice-chairman of the Soviet Government. The report was presented to a plenary meeting of the central committee of the Azerbaijan party on March 20, 1970.

As always happens in nomenklatura intrigues, these revelations took place in a very definite context—on this occasion the replacement of the first secretary, Akhundov. Aliev, who in Akhundov's time was president of the Azerbaijan KGB, set about exposing the corruption that had prevailed under his predecessor and, on the pretext of cleaning up the leadership, put his own people in leading positions. Between 1969 and 1972, responsible nomenklatura posts were filled by 1,983 KGB men.[10] But in 1973 it was obvious that Aliev's lieutenants, now in positions of responsibility, were no less corrupt than their predecessors.[11] Aliev was made a Politburo member. His successor is Bagirov. But today corruption still flourishes in Azerbaijan, to such an extent that the Azerbaijanis speak with nostalgia of the (good) old days under Akhundov.

What else was to be expected? It has long been known in the Soviet Union that KGB nomenklaturists are just as susceptible to bribes as others. I recall a woman friend of my family's who lived in Abkhazie at the beginning of the thirties. After doing everything possible to get her sister out of prison, she offered the wife of the local chief of the GPU a massive gold watch chain; her sister was released the next day. A friend told me that a former schoolfellow of his who joined the KGB arranged to put him on a delegation that was going to the United States and immediately added, "I'm giving you the green light. You pay for your electric light, don't you? Well, then, you must pay for being given the green light, too." The price was 300 rubles.

This indulgent attitude to corruption is of course primarily attributable to the solidarity that exists among nomenklaturists, all of whom are equally keen to add to their material wealth. But there is also another reason for it.

Can an ordinary Soviet citizen hope to become trade minister of Azerbaijan? To do so, a factory or office worker, who at that time was earning 150 rubles a month, would have had to work for 138 years without spending a kopek. Except in the nomenklatura and circles close to it, where are people to be found capable of accumulating the sums required without reaching the age of Methuselah?

It is the nomenklatura that has the money. Thus Zemtsov reports that the first secretary of the Baku district committee, a man named Mamedov, was seen paying into his wife's savings book the sum of 195,000 rubles—or about 160 years' pay of an average worker.[12]

There are of course sections of Soviet society that are not part of the nomenklatura and yet have large sums of money at their disposal. These are successful criminal gangs who live in conflict with the law. But those people do not seek appointment to nomenklatura posts; on the contrary, their funds are tapped by the nomenklatura. Thus the president of the presidium of the supreme soviet of the Soviet Republic of Azerbaijan, Iskenderov, fixed the price of a pardon for someone sentenced to a long term of imprisonment at 100,000 rubles.[13] No doubt it was the prospect of substantial bribes from criminals that explained the high price of the post of district public prosecutor or chief of militia. The official pay of these people is in fact small; that of the former is from 150 to 180 rubles a month, and that of the latter is between 200 and 250 rubles.[14]

The price of a pardon varies, but generally greatly exceeds the venal nomenklaturists' monthly pay; a judge will want the equivalent of three or four months' salary, while a party secretary will insist on ten months'.[15] Criminals do not gain entry to the nomenklatura with their money, but nomenklaturists buy themselves advancement with criminals' money.

A position in the nomenklatura can in fact be bought only by someone who already belongs to it. Thus corruption makes a major contribution to the trend of making membership of that class hereditary.

5.   "AND OTHER ANTIPODES"

Azerbaijan is not an exception and not even the republic most plagued by graft. Three years after Akhundov's removal, the Georgian scandals were exposed. They touched the highest circles of the nomenklatura: the Politburo itself.

Vasily Mzhavanadze, the Georgian first secretary and nonvoting member of the Politburo, and Albert Churkin, the second (i.e., Russian) secretary, as well as their wives ("the two Tamaras," or "the Princesses Tamara" as they were dubbed by the Georgians), set the standards for bribery in the republic. It was just like Azerbaijan, only on a larger scale. Ministers' jobs were also sold according to a price list: a hundred thousand rubles for the minister of social security, two hundred fifty thousand to three hundred thousand for the minister of trade or of light industry. But the number of bidders was so great that a kind of auction would be held. Since all of this took place not in a market economy but in "real socialism," the job did not always go to the highest bidder. Other factors were taken into consideration, particularly a candidate's membership in the right group in the Georgian nomenklatura. The auctioneers were the central-committee secretaries, the chairman of the republic council of ministers—to be brief, members of the Georgian central-committee bureau, to which the Georgian ministries were subordinated.

The highest ranks of the Georgian party apparatus divided up the republic into spheres of influence, that is, restored the feudal system of vassalage.

The two Tamaras also participated in the selection of the republic's leaders and for huge bribes would push their candidates. The ladies collected their bribes not in rubles but in hard currency, precious stones, paintings by famous artists, or antiques.

But could it be that all this is lies and gossip? In the West the opinion (inculcated by Soviet propaganda) is firmly held that the regime in the U.S.S.R. is perhaps overly strict but will not tolerate any real corruption. After the publication of the German edition of this book, a West German reader kept writing me indignant letters; he could not bring himself to believe that the president of the Azerbaijan university accepted bribes for getting students admitted. For such skeptical readers I shall permit myself a long citation from an officially approved article published by a newspaper of the Georgian central committee and the council of ministers: *Zarya Vostoka* (Dawn of the East). The article appeared after a change at the top of the Georgian nomenklatura and the plenary session of the Georgian central committee that took place in connection with it; despite all the clichés, the article gives a sense of the atmosphere created by the nomenklatura's constantly throwing its weight around. The article is titled "The Party Leadership Is Up to Contemporary Problems." Here are some extracts from it:

"Favoritism, abuse of seniority, and careerism flourish because of family ties and corruption . . . wives and other family members start substituting for their highly placed husbands at work; in the narrow circle of family and friends, government policy comes to be decided." This in connection with the two Tamaras. And again about them and others of their kind:

"Mentioning the negative influence on the life of the party organization and condemning family influences, the unseemly role of relatives and protégés of several people in positions of responsibility, who sap their authority, members of the plenary session said that being related to workers in a leadership position gave no one special privileges. The only privilege of these people consisted of the fact that they had to feel a greater responsibility for their words, for their actions, for their way of living, for their conduct in society." There are not only family ties but also friendship and protection.

People "have been named to positions of leadership not for their business acumen and moral qualities but because of favoritism, friendship, family ties, according to the principle of personal loyalty." The paper mentions "the practice of several leaders dividing the republic into spheres of interest . . . and having their so-called 'lovers'—privileged individuals."

Not only individuals but even whole districts were privileged—for example, the Gori district, Stalin's birthplace.

"The kind of thing that the existence of privileged districts leads to can be clearly seen in the Gori district. During a single year, more than five hundred sixty controllers and auditors visited the district. However, knowing that it was an especially privileged district, they all returned with good reports, singing the leaders' praises." But praise-singing alone is not enough for making a career; it is necessary to pay money.

"Unworthy people have sometimes been appointed to leadership positions on the recommendation of incidental persons. More and more frequently the phrases 'The boss said so!' and 'That's what the mistress wants!' were heard in the cadre apparatus. In a host of cases, schemers, bribers, and extortionists were able to gain leadership positions by dishonest means. It was precisely during that period that it became possible to 'order' a minister's position for the schemer Babunashvili" (a reference to the sale of a ministry). "There are many such cases. . . ." "Corruption, bribery, graft, and narrow-minded self-interest entered cadre politics." "Frequently people whose hands were always outstretched ended up in positions of responsibility." And nobody dared to disclose all this. "Among many leaders a totally harmful opinion was cultivated: that it was undesirable to 'carry the straw out of the isba.' Facts concerning bribery, theft, and moral crimes, etc., were passed over in silence." Well, what are the prospects? The answer was ambiguous: "The toiling people of the republic are happy, counting on the victory of justice over elements that have gotten out of hand, who seek an easy profit at the expense of workers. However, there are certain malicious gossipers and other antipodes who show their true face in precisely such crucial moments. These persons are not at all interested in making changes; they count on everything continuing as before."

As it turned out, the "malicious gossipers and other antipodes" counted correctly, and the hopes of the average citizen were dashed. As always under real socialism, it was the "antipodes" of the working class —the nomenklatura—that won out.

The reader may say, "But all the same, the Georgian affair was exposed, and Mzhavanadze and Churkin were fired. Therefore, the truth triumphed." It was simply that Shevardnadze, the Georgian minister of internal affairs, remembering what happened in Azerbaijan, saw in Mzhavanadze's scandalous corruption a chance to get the first-secretary job, just as Aliev had. Carefully avoiding the chairman of the Georgian KGB, to make sure he would have no competition on that front, Shevardnadze prepared and led a campaign to expose corruption, enlisting support directly from Moscow. Apparently, someone in the Kremlin leadership was interested in such an exposure. I shall hazard the hypothesis that in this case it was the same as in the Azerbaijan affair: Andropov and Tsvigun supported their colleague, the head of the Georgian police, and Brezhnev attempted, as was his wont, to smooth matters over and punish only the less guilty. One way or the other, it was the triumph of Shevardnadze, not of truth, and he lost no time taking Mzhavanadze's job. Georgia did not become as a result an area of high Communist morality, but remained a republic where nomenklatura baksheesh was a way of life.

It should not be thought that only the republics in the Caucasus are like this. Soviet Central Asia is no different in this regard. Let us take as an example the most developed of the Central Asian republics, the Uzbek S.S.R.

In the spring of 1967 I was in Tashkent, the capital, in my capacity as the representative of the Soviet Committee for the Defense of Peace. I was accompanying a group of prominent West German guests of the committee. We were greeted by Yadgar Nasriddinova, the chairman of the Presidium of the Supreme Soviet of the Uzbek S.S.R., that is, the official head of the Uzbek state. Nasriddinova, a youngish Uzbek wearing a lilac dress, slowly described for us in a low voice the happiness of socialist Uzbekistan. She looked like the perfectly wise mother of the republic. After the German guests said good-bye and left, she changed. She asked us matter-of-factly if her performance had been a success and listened with pleasure to our compliments. She told us, gesturing energetically, what we should show the Germans in Tashkent and what we should not. Then she said, with obvious satisfaction, "Now I'm off to a Presidium meeting: execute and pardon." At the time, I thought that her happiness was just the expression of the feelings of a satrap who has achieved power over people's lives. I still did

not know that Nasriddinova got a hundred thousand rubles per pardon
—so that her pleasure was in anticipation of the baksheesh.

What happened to Nasriddinova? Was she brought to trial? No, she
climbed even higher up the nomenklatura ladder: she became the
chairman of the Council of Nationalities—the second chamber of the
U.S.S.R. Supreme Soviet. The next time I saw her was during the
November 7 parade, on the tribunal at Red Square. Later she became
U.S.S.R. deputy minister of the construction materials industries.

The nomenklatura does not punish its members for graft and other
crimes per se. If some nomenklaturist receives punishment, everyone
knows that it is because he lost out in some infighting and the accusation is being used against him. On the other hand, if it should come to
that, the sentence is usually very light, and even if he is sentenced to
imprisonment, he is sent to a special "colony for upper-level workers."
Even while doing time, a nomenklaturist cannot be expected to rub
elbows with ordinary Soviet citizens.

Mercifully saving bribers of the proper sort from punishment, the
nomenklaturist viciously punishes those who expose them. Accordingly,
on instructions from the Moscow City Committee, the KGB accused
Grishin, the head of the Moscow OBKhSS (Department for the Fight
Against the Theft of Socialist Property), of "abuse of authority."
Grishin had taken a major grafter to court: Galushko, the first secretary
of the Kuibyshev District Committee and a member of the bureau of
the Moscow City Committee. Grishin was arrested and convicted.

K. M. Simis, who was for many years a defense attorney in the Soviet
Union, describes an incident from his law practice: A tractor driver, a
party member, accused the director of a wood-processing plant of corruption. He was, on the instructions of the first secretary of the district
party committee, not only expelled from the party and fired from his
job, but brought to trial for slander. During the trial, the factory workers, with a great deal of courage, supported the tractor driver's charges,
but he was still convicted. No appeal to the Central Committee or the
U.S.S.R. Prosecutor could help him.

In the Soviet Union no one is surprised by this: they would be
surprised if it were any other way. For even at the very top of the
nomenklatura class, where privileges are in fact unlimited, bribery and
embezzlement are unavoidable. In the early 1970s Ekaterina Furtseva,
for a long time a member of the Presidium and a secretary of the

Central Committee, later demoted to Minister of Culture, had built a luxurious dacha for herself outside Moscow with ministry money. According to informed sources, the late academician N. N. Inozemtsev, former member of the Central Committee, director of the Institute of World Economics and International Affairs, followed her example. Why be bashful? Even in Khrushchev's times, Frol Kozlov, considered second in line behind Khrushchev, took bribes for appointments to important jobs, for halting court cases, and other such services. He received money and precious stones through his associate N. Smirnov, the chairman of the Executive Committee of the Leningrad City Committee.

Everything is permitted the nomenklaturist, as long as he acts in the interests of his class. The symbol of this in the Soviet Union and throughout the rest of the world is Stalin: his crimes are acknowledged officially, but he is nonetheless—officially—"an outstanding Marxist-Leninist" and, after Lenin, the greatest leader of the Soviet people.

6. ON GOOD AND WHOLESOME FOOD

Soon after the abolition of food rationing in the postwar period, a book was published in the Soviet Union called *On Good and Wholesome Food.* To the overwhelming majority of Soviet citizens the recipes were useless because of the unobtainability of the ingredients. But it was so successful with the gourmets of the nomenklatura that it soon became a collector's item.

Good and wholesome food is a matter of deep and perpetual concern to the nomenklatura. When one is invited to the home of one of its dignitaries, the variety and quality of the fare is always astonishing. Excellent canteens and buffets are a feature of nomenklatura offices, whether in Moscow or in the provinces, and meals are an agreeable ritual in a nomenklaturist's life.

At the Central Committee of the CPSU, the buffet opens at eleven o'clock and nomenklatura dignitaries soon start dropping in for a second breakfast. All the items on the menu are of the best quality and of exceptional freshness; they are also cheap. True, the portions are not lavish, but that has nothing to do with parsimony, for nothing is too good for the nomenklatura; it is simply that the comrades have to watch their waistlines. Black and red caviar is for sale in small saucers, and there are platefuls of salmon or sturgeon. *Kumys*, the celebrated beverage based on mares' milk from the eastern steppes, is always available, the yogurt is as creamy as could be desired, and the sweet cream cheese, always perfectly fresh, melts in the mouth.

At one o'clock the canteen opens. For a long time this was at October 25 Street, which is now the home of the Slaviansky Bazaar restaurant, with its noisy band and its rather tipsy customers, who drag their feet while dancing. But imagine the place in the days of its glory, when a KGB official in civilian clothes stood close to the big mirror in the vestibule checking passes while carefully selected, reliable waitresses flitted to and fro between the tables, and the majestic and self-satisfied murmur of nomenklaturist conversation filled the rooms.

Though it is not very far from the Central Committee building to October 25 Street—it takes ten minutes on foot and stretching one's legs for that period can be quite agreeable—the nomenklaturists ended by objecting to the fact that they were not sufficiently protected from scrutiny by the outside world during this short transit. They found it intolerable to have to rub shoulders with the ordinary Soviet citizens swarming in the streets around Dzerzhinsky Square, and the unaccustomed promiscuity upset them. Their uneasiness as usual found a convenient alibi in the necessity for political vigilance. They began muttering to one another that a foreign agent might well take photographs of everyone entering the place, just imagine it, comrades, and the next thing would be that photographs of all the officials of the Central Committee apparatus would turn up in the files of the CIA.

Unsurprisingly, the incontrovertibility of this argument was immediately recognized, and a modern three-story house was built in a narrow street adjoining the Central Committee building where there is a charming seventeenth-century church (the Holy Trinity of Nikitny). This building now houses the canteen. The address is 5 Nikitnikov Street, and nothing on the outside indicates the canteen's existence. Admission is restricted to holders of a Central Committee pass, which a KGB official at the entrance examines with the greatest care. Special passes are issued for persons who do not belong to the Central Committee apparatus but have business in the building. The staff of the Party High School and of the Academy of Social Sciences, attached to the Central Committee, are allowed to use the place an hour before closing time.

On the left inside the huge vestibule there is a kiosk with newspapers and periodicals, and the cash desks are at the back. The cloakroom is on the right. A door near the cash desk provides access to a special buffet at which one can buy every conceivable kind of delicacy. The prices are low, the quality is outstanding, and nothing like it has been seen in ordinary shops since 1928.

A modern-style elevator and a staircase are available to take one to the first or the second dining room. The latter is reserved for customers on a diet. The tables are for four. On a long side table there are kegs containing fruit and vegetable juices and a vitamin-rich drink based on rose hips. One fills one's glass oneself and puts a few kopeks in a saucer provided for the purpose.

The canteen is immediately opposite the building that houses the Central Committee foreign travel department, which is a hybrid organization halfway between the party apparatus and the KGB. It would be inadvisable for anyone to stop here and take photographs.

The cooking is excellent, and only first class produce is used. Here, too, the portions are not large. Consequently, one may well order three, four, or even five items from the menu. The prices are those one would pay for a wretched, unappetizing meal at an ordinary canteen at which workers are lining up for a meal at the same time.

The Central Committee canteen is used both by personnel not entitled to a *kremliovka* and the happy possessors of that privilege. The latter could of course use their cars to go to Granovsky Street or to the "government's house," where, as they say in Russian, everything is available except birds' milk (though to make up for that you can buy in the Central Committee buffets those delicious sweets called "Birds' Milk").

But nomenklaturists endowed with *kremliovka* coupons do not do that, for it is not advantageous. For one of those coupons can be exchanged for a meal that can be taken home; as we have already mentioned, a single portion is enough for a whole family. That is why the Central Committee canteen is used not only by heads of desks, consultants, and other high officials of the apparatus who have *kremliovkas*, but also by the powerful heads of divisions of the Central Committee, who are officially senior to ministers of the Union.

The buffet reopens before the end of the working day, and although all the Central Committee officials could go there again, usually they do not. A first-class meal is waiting for them at home, and having a snack at the buffet would be improper. Instead one can go to another place that is also called a "buffet" but is actually a luxury delicatessen where one can pick up things one has previously ordered, just as higher officials pick up their parcels in Granovsky Street.

The canteens of organizations controlled by the Central Committee are similar in style, though rather more modest. They are to be found at the Party Higher School, the Academy of Social Sciences, the Institute of Social Sciences, and the Institute of Marxism-Leninism. The menu may be a little less extensive, but everything else is the same, and the prices are low.

At the hotel of the International Department of the Central Committee, housed anonymously in a building at No. 12 Plotnikov Street, quite near the Arbat, meals are completely free. Foreign visitors can use the hotel restaurant and order whatever they like, including wine and spirits, all entirely free. The same applies to the central committee "hostels" in all the socialist countries; and it is notably the case in the guesthouse of the East German central committee, a sumptuous new building opposite the Märkisches Museum, in East Berlin.

The nomenklatura in the provinces is looked after in the same way. In all the capitals of the Union's republics, in every big regional center, there are central committee canteens to which the public has no access. They are not exact replicas of the Central Committee canteen in Moscow, but successful imitations.

We shall pass over in silence the quality and quantity of the nourishment provided for those at the topmost level of the nomenklatura, who are entitled to a so-called special diet, which is of course provided free of charge. Meanwhile ordinary Soviet citizens have to line up to buy poor-quality food at high prices. Let us repeat that a gulf divides the nomenklatura from the rest of the population.

7. HOUSING

The width of that gulf is even more striking when nomenklaturist accommodation is compared with that of ordinary Soviet citizens.

For the population at large the housing problem is so acute that it is actually admitted by the authorities. Party and government resolutions, and speeches and articles in the press, agree that, while Soviet citizens enjoy all the good things of life, the exception is the housing problem, which has not yet been satisfactorily solved. "Activity on a gigantic scale" is of course taking place in the building sector, and with every day that passes every citizen has a better chance of improved living conditions. Nevertheless the target announced at the beginning of the sixties, that every citizen should have a room to himself, is still far from having been reached. The Soviet norm is nine to twelve square meters of habitable space per person. In the West, as I have had occasion to note, that figure is generally not understood, or is taken to apply to a bedroom. And particularly rare are those who understand that twelve square meters of habitable space is not a guaranteed minimum, but a permitted maximum; space in excess of the norm was formerly simply confiscated, and in 1984 the rent was tripled. An area of about five square meters per person is considered to be a kind of minimum, though it is not guaranteed. A family living in those conditions is officially considered to be "in a situation of distress in the housing sector" and is put on the waiting list of the housing service of the district soviet. The wait is generally a long one.

None of this applies to the nomenklatura. Our head of desk has no truck with waiting lists or the district soviet, but is given an apartment in a building belonging to the Central Committee. Nevertheless every nomenklaturist is always trying to change his apartment for a bigger and more comfortable one. Conversation in nomenklatura circles continually revolves round moving, i.e., giving up good accommodations for better. Soviet newspapers are delighted when they are able to report that somewhere or other in the Soviet Union "a worker's family has improved its housing conditions." The subject is not new; immediately after the October Revolution the party ceremoniously set about installing working-class families in bourgeois homes. In 1920 the poet Mayakovsky celebrated in verse the installation of a working-class family in an apartment equipped with a bathroom, but no one has yet written a poem about nomenklaturists' moving into bigger and better homes. Meanwhile new and sumptuous residences are built in the best neighborhoods for the central, regional, or town committee of the party or the Council of Ministers, and are shown from a distance to tourists as new buildings reserved for workers.

Housing for the nomenklatura is built under special supervision and is not standardized or jerry-built. Good, solid buildings contain spacious apartments, quiet elevators, wide and comfortable staircases. In Moscow, residential complexes of this type are situated on the Kutuzovsky Prospekt or in the Kuntsevo district. There are also isolated buildings of this type in between ordinary buildings in central but quiet streets in the capital; one of these is the celebrated building in Granovsky Street facing the Kremlin canteen; another is the new building in Stanislavsky Street. In East Berlin there is a district that the Germans call the Volga German district, which means that that residential complex is inhabited by Germans who have a Volga official car.

The times have passed when victorious Communist workers emerged from their cellars to install themselves in the homes of the wealthy. Aristocratic homes and districts have reappeared under the real-socialist regime, and carefully selected workmen have access to them only to carry out repairs.

These homes are large; they may have as many as eight rooms. Especially important nomenklaturists may be allotted a whole floor, consisting of two adjoining flats turned into one.

The excessive size of nomenklatura apartments by Soviet standards is revealed by statistics. We quote from an official publication giving the number of inhabitants of the Soviet Union in 1975 and the habitable space available. The total population of 253,261,000 persons occupied 1,798,589,000 square meters of habitable space. The impressiveness of these figures running into thousands of millions no doubt explains why they passed the censor. Simple division shows that the number of square meters per inhabitant was seven. As we have seen, the figure of twelve square meters per inhabitant is a permitted maximum and not a guaranteed minimum, and there is still a long way to go before it is achieved for all.

In an overpopulated city like Moscow, with its 7.6 million inhabitants (1975), the situation is acute, and the waiting lists of persons admitted to be in a situation of distress in the housing sector, that is, having less than five square meters each at their disposal, are never-ending. In spite of that, the Moscow average is fifteen square meters per person, or more than double that of the rest of the country. This is explained by the large number of nomenklaturists living in the capital. Their spacious apartments make it appear on paper to be the best-off city in the Soviet Union so far as housing is concerned.

Taking into account the habitable space actually available, an average Moscow family of four ought to be occupying an apartment of sixty square meters *now*, and not in a radiant Communist future.

The causes of the Moscow housing crisis are not technical, but social. If the inhabitants of Moscow live in such overcrowded conditions, it is not because the habitable space available in Moscow is too small, but because the nomenklatura occupies too much of it, at the expense of workers who have been on a waiting list and have been living with their families in single rooms for years.

In talking about the nomenklatura, just as when one talks in general terms about the exploitation of man by man, for instance, one should guard against overlooking the actions of particular individuals, especially in this matter of depriving people of accommodation. Here is an example: The Institute of World Economy and International Relations of the Academy of Sciences of the U.S.S.R. had been promised a quota of accommodation for some applicants who were on a waiting list. It was of course impossible to satisfy more than one or two of them. As the allocation did not take place every year, the trade-union committee (of which I was then deputy president) rechecked the most urgent cases on the waiting list. A young assistant whose only accommodation was a corner of a room already lived in by someone else was at the top of the list, and a family each member of which had only three square meters came next. Then we heard that the promised apartment had been allocated, not to someone on the waiting list, but to the first deputy of the director, a former party secretary. This individual had dropped his original intention of buying a cooperative apartment, which would have cost him money, and accepted the accommodation offered, which was rent free to him. The size of the apartment was such that it exhausted the institute's quota for a long time to come. The man to whom it was allotted, who had a good business sense, was not proposing to live in it for the next few years, as he was on the point of leaving for New York, where a responsible post at the United Nations awaited him. He subsequently became Soviet ambassador to an African state. I do not mention his name, because he is not a monster, but an ordinary nomenklaturist and actually a rather likable one. But that is their class spirit.

Other explanations have been attempted. It has been claimed that a large amount of the habitable space in Moscow is reserved for diplomatic missions and foreign correspondents and that some nomenklatura officials must have accommodation suitable for representational purposes and entertainment.

These arguments do not hold water. The diplomats and journalists who work in Moscow live in accommodations smaller and worse than they are used to at home. The necessity of living in accommodations appropriate to one's status is merely a convenient excuse to mask a taste for luxury; any nomenklaturist will hasten to assure you that his most heartfelt wish is to live modestly, in conformity with Lenin's wishes, but alas, the necessities of representation force him to live in a big apartment. But they say that only to other people. Among themselves they boast unrestrainedly about their apartments, their furniture, and their pictures. Which of them ever entertains visitors from abroad in his home? Perhaps one of the deputy foreign ministers may do so from time to time, such as V. S. Semionov, now ambassador in Bonn, whose home is like a museum. The alleged necessity of living in accordance with one's status in order to impress foreigners is pure humbug. Consider the situation in the capitals of the various republics, where there are no diplomats to impress. The number of square meters per inhabitant in these places is as follows: Tallin, 14.6; Riga, 14.2; Kiev, 13.7; Vilna, 12.5; Minsk, 11.6; Kishinev, 11.5; Alma Ata, 11.2; Tbilisi, 11; Baku, 10.3; Erivan, 9.9; Frunze, 9.8; Ashkhabad, 9.7; Dushanbe, 9.5; and Tashkent, 8.6.[16] In other words, the situation does not differ radically from that in Moscow.

Only in Tashkent, which was severely damaged by earthquake in 1967, is the permitted maximum in the republic not exceeded, but the nomenklatura lives in luxury there, too.

The average Soviet citizen has at his disposal a habitable area of less than seven square meters, for the spacious homes of the nomenklatura are included in that wretched average.

8. THE DACHA

In addition to his apartment, our head of desk is allotted a country villa, a dacha.

In theory anyone who is granted a plot of land by the district soviet with permission to build on it or buys it with the consent of the soviet is entitled to a dacha. If it is to be built by a cooperative, authorization by the presidium of the cooperative is required.

These regulations, which in themselves are perfectly reasonable, undergo such class distortion in practice that in fact ownership of a dacha is restricted to the privileged. The district soviet grants building plots only to persons of consequence. The rule that the purchase must be made only with funds "derived from earned income" is strictly enforced. As a dacha near Moscow costs from seven thousand to twelve thousand rubles, it is obvious that an ordinary worker will never get the required authorization, since the purchase price represents between six and ten years' wages. He can never hope to save such a sum.

It is often suggested in the West that a dacha-owning class exists in the Soviet Union. The idea is not correct, but neither is it completely wrong; no such class exists, but ownership of a dacha is in fact bound up with the class nature of Soviet society.

Ownership of a dacha is primarily a privilege of the intellectual. The nomenklaturist class is not interested in such ownership. A dacha is put at our head of desk's disposal practically cost free. He quietly takes it over without having to pay out several thousand rubles (which he, unlike the worker, could afford), without having to chase after building materials that are chronically in short supply, and without having to trouble about supervising the construction or worrying later about repairs. The dacha, which belongs to the state, is available to him and his family for the whole summer. It is situated in an agreeable and easily accessible vacation area surrounded by a high fence to protect it from inquisitive eyes. The residential complex in which it is situated will include a good-quality grocery store, an excellent canteen, a cinema, a club, a library, and a sports ground. The rent will be merely symbolic. A well-maintained road will lead to the site, and our head of desk will travel there straight from Staraya Ploshchad in his official car, a black Volga with Central Committee license plates.

In winter he will leave his office as soon as he has finished work on

Friday and go to a Central Committee rest home, where an apartment will be awaiting him and his family and even his friends. Here, too, the food will be excellent and very inexpensive. Skis and skates are available free of charge, and so is the cinema in the evening.

Though our head of desk generally uses the same country house for many years, he never forgets that it doesn't belong to him. This is illustrated by the fact that, so far from showing any interest in its maintenance, he does absolutely nothing that might contribute to improving it. Hence the strange appearance of these holiday homes; there are no flowers around them, nothing but beds planted by the management; no one troubles to take a hammer and nail to fix a shaky board (dachas are always built of wood); instead, the slightest defect is reported to the management. The nomenklaturists lounge in their hammocks, go for walks, play tennis or volley ball, eat and drink on the terrace, go to the movies. There is a striking contrast here to the ordinary dachas, whose owners spend their time digging, hammering, plastering, watering from morning to night.

It is not that nomenklaturists, at any rate individually, shrink from physical effort. A substantial proportion of them are of peasant origin and would no doubt enjoy gardening. But it is not the custom. Physical work is beneath the dignity of a nomenklaturist, demonstrating yet again the collective contempt with which the upstarts of the nomenklatura regard the labor that is the lot of their class of origin; and that is how it comes about that men who grew up in the country are ashamed to plant flowers, and passionate automobile drivers sit in the backseats of chauffeur-driven cars.

It is just as improper for a nomenklatura official to own his own dacha as it is to own his own car. Infringement of this unwritten law would expose the offender to being suspected of being a free-thinker or being not very sure of his future in the nomenklatura. Consequently a head of desk who buys a dacha will do so in the name of his parents; if he buys a car, it will be in the name of one of his grown-up children or his brother. That is his way of avoiding any suspicion of having petit-bourgeois leanings, while enlarging his share of the collective property of the nomenklatura.

9. THE SONG OF THE TELEPHONES

The cheerful and cynical Nikolai Tikhonov, who for many years was president of the Soviet Peace Committee and secretary of the Writers' Union of the U.S.S.R. (he died in 1979), called one of his best-known poems *The Song of the Nails*. In it he sang the praises of those indomitable Bolsheviks who were so tough that the toughest nails in the world could be made of them, or so he claimed. The court poet was flattering the nomenklaturists, who deserve to be celebrated in another song, the song of the telephones.

We have already mentioned that when Brezhnev received the correspondents of the German journal *Stern* in his office in the Kremlin he proudly showed them his telephones. It would never have occurred to a Western politician to do such a thing, but to the No. 1 in the Kremlin it was a natural gesture.

To a nomenklaturist a telephone is a status symbol and hence an object of pride. A Soviet visitor who enters the office of a Western politician or businessman would be surprised to see only one. He expects to see a table covered with telephones, the sight of which, I don't know why, always reminds me of a herd of elephants.

A highly placed nomenklaturist must have at least six at his disposal. One is for internal communication and another is for communication with the outside world; both pass through his secretary's office. To prevent possible listening in, there are two other lines that do not pass through the secretary's office. Finally—and this is the nomenklaturist's greatest pride—there are two special government lines, one called the *vertushka* and the other the *Vé-Ché*. In some departments, the Foreign Ministry, for instance, these instruments are pompous affairs, adapted to the nomenklatura's bombastic bureaucratic taste; they are light gray and are decorated with the gilded official emblem of the Soviet Union. Let it be said in honor of the Central Committee that their telephones are perfectly ordinary.

Nomenklaturists in contact with the army have a direct line to the military authorities, and so have a seventh telephone.

Lenin had only one, old-fashioned telephone in his office in the Kremlin, but it was he who originated the vogue of the telephone. He had a small automatic switchboard (ATS) installed so that there should be no operators who might overhear the Kremlin leaders' conversations. Instruments with dials were then a novelty and were called vertushkas (from *vertet'*, to turn). All telephone systems have long since been made automatic, but the term vertushka survives as a popular as well as an official designation; in the Central Committee internal telephone directories, vertushka numbers are preceded by the letter V. The designation Kremlin-ATS (like the less usual *kremliovka* for vertushka instruments) also still exists, though it now comes under the heading of "switchboard of the KGB of the U.S.S.R."; the maintenance of the system has been handed over to the KGB to prevent telephone tapping.

In Lenin's time there were fewer than a hundred vertushkas. At the end of the twenties there were more than five hundred.[17]

Vé-Ché is an abbreviation for *vysokochastotny*, which means highfrequency. This is the government line for long-distance calls. Corresponding instruments are to be found in the higher agencies of the party and the government in Moscow and the capitals of the republics and regional centers. They have also been installed in Soviet embassies in socialist countries, but not in nonsocialist countries, where it is impossible to ensure that the line will not be tapped. In 1955, when the Soviet occupation of Austria came to an end, the Vé-Ché (or VČ) line that connected the Soviet High Commission in Austria (at the Imperial Hotel, in Vienna) with the Soviet Union was dismantled. Because of the enormous distances covered by the VČ network, the switchboard is not automatic. So you have to lift the receiver and tell the operator the town and VČ number of the person with whom you want to be connected.

Every year, the happy owner of a vertushka is sent a pocket-sized red book: the telephone directory. In it surnames are listed alphabetically, followed by the forename and patronymic and sometimes the department in which the person concerned works (this is always given when there is more than one person with the same name, but sometimes it is given for other reasons). The person's job and address are not given. Vertushka telephone numbers in Moscow always consist of four figures, so theoretically there could be ten thousand vertushka telephones in the capital. Actually there are far fewer.

An unwritten rule is that a vertushka telephone is answered directly by its proud possessor, who gives his surname when he picks up the receiver. This rule is observed even by members of the Politburo. Let us call the possessor of the instrument concerned Comrade Ivanov. If he is engaged or not in his office, his assistant or secretary will pick up the receiver and say, "Comrade Ivanov's telephone." Senior officials have an extension of their vertushka on their secretary's desk, but only the nomenklaturist can dial a number. Less senior personages do not have an extension, and in their absence the secretary has to hurry into their office and take the call. Those who do not have a vertushka are not explicitly forbidden to make a call on the vertushka, but they seldom do so.

With the VČs the system is rather different. There are not many VČ telephones, and their use is not restricted to those in whose names they are listed. They are used for important calls, for on the ordinary Soviet telephone system interurban communication is difficult. So it is not the big chiefs of the nomenklatura who use the VČ system, but their subordinates who need to do so in the execution of their duties. Finally, it is by way of the VČ system that the many telephoned telegrams of government origin, VČgrams, as they are called in nomenklatura jargon, are transmitted.

The passion for vertushkas has spread to the whole of the Soviet Union and its satellites. The capital of every republic and every regional center has its own vertushkas, and there is a similar system in all the real-socialist countries, at any rate the European ones. I have used them myself. During the war, Sovinform, the Council of Ministers information office, was accommodated in the building at 10 Stanislavsky Street previously occupied by the German Embassy (it is now the East German Embassy). The interior telephones left by the Germans were put at the disposal of the principal members of the Sovinform staff and called vertushkas (only the head of the Sovinform was allowed both a Kremlin vertushka and a VČ). Though these pseudo-vertushkas were completely unnecessary, they were dismantled and taken to the new Sovinform offices at 21 Zhdanov Street. Consequently there were no internal telephones for the East German Embassy staff when they moved in, but what mattered was that the Sovinform bigwigs kept their previous vertushkas, those striking emblems of superiority to ordinary mortals.

The elitist spirit of the nomenklatura was also illustrated by the episode of the Central Committee telephones. Here there was no need to install a local surrogate vertushka system for the benefit of the bigwigs, as all of them, including heads of desks and consultants, already had vertushkas. These comrades never use anything but a vertushka to communicate with each other, even if it is only to make a lunch appointment. One vertushka holder cannot call another on the ordinary telephone system without rendering himself suspect of false modesty or showing contempt for the facilities put at his disposal (which would be a "free-thinking" attitude).

The Central Committee problem was rather different. What could be done to mark off the Central Committee telephones used only by nomenklaturists from those of the small fry? When the Moscow telephone system was made automatic, a special system was established, the code number for which was K6, which was later changed to 296. The Kremlin, the Central Committee and the Moscow committee of the party, the NKVD, and the People's Commissariat for Foreign Affairs—in other words, all the departments in which all the responsible positions were held by nomenklaturists—were connected to it, and it was put under the supervision of the NKVD. It was maintained with special care and gloriously survived the rest of the Moscow telephone system. After the war, all the Moscow exchanges had to be rebuilt, and the opportunity was taken to adopt the high ringing-tone that is characteristic of telephones in the West. But right up to the beginning of the seventies those who dialed a 296 number were able to listen nostalgically to the low ringing-tone of the days before the war.

As the number of telephones reserved for the nomenklatura grew and grew, other code numbers had to be found. The Kremlin and the Lubianka (the KGB and Interior Ministry) were given the code number 224 and the Foreign Ministry was given 244, while the Central Committee and the Moscow party committee, familiarly referred to as Staraya Ploshchad ("Old Square"), in which the Central Committee buildings are situated, retained their old and familiar code number. For years the K6 system was used both for internal and external communication; to be put through to an internal number the code number K6 did not have to be used if one were dialing from the Central or Moscow committee offices, though to call the Kremlin or the Lubianka from the Central Committee you had to dial the complete number; to call Moscow, you had to use the code number 9. For a long time this system, which has now become commonplace, was considered a technical marvel, which enabled those with a K6 line to feel agreeably different from the great mass of subscribers.

During the sixties, when the novelty had worn off, it was suggested that it might be desirable for security reasons to separate the internal and external lines at the Central Committee to prevent internal conversations from being tapped. Security was not the real issue, of course (even when spy fever was at its height the K6 system was never suspect); it was merely the result of the desire of nomenklaturists who did not have access to the vertushka system for something to mark them off from ordinary members of the staff. This legitimate wish was soon granted; at the beginning of the seventies it was decided that the code number 296 should be used only for internal communication in the offices of the Central and Moscow party committees. The external lines of these agencies were given the code number 206, while the old, K6 system was transformed into an internal vertushka system reserved for communication between the Central Committee dignitaries.

Vertushka and VČ telephones can be used to discuss party, government, and military secrets. Vertushkas were therefore installed in the apartments and dachas of members and nonvoting members of the Politburo and secretaries of the Central Committee, as well as all the vice-presidents of the Council of Ministers and the big shots of the KGB, the Ministry of the Interior, and the armed forces. The alleged need for secrecy is a mere excuse for granting the nomenklatura elite an additional status symbol. A similar purpose is served by the telephones in senior officials' cars. The inadvisability of using a radiotelephone for confidential conversation is well known, for it is easy to listen in, but senior nomenklaturists insist on this attribute of power. Vice-presidents of the Council of Ministers—serious and very busy men—engaged in a bitter struggle to have their official limousines (Chaikas) equipped with this useless gadget, and the Central Committee secretariat ended by granting them their wish.

It is of course true that when using the ordinary Moscow telephone system one can never be sure of not being overheard, even by chance. It is not at all unusual to pick up the receiver and find oneself listening to a conversation between two strangers. But it can be embarrassing. Once, when I was in my Moscow flat talking on the telephone to the Vice-Minister of Foreign Affairs, Valerian Alexandrovich Zorin (the celebrated organizer of the Communist *coup d'état* in Czechoslovakia in 1948), our conversation was suddenly interrupted and a masculine voice calmly assured us that we had been talking utter nonsense. Zorin giggled nervously, and no doubt he subsequently used the incident to lecture his subordinates on the need for discretion on the telephone. Thus conversations on the ordinary telephone system are liable to be listened to, to say nothing of the systematic recording of the voices of suspect subscribers engaged in by the KGB and the systematic tapping of all international telephone calls.

But vertushka conversations are tapped too. Boris Bazhanov, who was Stalin's secretary, has described how he caught the future "genius of mankind" listening in on a telephone conversation between two vertushka holders.[18] As soon as he came into power, Stalin saw to it that the listening system was put on a systematic basis. Apropos of that, I was told the following story as long ago as 1950: A minister's assistant tried to play a bad practical joke; he called the assistant of another minister on the vertushka, said, "Malenkov speaking," and announced that the minister was wanted at the Central Committee the next day.

Before a quarter of an hour or twenty minutes had passed, anonymous voices informed the first minister that his assistant had been playing a practical joke and the second minister that Malenkov had not sent for him. So the vertushka conversation had been tapped. Vertushka and VČ holders know very well that their conversations are being monitored, but that does not spoil their pleasure in belonging to the favored few who have those instruments.

The explanation for this farce is the perfectly conscious need felt by these people to mark themselves off from the rest of humanity and to have dealings with no one outside the narrow circle of their own social class. Sometimes the limits of absurdity are reached. Thus it was decided that in official residences there should be no ordinary telephones, but only vertushkas. In 1970 I was confronted in Prague and later in Sofia with the baffling problem of how to communicate with the residence when I was in the town or communicate with the town when I was in the residence. Imagine my surprise one day when the telephone rang in the home of a Western Prime Minister and he picked up a (perfectly ordinary) receiver and talked to an ordinary unknown woman who wanted a pension after her husband's death and considered that this was a matter worthy of the Prime Minister's personal attention in his own home. She had no difficulty in getting through to him, as his number was in the directory.

10. IN NOMENKLATURIA

Once upon a time—it was before the October Revolution—Russian liberal intellectuals sarcastically translated the phrase *bien-être général en Russie* as "It's a good thing being a general in Russia." Since then the purifying storm of the October Revolution has blown itself out, and nowadays being a general in Russia is even better than it used to be.

But do generals and other highly placed personages really feel they are living in Russia? I have actually heard it suggested in nomenklatura circles that above a certain level in the hierarchy, nomenklatura officials behave as if they were living not in the U.S.S.R. but in another, entirely different, and special country.

Ordinary citizens are just as carefully isolated from that country, which we shall call Nomenklaturia, as they are from foreign countries. It is the country of the special, with special accommodations built by special builders, special country houses and vacation homes, special hospitals, out-patients' departments, and convalescent homes, special products sold in special shops, special buffets and canteens, special hairdressers, garages, gas stations, and license plates, a special information network, special kindergartens, schools, and institutions of higher education, special waiting rooms at stations and airports, and even a special cemetery.

A member of a nomenklatura family can spend his life from the cradle to the grave working, resting, eating, shopping, traveling, talking, or being ill without ever coming into contact with the Soviet people, whom he is supposed to be serving. The barriers that separate foreigners from Soviet citizens also separate the nomenklatura from the mass of the population, with the difference that, while foreigners are not allowed contacts with the citizens of the country, the nomenklatura imposes that ban on itself.

A detailed description of Nomenklaturia would take us too far afield. So let us take a swift bus tour of the geopolitically highly original country of real socialism.

It was discovered by Lenin on October 25, 1918. On that day, accompanied by his sister Maria and Krupskaya, his wife, he went for the first time to the country house that had been made ready for him at Gorky, near Moscow. It had been confiscated from a rich landowner named Reinbot, and it was the first "state dacha" in the history of Nomenklaturia. At the entrance Lenin was ceremoniously presented with a bouquet by the Cheka guards. The discoverers of Nomenklaturia inspected the whole house, "overcome with astonishment," as a journalist noted, "at the sight of the furniture, carpets, chandeliers, and Venetian mirrors in their gilded frames."[19] Lenin ordered everything to be left as it was and settled down comfortably in all this luxury, which he evidently did not find in the least disturbing. He modestly referred to the place as "our dacha," for it would have been embarrassing to call it "our estate" or "our summer palace." Thus "dacha" became the established term to designate the numerous *palazzi* subsequently built by the nomenklatura.

In 1920, while the civil war was still raging, the incipient nomenklaturists had developed such a taste for luxury that in September of that year a so-called Kremlin control commission was appointed for the purpose of examining "the question of Kremlin privileges" (that was the official term) and, as far as possible, "bringing them within bounds that would be acceptable to every party comrade." This was announced in the *Izvestia of the Central Committee of the Russian Communist Party* (which was what the CPSU was called at the time) on December 20, 1920, that is, between Stalin's birthday and Brezhnev's.[20] The result was modest; the commission and the newspaper that published this news item were abolished, but the privileges were not.

The Eleventh Party Congress, in 1922, settled for a less ambitious objective, namely "to put an end to *great* disparity between the pay scales of differing groups of Communists." In October 1923 a Central Committee circular was even more discreet; it simply criticized the "expenditure of public funds on the equipment and furnishing of the homes of leading figures," "the furnishing of official offices and private dwellings," and the "use of unbudgeted public funds for the country houses of certain officials." The circular concluded that it was necessary "to increase the salary of responsible colleagues to assure them of a minimum standard of living."[21]

In February 1932 the ceiling on party members' pay (the "party maximum," introduced by Lenin) was done away with, thus eliminating the last obstacle in the way of the nomenklaturists' rapid rise to material prosperity. At the time, there was an appalling famine in the Ukraine, but by now the nomenklatura was establishing itself as a class, and it began increasing its pay by means of secret decisions.

Here is the text of one of them. It is still top secret in the Soviet Union, but it is to be found in the so-called Smolensk Archive, which was taken from Germany to the United States after the war:

Not for publication. Decision No. 274 of the Council of People's Commissars of the U.S.S.R. and of the Central Committee of the CPSU dated 11.2.1936. *On increasing the salaries of leading district officials.*

The Council of People's Commissars of the U.S.S.R. and the Central Committee of the CPSU resolve that

1. From February 1, 1936, the pay of presidents of district executive committees and of first secretaries of district committees of the party is to be increased to 650 rubles in 50 percent of the districts and to 550 rubles in the other 50 percent, and the pay of deputy presidents of executive committees and second secretaries of district committees is to be increased to 550 and 450 rubles respectively; the salaries of managers of the agriculture, trade, and finance departments, managers of district branches of the State Bank, heads of the cultural and propaganda department of the district committee, and the secretary of the district committee of the Komsomol respectively are to be increased to 500 and 400 rubles respectively:

2. In accordance with a special list to be approved by the Orgburo of the Central Committee of the CPSU the presidents of 250 district executive committees and the first secretaries of 250 specially important party district committees are to be granted a salary of 750 rubles; the deputy presidents of district executive committees and second secretaries of party district committees are to receive a salary of 650 rubles;

3. These salary increases to be carried out within the framework of the 1936 budget.

The President of the Council of People's Commissars of the U.S.S.R.
Molotov.

The Secretary of the Central Committee of the CPSU
Stalin.[22]

At the same time, the nomenklatura established special canteens and shops for itself, its excuse being that during the first half of the thirties food and textiles had had to be rationed.

Having acquainted ourselves with the living and working conditions that prevail in Nomenklaturia at the present day and seen the apartments and the dachas, let us now take a look at another sector: the hospitals, convalescent homes, and out-patient departments.

There are many holiday resorts in the Soviet Union, but it would be difficult to find one where the Central Committee or the Council of Ministers does not have a sanatorium. Even if our head of desk took it into his head to "bury himself" in a small and out-of-the-way resort such as Berdyansk, on the Sea of Azov, where I was born, he would not have to mingle with the common herd in an ordinary rest home, for the town party committee has a dacha reserved for nomenklaturists. No matter how much he was willing to pay, an ordinary Soviet citizen could not gain admission to a rest home or dacha of that category.

Here nomenklaturists are among themselves. A surprising consequence is the extraordinary license that prevails in these places. Nomenklatura officials who for eleven months of the year maintain a façade of impeccable marital fidelity here make up for lost time, men and women alike. This is generally accepted, and everyone knows that there will be no difficulties with the party when they go home.

A characteristic feature of the nomenklaturist is his concern for his health. According to his own story, he exhausts himself in grueling work, and if you compliment him on how well he looks he replies that appearances are deceptive. But it is not his appearance that is deceptive, but the pretense that he is perpetually overworked.

He and his family are looked after by the Fourth Medical Administration of the U.S.S.R. Ministry of Health (formerly known as the Kremlin Medical Administration). The family is allotted to the Kremlin hospital and the Kremlin out-patients' department, where they will always see the same doctor. This luxuriously appointed medical complex occupies two buildings on the Kalinin Prospekt at the corner of Granovsky Street and a little road near the Arbat. Malicious tongues say of it, *"Poly parketnye, vrachi anketnye"*—"parquet flooring and doctors picked by questionnaire"; and the doctors are indeed selected for their political qualifications. They are not expected to do much doctoring, but simply to chat pleasantly with their patients. If a nomenklaturist complains of anything that shows signs of being at all serious, he is referred to a consultant. The consultants are eminent specialists, members of the Academy of Medical Sciences of the U.S.S.R., and the best of them are personal physicians to the Soviet leaders. In 1952, when Stalin cooked up the famous "doctors' plot," the whole of the Soviet medical elite vanished into the underground cells of the Lubianka, the KGB headquarters. The old dictator had no confidence in doctors picked by questionnaire, so when he was taken ill in the middle of the doctors' plot he had no medical attention. He died of a stroke while his personal physician, Professor Vinogradov, was chained in a cell in the Lubianka, where he was periodically beaten by the dictator's own orders.

The Kremlin hospital equipment and pharmacopocia are imported from the West (the nomenklatura never relies on local medical skill and pharmacology when its health is at stake). The food and nursing are outstanding, and the staff are numerous, well trained, and smiling. This is in striking contrast to conditions in ordinary hospitals, where every corridor is encumbered with beds, the staff is inadequate, and the food so bad that it is impossible to manage without food parcels sent in by one's relatives. Convalescent and chronically ill nomenklaturists are sent to an annex of the Kremlin hospital in the wooded park of Kuntsevo, outside the city.

A Soviet writer, A. Bek, has described the Kremlin hospital in a novel about the life and death of a nomenklaturist. The patient's "room" consists of "an office, a bedroom with a balcony, a bathroom, a vestibule leading directly to a carpeted staircase." This "bright and spacious apartment" is furnished with soft armchairs, carpets, expensive statuettes," and on the wall there are pictures "in massive gilt frames."[23] This apartment is in the semiluxury category. The mind boggles at the thought of what the luxury category must be like.

Let us turn our attention to the transport sector in Nomenklaturia.

We have already mentioned that our chief of desk can live in comfort, work, and rest without ever coming into contact with the Soviet people. Even in the course of his travels across the vast spaces of the Soviet Union he can avoid all contact with his compatriots. He obtains his rail or air tickets directly from the Central Committee transport section, which is accommodated in an inconspicuous little house behind the Central Committee complex. The American journalist Hedrick Smith reports, with naïve Western indignation, an Intourist guide's complaints that places are kept vacant in all hotels, trains, and aircraft in case a high official should unexpectedly turn up. Soviet citizens have long since learned to take that for granted; they know that the best places are reserved for the government quota *(bronya)* and that tickets for them are not sold until thirty minutes before departure time. But ordinary people are never given the reserved rooms in hotels, which have no departure time, for a nomenklaturist might turn up at any moment.

Trains and aircraft are always overcrowded. Not till I arrived in the West did I discover that it is perfectly possible just to go to a station and buy a ticket. In the Soviet Union the lines at the advance booking offices are interminable, and a reserved seat is a great privilege.

Our chief of desk sets out in a black Volga with his ticket in his pocket. Instead of mingling with the vulgar mob at the station, he goes to a private waiting room called the waiting room for deputies to the Supreme Soviet. The officials whose duty it is to look after nomenklaturists are proud of this description, which sounds democratic and in harmony with the spirit of the constitution. No, it seems to say, the place is not reserved for big shots, but is an ordinary waiting room for the representatives of the people to whom we have given our votes. And who is to tell that for most of the time it is nomenklatura officials who use this room, with its upholstered furniture and soft carpets and special staff, and not deputies to the Supreme Soviet, the number of whom who are on the move at any one time is not sufficient to justify the existence of a vast network of such waiting rooms? There was also another problem. How was the existence of these places to be explained to foreigners, who were very conscious of not being deputies to the Supreme Soviet? The answer was simple. The words "VIP Hall," in English, appeared on the panel outside the door. Nobody was likely to be offended by being referred to as a very important person.

Polite staff—very different from those who deal with other travelers —take our head of desk straight to the train or aircraft some minutes before other travelers are invited to do the same; he must be spared the necessity of meeting people on the platform or in the gangways, and in his first-class sleeping compartment or in the first class on the aircraft he is among his fellows again. When the aircraft lands, the mobile steps are first taken to the first-class exit and our man walks down them, to be greeted by an assembly of local bigwigs. Only then are the other passengers allowed to get out. When he gets out of the train, he unfortunately has to mingle with *hoi polloi*, but not for long, for it is only a few paces to the "deputies' waiting room" on the arrival platform. An official car will be waiting for him at the exit to take him to the place where he will be staying in comfortable surroundings ideal for the preparation of his speech to the members of the party on some classical theme such as: "Unity of party and people."

Let us now turn to the subject of education in Nomenklaturia. Here, too, everything is for the best; the children of the nomenklatura have not been forgotten.

Certain difficulties had to be overcome. After the October Revolution it was announced that all children without exception were to have the same schooling. But at the time of the giddy ascent of the Stalinist nomenklatura, at the end of the thirties, special schools were established, making it appear that they did not want their offspring to mix with the children of ordinary folk. The official purpose of these schools was to train future artillery officers for the Red Army of Workers and Peasants (which was what the Soviet Army was then called), but in fact these were privileged establishments that had nothing whatever to do either with workers or peasants or artillery.

This military-proletarian camouflage has since been given up. Nomenklatura children are nowadays entered into special schools where they are taught in a foreign language (English, French, or German); the children of diplomats or other important persons employed abroad are sent to special boarding schools.

Also, at university level the children of nomenklatura dignitaries are saved from having to mingle with ordinary students. That is the reason for the existence of the Higher School for International Relations, in Moscow; here an elitist caste spirit prevails for which the Corps des Pages in the days of the czars provides the only parallel.

A number of institutions of higher education are reserved for the nomenklatura: the Central Committee's Party Higher School, the Foreign Ministry's diplomatic academy, the Academy of Foreign Trade, the Komsomol Central School, the military academies, the KGB Higher School and the Ministry of the Interior's academy. Some of these establishments accept only students who have already completed a course of study and have a certain amount of experience of the workings of the party. That is how the children of the nomenklatura are trained to take over responsible positions in it.

The taste for university degrees is very widespread in these exalted circles and has to be taken account of. Since 1947 there has been an institution in Moscow for granting doctor's degrees to nomenklaturists; this is the Academy of Social Sciences, attached to the CPSU Central Committee. I was for some years a member of the council of that institution, and I can say that in no ordinary university are such efforts made to extract a thesis from the future doctor. Each professor or lecturer has the same number of students as in other universities, but it is the production of doctoral theses that takes up most of his time (all that is required of him otherwise is that he publish one article a year). Admission to the institution is by decision of the Secretariat of the Central Committee of the CPSU at the request of republican or regional party committees. The students' living conditions are first-class. They live in a comfortable hostel inside the academy; the canteen food is excellent; their allowances are nearly equal in value to their teachers' salaries; and they are sent abroad for long spells to enable them to gather material for their theses. All this has nothing in common with the life of ordinary students, who live in overcrowded hostels, hurriedly eat Spartan meals in the university canteen, have a very small allowance, and do not go abroad even in dreams. Nevertheless their theses are on the whole better than those of their privileged colleagues. Everyone knows that theses written at the Academy of Social Sciences are invariably accepted, and that their standard is invariably low.

If the average student at this establishment is less gifted, it is partly due to the fact that selection is solely for political reasons. The special atmosphere that prevails in the place plays an even bigger part in bringing this about. A student who has been recommended by the party and approved by the Central Committee Secretariat knows from the outset that he has been considered in high places as being worthy of being granted a degree. Consequently if he fails to get one it must be the fault of his director of studies. The mere fact that students have already been enrolled in the Central Committee nomenklatura and that after receiving their doctorates they will immediately be appointed to positions of responsibility in the party apparatus results in their looking down on the professors who are feverishly writing their theses for them. The children of the Athenian aristocracy probably looked down on their slave schoolmasters in the same way.

According to figures quoted by Ilya Zemtsov, who worked for the science department of the Central Committee, 63 percent of the Central Committee staff have a degree, and in the case of the central committees of the republics the figure is 73 percent.[24] A big change from the first generation of a ruling class that boasted of not having finished secondary school!

The nomenklatura officially forms part of the "intermediate social stratum of intellectuals" and makes claims to culture. In a nomenklaturist's apartment one generally finds a full bookcase containing not only the classics of Marxism but also handsomely bound copies of Russian authors (including the émigré Ivan Bunin) and foreign authors in translation. It is difficult to tell whether these books are read or are merely decoration, but at any rate they have been bought. Nomenklaturists stick faithfully to their rule of marking themselves off from others by ordering books that are difficult to obtain. But a nomenklaturist's library never includes suspect books. After Khrushchev's downfall, his collected speeches were quickly removed from the shelves, as were copies of the periodical *Novy Mir*, which published Solzhenitsyn in 1962 and 1963. Pasternak's poems (the posthumous edition) or the works of Anna Akhmatova might still be on the shelves, but that is by no means certain. There must be nothing to suggest that the owner of these books has any "unhealthy interests," as it is so charmingly put.

Theater tickets are easily obtainable by nomenklatura officials. But it is not advisable for a nomenklaturist to acquire the reputation of being a theater fan, which would suggest that he was not a serious person and might raise doubts about his taste. Consequently it is the adolescent children of the nomenklatura or relatives and friends who have failed to secure admission to it who chiefly benefit from these theater tickets.

In fact the number of such friends is small, for the sagacious members of the ruling class quickly and correctly interpret the coded instructions that come down to them from above "that for security reasons" they should restrict their social contacts and as far as possible not make friends outside the nomenklatura. They also realize that these instructions are intended not so much to protect official secrets (a point on which in any case all nomenklaturists show the greatest discretion) as to protect the secret of the *dolce vita* led by the nomenklatura.

Let us glance at retirement pensions in Nomenklaturia.

Years have passed, the children of our head of desk have grown up and have themselves become nomenklaturists, and the time has come for him to enjoy his "well-earned retirement," as the saying is. Unlike ordinary citizens, he does not have to obtain a whole mass of references to support an application to the local social security office for a pension that will not exceed 120 rubles (152 U.S. dollars) a month. A resolution of the Central Committee Secretariat will entitle him to a personal pension on the Union scale, and he will continue to occupy a Central Committee apartment and take his vacations at a Central Committee rest home. A military nomenklaturist of general's rank will live in a dacha of which he is legally the proprietor, and if he wishes to build he will be granted a plot of one hectare instead of the .08 hectare ordinary people are allowed—in other words, twelve and a half times as much. Colonel-generals and generals (to say nothing of marshals) come into what is called the Defense Ministry's "paradise group" when they retire. They retain all their privileges—an official car with driver, an official apartment, an aide-de-camp, free rations and uniform, etc.— without having to do any work in return.

Western readers may well be tempted to object that a four-room apartment, a country villa, an official car, a pension of a thousand dollars a month is not to be sneezed at, it's true, but isn't a fortune.

The answer is that it is a fortune. Wealth is relative, and no arithmetical figures can be given for it. To the great mass of the Soviet population, what a nomenklaturist receives is a veritable fortune.

Above all, it is a privilege. Man is a social animal; he does not consider his situation in isolation, but in relation to that of other members of the society in which he lives. When you, dear reader, walk down the street, you have no particular feelings about it. But suppose a tyrannical authority forced all people to advance on their hands and knees and subsequently in its kindness allowed you to resume your normal stance; imagine how proud and delighted you would be. You would do everything in your power to "justify the confidence" placed in you, as they say in the U.S.S.R.

This way of looking at things is not peculiar to nomenklaturists. I have often noted with interest that Western journalists who have worked in Moscow look back with nostalgia to the time they spent there. There is no objective reason for this: it is extremely difficult to obtain any information apart from what has already been officially published; foreign correspondents are subject to continuous KGB surveillance; they can write nothing that upsets the authorities without exposing themselves to all sorts of unpleasantnesses or sanctions that may go as far as expulsion; contacts with the local population are minimal; all sorts of things, including food parcels, have to be sent from abroad; accommodation is worse than it would be in the West, and as non-Soviet citizens, they are not free to travel wherever they like. Living in Moscow can be interesting professionally to a Western journalist, but what is it that makes life there so attractive to him?

The answer is that it is his privileged status. In spite of all the inconveniences to which he is subjected, he is incomparably better off than the ordinary people of Moscow. To the latter, his apartment, though it is inferior to what he would have at home, represents an inaccessible marvel. They cannot buy things in special shops, and still less can they buy things from abroad. They cannot go abroad and buy things to bring back or have Western books and publications sent them, and they cannot talk politics freely. They creep on all fours while Western correspondents walk on their two feet—even though they have to bend—and this privileged status acts like a charm on their memory.

It is this privileged status that is all-important to the nomenklatura, though its material advantages must of course not be underrated.

We have looked at this very special country that is Nomenklaturia from the point of view—neither too high nor too low—of the head of a Central Committee desk. Now, Nomenklaturia is a mountainous country characterized by the fact that the higher the altitude the more fertile the soil and the more succulent the fruits.

The difference between the head of a desk and a deputy head of a division in the Central Committee leaps to the eye as soon as you enter their offices. You walk into the former's office straight from the corridor; it is comfortable, but small and characterless. The *zam. zav.* (deputy head of a division) has a smart office with a vestibule and a secretary who, to avoid any possibility of scandal or gossip, is generally no longer very young (the most exalted officials have male secretaries). When the head of a desk needs transport, he sends for an official car from the Central Committee pool, while the *zam. zav.* has a car and driver to himself. He does not go to a holiday home, but to a comfortable dacha suitable for use all the year round, with staff provided; and naturally he has a higher salary, *kremliovka* coupons of the first category, and a better apartment. Mounting still higher in the hierarchy, we reach the level of first deputy head of a division, who no longer belongs to the nomenklatura of the Central Committee Secretariat, but to that of the Politburo. So he has still greater privileges.

The first secretary of a regional party committee is a kind of omnipotent satrap, the other secretaries being merely his assistants. All these people not only have higher salaries, official residences and dachas, cars, free food, and special hospitals and convalescent and rest homes; they also have practically unlimited opportunities of drawing on the material wealth of their region. Now, the territory of a region is almost as big as that of an average European country.

The head of a Central Committee division perhaps enjoys fewer material advantages than these regional satraps, but he has one foot on the ladder to the top leadership of the nomenklatura. The head of a big division is also a secretary of the Central Committee and is thus one of those who take their place on Lenin's tomb and wave to the crowd on special occasions; he is one of those whose faces are recognized in press photographs and on television.

He is far higher in the world than our head of desk, and the two are not reunited even in death. When the latter dies, *Pravda* will print a brief announcement in a black border, or a brief tribute signed by a "group of comrades." The merits of a deceased head of a division or a first secretary of a regional committee will be the subject of a long obituary, accompanied by his picture and the signatures of members of the Politburo. But our head of desk will have no cause for complaint. His widow will not have to apply to a trade-union committee that will reluctantly grant her twenty rubles (26 U.S. dollars) for the funeral expenses, but will be given a state funeral, a convoy of Chaikas and black Volgas will follow the hearse, speeches will be made at the so-called lay funeral service, and after the return from the cemetery Armenian brandy will be drunk to the memory of the departed. In front of the luxurious bier, a brass band will strike up the famous

> You bravely fell in the terrific fight
> In the service of the workers
> You gave all to bring them well-being and light . . .

The desk head's burial will not take place in a cemetery for ordinary mortals, but in a special one at the Novodevichy monastery, where the remains of nomenklaturists lie in splendid stone tombs. Among them are those of Stalin's wife, Alliluyeva, and her relatives, Kosygin's wife, and Khrushchev. The widow, who will have completely taken over her husband's way of thinking, will complain bitterly that he never reached the highest level of the nomenklatura, which would have entitled him to burial in the Kremlin wall in Red Square; and she will note that dead generals are given military honors here in the Novodevichy cemetery, while her husband did not get them, though he loved nothing so much as pomp, power, and honors.

11. HOUSES ON OLYMPUS

And how do the highly placed comrades live who greet the crowd from the top of Lenin's tomb and are later buried in the Kremlin wall? A nomenklaturist who moved in those exalted circles once told me that they lived like the richest American multimillionaires.

The salaries of the Soviet leaders are top secret. But there are rumors that the salary of a secretary of the Central Committee of the CPSU, and even the Secretary-General is about a thousand rubles. That is of course much better than the average worker's 181 rubles a month but is far short of the multimillionaire level. So how is the difference made up?

In the first place, each of these people also has his pay as a deputy to the Supreme Soviet, as well as other fees. Much more important is that he has an open account at the State Bank that enables him to draw on public funds for any sum that he may need at any time. Secondly, he has no need to draw on that account or on his salary, as he does not need money, for at this level everyone lives in luxury at state expense without opening his purse. The *gensek* (Secretary-General) has only to pick up his vertushka and tell the head of the Central Committee administration to have a house or dacha built for him. He will have to sign a party decision to this effect, and some time afterward his new home will be fully furnished with every modern convenience, ready to move into, and carefully guarded.

The Secretary-General will thus be much better lodged than a big company chairman in a capitalist country. An idea of how "they" lived at the time is not to be obtained from Henri Barbusse's description of the little house in the Kremlin in which Stalin received him—while laughing behind his mustache at so much naïveté. But two houses in Moscow dating from the Stalin period enable one to see for oneself.

One of them, now the Tunisian Embassy, on the Sadovaya Ring, near Vosstania Square, used to be Beria's palace, and at the time it was inadvisable to walk along the big gray stone walls with bricked-up ground-floor windows—not that there was any inducement to do so with all those grim-looking individuals in civilian clothes standing about. Pedestrians used either to cross to the opposite pavement or at least walk in the roadway. Nowadays ordinary Soviet citizens still cannot enter the place because of the same grim-looking figures, now in militia uniform. But even if one is invited to an embassy reception there, it gives one a grisly sensation to walk through those parquet-floored rooms where revolting orgies took place with terrified girls taken there by Beria's bodyguard. In the basement, Beria himself tortured prisoners who were brought here for his entertainment. A selection of specially prepared and carefully looked-after instruments of torture were found there after his downfall. There are a number of small cells in the basement with heavy iron doors fitted with spy holes in which citizens of the country of the victorious socialism were kept and tortured by a member of the Politburo with his own hands, because he enjoyed it. There is also a small door that is kept firmly barricaded. Either it conceals some dreadful secret or, as rumor maintains, it provides access to an underground passage to the Kremlin.

Another, less macabre building was opened to the public about twelve years ago; this is where Maxim Gorky lived, and it has been turned into a museum. If after thirty years of hesitation it was at last decided to open to the public this baronial mansion that was the home of a proletarian writer, it was because the master of the house was, according to his own confession, only a "literary master craftsman" and did not belong to the ruling elite of the nomenklatura. But the brilliant chandeliers of the Gorky palace reveal the truth about its lifestyle even then. Stalin and members of his Politburo came here as guests, and they did not do so just to escape from their cramped apartments for a few hours and be able to stretch their limbs in comfort.

There is also in Moscow a monumental relic of the post-Stalin period, the Cuban Embassy, in the Pomerantsev Pereulok. Malenkov was not satisfied with what the old dictator provided for the members of the Politburo, that is, two apartments in Moscow: one in the Kremlin and the other in Granovsky Street, opposite the Kremlin canteen. So he had himself built a supplementary residence or, rather, a large palace, which later turned out to be big enough to house an embassy, complete with offices, reception rooms, and ambassador's residence. If he never benefited from all this, it was because Khrushchev unceremoniously threw him out.

But the nomenklatura did not exactly languish in poverty in Khrushchev's time either. Before Stalin's annihilation of Lenin's old guard, a cooperative estate of dachas, all of them small and simple wooden buildings, had been built for old Bolsheviks. It was called *Zavety Ilyicha* ("Lenin's testament"), but the people of Moscow ironically gave the same name to the palaces built on the Lenin Hills, behind Moscow University, for Khrushchev's "collective leadership."

There is a high, cream-colored stone wall with a heavy iron gate behind which are the guards. A house in the middle of a big garden is almost invisible from the street. Unless it is desired to have dealings with a *toptun*, which is what KGB guards in civilian clothes are called, loitering here is not advisable. But if you are one of the elect, your driver merely flashes his lights and the iron gate is opened. You advance through the garden, followed by the suspicious eyes of uniformed KGB officers, and you enter the palace through a heavy door. It is a huge, massively constructed building, decorated with wood carvings, marble statues, glass chandeliers, and open fireplaces. The reception rooms are on the ground floor, there is another suite of big rooms on the second floor, and the bedrooms are at the top. That was how the leaders of the party and the government were accommodated under Khrushchev. And how are they accommodated today?

The Lenin's Testament estate on the Lenin Hills is still unoccupied. The houses, furnished in neutral official style, are now used for distinguished foreign guests. The leaders of the party and the government have left their palaces for democratic apartments. One of them is theoretically secret, but the secret is known to everyone. A militiaman in uniform demonstratively stands guard outside No. 26 Kutuzov Prospekt, a Central Committee building. Next to the entrance there is a small red panel saying NO STANDING—PARKING PROHIBITED. Leonid Brezhnev occupied a five-room apartment there with his wife, Victoria Petrovna, and the rest of his family, and his neighbor was said to be Yuri Vladimirovich Andropov, then president of the KGB. The numerous wings of the building accommodate the families of middle-grade Central Committee officials. Ordinary citizens were actually allowed to cross the big courtyard without being subjected to an identity check. They could also rejoice that under the new Ilyich there was a return to the Leninist taste for simplicity.

In fact Brezhnev practically did not live there. The apartment was registered in his name, the domestic staff were in residence, and members of the family and Victoria Petrovna were sometimes to be seen there. But, like the other members of the governing elite, the supreme overlord lived in an official dacha near the village of Usovo, not far from Moscow, and the town apartment served the same purpose for him as the Kremlin cell served for Stalin. The Usovo dacha, incidentally, belonged to Stalin. It is known as the *dalniaya* (distant dacha), to distinguish it from the *blizhniaya* (near dacha), near Kuntsevo, where Stalin died. Khrushchev was the next occupant of the "distant dacha." As he had a sense of publicity, he allowed photographs of this two-story white palace, with its colonnades, balconies, and suites of reception rooms, to be published in the Western press.

12. BEHIND THE SEVENFOLD RING FENCE

The state dachas in the Moscow neighborhood are in a forbidden zone; high fences shelter the gardens from curious eyes, and they are heavily guarded. The nomenklatura upper crust keeps the people at a safe distance.

Some verses by Galich entitled *Behind the Sevenfold Ring Fence* illustrate what the people of Moscow think of these dachas:

> To the country—far from tensions!
> Rain refreshes our skin.
> Behind fences there are mansions,
> Our leaders live serene.

Here your grief is free and full,
Grass is here like silk,
Here are the wonderful
Candies "Bird's Milk."

Here are flora and fauna both
Highly cultivated ground.
From behind the fence plainclothes
Men are looking all around.

They pace to and fro, hats on,
Collars turned up.
In the house Stalin's falcon
Eats shashlik kabob.

And at night, at night all those
Who control Soviet power
Sit back to watch what they chose
It is sex movies hour.

The fat slug pants, mumbling "er,"
Gazing at the show.
He is very fond of her,
Marilyn Monroe.[25]

Everything in this picture is authentic, including the nighttime film shows that follow the Stalin tradition, with interpreters available from the state film committee who are much gratified by the confidence shown in them as well as by a good meal.

Evenings in these state dachas are incidentally much livelier than is imagined by the ordinary Soviet citizen, who goes to bed in his seven square meters of living space and winds his alarm clock to make sure that he won't be late for work in the morning. The dacha dwellers do not content themselves with gasping with pleasure at the sight of Marilyn Monroe's attractive form. But let us say no more, for in comparison with Beria's spare-time entertainments, what takes place is innocent enough.

We have mentioned that Lenin obtained a dacha in 1918. Other Soviet leaders began acquiring dachas in 1919, the unforgettable year when the ragged troops of the Red Army fought and died for the power of the Soviets on a quarter of a loaf a day. The process began, according to Svetlana Alliluyeva, when the revolutionary leaders "started using the numerous country houses or estates in the Moscow region that had been abandoned by their owners."[26]

Svetlana describes as follows the dacha occupied by Mikoyan as it looked from 1919 onward: "Inside are marble statues imported from Italy. The walls are hung with Gobelins [tapestry] and downstairs the windows are of stained glass. The garden, the park, the tennis court, the orangery, stables and greenhouses. . . ."[27] "At Mikoyan's dacha, even in winter, fresh green vegetables from his own hothouses were always served."[28]

The newspapers at the time were full of exhortations to the people to make sacrifices for the cause, but they can be combed in vain for any mention of the comforts their leaders provided for themselves.

In the twenties, when the leaders of the socialist revolution were still wearing Russian blouses and trying more and more clumsily to assume proletarian manners, they were already living like aristocratic landowners. Stalin's daughter's reminiscences seem to carry echoes of Turgenev's *A Nest of Gentlefolk:*

Our place . . . underwent endless transformations. At the outset my father had the woods surrounding the house cleared and half the trees cut down. He had clearings made and it became lighter, warmer and not so damp. He kept the woods cleared and tended, and had the dead leaves raked up in spring. In front of the house stood a lovely grove of young birches, all shimmering and white, where we children gathered mushrooms every year. Nearby was an apiary and two open spaces that were sown in summer with buckwheat, so the bees could make honey. Strips of open land had been left beside the tall, dry pine forest. Wild strawberries and blackberries grew there and the air had a special fragrance. . . . [My father] had fruit trees planted over large tracts and strawberry, raspberry and currant bushes planted in abundance. A small open space at a distance from the house was enclosed by chicken wire and neatly hedged with shrubs to make a run for turkeys, pheasants and guinea fowl. Ducks were paddling in a little pond. All this did not spring up overnight but developed bit by bit, so that we children grew up on what was actually a small estate with a country routine of its own—haying, picking mushrooms and berries, our own fresh honey every year, our own pickles and preserves, our own poultry.[29]

While all this was going on, the Soviet leaders, comfortably installed in their dachas, bitterly denounced the petit-bourgeois instincts of ordinary people who wanted to keep a few chickens for themselves.

The double standard introduced by Lenin—the greatest severity toward the people and the greatest indulgence for himself and his colleagues—was faithfully followed by his Diadochi. It was not yet the fashion to wear marshals' uniforms or well-tailored suits; Stalin still wore his soldier's tunic, and Bukharin, according to Svetlana, went about "in a long blouse and linen trousers and sandals,"[30] but that was purely for show.

The leaders insisted that ordinary children should be educated in accordance with the system devised by the Chekist Makarenko, while in their "nests of gentlefolk" their own well-cared-for, aristocratic offspring grew up under the watchful eyes of devoted nannies and foreign governesses. This phenomenon was not limited to the Politburo: the elegant Nelli, daughter of Colonel General Sumbatov-Topuridze, Beria's deputy, who grew up in a government dacha near Baku, told me about the lessons her governesses gave her in foreign languages, music, and both ballroom and Caucasian folk dancing.

In the twenties, according to Svetlana, the Soviet leaders lived "in a perfectly normal way."[31] It was only later that they began living in real luxury. After 1932 "they started building [my father] special dachas. My mother didn't live to see all this luxury paid for out of limitless public funds."[32]

There we have it: from public funds. Even then the luxurious way of life of the nomenklatura leaders was not paid for out of their regular income, even though this was disproportionately high. During the thirties, the Moscow newspapers reported a stirring incident that occurred after a military march-past in Red Square. A child had lost its parents, and Stalin came down from Lenin's tomb and approached it, intending to give it a ruble to enable it to get home, but he searched his pockets in vain. The purpose behind the prominence given to this episode was to impress readers with the fact that they were not the only ones with empty pockets, for Comrade Stalin was in the same position. This was nonsense, of course. Svetlana remembers the "monthly wages" that came "in envelopes" from the Central Committee and other sources. The drawers of his desk in the "near dacha" were full of these sealed envelopes.[33] Nevertheless the story is plausible. "He never spent any money," Svetlana wrote, "he had no place to spend it and nothing to spend it on. Everything he needed, his food, his clothing, his dachas and his servants, all were paid for by the government."[34] "To his table fish was brought from special ponds, pheasants and baby lambs from special nurseries; there would be Georgian wines of special vintage and fresh fruit flown from the south by plane."[35] And all that did not cost him a kopek. The expenditure was met by a special department of the Ministry of State Security. The sums involved were astronomical; General N. S. Vlasik, of the state security service, who was the head of Stalin's personal guard, "laid out millions in my father's name."[36]

Svetlana describes how this came about. After her mother's suicide,

> the whole household was run at state expense. Right away the size of the staff, or "service personnel" as they were called to avoid the old bourgeois word "servants," increased enormously. At each of my father's houses there appeared commandants, a detail of bodyguards, each with a chief of its own, two cooks to take turns during the day, and a double staff of waitresses and cleaning women, also working in two shifts. These people were all hand-picked by a special section for personnel and, of course, once they had been appointed as part of the household staff they automatically became employees of the MGB (or GPU as the secret police was still known). . . . Our household staff grew by leaps and bounds. It wasn't just in our house that the new system was put into effect, but in the houses of all the members of the government, at least the ones who belonged to the Politburo.[37]

In the homes and dachas of all party and government leaders in principle it was the same. "They were all paid for out of government funds and maintained by government employees."[38]

The children of the governing elite were not forgotten. This is how Stalin's son, Vasily, lived, according to his sister, Svetlana: "He lived in a big government dacha. It had an enormous staff, a stable and kennels, all, of course, at government expense. . . . They gave him medals, higher and higher rank, horses, automobiles, privileges, everything."[39]

So lavishly did the nomenklatura leaders help themselves from the cornucopia, that the service personnel benefited from it too. The golden rain did not fall only on persons as close to Stalin as "snub-nosed young Valechka"[40] (Valentina Vasilyevna Istomina, Stalin's last mistress, who was his housekeeper at the "near dacha" and lived with him there till his death). The dacha staff and guards enriched themselves, and still do so to the present day. Of the senior officers Svetlana writes: "The one thing they wanted was to grab as much as they could for themselves. They all built themselves country houses and drove government cars and lived like Ministers and even members of the Politburo." An exception was the officer in charge of one of Stalin's dachas who "wasn't like that. He of course lived well too, but on a modest scale compared to the others. He didn't live like a Minister, for example, though it must be said that a member of the Academy of Sciences might have envied his apartment and his house in the country."[41] Corresponding members of the Academy of Sciences, like full members of the Academy, are among the most privileged of Soviet intellectuals.

After the war, according to Svetlana, Stalin acquired still more residences. In the early postwar period, when there were nothing but ruins all the way from the western frontier to the Volga, the building of dachas was resumed with renewed energy. Svetlana describes an official trip to the south by car that her father undertook in 1946 "to see for himself how people were living."[42] They were living in dugouts and ruins. "After this journey they started building more vacation houses in the south. They were now called government dachas. . . . A dacha was built at New Athos, another not far from Sukhumi, and a whole cluster was built on Lake Ritsa. Another dacha was built in the Valdai Hills."[43] All these buildings are still state dachas or government sanatoriums. "He went on building dacha after dacha on the Black Sea . . . and even higher up in the Caucasus Mountains. There were not enough old imperial palaces in the Crimea, all of which were at his disposal; so he built new dachas near Yalta."[44] He also had dachas in the north. "In addition to Kuntsevo and Zubalovo . . . my father had two other places outside Moscow alone. They were Lipki, an ancient estate on the Dimitrov Highway, with a pond, a wonderful house and an enormous park lined with tall lindens, and Semyonovskoye, a fine old estate that had a house built just before the war, large, spring-fed ponds dug by serfs in the old days, and extensive woods. Now it's a government dacha. Some celebrated meetings between party leaders and writers and artists have taken place there."[45] There were also numerous dachas in Georgia: a huge seaside house at Zugdidi, a palatial residence at Tskhaltubo and others besides. Stalin and his Politburo would have had to split themselves into pieces to be able to spend their vacations in all these dachas. Svetlana recalls that "my father seldom visited either place [i.e., Lipki or Semyonovskoye], sometimes not for a year at a time, but the staff always expected him at any moment and was in a constant state of readiness."[46]

And what were the dachas of other members of the Politburo like? Let us see what Svetlana has to say about them: "Beria's dacha was sumptuous, immense. The big white house stood among tall spruces. The furniture, the wallpaper, the lamps had all been made to the architect's designs. . . . There was a film-projection room, but then such rooms existed in all the leaders' dachas."[47] "Molotov's apartment in town and his dacha were distinguished by good taste and luxurious furniture. . . . his home was far more lavish than any other such residence. . . ."[48] "Voroshilov loved splendour. His dacha near Moscow was about the largest and most sumptuous in existence. . . . The houses and dachas belonging to Voroshilov, Mikoyan and Molotov were crammed with fine rugs, gold and silver Caucasian weapons, valuable porcelain . . . jade vases, carved ivory, Indian silks, Persian rugs, handicrafts from Yugoslavia, Bulgaria, Czechoslovakia. It was hard to imagine valuables that did not decorate the abodes of these 'veterans of the Revolution.' . . . The mediaeval custom of vassals paying tribute to their overlord had been resuscitated. Voroshilov, being an old cavalryman, received horses; he never gave up riding at his dacha. Neither did Mikoyan. Their dachas had become luxurious estates with fine grounds, hothouses, stables, all of it maintained and further developed at government expense."[49]

There was really no difference between the dachas of the elite and feudal estates. There were the same rare and precious objets d'art and the same family portraits. Of Voroshilov, Svetlana says: "Extremely poor portraits of all the members of his family—the work of Alexander Gerasimov—'court academician of art'—decorated the walls of his dacha. . . . And, of course, payments to the 'court academician of art' for his creations were made by the state."[50]

Like the aristocracy in their country houses, the dignitaries of the nomenklatura had big libraries installed in their dachas, but these did not cost them a kopek. Svetlana says: "Voroshilov, Molotov, Kaganovich, Mikoyan, all had the same libraries as the one in my father's apartment in the Kremlin. In accordance with a standing regulation, all

newly published books were sent to these people by the publishers.
. . . Needless to say, no-one paid for the books."[51]

In Moscow at that time—and not in Moscow only—it would have
been hard to find a basement in which people were not living in the
most appalling, overcrowded conditions—small, dark, damp cellars that
have nothing in common with the spacious basements of buildings in
the West.

The higher-ups were fond of their dachas and saw to it that they
were not neglected. It was said that during the battle for Moscow in
1941 some troops under the command of a lieutenant did some damage in a dacha belonging to A. A. Andreyev, who had the reputation of
being one of the least arrogant members of Stalin's Politburo. He had
the lieutenant shot.

Andreyev in fact suffered no loss as the result of this incident. The
country houses of important persons, having been built free of charge
in the first place, were of course rebuilt free of charge also. Svetlana
tells us: "Voroshilov's big, three-storeyed dacha with its immense library was burned to the ground after the war through the carelessness
of a small grandson. . . . But the dacha was soon rebuilt as large as
ever."[52]

A woman student whom I knew, Milena Klimov, daughter of a corresponding member of the Belorussian Academy of Sciences, visited a
state dacha toward the end of the war. I remember how her eyes shone
with pleasure and pride while she imitated the fashionable way of talking that prevailed in those circles and enthused about the delightful
atmosphere, the marvelous dishes that were served, the beautiful light-
ing of the garden. The fact that there was a war on was apparently
ignored in those state dachas. If it is true that a head of a desk in a way
lives in another country, it can be said that at the highest levels of the
nomenklatura they wish to live on another planet.

The building of new dachas continued after Stalin's death. The best-
known is unquestionably that at Pitsunda, which was built for Khrushchev. Pitsunda Bay, on the Black Sea, not far from the well-known
watering place of Gagry, is famous all over the world for its ancient
pine trees, and a great deal of publicity had been given in the Soviet
press to the scientific importance of that conservation area. That did
not prevent a large part of it from being enclosed by a high concrete
wall behind which a dacha was built, complete with its own private

moorings. In 1959 I saw two secret police agents hurrying obsequiously in the direction of a big white outboard motorboat that was just arriving and laying down a red carpet on the sand; a few moments later, Khrushchev disembarked and walked with measured tread toward his dacha.

Along the road beside the sea are a number of small stone houses in which these guards live with their families. All the warnings about security do not prevent them from leasing their villas to summer vacationers.

And what is there behind the wall? Here is an extract from the memoirs of Hans Kroll, who was the Federal German Ambassador to the Soviet Union and was a guest there. The Pitsunda dacha, he says, is situated "in a large and magnificent park planted with rare old trees, and is, of course, surrounded by a fence and is obviously very strictly guarded." He was especially struck by "a sporting complex in ultramodern style designed by a celebrated Moscow architect which had just been completed. There is a huge swimming pool the glass walls and roof of which open when a button is pressed, and then there are a number of halls for gymnastics and games, with showers and changing rooms, and a splendid wide terrace with a view over the Black Sea, which is immediately in front."[53]

If our head of desk manages to avoid all contact with the Soviet population, those at the top of the nomenklatura are sheltered behind a sevenfold fence.

In accordance with the Stalinist tradition, the dignitaries of the nomenklatura travel in ZIL armored cars equipped with telephone and greenish, bulletproof windows; they are escorted by KGB agents in civilian clothes. For security reasons the license plates are changed almost daily. They have a large number of cars at their disposal. Brezhnev's collection of cars was often mentioned in the West, but his colleagues were also well provided for. Once more, it was Lenin who originated this automotive inflation. In the spring of 1922 he already had six cars in his garage, which, in his own words, were kept "under particular GPU supervision."[54]

Nomenklatura cars are still protected in the same way. Stalin used to have an escort of four vehicles full of security guards. Under Khrushchev this was reduced to two, but since then it has been increased again. Special KGB service stations provide high-octane gasoline for all these vehicles.

Ministers of the Soviet Union use the ordinary airline services but have the whole of the first class to themselves; when they travel, the door between first class and second is kept securely closed. More important persons can use special aircraft maintained for the purpose by a special regiment of the Soviet Air Force. Soviet leaders used to use the Tsentralny airport, but now they take off from Vnukovo II. These aircraft are very comfortably equipped: the accommodations include sitting room, office, bedroom, and kitchen. I once had the privilege of traveling in one of them; it did not belong to one of those at the very top of the tree, but to a mere marshal of the Soviet Union—and I can confirm that the comfort left nothing to be desired.

The Stalin tradition requires the protection of the nomenklatura elite to be entrusted to the Ninth Department of the KGB—in nomenklatura jargon *devyatka*, "the nine," which was established specially for the purpose. Protection is interpreted in the broadest sense. Though the foreign terrorists supported by the KGB represent no threat whatever to the Soviet leaders, the lives of the latter are assumed to be in perpetual danger; so all their moves are accompanied by a meticulously worked-out series of security measures.

Senior nomenklaturists do not use the deputies' waiting room in the course of their travels. Their ZILs and Chaikas drive straight onto the tarmac and take these gentlemen to their residence or their dacha immediately after landing. When they go abroad, their luggage and passports are looked after by staff of the *devyatka*. The latter have access to all parts of the airport and throw their weight around in a very self-assured manner. I was once present at a painful scene. One of these KGB bullies who had come to Sheremetyevo airport to fetch Kosygin's daughter's luggage (she was a member of our delegation) graciously allowed Professor A. P. Vinogradov, Vice-President of the Academy of Sciences of the U.S.S.R., to use a reserved exit. You should have seen the old man, who was one of the luminaries of Soviet science, trotting with an expression of servile gratitude on his face behind that lackey of the nomenklatura, who gave himself airs and behaved as if he were of more importance than his aged protégé. In Nomenklaturia he was indeed.

As we have seen, middle-grade nomenklaturists can buy things in special shops. When the top flight of the nomenklatura go abroad, they have their shopping done by subordinates or persons of confidence in the Soviet embassies or trade missions.[55] In Moscow they have no need of third parties. On the third floor of the GUM store there is a *spetsektsia* (a special department officially called Section No. 100), access to which is an exclusive privilege of the families of the highest dignitaries. Imported goods of excellent quality, the mere existence of which is unknown to the ordinary Soviet consumer, are sold there at low prices. Soviet products such as, for instance, magnificent furs that are obtainable at no shop that is open to the public, are also on sale.

Svetlana says that her father one day asked her with a frown if the clothes she was wearing were Soviet or foreign-made, and he was filled with patriotic pleasure when she told him they were Soviet-made.[56] I knew Svetlana well in 1943–44, when we were both students of history at Moscow University. If her short squirrel coat, her dark English outfits, her brightly colored silk blouses and smart flat-heeled shoes—all things that we had never seen—were really made in the Soviet Union, it must have been in the remote and mountainous country of Nomenklaturia.

The fashion for Russian things unsuccessfully introduced by Stalin belongs to the distant past. The present leaders of the nomenklatura and their families are not troubled by patriotism and wear luxurious articles of clothing from abroad. Only the furs are Soviet, as before. Brezhnev's daughter Galina liked showing her guests at her state dacha near Moscow a collection of valuable furs arranged in a wall cupboard that opens when a button is pressed. That is the sort of thing that the ordinary Soviet citizen will never see, except in films about the lives of American millionaires.

The flats and dachas of the men at the summit of the nomenklatura also contain libraries abundantly provided with books that have cost them nothing; the publishers of political or literary works have to send them free copies. The theater also costs them nothing; a stage box is reserved for them when they go there in the company of distinguished foreign guests, unless they prefer the government box on the left of the stage facing the box reserved for the management. *Devyatka* bodyguards in civilian clothes are on guard outside the door on these occasions. There is no need to leave the box, which has a private bar and a toilet.

13. ISOLATED CLASS

This lifestyle results in a special mentality. I myself had occasion to savor it for a few days in Sofia in the summer of 1970, when I was there with M. D. Millionshchikov, first vice-president of the Academy of Sciences of the U.S.S.R. and president of the supreme soviet of the Russian Soviet Federated Socialist Republic (R.S.F.S.R.), and A. P. Vinogradov, the vice-president. We were accommodated in a government palace that had belonged to the sister of Czar Boris of Bulgaria and later to Vasil Kolarov, the former Bulgarian Communist leader. It is in a quiet street near the center of the city. Everything is as it should be: a wall with a heavy iron gate, guards by the entrance, and a shady garden at the back. To the right of the front door two Chaikas with governmental license plates and dignified chauffeurs waited. There was a large staff, but we had dealings with only one of them, no doubt the chief steward. You could ask him for anything you liked, and the dish, the wine, or brandy you wanted would be produced immediately. In a small office next to the drawing room there was a telephone—the Bulgarian vertushka. When we had had enough to eat and drink, we had only to beckon and a Chaika drove up immediately; an agent of the security service opened the door and off we went through Sofia, keeping to the middle of the road and dutifully saluted by the police. After the meetings, banquets, and receptions the Chaika would reappear and whisk us back to the palace. A few days of this made one feel completely detached from real life. I very soon found this intolerable and started going for walks. But it is of course perfectly possible to get used to it. A man as dynamic and sociable as M. D. Millionshchikov, who lived in a single-family house in Moscow and always stayed in government residences when he traveled in the various republics of the U.S.S.R. or in the countries of the Eastern bloc was capable of spending hours sitting in the garden in the warm Bulgarian sunshine without being worried in the least by this splendid isolation.

Yes, it is perfectly possible to get used to it, but it ends by blunting one's sensibilities and completely insulating one from humanity and ordinary life. Stalin tried to find a remedy by watching films that—so he believed—showed him the life of the people. At the Twentieth Party Congress, Khrushchev made fun of him for having no sources of information other than films, but soon we learned that he relied on them himself, though they were newsreels. In fact neither Stalin nor Khrushchev really knew how the people whom they governed lived. Svetlana recalls that Stalin was completely ignorant of current prices and knew only prices of the prerevolutionary Russia.[57]

The Stalin tradition of ruling the people without having even an approximate idea of how they live remains intact. Contact between the leaders of the nomenklatura class and the people are limited to official visits to the federated republics or to the regions in the course of which they are—not unwillingly—shown Potemkin villages by zealous subordinates. If banquets and meetings leave any time for this.

The nomenklaturists have dug a gulf between themselves and their subjects. With their hearts full of anxiety and contempt, they shelter themselves behind their sevenfold fences and the KGB, talking in the meantime about their "links with the masses" and denouncing as renegades those who publicly express their dissatisfaction with the nomenklatura regime. But isn't it the nomenklatura class, the class of *déclassé* officials, that by reason of its nature and lifestyle has become a class of outsiders? What else is one to call a class of persons that actually live like foreigners in their own country?

That, then, is how the nomenklaturists live. There is no point in comparing it with the way of life of the privileged classes in the bourgeois West. The essential feature of capitalist society is not privilege, but money; in real socialist society it is not money, but privilege. This makes the nomenklatura both arrogant and nervous, for it is well aware of the reactions that the constant growth of its privileges rouse in the population. The nomenklaturists are beginning to feel anxious; like rulers whose reign is terminable without notice, more and more they fear a fatal outcome. The following joke went the rounds of the nomenklatura in the seventies.

One day the mother of a Central Committee official, who lived in a kolkhoz, came to visit him. She was shown his luxurious Moscow apartment and his dacha and was given excellent *kremliovka* meals. Unexpectedly she wanted to go home as quickly as possible.

"What's the matter, Mother?" her son asked. "It's lovely here; why don't you want to stay?"

"Yes, it's certainly lovely here," the old woman replied, "but it's dangerous. Suppose the reds come?"

NOTES

1. *Struktura sovetskoj intelligencii*, Minsk, 1970, pp. 122–23.
2. *Pravda*, June 28, 1975.
3. Lenin, *Collected Works*, Vol. 29, p. 113.
4. *Krokodil*, 1969, No. 4.
5. Hedrick Smith, *The Russians*, New York, London, 1976.
6. A. Pravdin, "Inside the CPSU Central Committee," *Survey*, autumn 1974, Vol. 20, No. 4 (93), p. 103.
7. Ilja Zemcov, *Partija ili mafia? Razvorovannaja respublika*, Paris, 1976, pp. 33–34.
8. Ibid., p. 41.
9. Ibid., p. 35.
10. Ibid., p. 89.
11. Ibid., pp. 92–93.
12. Ibid., p. 30.
13. Ibid., p. 57.
14. Ibid., p. 26.
15. Ibid., p. 27.
16. *Vestnik statistiki*, 1975, No. 11, pp. 89, 92.
17. Boris Bajanov, *Avec Staline dans le Kremlin*, Paris, 1930, p. 119.
18. Boris Baschanow, *Ich war Stalins Sekretär*, Berlin, 1977.
19. *Izvestiya*, Jan. 22, 1978.
20. *Izvestiya*, Dec. 20, 1920.
21. Quoted from R. A. Medvedev, *K sudu istorii. Genezis i posledestvija stalinizma*, New York, 1974, p. 1085.
22. U.S.A. National Archives, Miscellaneous Russian Record Collection. Call number 10732, microcopy No. T 88, roll No. 1, list 57.
23. Alexander Bek, *Die Ernennung*, Frankfurt a.M., 1972, p. 134.
24. A. Pravdin, op. cit., p. 102.
25. A. Galic, *Pokolenie obrečennych*, Frankfurt a.M., 1974, pp. 228–29.
26. Svetlana Alliluyeva, *Twenty Letters to a Friend*, London, 1967, p. 34.
27. Ibid.
28. Svetlana Alliluyeva, *Only One Year*, London, 1969, p. 382.
29. S. Alliluyeva, *Twenty Letters to a Friend*, London, 1967, p. 34.
30. Ibid., p. 37.
31. Ibid., p. 39.
32. Ibid., p. 40.
33. *Only One Year*, p. 365.
34. *Twenty Letters*, p. 219.
35. *Only One Year*, p. 364.

36. *Twenty Letters,* p. 220.
37. Ibid., p. 135.
38. Ibid., p. 137.
39. Ibid., p. 224.
40. Ibid., p. 137.
41. Ibid.
42. Ibid., p. 200.
43. Ibid.
44. *Only One Year,* p. 370.
45. *Twenty Letters,* p. 139.
46. Ibid.
47. *Only One Year,* p. 388.
48. Ibid., p. 382.
49. Ibid., p. 378.
50. Ibid., p. 379.
51. Ibid., p. 380.
52. Ibid.
53. Hans Kroll, *Lebenserinnerungen eines Botschafters,* Köln, 1967, p. 483.
54. Lenin, *Collected Works,* Vol. 45, p. 556.
55. In 1954 there were sensational reports in the Western press that G. M. Malenkov, then head of the Soviet Government, ordered his hats from Italy. In fact there was nothing unusual in such purchases.
56. S. Alliluyeva, *Twenty Letters,* p. 61.
57. Ibid., p. 219.

6

The Dictatorship
of the Nomenklatura

We have a party, a governing party. What do we want an opposition
for? People are always talking about freedom. What does it mean?
L. I. Brezhnev, in an interview with *Stern*, May 12, 1973.

The essential aim of the nomenklaturist class is to prevent a "red"
breakthrough at home while using "red" camouflage abroad to infiltrate into all the countries of the world. Let us begin with its domestic
policy; having dealt with the "dictatorship of the proletariat," which
never existed, let us take a look at the very real dictatorship of the
nomenklatura.

1. IS THERE SOVIET POWER IN THE SOVIET UNION?

At first sight that question may seem absurd. Power in the Soviet
Union, whether for good or evil, is obviously Soviet power.

But is it so obvious? The theory has been worked out in great detail.
In the Soviet Union, Lenin is frequently claimed to have discovered
that soviets (councils) were the form of state organization assumed by
the dictatorship of the proletariat. The statement has a certain importance in spite of the fact that the dictatorship of the proletariat never
existed, for soviets were in fact formed and Lenin saw in them indeed a
means of exercising state power.

Up to the revolution of 1905, Lenin and all the Bolsheviks followed
Marx and Engels in believing that in the transitional period between
the socialist revolution and the communist classless society, the form

assumed by the state would be of the type of the Paris Commune, of 1871. When councils (soviets) arose spontaneously and independently of the program of any party in the revolutionary Russia of 1905, Lenin saw in them the form of state imposed by the march of history and wrote: *"This* power is of *the same type* as the Paris Commune, of 1871."

The fundamental characteristics of this type are "(1) the source of power is not a law previously discussed and enacted by parliament, but the direct initiative of the people from below . . . (2) the replacement of the police and the army, which are institutions divorced from the people and set against the people, by the direct arming of the whole people; order in the state under such a power is maintained by the armed workers and peasants *themselves,* by the armed people *themselves;* (3) officialdom, the bureaucracy, are either similarly replaced by the direct rule of the people themselves or at least placed under special control; they not only become elected officials, but are also subject to recall at the people's first demand; they are reduced to the position of simple agents; from a privileged group holding 'jobs' remunerated on a high, bourgeois scale, they become workers of a special 'arm of the service' whose remuneration *does not exceed* the ordinary pay of a competent worker. This, and this *alone,* constitutes the *essence* of the Paris Commune as a special type of state."[1]

Now, the form taken by the state in the Soviet Union is the exact opposite of Lenin's model; it departs radically from every one of the points mentioned by him. For in the U.S.S.R. the people are completely subject to orders from above, they have no arms in their possession, there are a large army and a large police force, the political bureaucracy is not just paid on a "bourgeois" scale but actually constitutes the governing, exploiting, and privileged class. Thus in the light of Lenin's teaching we are entitled to ask whether when one can talk of soviet power in the Soviet Union.

In the first decades after the October Revolution, writers on the Soviet constitution returned to the argument that the soviets were the form of state organization that corresponded to the phase of dictatorship of the proletariat. They maintained that, while the bourgeois state was based on the separation of powers, an idea now hopelessly obsolete, the soviets represented the principle of the unity of power; they were both legislative and executive organs of proletarian government, and local soviets were consequently not mere municipal organs but organs of the state power. It was claimed that this system was more democratic than any parliamentary system.

No sooner had these theories, which were intended to support Lenin's, been published than the adoption of Stalin's 1936 constitution drove a horse and cart through these speculations. The much-vaunted unitary principle was dropped, and state and administrative powers were divided between higher, central organs and local organs. The powers of the latter, the soviets and their executive committees, were reduced to those of local authorities of the traditional type, while the higher organs of the state power, the federal and republican supreme soviets, were elevated to the rank of lawmaking (in fact, law-publishing) organs, and the "superior organs of state administration," the Councils of People's Commissars (renamed Councils of Ministers after 1945) thenceforward played the part of executive organs.

The nomenklaturist now began proudly calling the supreme soviets "Soviet parliaments," though such a description was in no way justified.

The parliamentary masquerade was carried still further. The nomenklaturists tried to conceal the absence of all parties other than the governing party behind the fiction of the "Communist and nonparty bloc." No one knows by whom or where this bloc was formed, but candidates are appointed in its name, the number of Communists among the latter being in inverse proportion to the national percentages, for an absolute majority of voters are nonparty, while the absolute majority of candidates are members of the party. Brezhnev's 1977 constitution brought about no change in the structure of the organs of power.

The Soviet system is not of course a parliamentary system, but it is not a soviet system either, since it does not possess a single basic characteristic of the latter as defined by Lenin and the theories we quoted above. The principle of a strict separation of powers has replaced the unitary principle. All that has survived of the "power of the soviets" is the word soviet (council). But the term "council" is used in a great many countries. In many of them the Cabinet is called the Council of Ministers. Under the Fourth Republic in France the Prime Minister was called President of the Council, the upper chamber of the Federal German Republic is called the Federal Council (Bundesrat), the Austrian parliament consists of a National Council (Nationalrat) and a

Federal Council (Bundesrat), and there are municipal as well as many other kinds of council all over Europe. The state councils so fashionable in Eastern Europe are not a novelty either. There was a Council of State in czarist Russia, and in Germany between the wars Adenauer was president of the Prussian State Council. But soviet power does not exist and has never existed in any of these countries, and it is the same in the Soviet Union.

It cannot be otherwise, even if one adopts the viewpoint of Soviet ideology. The latter is that soviet power is the form of state that corresponds to the phase of dictatorship of the proletariat. Now, according to the 1977 constitution, Soviet society has reached the phase of "developed socialism" and has therefore passed beyond that of the dictatorship of the proletariat. So how can the power of the soviets have survived? As a form without content? From the Marxist point of view that is impossible. Like the dictatorship of the proletariat, the power of the soviets has fulfilled its historical mission and has reached the end of its life, making way for a new type of state, the state of the whole people. All this could have appeared word for word in a report by Brezhnev, Andropov, or Chernenko.

When we say that there is no such thing as the power of the soviets in the Soviet Union, we are merely saying what the ideologists of the nomenklatura would have to admit if they took seriously their own theories about the "dictatorship of the proletariat" and the "state of the whole people" that has succeeded it. They do nothing of the sort, for they are well aware that all this is nothing but fiction. Nevertheless, as we have gotten into the habit of thinking that the power of the soviets must exist in a Soviet state, they take advantage of the fact and continue to claim that it exists.

Power in the Soviet Union is exercised not by the soviets but by the party leaders, i.e., the nomenklaturists. "Soviet power" is merely a euphemism that serves as a façade for the dictatorship of the nomenklatura; the state form corresponding to that dictatorship is not the power of the soviets, but Stalinist pseudo parliamentarism.

2. THE "DIRECTIVE ORGANS"

In Chapter 3 we described the process of political decision making in the U.S.S.R. and the process by which the nomenklatura was formed. In this chapter we shall try to show how the system works at the highest level, where policy is made and supreme power is exercised.

The phrase "directive organs" has established itself in nomenklatura jargon. It indicates the tip of the power pyramid; it expresses the fact that here we have to do with the supreme organs that issue instructions to the rest. Use of the term has spread from common parlance into administrative terminology, in which it indicates the Central Committee of the CPSU. Sometimes the nomenklatura uses the equally suggestive term "authority" instead. There are many authorities in the luxuriant bureaucracy of real socialism, but there is only one Authority. When a decision by Authority is spoken of, the initiated understand that the reference is to the Central Committee of the CPSU.

The term Central Committee of the CPSU has various meanings; it may refer to (i) the plenum of the CPSU (i.e., all the members elected to it by the party congress); (ii) the Politburo and Secretariat of the Central Committee; (iii) the Central Committee apparatus.

Though they are not mentioned in the constitution, the supreme organs of state are neither the plenum nor the apparatus, but the Politburo and the Secretariat of the Central Committee. When a layman penetrates to one of the offices of the Central Committee apparatus, believing himself to be actually in the holy of holies of the Central Committee, he is taken aback to hear it said that "this question must be submitted to the Central Committee," or "we cannot decide it; the agreement of the Central Committee is essential."

The explanation is simple: by Central Committee the nomenklaturists mean the Politburo and the Secretariat of the Central Committee, the two organs that jointly control the state machine. The Politburo and the Secretariat constitute the real government of the Soviet Union; the Council of Ministers has executive powers, but is not a government in the political meaning of the term. An even more modest role is played by the Presidium of the Supreme Soviet, which is a symbolic body practically without real power. The Politburo and the Secretariat of the Central Committee are the Soviet equivalent of a cabinet. It is not by chance that the phrase "this must be submitted for government approval" can frequently be heard in the corridors of the Council of Ministers; the users of the phrase themselves are supposed to be the government, but they know very well that the real government is the "directing organs."

That they are the most important bodies in the country is shown by the prominence given to them in all Soviet publications. When the country's leading political figures are listed, the voting and nonvoting members of the Politburo and the secretaries of the Central Committee are mentioned first; the offices they hold are not mentioned, for it is assumed that everyone knows them. Next come the vice-presidents of the Presidium of the Supreme Soviet, the vice-presidents of the Council of Ministers, and other eminent bureaucrats in the nomenklaturist hierarchy, with the offices they hold. In Stalin's time the order in which names appeared was not alphabetical, but was decided by the dictator himself. Under Khrushchev it was alphabetical. Under Brezhnev and Andropov their names come first, followed in alphabetical order by those of the members of the Politburo, the nonvoting members (still in alphabetical order), and the secretaries of the Central Committee (arranged in order of seniority in that organization, illustrating the hierarchical structure of the Secretariat).

Should the Politburo be regarded as the supreme legislative authority and the Secretariat as the supreme executive authority? That is too legalistic an approach; it offers only a pale reflection of reality and so is not very relevant. The Secretariat of the Central Committee cannot be regarded as the executive organ of a Politburo legislature; the nature of the relationship between the two cannot be established by analogy, for they are the result of a special historical development. The names of the two organs seem colorless enough, but better ones could not have been found. It is polit-bureaucracy that exercises sovereignty over the society of real socialism, and no more appropriate term than Politburo could be invented to indicate its highest organ. Under real socialism, government is exercised by what Trotsky called the hierarchy of secretaries, i.e., the core of the nomenklatura. Hence the popular saying "In the beginning there was the matriarchate, then there was the patriarchate, and now there is the Secretariat." What could the second-highest organ in this society be called except the Secretariat?

3. THE SECRETARY-GENERAL

There is a widespread view that the country is governed by the Secretary-General of the Central Committee, but it is mistaken. To convince oneself of that, it is sufficient to ask this question: If policy was autocratically laid down by personalities as different as Stalin, Khrushchev, Brezhnev, and Andropov, how did it come about that the most significant features of that policy remained unchanged?

The answer is that the country is governed not by the Secretary-General but by the nomenklatura class; the policy followed by the Central Committee is not that of the Secretary-General but that of this class. The guidelines of that policy were laid down by Lenin and Stalin, the fathers of the nomenklaturist class, in conformity with its requirements, and it is that which is largely responsible for their reputation as autocratic leaders. They unquestionably exercised paternal authority over a ruling class that was not yet firmly in the saddle, but as we have already pointed out, at the same time they were dependent on it. On the other hand, Khrushchev and, to an even greater extent, Brezhnev and Andropov, were never anything but supreme executants of the nomenklatura will.

The Secretary-General is the top nomenklaturist and is consequently the most powerful man in real-socialist society. As Lenin noted a few months after Stalin's appointment, immense power is concentrated in his hands. Anyone who tries to assume leadership of the nomenklatura without being assured of that position is inevitably thrown out, as happened to Malenkov and then to Shelepin.

The question is not whether the Secretary-General has great power (he has), but whether his power is the only one in the country (the Politburo, the Secretariat, and the apparatus being subordinate to him at differing levels).

He is the head both of the Politburo and of the Secretariat, but his relations with the directive organs of the nomenklaturist class are not those of a commander and his subordinates.

Two phases must be distinguished in a Secretary-General's relations with the Politburo and the Secretariat. In the first, the members of both bodies will have been taken over from his predecessor; in the second, most members of both bodies will be his own protégés.

It is impossible to make one's way in the nomenklatura class without a great deal of support, so it is essential to join a faction in which everyone helps everyone else while at the same time trying to undermine rival factions. Anyone with ambitions for a career in the nomenklatura will concentrate on forming such a faction and will take advantage of every opportunity of winning over useful persons; personal likings play only a subordinate part in this process.

The leader of such a faction will try to secure admission to the faction of a senior nomenklatura official, the higher the better, and thus become his vassal, taking his own faction with him. The consequence is that the unit in the power structure of real socialism is a group of vassals subject to an overlord; the number of vassals depends on his rank in the hierarchy. He protects and uses his influence on behalf of his vassals, who in return support him with all their might, sing his praises, and show him an apparently undying loyalty.

But this loyalty has strict limits. It is only to the outside observer that relations between overlord and vassals seem idyllic. While demonstrating constant obsequiousness to his overlord, the vassal, however successful his career may hitherto have been, aspires to one thing only: to seize any opportunity that may present itself to supplant him. That is the rule in every nomenklaturist clan, right up to the Politburo and the Central Committee Secretariat. When a Secretary-General leaves, his successor, that is, the most successful of his vassals, takes over the leadership of his predecessor's followers, and he is then faced with the task of putting his own followers in the leading positions and ending up with these at the pinnacle of the nomenklatura, thus bringing about the second phase of his relations with the latter.

Approval of his appointment to the post of Secretary-General amounts to formal recognition of his sovereignty, but his former fellows in fact regard him as an upstart who has managed to overtake them. At best, they regard him as *primus inter pares.* Hence the appointment of a new Secretary-General is invariably accompanied by a reaffirmation of the principle of collective leadership.

The objective of the new Secretary-General is to concentrate unrestricted power in his own hands, and he is in an excellent position to do so. The major difficulty is that everyone is aware of his intentions. He cannot, at any rate at first, afford to get rid of his enemies in the Politburo and the Secretariat, because the latter, having reached the top level in the nomenklaturist class, will each have a large number of vassals. So he has to be on excellent terms with them all; every single one of them must regard him as a lesser evil. Meanwhile he must use his ingenuity to form a coalition against those who stand in his way and eventually get rid of them, at the same time doing everything he can to secure the appointment of his own followers to leading positions. The usual method is to have his vassals appointed to positions that give access to the highest nomenklatura posts.

It is a highly complicated game of chess. That is why securing appointment to one of the highest positions in the nomenklatura is a painfully protracted business. What counts is not the applicant's political suitability (still less his administrative ability) but the adeptness of his political maneuvering. The power of the Secretary-General is consolidated to the extent that he succeeds in putting his vassals in commanding positions in the nomenklatura or in positions that give access to them. The ideal, which was achieved by Lenin and Stalin, is to be the overlord of vassals selected by oneself. In these conditions there is no more talk of collective leadership, the Politburo and the Secretariat are reduced to the role of assistants to the Secretary-General, and the second phase of the relations between them begins. That is how the situation in the Central Committee develops; there is a transition from collective leadership to the apparent autocracy of the Secretary-General.

This conclusion is not a product of speculation; it merely takes account of what happened under Stalin, Malenkov, Khrushchev, and Brezhnev. If the optimal situation is not reached (the Brezhnev government was an example of this), the strengthening of the Secretary-General's position leads to a situation in which the nomenklaturist leaders who were not followers of his find it politic to grant him their allegiance. But he cannot rely on his vassals, old or new; let us not forget that Brezhnev belonged to Khrushchev's faction, which did not prevent him from becoming involved in his overlord's downfall. The peculiarities of Andropov's coming to power will be analyzed in chapter 8.

What does such a faction look like in practice? Let us take a concrete example. If one takes a look at the top nomenklaturists under Brezhnev, it is impossible not to be struck by the surprisingly large number that came from Dnepropetrovsk. Andrei Pavlovich Kirilenko, member of the Politburo and secretary of the Central Committee, had been first secretary of the regional committee of Dnepropetrovsk; Vladimir Shcherbitsky, another member of the Politburo, succeeded him in that post after filling various responsible positions in the neighboring town of Dneprodzerzhinsk. Nikolai Alexandrovich Tikhonov, a member of the Politburo, was a graduate of the Dnepropetrovsk College of Metallurgy and worked in that city for many years, lastly as president of the economic council of the Dnepropetrovsk region. Other metallurgists from the same school were I. V. Novikov, Vice-President of the Council of Ministers of the U.S.S.R.; G. E. Tsukanov, the head of Brezhnev's Secretariat; General G. P. Tsinev, vice-president of the KGB; and N. A. Shchelokov, the Minister of the Interior and a former president of the Dnepropetrovsk town soviet. Pavlov, head of the administrative service of the Central Committee of the CPSU, was a graduate of the Higher School of Metallurgy at Dneprodzerzhinsk, and Brezhnev's assistant, A. I. Blatov, was a graduate of the Dnepropetrovsk railway engineers' higher school. The list goes on and on.

What, we wonder, does Dnepropetrovsk have that is so special? The puzzle will look less baffling if we mention another metallurgist who came from the Dnepropetrovsk area, and more specifically the town of Dneprodzerzhinsk, namely L. I. Brezhnev. That was where he began his nomenklatura career. Before and after the war he was secretary of the Dnepropetrovsk regional committee, a post in which he preceded Kirilenko and Shcherbitsky, and he was subsequently appointed first secretary of the Moldavian Communist Party's central committee. Accordingly the following comrades of his from this Moldavian period were also to be found at the top of the nomenklatura tree: Konstantin Ustinovich Chernenko, Brezhnev's heir and Andropov's successor as Secretary-General (we will picture him), was formerly head of the Moldavian central committee propaganda department; General S. K. Tsvigun, first vice-president of the KGB (and Brezhnev's brother-in-law), a former vice-president of the Moldavian KGB; Sergei P. Trapeznikov, head of the science and education division of the Central Committee of the CPSU, a former head of the Moldavian party higher school; and finally Shchelokov, Minister of the Interior, whom we have already mentioned, a former first vice-president of the Moldavian council of ministers under Brezhnev and then second secretary of the central committee of the same republic.

That is the utterly prosaic explanation of the Brezhnev-era overrepresentation at the highest level of Dnepropetrovsk and Moldavia. Those regions must be regarded as a breeding ground not of Russian genius but of the Brezhnev clan. That these people were Brezhnev's protégés was frankly admitted at the ceremony in September 1977 at which Shcherbitsky was decorated with the Order of Lenin and a second gold star as a Hero of Socialist Labor. On this occasion Brezhnev said, "We all, and I myself even more perhaps than many other comrades, know very well how much energy, determination, and Bolshevik ardor you have devoted to the progress and prosperity of the Soviet Ukraine. I well remember your work in the factory where I, too, once worked." Shcherbitsky hastened to reply, "Dear Leonid Ilyich . . . I have always been and I shall always be proud that nearly the whole of my active life has been under your leadership."[2]

Another member of the Brezhnev clan was Konstantin Katushev, a former secretary of the Central Committee, then Vice-President of the Council of Ministers of the U.S.S.R. His father was a close friend of Brezhnev's. Katushev is the Soviet ambassador to Cuba now.

The clan also included able specialists and technicians, for Brezhnev was good at attracting ability. Highly qualified experts who were not among his youthful friends included his assistant Andrei Mikhailovich Alexandrov-Agentov, an experienced diplomat; Leonid Mikhailovich Zamyatin, head of the Central Committee international information department, and Vadim Valentinovich Zagladin, first deputy head of the Central Committee international department. Nevertheless it is not ability, but the Secretary-General's favor that decides appointments, as shown by the above-mentioned Trapeznikov, a dogmatic and untalented historian of the party and a provincial who succeeded in attracting the surprisingly unanimous opposition of the members of the Soviet Academy of Sciences. The low esteem in which he was held was shown when he suffered a humiliating setback upon applying to become a corresponding member of the academy; his rejection was an unusual blow to a man who was appointed to preside over Soviet science. The members of the academy only granted him the title ten years later. He left his position only after Brezhnev's death.

The gradual concentration of power in the hands of the Secretary-General that takes place in the secrecy of the "directive organs" is reflected in the outside world in the development of his personality cult. This term made its first appearance in Soviet political jargon in connection with Stalin's dictatorship. But the de-Stalinizer Khrushchev was also accused after his downfall of having promoted a personality cult. In these circumstances, one is reminded of Marx's ironic remark that history always repeats itself, first as tragedy and then as farce. Marx did not envisage yet another repetition. The reaction to the Brezhnev cult was amusement combined with boredom. People began to realize that every new Secretary-General would inevitably develop into a political and military genius, a great theorist, and a champion of peace. Andropov's and Chernenko's rules confirm this.

The cult of the Secretary-General's personality is an outward sign of the second phase of the concentration of power in his hands; at the same time it is his exclusive privilege. There are of course rudimentary cults of the first secretaries of federated republics, regions, towns, and districts. Flattering references are frequently made to the talents of the leader of the local nomenklatura, but the latter will take care not to be carried away by the impetuous flood of simulated admiration, for the personality cult is the prerogative of the Secretary-General, whose exclusive right to it has been but reinforced in the course of years. In the forties it was still usual in official documents at the level of the party concerned to make flattering references to the first secretaries of federated republics, regions, towns, and districts, but nowadays it would be inconceivable.

To the nomenklaturists the Lenin cult, which sometimes assumes grotesque dimensions and is the object of many amusing jokes in the Soviet Union, serves as measuring rod. That does not prevent every Secretary-General as supreme chief of the nomenklaturists from vigorously promoting the cult of his own personality. The ideal—so far achieved only by Stalin—is to be put on a par with Lenin. Henri Barbusse found a neat phrase for this in his naïve little book about the dictator: "Stalin is the Lenin of the present day," he wrote.

In these ideal circumstances, the cult of the living leader takes the place of the cult of the dead one. Marx and Engels being dead, Lenin became the living god of Marxism, and when he died, someone had to be found to take his place. The obvious candidate was nomenklaturist No. 1, the Secretary-General of the party Central Committee.

4. STRUGGLES FOR POWER IN THE KREMLIN

The Byzantine personality cult of the Secretary-General does not conceal from the rest of the world the permanent struggle for power that goes on at the highest level of the nomenklatura. The public in the West often hears about "struggles for power in the Kremlin" and wrongly associates these with the idea of perpetual differences of opinion and dramatic debates similar to those that enliven Western parliaments. Nothing of that sort takes place in the Central Committee. There is a constant struggle, but it does not take the form of parliamentary debate. It is a long-drawn-out affair involving lying in wait for years, in the course of which intrigues develop of a subtlety probably inconceivable to Western politicians. Only in the last phase, when it is desired to attach a damaging political label to the "errors" of an already beaten opponent, is eloquence resorted to (though one hesitates to use the term of the speeches written in nomenklaturists' bureaucratic jargon that these orators are content to read). Until the trap has been snapped shut, there is no public taking of sides; on the contrary, every effort is made to lull the opponent's suspicions by reiterated demonstrations of friendship.

That is why trying to deduce differences of opinion in the highest circles of the nomenklatura from differences of nuance in official speeches is not a very profitable exercise. Nuances can certainly be detected, but sometimes they are connected with the nature of the speaker's office, sometimes with the kind of audience to whom the speech is addressed. The West should accustom itself once and for all to the idea that there is nothing personal about speeches by nomenklatura leaders; they are drafted by the apparatus and officially approved by the Central Committee.

The most important prize in the struggle for power inside the Central Committee is the post of Secretary-General. As there can be only one winner, the contestants try to secure the best possible starting positions. The contestant with the best chance is neither the strongest nor the ablest. The prize usually goes to the least able and most harmless-seeming member of the Politburo. That was what Stalin seemed to be in comparison with the other members of the Politburo at the beginning of the twenties, and the same applied to Khrushchev when Stalin died (while Malenkov had the reputation of being a strong man).

After Khrushchev's downfall, Brezhnev had the reputation of being a weak provincial, and Shelepin was regarded as the strong man. In the days of elected monarchies in the Middle Ages, care was taken to seat the weakest candidate on the throne, and the princes of the nomenklatura prefer to elect their Secretary-General on the same principle.

> Where are they, the noisy and mourners?
> They are gone, and forgotten, and deadly cold
> And the silent ones are the owners
> Of the might, because silence is purest gold.[3]

As an example, let us take a look at Brezhnev's campaign against Shelepin. A great deal appeared in the Western press about the events of that time, but the essential facts are still unknown. What was Alexander Shelepin's career? At the end of the thirties he was a student at the Moscow Institute of Philosophy, Literature and History (MIFLI), which was then fashionable in the intellectual circles, and he became secretary of the MIFLI Komsomol committee. He was a model of strictness and vigilance, as was the custom at the time. When a girl student at MIFLI whom I knew lost her Komsomol membership card, Sasha Shelepin gave her a memorable dressing-down: "Do you realize what you have done?" he shouted. "You have handed your card over to the enemy. While you sit here, a traitor, a spy, a saboteur is busy infiltrating into the Komsomol central committee with the aid of your card."

It was not an enemy, but Shelepin himself, who came into this committee. When the war broke out he, as secretary of the Moscow city Komsomol committee, was given the task of selecting Komsomol members to carry out real and not imaginary espionage and sabotage behind the German lines. One of those he selected was the schoolgirl Zoya Kosmodemianskaya, who was described by her schoolfellows as an uncommunicative child who was ill-treated by her parents and hated her mother.[4] She was given the cover name of Tanya and sent on sabotage missions, but the Germans caught and hanged her in the village of Petrishchevo, near Moscow. With the noose around her neck she called out, "Stalin is with us. Stalin will come." This resulted in her becoming a national heroine.

The careers of her publicity-seeking mother and above all Shelepin himself were founded on this unhappy child's death. An acquaintance of mine was witness to the incident that determined his meteoric ascent. He happened to be in the office of N. A. Mikhailov, the first secretary of the Komsomol central committee, just when Stalin telephoned to ask the name of the comrade who had selected the girl, and when he was told, he said, "He's a good man; you must keep your eye on him." After that there was no stopping Shelepin, who nearly became Stalin's third successor.

He became in succession first secretary of the Komsomol Moscow committee, first secretary of the Komsomol central committee, president of the KGB, and finally a candidate for the Presidium (as the Politburo was called then) and secretary of the Central Committee of the CPSU. At the same time, he was a Vice-President of the Council of Ministers. He took advantage of this extremely strong position to set his sights at the post of Secretary-General.

Shelepin made careful preparations and spent years building up his following and using his influence on their behalf. He recruited only useful people, people with "prospects," as they say in nomenklatura jargon. I particularly remember the indignation of a former fellow student of his at MIFLI who one day telephoned him when he was first secretary of the Komsomol central committee. Sasha, he said, coolly told him he could not remember him and replaced the receiver. But Shelepin's memory of comrades who might be useful to him did not fail him; he put them on the Komsomol central committee and later gave some of them key positions in the KGB. When he was elected to the party Central Committee, he gave the position of president of the KGB to Semichastny, who had previously succeeded him in the position of first secretary of the Komsomol central committee; and he placed his former Komsomol comrades in the most varied positions of responsibility in the party apparatus. Young careerists of the Komsomol apparatus (nicknamed "Mao's Red Guards") started making themselves at home in high places of the nomenklatura.

That was the situation at the time of Khrushchev's downfall, which was organized by Shelepin and Semichastny. While Khrushchev was staying at the state dacha at Pitsunda they surreptitiously managed to have him cut off from the outside world, so preventing his followers from warning him about the planned palace revolution. They also organized his transport from Pitsunda to the meeting of the Presidium of the Central Committee at which he was informed of his dismissal.

Shelepin certainly had nothing but his own interests in mind in carrying out this risky operation. Let me mention a hitherto unknown fact without a knowledge of which the whole course of events is incomprehensible. When Khrushchev was overthrown, *it was not Brezhnev, but Shelepin, who was expected to become First Secretary of the Central Committee;* a resolution to this effect had already been drafted. But it was agreed that Brezhnev should be elected to the position provisionally in order to conceal the real background of the conspiracy, and it was intended that the position should subsequently revert to Shelepin.

But how were the dignitaries of the nomenklatura to guard against an excessive concentration of power in Shelepin's hands? The Central Committee plenum that deposed Khrushchev passed an unpublished resolution to the effect that the posts of First Secretary of the Central Committee and President of the Council of Ministers must no longer be held by the same person. There were plain indications that the Shelepin faction was dissatisfied with that decision.

It is doubtful that the members of the Presidium were ever willing to have Shelepin as First Secretary, for his dictatorial tendencies were familiar enough. It is impossible to avoid the impression that the members of the Presidium simply tricked him. They needed him, for without the support of the KGB, which he controlled through Semichastny, the conspiracy could not have succeeded. The promise of the post of First Secretary was the price he was paid for his part in overthrowing Khrushchev, but the Presidium of the Central Committee obviously had no intention of keeping its promise.

That is the only possible explanation of Mikoyan's anti-Shelepin speech to the Central Committee; he paternally warned them that if they elected Shelepin to the post of First Secretary, they "would have a great deal of trouble from that young man." Mikoyan, who never needlessly exposed himself and, moreover, had nothing against Shelepin personally, would never have risked Shelepin's vengeance if he had not been certain that the Presidium of the Central Committee would follow his advice.

Shelepin was promoted from nonvoting member to member of the Presidium of the Central Committee, and Semichastny became a member of the Central Committee, but Brezhnev remained First Secretary because, as we pointed out above, he was regarded by the old members of the Presidium as the lesser evil. Also, Mikoyan felt he had nothing to fear from Brezhnev; though he had long since retired and left the Politburo, the wily old man retained the privileges that went with his former office until his death, in 1978. Brezhnev was of course well aware of how precarious his position was, as the following incident reminded him; if a recording of the opening ceremony of the Twenty-third Party Congress broadcast by the Soviet radio still survives in the West, there will be no difficulty in checking it: When the name of Shelepin was announced in the course of the election to the party Presidium, thunderous applause broke out in the hall. Brezhnev's supporters then applauded just as vigorously at the announcement of each of the names that followed, even of people who were very little known. The demonstration by Shelepin's followers showed that they had not yet given up hope and that steps to deal with them must therefore be taken immediately.

Shelepin was the only member of the Politburo who as president of the steering committee of the party and the state was both secretary of the Central Committee and vice-president of the Council of Ministers. To deprive him of that privileged status, the Central Committee simply abolished the steering committee and substituted for it a "people's steering committee." Shelepin thus lost his post as vice-president of the Council of Ministers, and he was not of course elected to the presidency of the people's steering committee. But he still had the even more important post of secretary of the Central Committee, so Brezhnev made another move. The post of president of the All-Union Trade Union Federation, though it had no real power, was exalted enough to be filled by a member of the Politburo, and Shelepin was suddenly appointed to it, with the result that he had to resign his Central Committee secretaryship. Now it was obvious that he had lost the game. Brezhnev had dislodged him from his strongest positions and routed his whole clan.

Semichastny lost the presidency of the KGB and was sent to Kiev to become vice-president of the Ukrainian council of ministers. To get rid of Romanovsky, another of Shelepin's followers, who was a member of the government and former secretary of the Komsomol central committee, the department he headed was abolished (this was the state committee for cultural relations with foreign countries, which came under the Council of Ministers), and he was appointed Ambassador to Norway. I had known him since my student days and often met him. A short time before, he had ceremoniously greeted me from the back of his Chaika (he was always driven from his office to the Kremlin restaurant, though it was only five minutes' walk away), but after the abolition of his committee he came to our Institute of Economics and International Relations and waited humbly outside the door to apply to have his name entered as a candidate for a doctor's degree. We have already mentioned what happened to Reshetov, the deputy head of the Central Committee information division. Similar stories could be told about many other members of the Shelepin clan.

Shelepin himself often opposed Brezhnev in the Politburo, and that explains in particular his vote against the decision to march into Czechoslovakia. But no attempt was made to throw him out; it was said in the party apparatus that this was what Brezhnev wanted; his presence in the Politburo was a reminder to other members that if they did not do as Brezhnev wished, Shelepin would be able to fight back and take his revenge.

He was not expelled from the Politburo until Brezhnev fell ill and his retirement came within the bounds of possibility. Shelepin was finally disposed of in complete accordance with the principles of nomenklatura intrigue. He was sent on a mission to England, where he was received with completely predictable demonstrations and protests, for in his capacity as president of the KGB he had personally decorated the killer Stashinsky with the Order of the Red Banner for murdering two Ukrainian *émigré* leaders in Munich. These demonstrations, far from being denounced in the usual manner as "provocations by Fascist elements," were used as a pretext to expel Shelepin from the Politburo. Soon afterward he was dismissed from his post as president of the trade union federation and his political annihilation was complete.

In nomenklatura circles the destruction of the Shelepin faction was jestingly described as the only operation ever carried out by Brezhnev with single-minded thoroughness. We will see it in Chapter 8. When they are engaged in the struggle for power, which is the most important thing in the world to them, the political managers of the nomenklatura fight tooth and nail.

Involvement in operations of this kind is not restricted to the highest levels of the nomenklatura. Obviously the leaders entrust their secrets only to the small number of people in whom it is essential to confide. When Khrushchev was dismissed, the Central Committee staff discovered what was going on only indirectly; the extreme nervousness of the Central Committee secretaries, the simultaneous arrival of leading party officials from the federated republics and the regions, and the fact that Khrushchev's name suddenly vanished from the newspapers enabled them to draw their conclusions. But the upper crust of the nomenklatura in the provinces were in the know. Shauro, who was then secretary of the Belorussian central committee (he is now head of the cultural division of the Central Committee of the CPSU), later told us in Minsk that the Belorussian leaders knew in advance of Khrushchev's dismissal; that was how the consent of the nomenklatura to his downfall was obtained. The dictatorship of the Secretary-General is the dictatorship not of an individual but of a class that needs consensus at the top level. The collective dictatorship of the Politburo and the Secretariat and the apparently personal dictatorship of the Secretary-General are merely the two faces of the dictatorship of the nomenklatura.

5. THE POLITBURO

The Politburo dates from after 1917. The second congress of the Russian Social Democratic Workers' Party elected two leading bodies, the Central Committee and the editorial board of *Iskra*, of which the latter was the more important. *Iskra*, a clandestine journal circulated throughout Russia, was intended to be the foundation on which the party was to be built up and through which it was to be led. The role of the Central Committee was secondary, though it was intended to be the controlling body when the party's growth had been substantially completed. But when the party split into Mensheviks and Bolsheviks, Lenin had to establish a controlling agency of his own, the Bureau of the Bolshevik ("majority") committee as a counterpart to the Menshevik central committee. The Central Committee of the Bolshevik party was elected at the 1912 conference in Prague and was subsequently enlarged (it was then that Stalin was co-opted).

It was smaller than the present Politburo. The question of setting up any kind of additional organization within the framework of the Central Committee did not yet arise. A political bureau on a temporary, provisional basis was first appointed at the Central Committee meeting of October 10, 1917, which is rightly considered a historic date, for it was at that meeting that armed insurrection against the Provisional Government was decided on. The appointment of the Politburo in no way implied a transfer of political power from the Central Committee to this new body, which was established on a permanent basis at the eighth congress, in March 1919, to deal with urgent matters that required immediate attention and report to the next fortnightly meeting of the Central Committee. The Orgburo, responsible for all organizational matters, was appointed at the same time. Thus the Politburo, like the Orgburo, was originally a subsidiary body of the Central Committee and not the assembly of gods superior to it that it became under Stalin and has not ceased to be since.

In Stalin's time it consisted of cronies of the dictator, some of whom were closer to him than others. For a long time, Molotov was officially called "Stalin's closest friend and comrade-in-arms," but he lost favor after the arrest of his wife, P. S. Zhemchuzhina. Kaganovich, who was very close to Stalin, shared with Yezhov and more rarely Voroshilov the privilege of being known as "Stalin's people's commissars." Other close associates were Zhdanov and Beria, and before he died Stalin put his trust in Malenkov. When a member of the Politburo became unpopular with him, Stalin had no hesitation in having him cold-bloodedly liquidated, as happened to Voznesensky.

These patriarchal ways ceased after Stalin's death. The President of the Council of Ministers and the principal secretaries of the Central Committee are now assured of a place in the Politburo, as are the president of the KGB and the Defense and Foreign ministers, the first secretaries of the biggest federated republics (Ukraine and Kazakhstan), those of less important republics, who enjoy the privilege in turn, and finally the first secretaries of the Moscow and Leningrad party committees. This is an example of the trend toward conservative stability and the establishment of definite rules that accord with the wishes of the nomenklatura class.

Since it no longer consists of a clique of friends, but of persons selected more or less on a representative basis, relations inside the Politburo are extremely complex. Appointments to important posts are always painfully protracted, because relations of strength in the Politburo are delicately balanced; anyone appointed to these posts is generally a man of straw, a vassal of one of the members of the

Politburo. Even the speeches published on the occasion of Brezhnev's seventieth birthday alluded to his skill at "integration."

In the countries of Eastern Europe, the rules of the political game and of making a career differ from those in the West. An ambitious Western politician must attract attention and try to stand out of the ruck, since his advancement depends on the favor of as large as possible a proportion of the active members of his party or the electorate as a whole. A leading politician in Eastern Europe must stake everything on the goodwill of the Secretary-General and, if not the support of, at any rate the absence of opposition from, other leading figures. He must therefore concentrate on not standing out of the ruck, on not drawing attention to himself; he must create the impression of being innocuous and even rather dumb in the eyes of his colleagues. That was how Stalin, Khrushchev, Brezhnev, and later Chernenko rose to the top. Thus unless he is already Secretary-General, any leading political figure who distinguishes himself in any way is only putting his head in the noose; that was the fate of Trotsky, Bukharin, Kirov, Tukhachevsky, and others under Stalin, of Molotov and Marshal Zhukhov under Khrushchev, and of Shelepin under Brezhnev.

Another handicap to a Soviet leader is youth. Everyone knows that the members of the Politburo are old men. The election of a relatively young man to the Secretariat always leads to a wave of speculation in the Western press that here is the coming man. But generally it is the young and not the old who are thrown out of the Politburo. That is what happened to any number of young men, from Mukhitdinov, who from being a member of the Presidium and secretary of the Central Committee plunged to being deputy president of the Association of Consumer Cooperatives and then to being Soviet Ambassador to Syria. The same thing happened to Poliansky, who was born on November 7, 1917, the day of the October Revolution, and became a member of the Politburo and First Vice-President of the Council of Ministers, only to lose both posts and become Ambassador to Japan. Demichev, a nonvoting member of the Politburo, was transferred from the post of secretary of the Central Committee for ideological questions to the subordinate post of assistant to the Minister of Culture. Katushev was removed from the Central Committee secretariat to become one of the many vice-presidents of the Council of Ministers, then Ambassador Ryabov, another young eagle on the secretariat, had an even greater fall, to the position of deputy vice-president of the Council of Ministers. Youth is no guarantee of access to the top of the nomenklatura class; on the contrary, it is sure to rouse the mistrust of the old men who cling stubbornly to their power and privileges and reject anyone younger than they who might play a political role currently or in the future, or who shows signs of being an independent political personality.

It would be wrong to conclude from this that those who gain entry to the Politburo and remain in it are a collection of incompetents. On the contrary, they have to possess an extra qualification, that of being able to conceal their real political talents while not creating the impression of being incompetent or insufficiently qualified. Though all of them except the Secretary-General seem colorless, the members of the Politburo and the Central Committee Secretariat are very astute politicians.

How does the Politburo work?

It meets once a week, on Thursdays, in accordance with the practice initiated by Lenin. There was nothing fortuitous about the choice of that day; it enables a report of the proceedings, including the resolutions passed, to be printed on Friday. Copies are in the hands of the heads of the administrative offices concerned first thing on Monday morning, and the latter are able to see to their execution.

The form in which questions submitted for decision to the Politburo and the higher organs of the nomenklatura are drafted was laid down by Lenin, and his instructions are still in force. The following rules applied to the drafting of submissions to the Council of People's Commissars:

(a) The subject matter must be briefly stated. A simple indication (of the type *re* so-and-so) is not sufficient; the full implications of the question must clearly emerge.

(b) What action is it suggested that the Council of Commissars should take? (E.g., grant funds, pass a particular resolution, etc. The raiser of the issue must state clearly what he wants.)

(c) Does the question come within the competence of other commissars? If so, which? Any written documents?[5]

That is the form in which questions submitted to the Politburo still have to be presented.

Brief minutes are taken of Politburo and Secretariat meetings; they merely state what resolutions have been passed and give no clue to the nature of the discussion; they are the only official documents that exist about these meetings. The resolutions are put in a thick file in a dark red envelope and brought by KGB courier to all the members of the Central Committee. The latter keep them in their safes and return them with their signatures to confirm that the contents have been noted. Really secret resolutions are not circulated in this way; they are put in a so-called "special portfolio," and the minutes of the meeting mention only the number of the resolution and the administrative office that submitted it, stating that the resolution is in that portfolio. Members of the Central Committee apparatus in responsible positions have access to it (they lost that privilege after the events in Czechoslovakia in 1968). The files are then destroyed, except for a few copies that are kept in the Central Committee records and are eventually handed over to the party record office in the Central Committee Institute of Marxism-Leninism.

The use of the "special portfolio" dates back to Lenin. Bazhanov, who was Stalin's secretary and thus also secretary of the Politburo, tells us that the phrase used nowadays, "Such-and-such question . . . see special envelope," occurred in the minutes of the first meeting of the Politburo that he attended, on August 23, 1923. Not many people have seen that envelope since. Bazhanov kept it in his office safe, to which he alone had the key. "Members of the Central Committee entitled to consult these documents have first to seek Central Committee authorization; only if the reply was favorable was I allowed to let them see them. But I must mention that this never happened in my time."[6]

The use of "special portfolios" is not confined to the Central Committee; they also exist in the central committees of the parties of the federated republics and in regional and territorial committees.

When the secret archives of the nomenklatura are made available to scholars—which is the fate of all archives, however inaccessible they may be—documents of supreme importance will come to light. But none of them will be as important as the minutes of the meetings of the Politburo and the Secretariat, for in spite of their dryness they will tell us how those two bodies ruled a vast country day after day, week after week, for decades, exercising the class rule of the nomenklatura.

6. THE SECRETARIAT

The origins of the Central Committee Secretariat date back to the prerevolutionary period, when it was still a purely administrative body. In 1917 it acquired a certain independence, as it was responsible for correspondence with the various Bolshevik committees in the country, but, like the Politburo and the Orgburo, it attained the status of a permanent organ of the Central Committee only at the Eighth Congress.

At first it was a mere appendage of the Orgburo and consisted of a secretary aided by five assistants (who rapidly increased to thirty). After the Ninth Congress, in March and April 1920, it became an autonomous body; it was decided that it should consist of three members of the Central Committee, all of them permanent members of the Central Committee apparatus. It was thus that the posts of secretaries to the Central Committee were established (one of them was a "responsible secretary"); the work of the Secretariat consisted of dealing with day-to-day organizational and executive business, while the Orgburo was responsible only for the "general direction of the organizational work of the Central Committee." At that time, the Secretariat staff already numbered one hundred fifty, but it increased to six hundred in the year before the Tenth Congress.[7] In the past ten years the number of secretaries has varied between ten and twelve. The Secretary-General's responsibility covers the whole field; the other secretaries are responsible only for their special fields, e.g., party organization, ideology, national defense, industry, agriculture, the international Communist movement. Under Stalin there was also a secretary for personnel and another for state security. Nowadays personnel work is divided up among the various divisions of the Central Committee, and the Administrative Department comes under the secretary responsible for party organization. As we have already pointed out, all the members of the Politburo are of equal rank in the party hierarchy except the Secretary-General, whose primacy is admitted; in the Secretariat, however, there is a definite hierarchy.

The first dividing line is between secretaries who are also members or nonvoting members of the Politburo and those who are not; the difference is so great that they could well be called secretaries and under secretaries. Thus Mikhail A. Suslov, member of the Politburo and a

Central Committee secretary, was unquestionably a man apart, for he was the supreme authority on questions of ideology and the international Communist movement. Boris N. Ponomarev was one of the secretaries of lower rank, but as a candidate for the Politburo he was on the point of changing his status; his field is relations with Communist parties in nonsocialist countries; his colleague Konstantin Rusakov deals with the parties in the socialist countries; Mikhail Zimyanin is secretary for ideological matters; Chernenko, before becoming Secretary-General of the party Central Committee, dealt with questions concerning the party organs and organization, while Ivan V. Kapitonov and Egor Ligachev were "under secretaries" in the same field. After Suslov's death, Chernenko also took over responsibility for questions of ideology.

The differences in status among Central Committee secretaries are strictly taken into account when draft resolutions are circulated. These are not submitted to all, or even most, of the secretaries, as the approval of only five out of twelve is required for a resolution to be adopted. The general department of the Central Committee, which is responsible for circulating the drafts, first obtains the approval of the secretary in whose province it comes, and then arranges things so as to obtain the signature of at least one or two of the senior secretaries. The heads of the general department are men of great experience who know all about the likes and dislikes of the Central Committee secretaries and are thus in a position to hold up resolutions or even cause them to fail.

Each Central Committee secretary has a small secretariat of his own. The seniors have two assistants and two secretaries, and the juniors have to manage with one assistant and two secretaries. The secretaries' secretaries work every day from morning till night to cope with the day's work load. Like the secretaries' assistants, they belong to the Secretariat nomenklatura and are entitled to kremliovka rations and a vertushka. The secretaries' assistants have the rank of candidates for the position of deputy head of a Central Committee division, and the secretaries that of candidates for the post of head of a desk.

If you are walking on the pink-and-green carpet on the parquet flooring of a corridor in the Central Committee building and find yourself having to go a long way before you come to a door, it means that the office of a highly placed official is on the other side of the wall. Eventually, you reach a door upholstered in dark synthetic leather with an ordinary glass-covered nameplate bearing the initials and surname of one of the leaders of the Soviet Union. You go in and find yourself in a big antechamber, in which a young man is sitting at a light wooden desk; he is the secretary's secretary. On his left is a small table with a battery of telephones. There are two doors, one leading to the huge office of a secretary of the Central Committee and the other to the smaller office of his assistant. There is no trace of luxury in this holy of holies. The room (like everything else in the Central Committee building) is dazzlingly clean. It is austere, functional, and unrelieved by any personal touches; there are no photographs of wife or children, and no reading matter unconnected with the work of the office. On one wall there hangs a portrait of Lenin. There is a big, plain desk with a standard lamp on it, and on the left is a small table with the telephones, and there are also a long conference table and a safe. A door at the end of the room leads to a rest room with a bed, a refrigerator, a small table, and an armchair, and behind it there are a toilet and a shower. All these offices are alike in their impersonality; Lenin's office in the Kremlin is just as severely practical, but in comparison with this soulless functionalism it seems comfortable and homelike. This anonymity is not deliberate, but it is significant; it is not the omnipotent party secretary who reigns here, but the anonymous class of nomenklaturists that reign through him.

7. ARE CONFLICTS BETWEEN POLITBURO AND SECRETARIAT CONCEIVABLE?

The Politburo and the Central Committee Secretariat are twin bodies. Is conflict between them possible, or are the relations of strength so disproportionate as to put any confrontation out of the question? The answer to the last part of the question is no. The powers of the two bodies are perfectly comparable. Membership in the Politburo confers enormous privileges, but it has its Achilles' heel: it confers no office, while the Secretariat is the supreme administrative body in the nomenklaturist state.

The position of President of the Council of Ministers is certainly senior to that of any of the twelve Central Committee secretaries, but the presidium of the Council of Ministers and its President in fact hold positions junior to those of the Secretariat and its Secretary-General. Hence all the Central Committee secretaries must be classified as among the supreme leaders of the country, while that applies only to the President and the First Vice-President of the presidium of the Council of Ministers. There are a number of members of the Politburo who have less power than any Central Committee secretary. This applies, for instance, to the first secretaries of the central committees of the federated republics. That does not mean that their powers are small; they are small only in comparison with the enormous power of the Central Committee Secretariat, which controls the omnicompetent central party apparatus, to say nothing of the ministries and other administrative bodies. In practice the Secretariat exercises as much authority in all the country's affairs as the Politburo. Though it is nominally subordinate to the latter, many more levers of power are in its hands. This diarchy has naturally led to conflicts. We shall ignore differences on secondary matters and concentrate on three major clashes that have taken place.

The first was between Stalin, who was then head of the Secretariat, and Trotsky, Kamenev, Zinoviev, Bukharin, and Rykov. Commentators on this confrontation have generally merely drawn attention to the skill with which Stalin divided his opponents and then played them off against one another. This overlooks the fact that the conflict was primarily between two controlling bodies and that it ended with the victory of Stalin's Secretariat and the taking over of the Politburo by his supporters.

The second clash is less familiar; it took place in 1953–54, after Stalin's death, when his successor, G. M. Malenkov, failed to secure the post of Secretary-General. It is known to few that as early as 1952, when the prospect of Stalin's death began to loom on the horizon, his successors obtained his consent to the abolition of the post. For a long time, he had signed his name not as Secretary-General but simply as secretary of the Central Committee. He had every reason to assume that his name carried more weight than the title of Secretary-General.

After his death, this resulted in the paradoxical situation that every party committee, from those of the federated republics downward, had a first secretary, while the Central Committee of the CPSU did not have one, the object being to prevent Malenkov from slipping into Stalin's empty chair.

In the period immediately after the dictator's death, in March 1953, speeches at meetings held to commemorate him ended in the stereotyped phrase "Eternal glory to J. V. Stalin, President of the Council of Ministers of the Soviet Union and secretary of the Central Committee of the CPSU. Long live G. M. Malenkov, President of the Council of Ministers of the Soviet Union and secretary of the Central Committee of the CPSU." This was very reminiscent of *Le roi est mort, vive le roi.* Then, suddenly, the Presidium of the Central Committee relieved Malenkov of the post of secretary on the pretext that it was impossible to combine the position with that of President of the Council of Ministers, which required all the energies of the holder of the position. Any reference to the precedent created by Stalin would have been presumptuous.

In these circumstances, Malenkov tried to diminish the role of the Secretariat and the Central Committee apparatus subordinate to it. Though this was not mentioned in the press, he began by referring to himself as "presiding over" (not "president of") the Presidium of the Central Committee and claiming that the Secretariat was merely an administrative body. It was then that Khrushchev was elected to head the Secretariat, since it was believed (wrongly, as it turned out) that he did not have the qualities of a Malenkov.

The latter set up big departments under the Council of Ministers, to which he tried to have the functions of the Central Committee departments transferred. But once more it was the Secretariat that won the day. The party apparatus led by Khrushchev quickly succeeded in checkmating Malenkov and forcing him to resign, at the beginning of 1955.

The third major conflict between the Politburo and the Central Committee Secretariat took place in 1957, when the Central Committee Presidium decided, eight votes to four, to relieve Khrushchev of his office. The three secretaries who were also members of the Presidium, that is, Suslov, Furtseva, and Khrushchev himself, voted against the resolution (the fourth was Mikoyan).

The Central Committee apparatus loyal to the Secretariat, assisted by Marshal Zhukov, hurriedly organized a meeting in the Kremlin of about a hundred members of the Central Committee who constituted themselves a plenary meeting of the Central Committee and backed Khrushchev in defeating the majority of the Presidium.[8]

It would be wrong to regard these events as merely a revolt of members of the Central Committee against the Presidium; the operation was conducted by the Secretariat from beginning to end; Shepilov, the only Central Committee secretary who joined the anti-Khrushchev majority on the Presidium, suffered exemplary punishment; he was thrown out of the Secretariat and then expelled from the party and the Academy of Sciences. This was the third time the Secretariat emerged victorious from a conflict with the Politburo.

It would be wrong to conclude from these repeated successes that the Secretariat is more powerful than the Politburo. But it is safe to assert that, when it comes to the point, it is no weaker.

The independence of the Secretariat is also shown by official figures. Between the Twenty-fourth and the Twenty-fifth congresses, i.e., in five years, the Secretariat in the course of its work of checking the execution of party decisions examined "more than eighty cases," or an average of only sixteen a year, which shows that that is not its most important task. The preparation of working papers for meetings of the Politburo is obviously not its most important task either, as during the same period it met only 205 times, while the Politburo met 215 times.[9] The Politburo and the Secretariat work in tandem and jointly constitute the machinery that makes the political decisions of the nomenklatura.

8. THE CENTRAL COMMITTEE APPARATUS

Westerners think of the Soviet leaders as deliberating in the Kremlin day and night. As the omnipotent leaders of a superpower, they must be faced with an almost infinite number of decisions, and the Western observer cannot see how they can possibly also have time not only to sleep but also to attend banquets and receptions, go abroad, travel from one end of the Soviet Union to the other, spend weeks in their dachas near Moscow or on the Black Sea, love their wives and nonwives, go shooting and fishing, and enjoy all the other pleasures of the nomenklatura life. The question has not been made any easier to answer by

Svetlana Alliluyeva's description of the long drinking nights at Stalin's dacha. Political questions were certainly discussed there occasionally, but the Soviet leaders spent most of the time telling each other old stories, getting drunk, and outdoing each other in flattering their host.

Meanwhile the machinery goes on working, political decisions and actions go on being taken, and everything seems to come from this small group of old men. What sort of persons are they? Geniuses? Creatures endowed with a superhuman capacity for work?

They are neither. If, like Lenin, they tried to think of everything and do everything themselves, they would long since have died from overwork, as he did. But they take it easy and reach an advanced age in astonishingly good physical condition. The secret of this gerontological phenomenon lies in the huge nomenklatura apparatus that thinks and works for the members of the Politburo and the Secretariat. The wrong idea that Westerners have of the load of work borne by the leaders of the nomenklatura is based on a methodological error; they overlook the fact that the decisions made are only the final phase of a complicated process. The Politburo and Secretariat are only the last, though highly important, cogs in a mechanism that has taken half a century to construct and perfect.

We have already noted that the way in which Central Committee decisions are reached is not that which prevailed in Lenin's time. His *Complete Works* includes the texts of many resolutions by the Central Committee and the Council of People's Commissars that were drafted by him. There are few of these in Stalin's works and none in Khrushchev's or Brezhnev's. Lenin's office in the Kremlin is crammed with reference books, dictionaries, works on the most varied subjects, and it comes as no surprise that the present General Secretary's was quite different; it contained nothing but telephones, push buttons, a long conference table, and in a prominent position a clock.

That does not mean that the General Secretary works less than Lenin, but his work is differently organized. He does not have to look into reference books, for an aide brings him all the information he needs, carefully checked and typed out before being submitted to him in a Morocco leather file. And it is not served up raw, but in the form of a resolution, a report, or a draft of an after-dinner speech. The text is produced by specialists, and every word has been carefully weighed and scrutinized from every possible angle. Can the Secretary-General pick up a piece of paper and do all this better himself? Of course not. All he has to do is to add his signature or make the prepared speech without bothering too much about it. One of the jokes that went the rounds is very revealing: "I asked you for a ten-minute speech, and it took me twenty minutes to read through this," the Secretary-General says to his aide. The man replies nervously, "I put two drafts in your file."

Western politicians also have speeches written for them, but the system is different. A president, a prime minister, or a party leader will use a ghost with a personal style that appeals to him, while in the socialist countries the ghosting is done by the apparatus, the text passes through a large number of hands, the first draft is often by several persons, each of whom is qualified for a particular subject. I myself, for instance, regularly drafted the messages of greeting that Khrushchev sent to participants in the Pugwash conferences. They were reproduced practically unaltered in the Soviet press. Khrushchev did not use a single ghost; his speeches were drafted by various hands.

It is not my intention to cast doubt on the ability of nomenklaturist politicians. Khrushchev could not write, but he was a good speaker and a born demagogue, and his taped memoirs are of great interest. Brezhnev and Andropov are not mere bureaucrats with limited horizons; they have always shown great political skill (within the categories of real socialism, of course).

The role of the apparatus is certainly not limited to the drafting of resolutions, reports, and speeches; it also influences the formation of the leaders' views. We stressed in the previous chapter how remote the nomenklatura leaders are from ordinary life. All their information comes to them through the apparatus. The average Soviet citizen culls information about national and international affairs in dribs and drabs, while those at the summit of the nomenklatura have a flood of information from the most varied sources: from ministries, public authorities, the Central Statistical Office, Tass correspondents, satellites, KGB spies, embassies, commercial missions, the radio monitoring services, foreign Communist parties, and foreign diplomats. Nevertheless they seem dissatisfied; no ruling class in the world has such a passion for information. In spite of that, the Soviet leaders are not among the best informed in the world. Svetlana Alliluyeva tells us what the table talk was like when the Politburo met at Stalin's dacha:

Everything was the same as ever at the table—not a single new word. It was as though the outside world didn't even exist. Could it really be that all these people sitting here hadn't gleaned a single fresh or interesting piece of information from anywhere in the world that day? These people had access, after all, to more facts than anybody else, but they certainly didn't show it.[10]

The reason why the talk was so dull was certainly not to protect state secrets; the leaders of the nomenklatura class are simply not very well informed, and their curiosity is selective; they are curious only about things that affect their careers.

How is the ocean of available information reduced to the thin little trickle from which members of the Politburo and the Secretariat derive their knowledge?

No matter how important the subject may be, a strict rule applies to all the material submitted to them. The case for making a proposed decision must not take up more than two typed pages, and for background information the limit is five pages. The drafters of these papers are expected to write for an imaginary reader having no preliminary knowledge of the subject.

That is the form in which they reach the aides of the country's leaders. At this stage the material is passed through a fine-toothed comb, superfluities are eliminated, unpleasing news is glossed over, and the whole is greatly abbreviated. Thus what comes to the notice of the nomenklatura leaders is no more than a retouched précis of a résumé. It is well known, however, that they pay particular attention to the daily KGB report on the internal political situation (a similar report by the local KGB on the situation in each of the federated republics is submitted to the first secretary of the party's central committee in each of these republics.

Such a system provides a certain amount of half knowledge and an illusion of being well informed. The aged leaders cast a hurried glance at the brief, carefully chiseled phrases, every word of which is pregnant with meaning if one takes the trouble to think about them. As this trouble is not taken, the only purpose served by these papers in practice is to act as cover for their authors, for they are written in such a way as to make it impossible to criticize them later for having distorted or omitted anything. Not much of all this sticks in the memory of the nomenklaturist leaders, apart from items that rouse their interest for one reason or another, and even then the memory is vague and fragmentary.

More abundant information on any particular subject is of course available if they want it, but they don't. You can't keep abreast of everything, of course; there simply isn't time, and in any case there's no need for it, as there's no opposition and the leaders of the nomenklatura have long since become accustomed to hearing all their decisions praised to the skies by their toadying entourage and the people have been silent and resigned for a long time now.

The Central Committee apparatus exercises power by the nomenklaturist class not only by keeping the "directive organs" informed and drafting their resolutions; it also gives orders. This is extremely important, for large as is the number of decisions made by party bureaus and secretariats at all levels of the nomenklatura, it is minute in comparison with the orders given orally or by telephone. It is useless to protest to a higher agency of the party against an order given at a lower level. The class cohesion of the nomenklatura apparatus is such that a senior official will never publicly repudiate any action by a subordinate; at most he may reprimand him in the privacy of his office, while the protester can regard his career as ended, for he has exposed himself to the vengeance of the apparatus, which will not rest until it has struck him down. At the time of Stalin's purges there was still a chance that a high official of the apparatus might take advantage of a complaint to settle accounts with a rival. Nowadays nothing is to be hoped for from that quarter, for in the post-Stalin era, *esprit de corps* at the expense of the outsider has practically the force of law.

With the state apparatus, things are different; here it is possible to take a complaint to a higher level, and it may even reach the party apparatus by that route. But there can be no questioning of a decision by the party apparatus, for the latter is not an ordinary official body, but the command post of the governing class.

Could there be a displacement of the axis in the system of the dictatorship of the nomenklatura? In other words: could the historically formed core of the nomenklatura—the party apparatus, the direct continuation of "the organization of professional revolutionaries"—be replaced by another apparatus: of the security forces or the military? In short, could not the dictatorship of the nomenklatura be reborn as a military or police dictatorship?

Attempts have been made. After the Bolshevik victory in the civil war, Trotsky, who was a weak politician but a capable military leader, supported the militarization of the entire society. He insisted on the universal introduction of military discipline and the creation of "labor armies" and at the same time strongly opposed the party apparatus and "apparatchiks." Therefore the struggle between Trotsky and Stalin took on the character of a fight over who would occupy the central place in the system: the party apparatus or the military. Stalin won, and the party apparatus with him. But ever since, the party apparatus has been afflicted with the fear of "Bonapartism," the attempt by the military leaders to play a decisive political role. An expression of this fear was Stalin's eradication of Marshals Tukhachevski, Bliucher, et al., as well as Marshal Zhukov's disgrace after the end of the war.

The name of G. K. Zhukov is linked to the second attempt to establish a military dictatorship in the country. In the summer of 1957, Khrushchev, with great difficulty, managed to fight off the so-called antiparty (really, Stalinist) group in the Central Committee of the Presidium (Molotov, Malenkov, Kaganovich, and others) thanks to support from Zhukov. Having become a member of the Presidium shortly thereafter, Zhukov, apparently, decided to fill the vacuum that had formed and establish a dictatorship. There is nothing surprising about it: Zhukov was a popular war hero who was known for his cruelty and inflexible will. I had a chance to converse with him and was struck by the intense imperiousness in his gloomy expression and the fierce decisiveness of his laconic sentences.

But those are not the qualities that lead to success in the struggle for power at the top of the nomenklatura. In October 1957, Zhukov was sent on a trip, which lasted several days, to Yugoslavia and Albania; in the meantime his removal was prepared. It was announced at exactly the moment he was arriving back in Moscow. Stepping off the plane, the marshal discovered that his position as U.S.S.R. Defense Minister had been taken over by Marshal Malinovsky, and that a plenary session of the Central Committee was meeting to discuss "the Zhukov case." Although the news reports about the plenary session contained only an allusion to Zhukov's "Bonapartism," we know from Khrushchev's memoirs that Zhukov was accused of plotting a military takeover.[11]

The nomenklatura's fear of the military's taking power was shown by the fact that after Malinovsky's death—it is said—the appointment of then-secretary of the Central Committee Ustinov to the position of Defense Minister was under discussion, and it was only the vocal dissatisfaction of the high military command that led to the appointment of the diplomatic Marshal Grechko. However, Grechko's successor turned out to be Ustinov after all—the head of the Soviet defense industry. Accordingly, Brezhnev's Politburo had two marshals of the Soviet Union (Brezhnev and Ustinov) and one general of the army (Andropov) but nonetheless no one from the military.

Even if attempts to give the nomenklatura's rule the form of a military dictatorship have not met with success, the striving to establish a police dictatorship has not been as fruitless. The Yezhov terror was simply one variant of NKVD power within the state.

However, that power was limited. An influential official in Baku once told me, quite correctly, that "after the Twentieth Congress we have a false image of the Yezhov period. In reality, at every level—district, city, region, and republic—the question of repression was not decided by the NKVD head in isolation but with the first secretary of the party committee." In Chapter 9 the reader will find documents illustrating this point. But all the same, if the party apparatus felt it necessary to take preventive measures against the military takeover, the state security organs had to be constantly held in check.

The party apparatus' success was based on the nomenklatura class structure, described in Chapter 4. But the struggle between the military-industrial complex and the state security organs made the task easier. Such a struggle is characteristic, apparently, of any totalitarian system: there was one in fascist Italy and one in Nazi Germany. In that situation the party apparatus has the pleasant task of acting according to the classical maxim of "divide and conquer."

The liquidation of Marshal Tukhachevsky, Gamarnuk, Yakir, and other military leaders was the result of a complex NKVD operation. Hitler's intelligence was provided with forgeries showing Tukhachevsky's "treason"—and this information was sent back to Stalin through Czechoslovakian President Beneš. Since even more highly placed persons were liquidated in 1937 without any such proof, such a complicated move shows that the initiative was most likely not Stalin's but the NKVD's, in an attempt to convince Stalin to take measures against the military. Military leaders have never forgotten. Beria's removal was accomplished not only with the active *support* of the military, but by them directly.[12]

A new attempt to put the police and military stabilizers of the nomenklatura at the center of the class was undertaken with the completion of the Brezhnev period. This attempt is described in Chapter 8. It was preceded by the experiment with police-military rule of Jaruzelski, in Poland.

It is difficult to predict the future of such attempts to displace the axis of the nomenklatura system. We may suppose that they will continue as a manifestation of the historical aging of the nomenklatura.

9. THE KGB

No dictatorship can manage without terror. The myth of a dictatorship of an "overwhelming majority" over a "tiny minority," launched by Marx and Engels in their youthful writings and later taken up by Lenin, has never become a reality. Dictatorship is and always will be the rule of a small minority over an overwhelming majority, a minority that can consolidate its power only by intimidation and coercion, i.e., by terror.

A dictatorship is always a police state. That does not necessarily mean that the police in that state—at any rate the ordinary police—are especially efficient; the Soviet "militia," for instance, is pitifully trained and poorly equipped, which means that the country is far from being a haven of personal security. The crime rate is perhaps lower than in the United States, but higher than in Western Europe. A police state has a powerful *secret* police, whose task is to catch not thieves or murderers, but dissidents. In the Soviet Union it is a large, well-trained and well-equipped force.

Orwell correctly noted the propensity of dictatorships to euphemistic camouflage of their bloodhounds; in *Nineteen Eighty-four* the secret police are agents of the Ministry of Love. The nomenklatura does not go as far as that, but it has tried out a large number of high-sounding names for its secret police, such as Cheka, the Russian acronym for All-Russian Extraordinary Commission for the Suppression of Counterrevolution and Sabotage; GPU, or State Political Administration; NKVD, or People's Commissariat for Internal Affairs; NKGB, or People's Commissariat for State Security; MGB, or Ministry of State Security; MVD, or Ministry of the Interior; and finally KGB, or Committee for State Security. All these apply to one and the same agency, set up in December 1917, only a month after the October Revolution. Soviet citizens cope with these periodic changes by simply talking about the "organs."

Nomenklatura propaganda tirelessly exalts the humanity and generosity of these "organs." It has turned Felix Dzerzhinsky, their first head, into the fearless champion of the revolution, and statues of him are to be seen outside all KGB buildings (in Moscow as elsewhere) and the only decoration in its offices is often his portrait. I once gave a lecture to the KGB of the federated republic of Lithuania at Vilna; a huge portrait of Dzerzhinsky hung on the wall of the lecture room; it almost filled the space from the ceiling to the floor, and so striking was it that everyone in the hall felt transfixed by his piercing, suspicious gaze.

How did the "organs" (then called the Cheka) work under the command of that fearless champion? Professor Miliukov notes dispassionately that "every department of the Cheka in the provinces had favorite methods of torture. At Kharkov people were scalped and the skin of their hands pulled from the bone like a glove. At Voronezh they put their victims naked in barrels spiked on the inside, and rolled them, applied red-hot five-pointed metal stars to people's foreheads, and crowned priests with wreaths of barbed wire. At Tsaritsyn and Kamyshin limbs were amputated with a saw. At Poltava and Kremenchug impalement was used. At Ekaterinoslav people were crucified or stoned. At Odessa officers were roasted alive or dismembered. At Kiev victims were put into coffins containing decomposing corpses or were buried alive and dug up half an hour later."[13]

If that is what happened in the provinces it is easy—or difficult—to imagine what happened in the Lubianka in Moscow. In a novel published in Moscow in 1923, Ilya Ehrenburg (not the depressed and embittered Ehrenburg whom I met in the fifties, but a man who had just returned from emigration and was still intoxicated with the atmosphere of freedom he had breathed in Paris) said of the Lubianka: "They took possession of the building . . . an ordinary building. They installed themselves there, and committed such atrocities that passersby shuddered even in the heat of summer and crossed to the opposite pavement. It is sufficient to startle somebody out of his sleep by calling out 'Lubianka,' and he will lower his eyes, look at his bare feet, say good-bye to his family and, even if he is a vigorous young giant of a man, he will start sobbing like a small boy."[14] Ever since the time of Lenin and Dzerzhinsky, the Lubianka has been a place "where blood flowed, where they crushed your soul, where a mere urchin in a cap gave himself the airs of a Genghis Khan."[15]

Colonel Stepan Gavrilovich Korneyev, of the state security service (who became later known to Western scientists as head of the international relations department of the Academy of Sciences of the U.S.S.R.), one day asked me if the mere sight of the Lubianka was really enough to terrify me. "Many people say they're frightened even when they pass our building, where so many horrors are said to have taken place," he went on.

There is no doubt about the innumerable crimes that have been committed in the Lubianka. But the thugs of the old days have disappeared, and the sinister-looking types to be seen in the neighborhood in Stalin's time are to be seen no more. The coldness and fixity of their gaze betrayed the nature of their occupation. Was it a reflection of their corrupt souls or a mark of the revolting work to which they devoted themselves day and night?

In the course of 1951 I had to share a room with one of those individuals for a month in a resort near Kaliningrad (the former Königsberg). On the very first day, a friend of mine said to me, "Who is that type with the eyes of an assassin?" He had told me himself that he was an MGB investigator and worked at the Lubianka. "I'm overworked," he hoarsely complained. He was thin, hollow-chested, and chain-smoked. Also he was a person of appalling vulgarity: crude, uneducated, and with a perpetual scowl; he never read anything. Later he struck up a friendship with a woman who had the same look in her eyes, and one day he confided to me that they "worked in the same field of production." "And what do you produce? Corpses?" I felt tempted to ask him, but it would have been equivalent to suicide. When his leave was over, he went back to Moscow to resume his murderous activity as master of the life and death of those who fell into his hairy hands.

From the nomenklatura point of view these people were the "glorious Chekists," who were supposed to be examples to us all. At one time, informers were held up as examples to be followed. Refusing to inform was a punishable offense, but the nomenklatura tried to use persuasion as well as force, and wanted to make us proud of being informers. For this purpose it instituted the cult of Pavlik Morosov, a schoolboy who listened in to his kulak father's conversations and reported them to the GPU, with the result that his father was shot. After the boy's family had silenced the young hero in the only way that was open to them, monuments were erected in his honor (one of them is in Moscow), and schools and groups of pioneers were named after him. We were taught that informing was a perfectly normal action. During the great purge, schoolchildren whose parents had been arrested had to appear at Komsomol meetings. "How could you, a member of the Komsomol," they were always asked, "live under the same roof as an enemy of the people [the child's father or mother] without unmasking and denouncing him [or her] to the NKVD?"

An enormous number of books, enough to fill a library, have been written about the "organs" and the police regime in the Soviet Union. The object of what follows is to draw attention to a detail that is overlooked in most of them.

In their accounts of the crimes of the Cheka-GPU-NKVD-MGB-KGB, these authors create the impression, whether deliberately or not, that the "organs" consist of fiends possessing almost supernatural powers. That is wrong, and it was wrong even in Stalin's time, when there was more reason to believe it. P. I. Pavlovtsev, head of the personnel department of the Soviet Information Office, who had worked in the "organs" for many years, said at the beginning of the fifties, when Stalin was still alive: "The MGB is not an icon, but a Soviet state agency." Pavlovtsev's personal tastes are responsible for the icon metaphor, but his statement is correct. The KGB is a nomenklatura department; it is populated not by demons with supernatural powers, but by nomenklaturists who are neither better nor worse than those in other departments. If that was true during the great purge, it is even truer today.

Communist propaganda still depicts the staff of the KGB as proletarians defending the revolution with their horny hands. Many Westerners visualize them as brilliant degenerate intellectuals, a mixture of Sherlock Holmes and James Bond, which is equally remote from reality. The staff of the "organs" are in fact well-paid bureaucratic types who cling tenaciously to their jobs and do their best to impress their superiors with their zeal. Intellectuals who exceptionally find their way into the KGB are quickly rejected by it, or at any rate do not get very far in it.

The staff of the organs work with military precision and show unwavering obedience to their chiefs. They do not think in logical categories, but in the pseudo-psychological categories of the professional policeman. Their basic view is not to believe anything whatever that anyone says, since people can have no principles; all people want is as comfortable a life as possible, for the sake of which they are willing to do anything whatever. Hence the KGB view that dissidents are psychological deviants is put forward partly in good faith.

They are extremely conservative; their purpose in life is to prevent Soviet society from making the slightest move in the direction of liberalization. They naturally feel a secret nostalgia for the Stalin era, when they were feared by everyone, including the highest officials in the nomenklatura, the golden age when (as nomenklaturists generally put it) "order" and "authority" were not just idle words. They would not be averse to a restoration of such "order," but they do not want a resurrection of a reign of terror of the Yezhov or Beria type, which would inevitably involve bloody purges of their own ranks. They constitute one of the vital pillars of the nomenklatura ruling class; they want security, like the latter, and would like to be assured of it forever.

Do they realize they are doing dirty work? Yes, but they do not seem to feel any moral conflict as a result. They consider defense of their class supremacy and privileges to be vital, and they justify their methods by convincing themselves that all men are swine. Any remaining scruples are quenched by the cultivation of a caste spirit, a feeling of superiority to ordinary mankind, and the officially promoted myth of Chekist heroism and inflexibility in the face of the enemy, loyalty, and other S.S. virtues. Their ideology is completely summed up in Himmler's phrase "Our honor is loyalty." In the countries liberated from Fascism, honor is once more called honor.

The innumerable victims of nomenklaturist police terror are rightly pitied, but the officials of the KGB deserve pity too. Though they are untroubled by remorse, they are aware of the revulsion they inspire in their fellow citizens. In Stalin's time they proudly went on wearing their blue uniform and cap with their "honorary Chekist" badge after they retired on pension, but nowadays they try to conceal their Chekist past, and people shun them. You never meet them on social occasions, even in nomenklaturist circles. The only persons who do not avoid them are public prosecutors and magistrates.

That attitude to the "organs" is not confined to intellectuals, but is shared by the workers, as has been shown for a long time by the facetious question: Are you a man or a militiaman? (Both MVD and KGB agents are popularly known as militiamen.)

Interesting evidence of their psychological capitulation in the face of general aversion is provided by a method they use when they want to discredit someone; they simply spread the rumor that he is a KGB agent. Could there be better evidence of their inferiority complex?

The KGB is a Soviet government department, and so its work is subject to planning and it must render an account of how the plan has been carried out. Its hierarchical system is particularly complicated, but apart from that it works like any other Soviet department, with rewards, reprimands, party meetings, Komsomol meetings, successes and failures, passivity and intrigue, lack of imagination and too much of it, sycophancy—everything. But nowhere is there any trace of the infallibility and mythical astuteness attributed to it by credulous readers of the Western press.

For decades the "organs" have been accustomed to dealing ruthlessly with helpless, frightened people. All they need for this is the heavy hand that has been in uninterrupted use since Dzerzhinsky's time. Whether they would turn out to be intellectually or organizationally equipped to cope with an intelligent adversary who refused to be paralyzed by their reputation is doubtful.

Is there any assurance that the KGB will never again engage in a purge of the Yezhov type? Such a development seems unlikely, but there can be no certainty in the matter. There have been periods (such as that of the New Economic Policy, for instance) when people believed that the "organs" were becoming more moderate, but another outbreak of terror soon put an end to the illusion. This was notably the case in the period that preceded the Great Purge. Here is a statement made by a nonparty Soviet journalist to Hermann Pörzgen, correspondent of the *Frankfurter Zeitung:* "Anyone who enjoys privileges does everything possible to preserve them. The need for legal safeguards is reinforced. The GPU itself has fallen victim to that development. It used to be a completely independent, sovereign, secret police force. Now it is a normal department of state bound by law, an agency that can no longer interfere at any rate in the existence and rights of other officials."[16]

That statement could be repeated word for word today, but it dates from 1936, when the shadow of the Great Purge was beginning to loom over the country. So we prefer to refrain from repeating a prediction that has been proved wrong once already.

10. SEMICOLONIES OF THE NOMENKLATURA

So far we have been concerned with the organization of the nomenklatura dictatorship at Union level; as the U.S.S.R. is a federal state, we still have to consider the structure of the organs of power in the federated republics.

That structure is a replica of the leading agencies of the central nomenklatura, with one notable difference: there is no such clear subdivision into politburo and secretariat; instead there is a central-committee bureau that includes all the secretaries, the president of the council of ministers, and the president of the supreme soviet of the federated republic, and a few more of the most important dignitaries of the local nomenklatura. The Central Committee secretariat exists, but here it plays a less important part than in Moscow.

The governing body of a federated republic is the Central Committee bureau. It, too, meets once a week, makes decisions, appoints nomenklaturists to various offices, and regulates citizens' lives. Like their counterparts at the center, the secretaries of the central committee and their apparatus issue orders and have their vertushkas and their VČs, are protected by KGB bodyguards, live in huge flats and state dachas, use official cars, receive Central Committee pensions and special rations, and have access to special restaurants; in short, they enjoy the same privileges as their Moscow colleagues.

But Moscow is far away, and to the average citizen of a federated republic, power means the local nomenklatura. Only the few highest officeholders in the republic have access to the central nomenklatura. They are in daily touch with their superiors in Moscow, sometimes to listen to friendly (but categorical) advice, sometimes to be reprimanded; subordination is inherent in their position.

Theoretically these republics are sovereign national states that are voluntary members of the Union, from which they have the right to secede. To Communists the traditional answer to the nationality question is the right to self-determination, which has been proclaimed in all the documents of the CPSU on the subject ever since its creation. All the same, Lenin liked to say, when occasion arose, that while the right to secede was one thing, its expediency was another. The right of secession from the U.S.S.R., reaffirmed in successive constitutions (in Article 72 of the 1977 constitution), is obviously a mere fiction, for no procedure is laid down by which it could take place. Moreover, any suggestion that the republics should be granted greater autonomy—let alone secession—is frowned on as propaganda for bourgeois nationalism and is a punishable offense.

Are the national republics national states or locally administered colonies?

According to the historical record, all the Central Asian and Transcaucasian republics were colonies. In the age of the great discoveries, Muscovy had no access to warm water, so was unable to acquire a colonial empire overseas. Colonial expansion therefore followed a different course. The principal stages in the creation of the Russian Empire were the conquest of Siberia, where the local population was exterminated as methodically as the American Indians; the annexation of the backward states of Central Asia; and the conquest of the Caucasus. The creation of a colonial empire on the Eurasian mainland was a brilliant success. The empires with overseas colonies have disintegrated, while the Soviet Union has preserved intact all the colonies of czarist Russia.

The history of the other republics is more differentiated. The Baltic republics and Moldavia are in the Union as a result of military occupation. The R.S.F.S.R. (Russian Soviet Federated Socialist Republic) includes, besides Russia properly so-called, the colonized territories of Siberia, the extreme North and the Far East, as well as East Prussia (the Kaliningrad region) acquired as a consequence of the Second World War, and the Kuriles. The Ukraine and Belorussia were not colonized, but came under the sway of the princes of Muscovy at the time of the "gathering in of Russia," their population being ethnically related to the latter. But that does not imply that the national question is less acute in the Ukraine than in other republics.

Thus we see that twelve of the fifteen federated republics were acquired either by colonization or by conquest, and that more than three quarters of the territory of the R.S.F.S.R. was acquired by the same means. Thus the question is not whether the federated republics were colonies, but whether they are still colonies today. I have been many times to various federated republics, and have had a close-up view of how they are governed by their vassal nomenklaturas. This made it clear to me that the question is not easy to answer.

The first thing that strikes one is the absence of what traditionally is the chief characteristic of a colony, namely the privileged status of citizens of the home country. The Russians who live in the republics enjoy no privileges and are merely a minority against whom the hostility felt by the local populations for their nomenklatura masters in Moscow is often directed. This hostility does not of course extend to open persecution, which would inevitably lead to Moscow's intervention, not to ensure the safety of the Russian minority but to punish the hatred of nomenklatura rule that manifested itself in the guise of persecuting Russians. The life led by Russians in the national republics is, generally speaking, not very agreeable; also it is members of the local population whose careers are favored, while Russians, so far from being regarded as masters, are dependent on the local people and are in a disadvantageous position in comparison with them.

In spite of that, all the political power in the republics is exercised by Russians, but Russians of a different type; they are not expatriates, but nomenklaturists put there by the Central Committee of the CPSU, and they fill some key positions in the republic. There is an unwritten law that the second secretary of the central committee of the party in a republic must be a Russian sent by Moscow. Sometimes a Moscow nomenklaturist is appointed first secretary; Khrushchev, for instance, was sent to the Ukraine after spending many years as first secretary of the Moscow committee, and Kaganovich was his temporary successor in that position. Brezhnev was first secretary in Moldavia and in Kazakhstan. But if the first secretary is a national, the second secretary of the central committee in the republic will be a Russian.

The other secretaries of a republican central committee are generally nationals of the republic, but each of them is under the supervision of a

Russian. If, for instance, the secretary for ideology is a non-Russian, the head (or deputy head) of the central committee propaganda department will be a Russian. In nearly every republic the president of the KGB will be a Russian, and the KGB apparatus will be predominantly Russian. Also, the military command will be Russian. Non-Russians who reach high positions are generally officials who have not lived for a long time in the republic of their origin, but have become Russified, often have married a Russian woman, and have attended party higher schools in Russia or the Academy of Social Sciences of the Central Committee of the CPSU. When one meets one of these people, one feels immediately that they are really half Russian.

Are the federated republics colonies or sovereign states, then? The answer is that they are neither the one nor the other. I prefer to call them semicolonies.

In the terminology of Soviet ideologists, that phrase refers to the Third World states that are dependent on the West, but it perfectly describes the status of the Soviet federated republics: they are totally dependent countries, are hardly more than administrative units, and are integral parts of the Soviet nomenklaturist state. Their administrative personnel is mainly recruited from the nationalities, but the key positions are filled by commissars from the metropolis, and metropolitan troops are stationed on their soil. The official languages are the local language and Russian; newspapers, periodicals, and books are published in both languages, and primary and secondary education is also bilingual. These are not sovereign states.

But they are not full colonies, either, for power is basically exercised by a nomenklatura of local origin; the representatives of the Russian nomenklatura are few, though their political weight is substantial. They sensibly do their best to avoid offending the national susceptibilities. This attitude, and the discrimination against local nonnomenklaturist Russians, help to prevent the local nationality from becoming aware of its state of semicolonial dependence.

As for the nomenklaturists, they have no national feelings and are interested exclusively in their power and the privileges that flow from it. From that point of view they can be said to be real internationalists. In recent years they have begun claiming that the Soviet people represent a new kind of historical community; this is yet another way of masking the semicolonial regime imposed on the national republics.

In drawing attention to the semicolonial condition of the non-Slav republics, I do not wish to imply that there have been no successes there. On the contrary, the progress in industrialization, health, and education are obvious. These successes are most obvious in the most backward areas of Central Asia. True, daily life in the principal towns, and still more in the country, bears no resemblance to the picture painted of it by the nomenklatura. I have visited them several times, and there is a great deal of dirt, poverty, and lack of culture. The well-dressed and well-fed nomenklaturists, who stand out from the rest of the population, believe themselves to be Europeanized, while they are only Russified. But there are also hospitals, universities, theaters, libraries, and academies of science, even though they are on a modest scale. Progress in these fields is undeniable, though it would be wrong to assume that in the absence of the dictatorship of the nomenklatura these countries would have remained in the state they were in before 1917.

Do such achievements justify the regime? Consider South Africa, the most industrialized country in Africa. There are more schools, universities, and hospitals there than anywhere else in that continent. Does that justify the political regime? The same applies to the half colonies of the Soviet nomenklatura. Nearly two decades after the dismantling of the colonial system, and in spite of the factories, the mines, the national ballets, and the national choirs, the Soviet Union remains the world's last colonial empire.

11. IS THE NOMENKLATURA MARXIST?

When the wave of arrests and executions was at its height, in the autumn of 1938, Stalin took time off between signing death sentences to publish a work called *Dialectical and Historical Materialism*. In the very first paragraph of this work one notes with surprise the statement that "dialectical materialism is the world outlook of the Marxist-Leninist party," which amounts to saying that any statement made by the party is *ipso facto* historical materialism even if it departs from the theories of Marx. This simple way of propounding Marxist profundities without connection to Marx survived the Stalin cult; the dictator's work remained on the list of recommended reading on Marxism-Leninism even after the Twentieth Congress.

Marx himself lightheartedly remarked one day that he was not a Marxist, but his little joke turned out to be prophetic; to the nomenklatura, Marxism is not what Marx said or wrote, but what the party, i.e., the nomenklaturist class, says at any particular moment.

Is Soviet ideology Marxist or not? Ideas about what Marxism really is differ widely. Marx, for his part, believed it to be a scientific theory with a number of well-defined propositions. In that sense "Marxism-Leninism" of the Stalinist type is certainly not Marxism; the allegedly Marxist propaganda of the nomenklaturist class is dictated by tactical considerations and has nothing in common with any scientific theory.

An alternative view is that Marxism is the sum total of what Marx and Engels wrote in the course of their lives, from their schoolboy exercise books to their last will and testament, including marginal comments in their handwriting scribbled in the books they read. That uncritical kind of literal Marxism is not based on the essential content of Marx's theory, but on quotations that can be useful for any particular purpose.

The ideology of the Soviet nomenklatura is not Marxist even in that sense. True, it makes extensive use of quotations from the works of Marx and Engels, and employs Marxist terminology and some of Marx's ideas that suit its propaganda purposes. At the same time, it passes over in silence a whole series of Marxist principles, and some of his works are actually banned, for instance his *History of the Secret Diplomacy of the Eighteenth Century,* in which he says some exceedingly uncomplimentary things about the history of Russia.

Leninism, unlike Marxism, is not a theory or a hypothesis, but a strategy and tactics for the seizure of power decked out in Marxist slogans. Leninism is more familiar to the nomenklaturist class than Marxism is, but since the nomenklatura achieved power a long time ago now, Leninism is in a certain sense a relic of its past. The seizure of power in other countries is still on the nomenklatura program, so it is in foreign politics that it takes Leninism more seriously. But the subversive spirit of prerevolutionary Leninism is no longer appropriate to the nomenklatura policy in the U.S.S.R., so the nomenklatura has carefully eliminated it from its ideology.

As the new ruling class is anxious to conceal the existence of classes in Soviet society, the Marxist principle of the class approach to social phenomena is increasingly disappearing from Soviet ideology. The new approach is strongly marked by what Lenin called great-power chauvinism. This nomenklatura chauvinism should not be confused with Russian nationalism. The nomenklatura likes to describe everything connected with itself as Russian (and indeed it consists predominantly of Russians), but it extols Mongolian, Cuban, or Vietnamese virtues with almost equal enthusiasm. This is not socialist internationalism, for specifically Chinese, Albanian, or Yugoslav characteristics are not the subjects of comparable admiration. The chauvinism of the nomenklatura draws a sharp line not between Russian and non-Russian but between those who are subject to it and those who are not.

The Soviet press is full of chauvinist propaganda, and "Soviet patriotism" is exalted at every opportunity. To find anything similar in the Western press, one would have to go back to Hitler's Germany or Mussolini's Italy. Even the type of propaganda in those two countries closely resembled Soviet propaganda. The only difference is in vocabulary.

The basic element in official Soviet ideology is not Marxism, but the great-power chauvinism of the nomenklatura. It reflects the outlook of the déclassé careerists who have risen to the leadership of the great power—the Soviet Union.

There is a point that must be made here. This ideology assures the nomenklatura some popular support. The vitality of its chauvinism derives from the fact that it is less of a lie than the Marxist and Leninist elements in Soviet ideology. The masters of the nomenklatura are no Marxists (Marx would have turned away in disgust from the system they have established). They are not Leninists (the real Leninists were shot forty years ago in the cellars of the NKVD). But the overwhelming majority of them are Russians, and their great-power behavior and their chauvinism, with its emphasis on Russian patriotism, awaken an echo in the Russian people.

That is a factor that must not be underestimated; the Soviet nomenklatura owed its victory in the Second World War to patriotism (and to Hitler's policies). The Russian nobility, the governing class in czarist Russia, carefully isolated itself from the people, and at the same time managed to renew its links with the latter by means of pseudopatriotic ideology. The Leninists realized the advantages that the nobility drew from that maneuver, so in the years before the revolution they tried to break the ideological link between nobility and people by propagating the idea of class war and internationalism. When they secured power they, too, resorted to great-power chauvinism and passed over in silence the class problems of the society they ruled.

To sum up, the ideology of the nomenklaturist class is neither Marxist nor Leninist; it is Stalinist chauvinism. The chauvinism was erected by the feudal aristocracy, and Stalin and his heirs superimposed onto it Marxist terminology and ideas from Marx and Lenin that serve the interests of the nomenklatura.

12. XENOPHOBIA AND ANTI-SEMITISM

A corollary of this chauvinistic ideology is that the nomenklatura, while never ceasing to proclaim its internationalism, in fact cultivates its subjects' prejudices and mistrust of any individual of foreign extraction, encouraging them to regard him as suspect, as probably an enemy and a spy.

To foreign diplomats, journalists, and tourists, constant KGB surveillance results in unpleasantnesses such as being shadowed in the street and having one's telephone tapped and luggage searched in hotel bedrooms. Foreign residents in the U.S.S.R. have to put up with continual mistrust, which in Stalin's time almost inevitably resulted in catastrophe. A good example of what could happen to such unfortunates is provided by the experiences of a fellow student of mine at Moscow University. Because of his Swiss extraction he was not called up during the war. But in 1948, when he had finished his thesis (on Slavonic languages and literature), he was arrested by the MGB, tortured, and sentenced to twenty-five years' imprisonment. Eight years later, after the Twentieth Party Congress, he was released. The only explanation of this tragedy was that he had a foreign name.

Hand in hand with the xenophobia of the nomenklatura goes its anti-Semitism. At first this was camouflaged behind the slogan of the struggle against Trotskyism; later it was less effectively concealed behind that of the struggle against cosmopolitanism. Nowadays it takes the completely transparent form of the struggle against Zionism. These various labels ill conceal the inveterate anti-Semitism that the nomen-klaturists inherited from their previous social environment and perpetu-ate in their new-class community. It is good form among them to be outspokenly anti-Semitic; if one of their propagandists tries to deny it, disbelieve him, for it is a blatant lie. Nor should the slightest credence be placed in the small group of Soviet Jews whom the Central Com-mittee Secretariat sends abroad to demonstrate by their jobs that Jews in the Soviet Union have equal chances with Russians of securing ap-pointments. As a matter of fact, Jews in responsible positions are rare in the U.S.S.R.: General Dragunsky, Hero of the Soviet Union and Chairman of the Soviet "anti-Zionist Committee"; Chakovsky, editor of the *Literaturnaya Gazeta;* Professor Zivs, of the Institute of State and Law, of the Academy of Sciences; Guililov, professor at the Insti-tute of Social Sciences of the Central Committee of the CPSU; and a few others. I know several of these people; some are likable and gifted; they should not take it amiss if I say that the role they have agreed to play is a degrading one.

The anti-Semitism of the Soviet leaders seemed, strangely enough, to break out suddenly during the war with Hitler's Germany. It seemed to have leaped across from behind the German lines and infected the nomenklatura leaders. But appearances were deceptive, for the Stalinist nomenklaturists who secured jobs at all levels of the party and the administration during the Great Purge were already infected with the stubborn germ of anti-Semitism.

Kaganovich and Mekhlis, both of whom were Jews, remained mem-bers of Stalin's inner circle; Losovsky and Maisky, who were Jews too, remained deputies to Molotov, the Commissar for Foreign Affairs, but their days in these positions were numbered. The rising generation of Jews no longer had access to such heights.

As early as 1942, a secretary in the People's Commissariat for For-eign Affairs told a Jewish acquaintance of mine, with whom she lived and who wanted to marry her, that she wished to work in an Embassy abroad. As a Jew, he would not be allowed to go with her, and alto-gether to marry a Jew would only cause problems.

In the spring of 1944, when students who had just graduated from Moscow University (of whom I was one) were being vetted for political positions or for the Diplomatic Higher School, careful inquiries were made to find out whether any of us were Jewish or had Jewish antecedents. Mikhail Alexandrovich Silin, head of the personnel department of the People's Commissariat for Foreign Affairs and a future ambassador to Czechoslovakia, investigated my surname, and only when he discovered that it must originally have been an Orthodox priest's name did he say to me with an air of satisfaction: "So that's all right, then; Orthodox priests have never been Jews."

When Svetlana Stalin married Grisha Morosov, a Jew who had Russianized his name (his father still called himself Moros), Stalin was furious and refused to meet him. As soon as Svetlana divorced Morosov, Malenkov hastened to get rid of his own son-in-law Vladimir Schamberg (who was later my colleague for several years at the Institute of World Economy and International Affairs in Moscow; his eyes reflected a permanent secret sorrow at the inconstancy of fate).

Nowadays, there are hardly any Jews in the nomenklatura class. There is one in a high position, Veniamin Dymshits, a vice-president of the Council of Ministers, but there are no Jews in the Politburo, the Secretariat, or the Central Committee apparatus. Some half-Jews employed by the party apparatus claim to be Russian and have Russian names, such as Igor Sokolov and Alexander Berkov, consultants in the international department of the Central Committee. To the best of my belief, only one Jew, the gifted Lev Mendelevich, is employed in the Foreign Ministry. In the course of two decades of work for the Soviet secret service, he has deserved well of the nomenklatura.

There are said to be very few Jews in the KGB, and none in leading positions. In the federated republics and the bigger and smaller autonomous regions the picture is the same. They tell you with a knowing wink in the corridors of the Central Committee building how difficult it was to find a Jew (Shapiro) for the position of first secretary of the party regional committee of the Jewish autonomous region of Birobidzhan, and they add jestingly that Shapiro is sure to keep the job until his dying day, for no one will take the trouble to find such a rare bird all over again. The nomenklaturists allow Jews to work in the scientific field only with reluctance, but in music and journalism things are rather easier for them. Half-Jews with Russian surnames such as Arbatov and (the late) Inosemtsev reached a better position; both became members of the Academy of Sciences, directors of institutes, and members of the Central Committee, but they are exceptions. In the scientific field, the names of Jews are whenever possible excluded from lists, publication of their works is kept to a minimum, and the most varied reasons are found for refusing to allow them to go abroad, even to countries of the Eastern bloc, with the result that it is easier for a Jew to emigrate than to go abroad on a scientific mission.

To illustrate the harassment to which they are subject, let me quote from my diary for Thursday, March 4, 1971, when the following scene took place in the Central Committee department of science and education. Dramatis personae: Kuznetsov, inspector of that department, and Khromov, the chief of the historical sciences desk. The Jews involved were Mints, member of the Academy; Smirin, corresponding member of the Academy of Sciences; Davidovich, vice-president of the Soviet-East German historians' commission; Drabkin, holder of a doctorate in history and author of a big book on the German revolution of November 1918 that was also published in East Germany; Gefter, joint author and editor of a book that had been severely criticized; Melamid (alias Professor Melnikov), a specialist on West Germany who had gotten into trouble after an interview given to the German journal *Der Spiegel;* Tartakovsky, of the Institute of Marxism-Leninism; and Kremer, head of a department of the Institute of the International Workers' Movement. The non-Jews were L. N. Smirnov, president of the Supreme Court of the U.S.S.R., and Academician V. M. Khvostov, president of the Academy of Pedagogic Sciences of the U.S.S.R. and of the Soviet-East German historians' commission. At the time, I was vice-president of that commission, and I went to the Central Committee that day to submit the list of members of the commission for approval.

Here are my notes about what took place: "At 1600 hours saw Kuznetsov at the Central Committee. He took me to the new head of the history desk, Khromov. . . . He looked at the list of members of the commission and (with the exception of Mints, Smirin, and Davidovich) crossed out the names of the Jews: Drabkin because of the criticism of the Gefter volume; Melamid because of the *Spiegel* affair. He said Tartakovsky's place must be taken by Malysh, the head of his department; Kremer's frankly because of "the sensitivity of the East German comrades in national matters." He was pleased to see Smirnov's name on the list, for he had condemned Sinyavsky and Daniel. He asked me to tell all this to Khvostov within a week. Our talk to remain strictly confidential.

"I went to the March 8 celebration at the Historical Institute feeling very upset. The Jews will assume that the initiative for this came from me. I telephoned Khvostov, who immediately approved of it all."

I took these notes the same evening; they are an instant picture, not the result of subsequent reflection.

In the spring of 1949, Professor Golovenchenko had been specially appointed deputy head of the Central Committee propaganda division, to direct the campaign against "cosmopolitanism." He was a by-no-means-brilliant, but conscientious, round-faced Ukrainian who had been professor of history at the graduate school at which I was then writing my thesis. At a meeting of party activists at Podolsk, near Moscow, he said: "Look, we talk about cosmopolitanism. But what does it mean? Put simply, in workers' language, it means that all these Moseses and Abrahams want our jobs." By this time the campaign was coming to an end, and Stalin took advantage of this too frank statement to put an end to his job and send him back to our school.

The style has changed since then, and the bureaucrats of the nomenklatura no longer express themselves so crudely in public. But in private they express themselves even more freely. I have heard the theory that Jews corrupted everything in society with which they came into contact: Once a Jew has ensconced himself in a family, it is said, all its members are infected with the Jewish poison and are degraded in consequence. In this connection nomenklaturists mention without sympathy the fact that Brezhnev was married to a Jewess (but they hastened to add that he had not been living with her for a long time). They also liked recalling that Molotov had a Jewish wife.

Thus that xenophobia and anti-Semitism are even more deeply rooted in the ideology of the nomenklatura than their servile respect for the high dignitaries of the regime.

13. THE IDEOLOGICAL FRONT

The propagandists of the nomenklatura insist that the ideological struggle of real socialism against its enemies never ceases, and they talk about it in military terms: the "ideological front," the "ideological offensive," the "ideological enemy" are among the constantly recurring expressions. The ideological front is divided into economic, philosophical, historical, literary, and other sectors. The nomenklaturist class calls on the combatants on those fronts to show fighting spirit, alertness, intolerance, irreducible hatred, and other watchdog virtues.

One of the many myths current in the West about the Soviet Union is that nomenklaturist propaganda is extraordinarily effective, almost worthy of Goebbels, with the result that Soviet citizens are all convinced Bolsheviks. This is wrong. It is in fact practically impossible to find a convinced Communist in the Soviet Union. They are to be found only in nonsocialist countries. Nowadays nomenklaturist propaganda does not even take the trouble to try to make people believe what it says. Its aim is a different one, namely to make Soviet citizens understand that they must use a definite phraseology. This terminological constraint imposed on the population in general and intellectuals in particular has the following peculiarities: In the first place, Soviet propaganda no longer makes any serious attempt to persuade its readers or hearers of the correctness of its assertions and slogans, but confines itself to repeating them tirelessly with a view to engraving them in everyone's mind. Secondly, nomenklatura propaganda is inseparably connected with terror. If anyone dares to cast doubt on a propagandist claim or actually to deny it, the nomenklatura does not try to reason with or instruct him, but punishes him. The labor camp and the firing squad are not the only penalties available; the security agencies have almost unlimited powers and have full authority to make the punishment fit the "crime"; to an outsider the punishment may not seem especially severe, but to the victim it will be a heavy blow.

The object is to show not that the nomenklatura is right, but that it is necessary to agree with it. The proverb about the necessity of howling with the wolves is often heard in Soviet intellectual circles. The nomenklaturists are perfectly satisfied with this attitude, for they no longer believe in the possibility of persuading their subjects, but want them to abandon all hope of liberation from the ideological conformism imposed on them from above. Their knowing that they must howl with the wolves doesn't matter, so long as they go on howling.

The nomenklaturist class is terrified of voices other than their own reaching their subjects' ears; insidious ideas could lead to disharmony in the monotonous howling on the ideological front and persuade Soviet citizens to drop out of the chorus. So radical measures are taken to prevent this.

The Soviet citizen tunes in to a foreign radio station and hears a voice talking to him in Russian or some other national language of the Soviet Union. It is suddenly interrupted by an intolerably shrill whine similar to that made by a mechanical saw; the voice has been smothered by a jamming station. The nomenklaturists have plugged the listener's ears, but not their own. These transmissions are monitored and their contents transcribed by Tass for reproduction in a secret bulletin to be read at leisure by the nomenklatura higher-ups, to whom it is circulated. The towers of these jamming stations are to be seen in many big towns and in the capitals of the federated republics; they are expensive, for they are real transmitters with highly qualified staff, but instead of spreading information they stifle and smother human voices.

You have to travel only a few miles from Moscow or any other town where there is a jamming station for reception to be almost perfect. But it should not be concluded from this that the jamming is ineffective, for the intelligentsia are concentrated in the big towns, and are thus largely cut off from foreign broadcasts that do not suit the nomenklatura.

The jamming has been going on for thirty-five years, but the targets have varied. There was a time when all Russian-language broadcasts from abroad were jammed, and there was also a time when none of them were, with the exception of Radio Liberty and Radio Free Europe. But the Soviet radio committee was instructed to make reception of other Russian-language broadcasts as difficult as possible, so Soviet transmitters broadcast music on the same wavelength. Since August 1980, because of the Polish crisis, an overall jamming has been ordered. Nomenklaturists prefer smothering foreign broadcasts to answering them and, as the West does not protest, they do not see why they should change their ways.

14. WHAT DOES THE NOMENKLATURA THINK OF FREEDOM OF MOVEMENT?

What are you to do when you are so sickened by the dictatorship of the nomenklatura that you can no longer take pleasure in anything, neither the soughing of the wind in the birch trees, nor the waves of the Volga, nor the vast spaces of a country that stretches from the pole to the subtropics and from one ocean to the shores of the other? The commonsense answer is that you should leave.

The nomenklaturist class knows that this is what many of its subjects would like to do. What conclusion does it draw?

In Stalin's time, wanting to leave the Soviet Union was a grave crime against the security of the state. The notorious Paragraph 58 of the penal code of the R.S.F.S.R. made escape to a foreign country or a refusal to return from abroad an act of high treason. The penalty was death, or a long prison sentence, which in most instances amounted to the same thing. If a member of the armed forces deserted, the law in Stalin's time provided for long prison sentences for all the members of his family who knew of his intention to do so, and banishment for those who did not. Thus all the members of a soldier's family were hostages. In practice this law was applied to the families of all fugitives, whether military or not.

Things have changed since then, but not greatly. The law establishing the collective responsibility of a fugitive's family has been repealed. Paragraph 58 has been struck out of the penal code, but its place has been taken by Paragraph 64, under which escape abroad or refusal to return still constitutes high treason. This paragraph is in complete conflict with the international undertakings of the Soviet state deriving from the following conventions and agreements: (i) The Universal Declaration of the Rights of Man, adopted by the General Assembly of the United Nations on December 10, 1948, and in particular Article 13/2, which lays down that everyone has the right to leave every country, including his own, and to return to his own country.[17] The Soviet Union abstained from voting on this declaration, but subsequently accepted it. (ii) Article 5(d) of the International Convention on the Abolition of all Forms of Racial Discrimination, adopted by the General Assembly of the United Nations on December 31, 1965, which repeats the terms of Article 13/2 of the Universal Declaration of the Rights of Man.[18] The U.S.S.R. ratified this convention in 1969. (iii) The International Pact on Civil and Political Rights of December 16, 1966, Article 12/2 of which also states that everyone has the right to leave any country, including his own. The Soviet Union signed this pact and ratified it in 1973, and the Ukraine and Belorussia, the two federated republics represented in the United Nations, did the same. The pact came into force in March 1976.

Thus we see that the Soviet Union not only formally recognized in principle the right to freedom of movement proclaimed by the Universal Declaration of the Rights of Man, but by ratifying the convention and the pact formally committed itself to allowing its citizens the right freely to go abroad.

Moreover, so that possible restrictions on freedom of travel might be kept to a minimum, Article 12/3 of the pact lays down the precise conditions under which a signatory state may restrict that right; in particular, it specifies that no such restriction shall be imposed in the absence of legislation permitting it. No such legislation exists in the Soviet Union. On the other hand, there is also no legislation specifically guaranteeing Soviet citizens the right to leave the country. It is true that by Article 12/2 of the pact all the contracting parties are under an obligation to take the legislative and other steps necessary to guarantee the rights recognized under it.[19] But the Soviet Union is not in a hurry to take such steps.

Might it perhaps be tempted to justify its disregard of the pact by pleading the nonexistence of such legislation pending the necessary legislative action by the Supreme Soviet? This would probably take a long time, since such legislation has not been drafted in the Soviet Union (the 1977 constitution is silent on the subject of a citizen's right to leave the territory of the U.S.S.R.). But Soviet legislation prevents use of an argument of that kind. The *Principles of Civil Legislation in the U.S.S.R.* (paragraph 129) and the *Principles of Soviet Justice* declare that in the event of conflict between legislation in force in the U.S.S.R. and a commitment undertaken by the Soviet Union as a consequence of an international agreement, international law prevails. As we have just shown, the law in force is that of the international agreement quoted above: thus every Soviet citizen has the right to leave any country, including his own, the Soviet Union.

The theory is clear, but in practice the nomenklatura ignores the obligation to which it put its signature in a "spirit of détente." It controls the foreign travel of its citizens as strictly as ever. Behind the propaganda claim that it is a great good fortune to be born a Soviet citizen lies the secret nomenklatura belief that if they allowed their subjects to travel freely beyond the Soviet frontiers the country would be emptied. The existence of a huge repressive apparatus and that profound belief betray the nomenklatura's real view of the Soviet people's loyalty.

It is extremely difficult for a Soviet citizen to leave Soviet territory, whether for a few days or for good. The nomenklatura believes that every one of its subjects, whatever his age, who escapes from its control even for a minute is prepared to abandon his relatives, his friends, his home, his job, and his property to start a new life in a country free from its control. The overriding purpose of the difficult system of granting exit visas to countries outside the Eastern bloc is to prevent escape.

The problem is of course to select people who can be trusted, but the choice is not made, as might be expected, on the usual political grounds. Bitter experience has shown the nomenklatura that many of those who profess servile devotion while making a career under its aegis take the first opportunity to escape. A Central Committee official explained to me that the question of the loyalty of persons sent to capitalist countries was a very complex equation. On the one hand the factors tending to favor such a person's return had to be considered (his family, position, possessions, and privileges; his apartment, dacha, furniture; his age, lack of knowledge of foreign languages, poor chances of finding employment abroad, etc.). On the other hand were the factors which, in the eyes of the nomenklatura, stimulated the desire latent in all Soviet citizens to leave the country (difficulties at work, family or material problems, difficulties he or his relatives might have had with the nomenklatura, expatriate relatives, good prospects of finding work in the field for which he was trained, knowledge of foreign languages, etc.). This equation enables us to sketch a profile of a Soviet citizen with the best chance of being sent abroad. He is a member of the party, has been thoroughly successful in his profession, is a paterfamilias anxious about the future of his children, earns a good living, and has an apartment and a dacha. Neither he nor any of his close relatives has ever had any trouble with the Soviet security services or has been expelled from the party, he has no relatives living abroad, knows no foreign language, and has no prospects of or insufficient qualifications for finding a job in his own field.

When the nomenklatura sends a model citizen abroad it does not drop its extreme mistrust and goes on keeping him under surveillance from a distance; and it has no peace until it is certain he will come back again. In the jargon of the Soviet personnel departments, people are either "suitable for travel" *(vyezdnye)* or "unsuitable for travel" *(nevyezdnye)*. The handful of lucky ones are generally big shots and their aides; the unsuitable remainder are ordinary mortals.

It is curious to note that not a few Foreign Ministry officials are classified as unsuitable for travel; they include not only accountants, librarians, filing clerks, etc., but also members of the diplomatic service.

Persons such as we described above are not the only ones who are allowed to leave Soviet territory. It is possible to secure permission to go abroad and even to be put in the "suitable for foreign travel" category if, in the nomenklatura view, there are compelling reasons why you should return. Lev A. Artsimovich, a member of the Academy of Sciences, was allowed to go abroad, though he was not a member of the party and was well known for his critical nature. But he was a remarkable physicist, one of the fathers of the Soviet atomic bomb and a Hero of Socialist Labor, lived in a comfortable house, had a monthly salary (not including other payments) fifteen times greater than the average pay of a Soviet worker, and of course had a handsome dacha and an official car with chauffeur.

The case of the physicist Piotr Leonidovich Kapitsa, another eminent member of the Academy of Sciences, was more complex. His early years were spent in England, where he was working when he was invited to the Soviet Union to see the methods used in the physical laboratories there, but he was not allowed to return to England. Stalin hoped he would build an atomic bomb for him, and had a well-equipped physics laboratory built for him in Moscow, and a two-story villa, in which he still lives, was built for him in the big surrounding park. There was, of course, no question of allowing him to leave the country, even for an hour. Not till the beginning of the sixties did Khrushchev, after a talk with him, agree to his visiting the socialist countries. In the second half of the sixties, all due precautions having been taken, the septuagenarian was given permission to pay a short visit to Sweden. His sons Sergei and Andrei had made a career in the Academy of Sciences, and it was certain that he would return to the fold. But before he did so he had the pleasure of giving his nomenklatura warders a fright. He made an unauthorized trip to Denmark, from where he sent a telegram to the Presidium of the Academy informing them that he would be returning a little late. This must have put some of the Central Committee and KGB nomenklaturists into a cold sweat. Nevertheless their calculations turned out to be correct: the habits of a lifetime were stronger than the natural desire to get his own back for his kidnaping and his long captivity.

The difference between "suitability" and "unsuitability" for travel abroad can have consequences far more serious than having to spend your vacation in the Caucasus when you wanted to go to Finland. A refusal of permission to go to Finland may be attributed to a suspicion in higher quarters that you wanted to leave the country, i.e., are a potential traitor. The party organization and your superiors cannot turn a blind eye to this mark of distrust; people will start talking about you as a person whose loyalty is suspect, there will be no more promotions for you, and your superiors will try to get rid of you. I still remember the rumor that spread at the expense of the president of the trade-union committee of the presidium of the Academy of Sciences (his successor's name was already being bandied about) because his trips abroad took him only to socialist countries; since he never went to capitalist countries, presumably there were doubts in high places about his loyalty. In these conditions, an intriguer who wants to compromise a rival has merely to ensure that he is refused an exit visa. I have seen various methods used for this purpose, ranging from simple denunciation to the Central Committee commission for foreign travel to the most elaborate psychological maneuvers. Even if there is no reason whatever for suspicion, the nomenklatura "organs" rarely grant these visas; any excuse will do to justify a refusal. The Soviet Union, in spite of all the declarations, conventions, and pacts that are supposed to guarantee freedom of movement to its citizens, abides by the good old principle of refusing to let them go abroad.

15.   OFORMLENYE, OR HOW TO GET AN EXIT VISA

A citizen of a nonsocialist country who wants to go abroad simply picks up his identity card or passport, buys a ticket, and off he goes. In the countries of real socialism he has to obtain special permission, which is granted only at the end of a tedious process which in the Soviet Union is called *oformlenye*. The process is the same whether it is for a twenty-four-hour trip or a stay of several years. That is reasonable enough, of course, because if the object is to escape it is sufficient to cross the Soviet frontier for only a minute.

In this respect the rules in force at the Soviet Embassy in East Berlin are typical. Soviet citizens passing through East Berlin often apply for permission to visit the Western sectors of the city, but this is abruptly refused on the grounds that Central Committee authorization is necessary for such an excursion. When I arrived in East Berlin from Frankfurt in January 1968 and left my luggage at the Soviet Embassy, I asked to be taken to West Berlin for a few hours. This request caused consternation and dismay among the senior embassy officials. In their panicked anxiety about escape attempts, they were actually inclined to believe that I had returned to East Berlin from West Germany for the special purpose of dumping my luggage with them before escaping back to West Germany by way of West Berlin.

Permission to travel abroad is not granted to those citizens who just want to go. It is granted only (i) if an application to go abroad on official business is supported by the agency employing the applicant; (ii) if an organization (trade union or social organization) recommends that the applicant should be granted a tourist travel coupon or a document admitting him to a foreign rest home; (iii) if the applicant has a personal invitation from abroad.

In the first of the above instances (travel on official business), approval of a Central Committee foreign travel commission is required. In the second instance (tourism), the application has to be supported by the foreign travel commission of the applicant's town or regional committee or the central committee of a federated republic. In the third instance (private foreign travel), the visa and registration department (OVIR, part of the Internal Affairs Ministry) is responsible; actually it is under the control of the KGB. Members and nonvoting members of the Central Committee must have the approval of the Secretariat for a trip abroad.

There are some exceptions to these rules. Soldiers belonging to units of the Soviet Army stationed in the countries of the Warsaw Pact can travel throughout them with documents supplied by the Defense Ministry. Special rules apply to agents of the KGB and the Military Intelligence Service (GRU) of the Defense Ministry.

A few passports are issued with "open visas," meaning that the Central Committee has granted the holder the right for one year to pay official visits to the socialist countries or (more rarely still) any country in the world. That such passports are rare goes without saying; a mere handful of persons in the huge complex of the Academy of Sciences receive them, and officials of the Foreign and Foreign Trade ministries are only slightly luckier.*

There are three phases in the process of obtaining an exit visa: (i) the preparation of an "exit file"; (ii) examination of the file and making a decision on it; (iii) handing over the passport with exit visa, foreign exchange, and tickets.

1) The most important document needed for the exit file is a testimonial to the applicant's character somewhat on the following lines:

> Servilin, Ivan Ivanovich, born 1930, Russian, member of the CPSU, scientific assistant in the institute for various problems of the Academy of Sciences of the U.S.S.R. During his employment at the institute he has shown himself to be a highly qualified scientist specializing in the field of. . . . He is active in the party organization, leader of an agitational group, has been sent on a number of official missions abroad (list of countries visited follows, socialist countries first, capitalist countries second). Comrade Servilin is married and has two children. His political consciousness is highly developed, he is of irreproachable morality, and lives modestly in his personal life.
>
> The party committee and the trade-union committee of the institute of various problems of the Academy of Sciences of the U.S.S.R. recommend Comrade Servilin, I.I., for a scientific mission to [country] lasting [such and such a time] beginning on [expected date of departure]. This testimonial was approved by the party committee at its meeting on [date], minutes of the meeting [number].

A copy of this document has to be signed by the so-called "triangle," i.e., the head of the applicant's department, the party secretary of the department, and the trade-union organizer.

* The nomenklaturist class has been caught in its own net, for even nomenklatura bureaucrats cannot go abroad at their own sweet will. In 1969, when the German Communist Party apparatus moved from East to West Germany, I noted the satisfaction felt by leading members of the party at the prospect of acquiring West German passports and of being able to travel freely in the future; this in spite of the fact that the move obviously did not represent promotion for them, since from being members of the ruling class in the German Democratic Republic they were to be reduced to being mere officials of a small opposition party in the Federal Republic.

The certificate of good character is then submitted for confirmation to the institute party committee. It is dated, the number of the minutes of the committee meeting at which it was approved is noted on it, and it is signed by the "big triangle" (the director of the institute, the secretary of the party committee, and the president of the trade-union committee of the institute), and it is stamped with the institute stamp. The original document is then put in the applicant's file, which is kept in the personnel department.

Now the second phase begins. The file is submitted to the district committee of the CPSU, and the certificate of good character is submitted to the foreign-travel commission of the district committee, which summons Servilin for an interview. The three members of the commission subject him to a quarter of an hour of questioning on why he needs to go abroad. If he makes a good impression, they will report that they approve of his making the trip. On the strength of this, the district-committee secretary will write "approved" on the certificate of character, stamp it with the committee stamp, and add his signature. The certificate of character is then complete.

2. Two copies of a questionnaire have to be filled in. Two copies of a handwritten curriculum vitae used to be required as well.

3. A brief curriculum vitae (known as an *obyektivka)* is required, stating the essential facts about the applicant's career, with a chronological list of the educational establishments he attended, the jobs he has had, and his grade in the hierarchy.

4. A medical certificate is required, stating that the applicant is in good health and that he has been examined with a view to a journey to (country) lasting (such and such a time). To obtain this certificate he has to be examined by a number of specialists and have blood and urine tests. This certificate must be signed by his own doctor and the latter's superior (or his deputy).

5. Six photographs of the applicant are required.

6. The "directives" for the prospective traveler must be signed by the director of the institute and countersigned by the secretary of the department of the Academy of Sciences, who is a member of the Presidium of the Academy. This document is a long succession of commonplaces, saying, among other things, that the "traveler must respect the foreign-policy line of the Soviet Union and do his best to explain it," "must play an active part on the international mission" on

which he has been sent, etc. An interesting point is that the traveler must agree with the Soviet Embassy in the host country on the content of any statement made to the press or radio of that country. The instructions to delegations entrusted with important negotiations abroad are more sensible; they are countersigned by a secretary of the Central Committee. Instructions are not required for private trips abroad, but an exit tax of thirty rubles is payable if the destination is a socialist country and two hundred rubles if it is a capitalist country; and in the case of a private trip the file must include confirmation by the housing administration that the applicant lives where he says he does; it must state how long he has lived there and that his address has been reported to the police. It must also include a statement from his place of employment stating what work he does, how much he is paid, and the number of days' vacation to which he is entitled.

These documents complete the exit file. An accompanying letter is drafted by the foreign relations department of the Academy of Sciences and is signed by the chief scientific secretary of the Presidium of the Academy of Sciences. The file, together with the letter, are then sent by secret courier to the Central Committee. The second phase of the *oformlenye*, in which the matter is considered and eventually decided, now begins.

The file goes to the foreign-travel commission of the Central Committee, the hybrid organization (half Central Committee and half KGB) that we mentioned earlier. For travel to capitalist countries, the file has to be submitted forty-five days before the proposed date of departure; for socialist countries, thirty days is sufficient. If the documents are late, the chief scientific secretary has to address a special request to the commission, asking it to examine the file in spite of the delay. The Central Committee will generally accept the apology, while making it clear that this is an act of grace and favor on its part. Even in cases of extreme urgency, the time required for reaching a decision in the case of a proposed trip to a capitalist country will be about a week, because the procedure is complicated.

At the Central Committee foreign-travel commission, the file is dealt with by two officials, one of whom deals with the foreign travel of the personnel of the Academy of Sciences, while the other deals with the country to which the Academy is proposing to send its representative. The former submits the file to the Central Committee science division, and the latter submits it to one of the two international divisions of the Central Committee. If the trip is to a capitalist country, the department of the KGB that deals with the personnel questions is asked whether there is any objection to the applicant's proposed trip. If it is to a Warsaw Pact country, the KGB does not have to be consulted. Before the Berlin wall was built, the KGB's agreement was required for visits to East Germany, for in those days it was still possible to escape from there to the West.

This is another example of how nomenklaturists cover themselves when they have decisions to make; responsibility is spread so widely that in the last resort everyone, that is, no one, is responsible.

When the prospective traveler's file has been examined in both divisions, a report, either favorable or unfavorable, is drawn up. The report will be signed by both divisions jointly or, by mutual agreement, by one of them only. It is then sent to the foreign-travel commission. Meanwhile a reply will have been received from the KGB.

If both reports are favorable, the prospective traveler may be summoned for an interview. In Stalin's time everyone going abroad had to present himself for an interview at the Central Committee. A large number of persons being sent abroad would be present, and sometimes the meeting would be handled personally by Comrade Strunnikov, the deputy head of personnel for foreign countries. But there were also individual interviews with Central Committee instructors. On these occasions one had to read through and sign detailed instructions for Soviet citizens on how they were to behave abroad. These were several pages long, and most of what they said was obvious. There must be no personal relations with the local population. Vigilance is required against any provocative actions of the class enemy, and in the event of difficulties the Soviet diplomatic mission must be consulted. Some of the more remarkable details stick in one's memory. If one was traveling by train, for instance, one was told not to remain in a compartment with a foreigner of the opposite sex at night; the conductor should be asked to put one in another compartment; and in the absence of special permission there should be no contact with Communists in the country concerned and one should not attend their meetings. One was dryly informed that any infringement of these rules "would be dealt with extrajudicially," i.e., not by a court, but by the *troika*, the secret tribunal of three—which meant being sent to a concentration camp, if not an actual death sentence.

In the post-Stalin period things grew easier. The interviews were individual and were conducted in a friendly manner, and one had to attend them only if one was going abroad for the first time, or for the first time after a long interval. One was no longer threatened with severe penalties, but the instructions, which were unchanged, still had to be read through and signed.

Let us assume that all is well and that the travel commission authorizes the Academy of Sciences to send the applicant to the country concerned for the prescribed period of time. The decision is registered and given a number; an excerpt from the commission's minutes is immediately sent by KGB courier to the Academy of Sciences and the consular department of the Foreign Ministry. If the traveler is to leave immediately, the decision will also be communicated by telephone.

In any case, the decision is always made only very shortly before the time of departure. The Foreign Ministry has to apply for an exit visa and the Academy for a ticket without any assurance that they will be used. This is deliberate, for if the individual concerned intends to flee he must be allowed no time to make preparations. Soviet citizens awaiting permission to leave Soviet territory generally believe they are being watched, so they carefully avoid doing anything that they think might arouse suspicion; they do this even if they have not the slightest intention of fleeing.

Sometimes the Central Committee refuses an exit visa; the refusal is completely arbitrary and expresses the nomenklatura's contempt for those in its power. A frequently given reason is that the applicant has already been abroad this year. The agency that decided to send him abroad was of course well aware of that, as was the district party committee. So what was the point of the many hours of work devoted to dealing with his file, if the only result was to be a blunt refusal? But who would dare put such a question to the Central Committee? Everyone acts as if the decision were a revelation. Good gracious, so the man has already been abroad this year? How could we possibly not have noticed? The Central Committee apparatus does not tolerate any answering back. Anyone foolish enough to question the decision would be certain of not getting permission to leave Soviet territory for years.

Even nomenklaturists who are unquestionably "suitable for travel" can be victimized by an arbitrary decision of the Central Committee unless they are at the very top of the tree. Thus in 1970–71, when I was vice-president of the Soviet-East German historians commission, Lev N. Smirnov, who was then president of the Supreme Court of the R.S.F.S.R. (and is now president of the Supreme Court of the U.S.S.R.), was refused permission to go to East Germany for a few days on the grounds that he had already been to Sweden and there was quite enough for him to do in Moscow. All my efforts to obtain permission for him to go failed, though they were supported by the Central Committee science division. The mighty administrative division stuck to its refusal.

A similar instance occurred at the end of the sixties, when, to the general surprise, the Central Committee Secretariat rejected an application by M. D. Millionshchikov (who, as stated earlier, was first vice-president of the Academy of Sciences), who was to have gone abroad for a meeting with Western participants in the Pugwash movement. Millionshchikov, who had already sent a telegram announcing that he would be coming, was mortified by this insulting treatment and stayed away from work for several days. The refusal was not due to any suspicion that he wanted to flee to the West, nor did any consideration of high politics come into it, for Millionshchikov knew more about the Pugwash movement than the Secretariat; the explanation was simply that the higher level of the nomenklatura, as is its custom, wanted to remind one of its senior subordinates that it and no one else ruled the roost.

What happens when a favorable decision has been made? We now reach the final phase of the formalities. This, as we have seen, is necessarily very short. It includes a number of things: the handing over of the passport, with an exit visa, as well as foreign exchange and travel tickets.

As in many countries, there are three types of passport in the Soviet Union: ordinary passports, service* passports, and diplomatic passports. All three are theoretically valid for all countries, but Soviet passports are peculiar in one respect. For travel to countries of the Eastern bloc they carry the stamp of the Foreign Ministry of the R.S.F.S.R., while for travel to capitalist countries they bear that of the Foreign Ministry

* These are granted to civilians as well as military persons representing the U.S.S.R. abroad.

of the U.S.S.R. Thus if a Soviet citizen who has obtained an exit visa for Czechoslovakia, for instance, tries to cross into Austria or West Germany, the Czech police will stop him when they see the R.S.F.S.R. stamp on his passport.

As soon as information is received at the Foreign Ministry that the application has been successful, an official takes the traveler's passport from the safe (in the Soviet Union the holder of a passport does not keep it at home; the Foreign Ministry keeps it and hands it over only on his departure). By this time it will have been stamped with the entry visa of the country of destination as well as the exit visa; and it will now be sent by courier to the Academy of Sciences, where it will be handed over to the lucky recipient by the official of the foreign-relations department responsible for passports, and the recipient will have to sign for it. At the same time, the new passport holder's identity card will be taken from him and kept in a safe until his return. Members of the party or of the Komsomol have to hand over their membership cards to the Central Committee while they are away.

The prospective traveler will also be handed some strictly rationed foreign currency, the amount depending on the country of destination. If he is a member of a delegation, the secretary of the delegation will hand over the money in the aircraft. If he is on his own he will be given a money order enabling him to draw foreign currency from the Soviet Foreign Trade Bank, in Moscow. The train or air ticket has to be collected from the Academy transport department.

The traveler is kept under surveillance till the very end; he may be asked to get out of the train or aircraft at the last moment to be told that his exit visa has been canceled.

During this final phase the nomenklatura is not above laying traps, of which the following is an example. Professor Anikin, one of the most brilliant economists of the Institute of World Economy and International Relations (IMEMO), of the Academy of Sciences, was going to New York to work there for the United Nations for several years. He had been granted his visa and had his passport and air ticket, when an old schoolfellow whom he had not seen for ages appeared and asked him to buy various things for him in New York, giving him two hundred dollars for the purpose. Anikin did not like to refuse and took the money. On the eve of his departure he was summoned to the Central Committee foreign travel commission, where they casually asked him whether he had any foreign currency in his possession (which is strictly forbidden). Anikin was embarrassed. They immediately told him that they knew everything, that he had been about to break the regulations, and that in the circumstances he would not be allowed to go to the United States. A long succession of humiliating incidents followed; he was lucky to keep his post.

All these formalities, which seem to come straight from Kafka's *The Castle*, also apply to travel to Eastern-bloc countries, the only difference being that the KGB is not consulted.

For a short time in 1967 and 1968, Central Committee approval was not necessary for travel to COMECON countries, and files were dealt with by the travel commission of the Presidium of the Academy of Sciences, which was set up for the purpose. If that body gave its approval, the resolution had only to be countersigned by the State Committee for Science and Technology and the traveler could pack his bags. Though the system was still clumsy, it was more straightforward and no longer depended on the whims of a mysterious administration. But after the invasion of Czechoslovakia the new system was abolished by a decision of the Central Committee Secretariat, and applications for travel to the socialist countries were again subjected to Central Committee vetting. Personal friends in the Central Committee apparatus openly admitted that the events in Czechoslovakia were merely an excuse. The nomenklaturists put out of a job by the new arrangements were afraid of being downgraded to positions in which they would lose their vertushka and kremliovka, and they managed to persuade the Secretariat of the necessity of increased vigilance and stricter control of Soviet travelers to socialist countries whose loyalty could not be depended on.

Soviet citizens in the federated republics face even greater difficulties and dangers than the inhabitants of Moscow. It is not uncommon in Moscow to meet people who refrain from applying for an exit permit for fear of exposing themselves to the unpleasant consequences of a refusal. In the provinces, these people are more numerous; applicants' papers are not sent to Moscow, but to the central committee of the party of the republic concerned, and it is the central-committee bureau whose approval is necessary. Only when this approval has been obtained can the file be submitted to the foreign-travel commission of the CPSU Central Committee. As we pointed out above, it is the central-committee bureau of the federated republic that has the decisive voice. Few take the risk of applying to this assembly of capricious and conceited satraps for the sake of a trip abroad that would be enjoyable, but is not absolutely necessary. Rejection of an application by the local nomenklaturists would be evidence of their lack of political confidence in the applicant, and in those circumstances there would be nothing enviable about his future. It is largely for this reason that most Soviet citizens who go abroad, whether on business or as tourists, come from Moscow, though the people of that city constitute only 3 percent of the Soviet population.

Such is the actual position of Soviet citizens in regard to foreign travel. The gulf between practice and theory is wide, particularly in relation to the international commitments undertaken by the nomenklatura. In these circumstances it seems hardly fair to put desperate human beings who force an Aeroflot pilot to take them to the West on a par with terrorists who hijack and direct an aircraft to Libya or South Yemen.

16.   THE BARRICADED FRONTIER

From the Soviet citizen's earliest childhood, the nomenklatura tries to inculcate in him the belief that the imperialists are impatiently awaiting a favorable opportunity to assault him from every side, but the glorious Soviet frontier guards are perpetually on the watch and protect the frontier, preventing spies and saboteurs from infiltrating the Soviet Union.

As he grows up, however, the Soviet citizen stops believing this fairy tale and gradually begins to realize that the bolts and bars along the thousands of miles of Soviet frontier are for the purpose not of keeping out imperialists, but of keeping in Soviet citizens who want to escape from their nomenklatura masters. It has become customary to compare the Soviet frontier to the barbed-wire fence of a concentration camp; hackneyed though the comparison may be, I cannot think of a better one. The Soviet frontier is really like a concentration-camp fence. Everyone inside is assumed to be prepared to do anything for the sake of getting out, so everything possible must be done to prevent this. The

Soviet frontier differs from the Western frontiers of some of the socialist countries, which are more like frontline defenses, with fortified positions and minefields. It also differs from the Berlin wall, in not resem-
bling the wall of a prison. It is purely and simply a ring fence around a
huge concentration camp.

It makes no claim to being up to date and does not have the automatic firing devices that the East Germans have on their frontier; but
it is well equipped, and there are some technical innovations. Special
courses on the security of the international frontiers of the Soviet
Union are even given at KGB schools and at those of the Ministry of
the Interior.

No textbook on this dismal science is available to me, but let me
nevertheless try briefly to describe the equipment and security arrangements of a typical stretch of Soviet frontier. Approaching it from the
interior, there are three distinct zones:

(i) The frontier zone, i.e., the area adjacent to the frontier. Every
resident has to have a special permit, and he has a particular stamp on
his identity card. Permission has to be obtained from the militia to
enter the zone, even if only in transit. Special units of frontier troops
are responsible for security. Any unauthorized person found in the zone
is arrested, and his reasons for being there are investigated.

(ii) The fortified zone. This is about one hundred yards deep. Here is
a list of various so-called "frontier systems" to be found there:

(a) Barbed-wire entanglements supported by concrete posts covered
with a protective layer of metal. This zone is interrupted by numerous
corridors that can be opened electronically from observation posts.
When a guard telephones the post commander to ask to have a corridor opened he gives a password, which is changed daily. Posts at which
frontier guards can plug in the receiver suspended from their belts are
scattered about the neutral zone that follows the line of the frontier.
Low-voltage electric current causes the slightest contact with the
barbed wire to sound an alarm in the control post.

(b) Immediately beyond the barbed wire is a strip five or six yards
wide in which the earth is regularly turned over so that the footprints
of any fugitive would stand out distinctly.

(c) Next comes a system of concertina barbed-wire entanglements
supported on low stakes.

(d) Another "system" is concealed in the grass and brushwood, a veritable spider's web of steel loops. "Anyone who catches his foot in one of those loops falls to the ground, and when he tries to rise he is caught in another loop," as a Soviet frontier guard put it. "The harder you struggle, the more entangled you get. We had an exercise to test the system. Not one of us managed to get out of it."[20]

(iii) The neutral zone, or no-man's-land, as it is sometimes called, belongs to no one, but Soviet frontier guards, armed with submachine guns and accompanied by dogs, patrol it in pairs.

To make things even more difficult for would-be fugitives, the times of the changing of the guard and the route taken by patrols are frequently changed. In spite of their special identity card, residents in the frontier zone are not allowed into no-man's-land unless specially authorized and escorted by two armed soldiers. An order to shoot that to Westerners suggests the East German, rather than the Soviet, frontier has been in force for a long time among the Soviet frontier guards.

A frontier guard who shoots a fugitive is awarded a government medal "for valor," though shooting an unarmed man in the back with a submachine gun does not call for exceptional courage. Their political instructors tell the frontier guards the edifying story of a commander of a frontier post who managed to get away over the frontier but was "caught and shot by Soviet citizens."[21] If possible, however, fugitives are brought back alive, but it is doubtful whether or not this is to their advantage.

If, in spite of all the obstacles, the "violator of the frontier" manages to get away, it is likely that he will be pitilessly hunted down. Soviet military search parties often used to cross to West Berlin to try to catch fugitives, and during the occupation of Austria it was the same; Soviet troops were frequently sent to the Western sectors of Vienna to track down fugitives.

These manhunts are not confined to European countries under Soviet occupation. Armed "diplomatic couriers" were sent after Evdokia Petrova, the wife of a KGB "resident" (the head of the KGB in that country) who applied for political asylum in Australia. Lieutenant General P. K. Ponomarenko, Soviet Ambassador to the Netherlands, personally tried to drag into a Soviet aircraft a Russian tourist named Golub who had applied for political asylum. A lively tussle ensued, and Ponomarenko had to go back to Moscow, where he was given the chair of "illegal methods of working by Communist parties" at the Central Committee Institute of Social Sciences.

There can of course be no legal justification for hunting down fugitives outside Soviet territory. When this type of operation is carried out, the Soviet authorities bank on nonintervention by the Western authorities, expecting their tacit approval of the hunting of Soviet refugees in their national territory like runaway slaves. Sometimes this assumption turns out to be correct. Readers may still remember how the master of an American ship handed over a dissident Soviet sailor named Simas Kudirka who took refuge on his ship in international waters. Simas was promptly beaten up under the eyes of the complacent skipper and was sent to a camp in the Soviet Union. A less familiar fact is that under Soviet pressure, Finland (to say nothing of the socialist countries) hands back to the Soviet authorities fugitives who expected to be granted political asylum on its soil. The Soviet Union shows its neighbor little gratitude for this. Otto Kuusinen, who headed a so-called Finnish people's government after the Soviet attack on Finland in 1939, was not extradited to Finland, but was elected a member of the Presidium and a secretary of the Central Committee of the CPSU.

Even when Soviet pressure fails and the bloodhounds are cheated of their prey, the vengeful nomenklaturists do not give up. They use KGB agents camouflaged as diplomats to keep *émigrés* under observation, and try to discredit them by spreading slanders about them. Standardized, forged, or falsified documents devised by the KGB disinformation department are circulated for the purpose of showing that these *émigrés* are impostors or common criminals or even KGB agents, which, as I said earlier, shows how well aware the "organs" are of the reputation they enjoy.

A KGB book of wanted persons exists, naturally marked "top secret." Its long, bureaucratic title is *Alphabetical Index of Agents Employed by Foreign Espionage Services, Traitors to the Fatherland, Members of Anti-Soviet Organizations, and Other Wanted Criminals;* the names listed are not those of spies, but of persons who have escaped from the Soviet Union.

A copy of the book reached the West in 1976. It contained a list of persons considered to be "traitors to the fatherland"; they had fled abroad and been sentenced *in absentia* to long terms of imprisonment (from ten to twenty-five years) or to death. The book shows that Soviet justice still has no statute of limitations, for it included the name of Igor Guzenko, once employed in the cipher department of the Soviet Embassy in Canada, who more than thirty years before gave the Canadian authorities the names of Soviet agents who were engaged in nuclear espionage in Canada. Sentences pronounced decades ago are still in force.[22]

Several attempts have been made to carry out these sentences. Refugees have been kidnapped or murdered, and a so-called special technology *(spetstekhnika)* was developed for the purpose. In the fifties a silent electric pistol that was camouflaged as a cigarette box and fired tiny bullets poisoned with cyanide was used. Toward the end of the fifties a new model was produced, a pocket instrument with which a phial containing prussic acid could be fired in the victim's face; inhaling the fumes was sufficient to cause immediate heart failure. The fumes quickly dissipated, and if a post-mortem was held, the only possible finding would be death from natural causes. This technique made it possible to conceal the crime as well as the weapon. These triumphs of Soviet technology came to light because a KGB officer, Khokhlov, defected in 1953, rather than commit the murder required of him. Stashinsky committed two murders (1957 and 1959) and was decorated for it. Then he repented and defected in 1961. Both have been sentenced to death *in absentia,* and their names appear in the "wanted" book. One attempt to kill Khokhlov has been made already; this was at Frankfurt in September 1954, where the latest technical achievement, a radioactive poison, was used.

We know from statements made by Khokhlov and Stashinsky that the Soviet security services have a special department for political murders and kidnappings abroad. After the war it was known as the Spetsburo, then it was called Department No. 13, and then Department V. KGB agents refer to it as the "wet affairs department" *(otdel mokrykh del).* For a long time the head of this rather special agency was General Sudoplatov. He was removed from the post after Beria's downfall, but his family was not disgraced; a very attractive lady bearing the name Sudoplatova was in charge of the theatrical booking office in the Central Committee hotel for foreign guests in Plotnikov Street.

Although, at the time, these piquant details were abundantly commented on, the Western press largely overlooked the fact that for every murder there was a special resolution of the Central Committee. Sooner or later the archives of the Central Committee will be opened, and it will be extremely instructive to read the resolutions prescribing the "executions" abroad.

The Soviet frontiers are locked, bolted, and barred, and the friendly and agreeable frontier guard who examines your passport at Sheremetyevo airport is just as much part of that barrier as the killer with his prussic acid or radioactive poison or "Bulgarian umbrella." The "organs" are internal mechanisms of the lock, and it is the nomenklatura that holds the key.

We have not dealt exhaustively with the domestic policy of the nomenklatura class, but have merely drawn attention to its principal features. A great deal more could be said and many details added, but the conclusion would still be that power in the Soviet Union is the dictatorship of the nomenklatura.

NOTES

1. Lenin, *Collected Works*, Vol. 24, pp. 38–39.
2. *Pravda*, Sept. 30, 1977.
3. Alexander Galič, *Pesni*, Frankfurt, 1969, p. 9.
4. Cf. Vladimir Gusarov, *Moj papa ubil Michoelsa*, Frankfurt, 1978, p. 115.
5. Lenin, *Polnoe sobranie socinenij*, Vol. 54, p. 384.
6. Boris Baschanov, *Ich war Stalins Sekretär*, Frankfurt, 1977, p. 60.
7. E. H. Carr, *A History of Soviet Russia*, New York and London, 1951, Part I, pp. 204–205.
8. See also R. Medvedev and Zh. Medvedev, *Khrushchev: The Years in Power*, New York, 1976, pp. 76–78.
9. *Voprosy Istorii KPSS*, 1976, No. 12, pp. 33, 36.
10. Svetlana Alliluyeva, *Twenty Letters to a Friend*, New York, 1967, pp. 208–209.
11. *Khrushchev Remembers*, Vol. 2, New York, 1976, p. 11.
12. See N. Khrushchev, *Vospominanija: Izbrannye otryvki*, New York, 1979, p. 154. The English translation omits many details: See N. Khrushchev, *Khrushchev Remembers*, Vol. 1, New York, 1971, p. 362.
13. P. Milyukov, *Rossiya na perelome*, Vol. I, Paris, 1927, p. 193.
14. Ilya Ehrenburg, *Zhizn i gibel' Nikolaya Kurbova*, Moscow, 1923, p. 76.
15. Ibid., p. 8.
16. Hermann Pörzgen, *Ein Land ohne Gott*, Frankfurt, 1936, p. 70.
17. *Human Rights*. A compilation of international instruments of the United Nations, New York, 1973, p. 2.
18. Ibid., p. 25.

19. Ibid., p. 8.
20. *Posev*, 1977, No. 4, p. 37.
21. Ibid., p. 41.
22. *Posev*, 1976, No. 12, pp. 29–31, and following numbers 1977–78.

7

The Claim
to World Hegemony

The socialist world is expanding; the capitalist world is shrinking. Socialism will inevitably succeed capitalism everywhere. Such is the objective law of social development. Imperialism is powerless to check the irresistible process of emancipation. Our epoch, whose main content is the transition from capitalism to socialism, is an epoch of struggle between the two opposing social systems, an epoch of socialist and national liberation revolutions, of the breakdown of imperialism and the abolition of the colonial system, an epoch of the transition of more and more peoples to the socialist path, of the triumph of socialism and communism on a worldwide scale.

Party Program of the CPSU, Moscow, 1961

The expression "candidate for world hegemony" is familiar to every Soviet newspaper reader as a label applied to every imperialist power. It was first applied to British and French and later to German and American imperialism. Nowadays it has become so hackneyed that the Soviet reader ignores it. Nevertheless it is not totally devoid of meaning; there really is a candidate for world hegemony.

1. AN AGGRESSIVE CLASS

Nomenklatura propaganda claims that Soviet foreign policy is peaceful, because in the conditions of real socialism there are no classes or groups whose interests lie in aggression and expansionism. Soviet society consists of workers, kolkhoz peasants, and working intellectuals, and how would they benefit from aggression? That is true enough. Neither workers nor kolkhoz peasants nor intellectuals have anything to gain from aggression or expansion. But Soviet society does not consist only of those groups; as we know, it also includes the ruling, nomenklatura class.

The most important thing about that class is not property but power; the extent of that power determines the extent of its privileges, including the share of the collective property that each one of its members manages personally to appropriate. There are only two ways of increasing that share: (i) individually, by climbing as high as possible up the hierarchical ladder; (ii) collectively, by increasing "socialist property."

Anyone with firsthand knowledge of the nomenklatura knows that nothing is more important to its members than their careers. They have a highly developed sense of their common interests and are unquestionably able to act as a class; that is not the result of any lofty altruism on their part, but of the structure of the nomenklatura class as the collective possessor of both power and property.

In the domestic field the nomenklatura exploits the basic producers, and as we saw earlier, the economic system it has created is unproductive. But a substantial improvement in productivity is inconceivable without a change of system, something unacceptable, since it would interfere with the nomenklatura's unrestricted monopoly of power. It therefore aims at external expansion, the establishment of its rule over foreign countries and the exploitation of their wealth.

Before the revolution, the Leninists proclaimed that they would grant independence to all the colonies of czarist Russia, but even in Lenin's lifetime various pretexts were found for keeping them under control and then turning them into federated republics of the Soviet Union. In 1920 the Bolshevik government tried to grab Poland, and a so-called Polish Soviet government (of which Dzerzhinsky, the head of the Cheka, was a member) traveled in the Red Army baggage train. The songs of the newly formed Red Cavalry proclaimed, "We want Warsaw, we want Berlin," and Soviet writers of the time echoed them with the chorus: "We want Europe."

This first onslaught failed, and the Red Army had to retreat from Warsaw. Lenin's delegates to the Geneva conference in 1922 claimed that they were merely "merchants" and that world revolution was a secondary matter.[1] But the nomenklatura did not abandon the idea of subjecting foreign nations, and started making long-term plans. We mentioned above the primacy given to heavy industry for the purpose of building up a military potential worthy of a great power. The war machine was created against a background of propaganda, and the nomenklatura never ceased repeating that the imperialists might attack the Soviet Union at any moment.

It was not Nazi Germany that they had in mind. A study of the Soviet press in 1930 (when there was still close military cooperation between the U.S.S.R. and Germany) shows that the nomenklatura justified its armaments by the threat of a "crusade" against the Soviet Union that was apparently to be proclaimed by the Pope. Some years later Stalin was to ask jestingly how many divisions the Pope had, but in 1930 the nomenklatura pretended to believe that the Pope's moral crusade represented a serious military threat.

The real threat subsequently posed by the Third Reich did not put a brake on the nomenklatura's expansionist appetite. On the contrary, Hitler's initial successes merely stimulated it. As a result of their secret pacts with him, they succeeded in the first year of the Second World War in acquiring the western Ukraine, western Belorussia, Latvia, Lithuania, Estonia, Bessarabia, and northern Bukovina. The bards of the nomenklatura were once more able to produce triumphant hosannas. On the eve of the war (in which he was to be killed) the young poet Pavel Kogan predicted with enthusiasm:

> We shall yet reach the distant Ganges,
> Give our lives on the battlefield,
> So that from Japan to Great Britain
> May shine my country's sword and shield.

The nomenklatura empire expanded indeed. It kept the spoils that Hitler left it in return for its neutrality in the war against the Western democracies, and it got those left it by the Western democracies in return for its support in their struggle against Hitler. The democracies felt themselves under an obligation to reward the resistance put up by the nomenklatura, which in fact was doing no more than fighting to save its skin, and they did so generously.

The nomenklatura obtained East Prussia, South Sakhalin, and the Kurile Islands, and Poland, Bulgaria, Czechoslovakia, Hungary,

Romania, Yugoslavia, Albania, East Germany, eastern Austria, and North Korea were left to its control; Finland was put at its mercy. The magnitude of these gifts will be appreciated if one looks at a globe. They were given voluntarily at a time when the relation of forces did not justify them. It was not because of those territories that the cold war started, but because the Stalinist nomenklatura wanted more. East Germany was not enough; it wanted West Germany, and of course West Berlin, too; it wanted not just eastern Austria but the whole country, South Korea as well as North Korea, to say nothing of Greece, Trieste, the Dardanelles, Kars and Ardahan (in Turkey), northern Iran, China, Indochina, and even a colony in Africa, the former Italian Somaliland. Let us take another look at a globe and consider the territory the nomenklatura wanted in 1952 and compare it with that under its control ten years earlier, in 1942, when the front went around Leningrad and extended to North Caucasus by way of Moscow and Stalingrad. We shall see how much it has succeeded in swallowing. Moreover, its jaws are still gaping wide: Cuba, South Yemen, Angola, Ethiopia, Afghanistan, Vietnam, Laos, and Cambodia have joined the group of countries in which it has succeeded in establishing itself, with varying degrees of success.

Sometimes the jaws have snapped on nothing, but that has been rare. What interests us here is not so much the *results* of nomenklatura policy as its expansionism as such, for it is never absent from its consideration of foreign policy. As an example, let me quote an anecdote from Churchill's memoirs: In 1945, at a banquet given by the British at the Potsdam conference, Stalin suddenly started asking those present for their autographs. "Stalin's eyes twinkled with mirth and good humour. . . . I filled a small-sized claret glass with brandy for him and another for myself. We both drained our glasses at a stroke and gazed approvingly at one another. After a pause Stalin said: 'If you find it impossible to give us a fortified position in the Marmora, could we not have a base at Dedeagatch?' "[2] Stalin had never been interested in collecting autographs, he did not like brandy, and all this was just playacting. What he was interested in was a base for the Soviet Navy.

The nomenklatura is by its very nature an expansionist and, therefore, aggressive class. There is no mystique about its aggressiveness; it is the direct consequence of its inexhaustible thirst for power. It is a mistake to suppose that there is no class in the Soviet Union that has any interest in expansionism and aggression. There is such a class, the ruling nomenklatura.

2. THE TRADITION

I once said to Professor V. M. Khvostov, head of the Foreign Ministry archives department and a member of the Academy of Sciences: "Vladimir Mikhailovich, I understand why Soviet scholars are not allowed access to diplomatic documents later than 1917, but why are czarist diplomatic documents of the second half of the nineteenth century just as inaccessible to them?"

Khvostov answered me dryly, emphasizing every word. "Because Russian diplomacy was faced with foreign-policy problems similar to our own, and in certain instances it made decisions identical with our own. We have no interest in publicizing that." It was thus not a vague feeling on the nomenklatura's part that there might be some fortuitous resemblances between the two, but the continuation of a tradition, an actual link between the diplomacy of the nomenklatura and that of the czarist aristocracy.

Marx said things (that are never quoted in the Soviet Union) about the objectives and methods of that policy, which has survived to the present day: "Russia is decidedly a conquering nation."[3] "As to Russia's antipathy against aggrandizement, I allege the following facts from a mass of the acquisitions of Russia since Peter the Great.

The Russian frontier has advanced.

Toward Berlin, Dresden and Vienna about	700 miles
Toward Constantinople	500 "
Toward Stockholm	630 "
Toward Teheran	1,000 " "[4]

Since Marx's time, these frontiers have advanced still farther. "But the traditional manner in which Russia pursues those objects, is far from meriting that tribute of admiration paid to it by European politicians. If the success of her hereditary policy proves the weakness of the Western Powers, the stereotyped mannerism of that policy proves the intrinsic barbarism of Russia herself."[5]

In using the word barbarism Marx was carried away by his feelings, but the inference is plain; he was referring to the backwardness of feudal Russia, and by Russia he meant neither the country nor its people, but the ruling class of the time. The masters of the nomenklaturist state proclaimed at the time of their state's creation that they were going to make a complete break with the whole policy of czarist Russia, but instead they stubbornly pursued the expansionist policy of the czars.

3. FOREIGN POLICY PLANNING

A country's foreign policy is a product of its domestic policy; it is the form in which the national regime manifests itself in the international arena, something upon which Lenin insisted:

> It is fundamentally wrong, un-Marxist and unscientific, to single out "foreign policy" from policy in general, let alone counterpose foreign policy to home policy.[6]

Nomenklaturist control of the Soviet Union is unchecked by parliament or an opposition. Economic planning automatically results from the nomenklatura's economic monopoly; in the same way, foreign-policy planning follows from its political monopoly. Planning, in fact, is the great strength of the nomenklaturist foreign policy, against which parliamentary democracies cannot compete. At best, their governments can plan only until the next election. As soon as an election is over, the Western political parties begin preparing for the next. As a party's purpose is to obtain a majority and everything else is a means to this end, a strange phenomenon in the field of foreign policy may result: the governing party may opt for a vote-getting policy in lieu of one that might be advantageous to the state. This is a weakness obvious to every person coming from countries subject to the nomenklatura. There, foreign policy can be planned for the long term, without bothering about public opinion or elections. Nothing but the interests of the nomenklatura class need be taken into account.

At the end of the sixties, the Central Committee established the Department for the Planning of Foreign Policy Activities (UPVD), in the Foreign Ministry. This was to be a research institution, with highly paid expert officials, called counselors, senior counselors, and chief counselors. Foreign-policy planning departments on the Soviet model were set up in the foreign ministries of most of the East European countries. All this being said, we must not think that it is they who plan foreign policy. Professor Harry Wünsche, who was then head of the East German department, told me what their work really consisted of: "We can plan only single steps in foreign policy," he said. "Real foreign policy is not planned by us, but by the Central Committee." That applies completely to the UPVD: "Our diplomacy is subordinated to the Central Committee,"[7] Lenin himself said.

4.   AGGRESSION AS DEFENSE

Might it be possible that the nomenklatura is really concerned primarily with defense? There are perfectly serious persons in the West who believe that the Soviet leaders are morbidly obsessed with national security.

In his "oath" on Lenin's tomb Stalin said, "Lenin never regarded the Republic of Soviets as an end in itself. He always looked on it as an essential link for strengthening the revolutionary movement in the countries of the west and the east, an essential link for facilitating the victory of the working class of the whole world over capitalism. Lenin knew that this was the only right conception, both from the international standpoint and from the standpoint of preserving the Republic of Soviets itself."[8] That is why Lenin and Stalin believed that Lenin's tirelessly reiterated slogan of a "world republic of soviets" was essential to the survival of the Soviet Union.

Why does a class that believes it to be scientifically certain that its rule heralds a radiant future for the whole of mankind feel threatened by the existence of another system that it believes to be doomed? The answer is simple: Its talk about the inevitability of Communist victory on the world scale is mere propaganda for the purpose of demoralizing the West and persuading the Soviet people that all hope of change is illusory.

Nomenklatura thinking is not based on apocalyptic visions, but is severely practical. It knows very well that the standard of living in the

West is much higher than in the Soviet Union, and that the West enjoys a degree of liberty inconceivable to Soviet citizens; it also knows that its subjects know that, and that it is able to contain them only by perpetual intimidation. But it cannot count on intimidation forever and is terrified of what will happen on the day its subjects tire of living in fear.

Because the mere existence of a free and affluent West shows its subjects that the capitalist system, in spite of all its faults, provides better living conditions, the nomenklatura believes that that day might come. As this has nothing to do with any provocative attitude on the part of the West, but is a consequence of its mere existence, no amount of détente or "good conduct" on its part will cause the Soviet leaders to depart from their general line and abandon their objective of destroying the Western system. The same consideration underlies nomenklatura policy in the countries of the Third World. Lenin and Stalin expected that when colonialism had been abolished, states of the Soviet type would arise everywhere on its ruins. Reality has neither confirmed nor refuted this idea; after becoming sovereign states, the former colonies and dependent territories were faced with a choice between the "Japanese" path, leading to a society of the Western type, and the "Cuban" path, leading to a society of the Soviet type. The former turned militarist Japan into a peaceful and prosperous country experiencing giddy economic growth; the latter turned Cuba, an island of sugarcane plantations and pleasure establishments, into an economically ruined country, a bellicose power that sends its troops to conquer Africa.

The nomenklatura fears that the countries of the Third World will take the Japanese path and make the Western system even more predominant on the world scale, permitting it not only to survive but to triumph. It therefore tries to force the developing countries down the Cuban path, which explains its dogged neocolonialist expansionism in Asia, Africa, and Latin America.

Thus we see that the idea of defense is actually an inherent part of the nomenklatura's aggressiveness and is, in fact, the most dangerous element in its ruthless policy of expansion. There is nothing paradoxical about that statement. If expansionism were merely an idea, a whim of the nomenklatura, it could be dropped like any other, but since its power and privileges, and hence its existence as a class, are at stake, it cannot drop it.

The question of the best defense against the automatic aggressiveness and expansionism of the nomenklatura class is no easy one, and falls outside the scope of this book. Here we shall only try to point out how this automatism *cannot* be overcome. Trying to persuade the nomenklatura that the West is not determined to break its power and represents no threat to the real-socialist system is useless. The nomenklatura knows that the West is a danger to it. The danger is not of military attack, as the nomenklatura propaganda claims, but takes the more insidious form of spontaneous dissolution from within—which the nomenklatura never mentions. To stop being a danger in this way, the West would have to sacrifice its liberty and prosperity, everything that so advantageously distinguishes it from real socialism.

The two systems now existing in the world are incompatible; they cannot converge, for the differences between them are fundamental, and coexistence between them could be only a passing phenomenon. Coexistence, whether peaceful or not, can only take the form of conflict. Real socialism aims at the destruction of its rival, to which it attributes intentions identical with its own. That is the reality of the situation. It should not be supposed that I am on the side of advocates of the cold war; I am merely stating what the Soviet nomenklatura tirelessly repeats.

That being the case, is there any alternative to war?

5.   DO THE RUSSIANS WANT WAR?

That is the title of a song by Yevtushenko that is popular in the U.S.S.R. and is invariably included in the musical program that follows peace meetings. The answer given to the question is obviously no. The Russians don't want war, we are told, for they know only too well what it means. But the Russians are not a homogeneous entity with a unanimous will; on the one hand there is the Russian (Soviet) people, and on the other there is the Russian (Soviet) nomenklatura. With twenty million dead and ten million disabled, the people of the Soviet Union indeed know about the horrors of war, and they certainly don't want another. The war experience of the nomenklaturists, however, was quite different. They allocated to themselves tremendous privileges, in particular the agreeable one of sending others to their deaths while they were enjoying special rations, promotion, medals, and decorations and playing the part of heroes of the "Great Patriotic War." Victory, gained at the cost of appalling devastation, brought them new subjects to rule over, foreigners who were previously out of their reach, and made them the prestigious masters of a world power. No, the Russians don't want war. But can the same be said of their ruling class, the nomenklatura?

Not a few politicians in the West believe that the Soviet Government would not hesitate to plunge into a war with the West if the latter showed itself to be unyielding, and that it is therefore advisable to give way to it in everything. That kind of attitude merely emboldens the nomenklatura, which then flexes its muscles and makes bellicose noises as if it wanted a fight.

Does it want a fight? Not in the least.

In the course of visits to a wide variety of countries, I have had occasion to meet representatives of the ruling classes of those countries. None of them showed signs of particular courage, but nowhere have I met a ruling class so preoccupied with the safety of its own skin, so concerned for its own prosperity and careers, as the nomenklatura. It is difficult for me to keep from smiling when I hear horrific stories told by Westerners who persist in thinking of these bureaucrats as if they were heroes of ancient times.

It is this notion that is wrong, and Yevtushenko who is right. Neither the people nor the nomenklaturists want war. The latter are frightened of war. What worries them is not the likelihood of millions of dead (how could that be expected of the heirs of Lenin and Stalin?); they are frightened for themselves. They fear a nuclear war, but not because of the appalling loss of human lives and the risk that our civilization might be destroyed. They would be ready to pay a heavy price for victory and would be perfectly willing to send millions to their deaths (as they callously did in the Second World War), but only on certain conditions, namely the certainty of (i) not becoming casualties themselves and (ii) preserving their power intact. Now, the use of nuclear weapons can assure neither the one nor the other. The nomenklatura can obviously try to ensure its survival and that of its acolytes by the construction of antiatomic shelters (which it already does under cover of civil defense). But even if this saved their lives, these measures would not enable them to maintain themselves in power, for the whole infrastructure of that power would be destroyed and there would be no more subjects for them to rule over. If, at the end of a nuclear war, they crept out of their concrete holes to tread a devastated atomic waste carefully deactivated by their minions, their power would be at an end.

That is why they call so insistently for nuclear disarmament—their opponents', of course, not their own, and that is why they are opposed to international verification. They try to pass off their fear of nuclear war as concern for the survival of humanity.

The nomenklatura wants, not war, but victory. Its aim is to win the struggle between the two systems without fighting, and it makes a show of pugnacity for the purpose of persuading the West that communism is preferable to catastrophe, that it is better to be Red than dead. It creates the impression that it is ready to attack those who stand in its way, and that giving in to it is merely political realism.

All these threats are nothing but a bluff.

Let us consider the past actions of the nomenklatura. What countries has it attacked? (i) Poland in 1920, immediately after it became independent, making use of a border conflict; (ii) Poland again in 1939, after it had been defeated by Hitler's Germany; (iii) in 1939, tiny Finland; (iv) in 1940, the countries conceded to it by Hitler: Latvia, Lithuania, and Estonia; (v) in 1944, Bulgaria, after it had been abandoned by its allies; (vi) in 1945, Japan, immediately before its surrender; (vii) in 1956, Hungary, where a revolution was taking place; (viii) in 1968, unresisting Czechoslovakia; (ix) in 1979, Afghanistan. In other words, it has carried out plenty of invasions, but always of weak countries and after covering itself in advance. It made sure of Hitler's agreement before occupying eastern Poland, Finland, Latvia, Lithuania, and Estonia; of American and British agreement before acting against Japan and Bulgaria; and of China and other real-socialist countries before invading Hungary. The invasion of Czechoslovakia was carried out in collaboration with other countries of the Warsaw Pact, and only after making sure that there would be no military resistance. Particularly treacherous was the attack against Afghanistan.

Thus the nomenklatura attacks only the weak. And what happens when it meets resistance?

In 1920, when Poland refused to yield or to recognize the so-called Soviet government appointed by the invaders, Lenin hastened to make peace. In 1939, Latvia, Lithuania, and Estonia surrendered and were incorporated into the Soviet Union, while Finland defended itself, remained a sovereign state, and did not even become a "people's democracy." After the Second World War, an attempt was made by Moscow to seize control of Iranian Azerbaijan, but Teheran put up fierce resistance and the nomenklatura beat a retreat. They also withdrew from Greece after backing a civil war from 1944 to 1949 in the hope of turning that country into a "people's democracy." In spite of all the threats and insults flung at Tito's Yugoslavia, they made no attempt to invade that country, for they knew they would meet resistance. The blockade of Berlin in 1948 and Khrushchev's ultimatum about that city ten years later were aimed at imposing a peace treaty on the two Germanys on Soviet terms, but they were dropped when it became clear that the West was not going to give in. Whenever it meets with firm resistance, the nomenklatura withdraws. When it installed its rockets in Cuba in 1962, it took fright in the face of America's determination to defend its security, and the rockets were reembarked under the demonstrative supervision of the United States Air Force. After the invasion of Czechoslovakia by the troops of the Warsaw Pact, while some Western politicians were anxiously wondering where the Soviet divisions were going to stop, the Bucharest government, which knows the mentality of the nomenklatura only too well, let it be known that Romania would defend itself if it were invaded, and to back this statement Romanian guards demonstratively destroyed an adventurous Soviet tank. Though the Romanian military potential is not great, the nomenklatura made no attempt "to go to the aid of Romanian socialism." It left Yugoslav, to say nothing of Chinese, socialism similarly unrescued. In spite of its treaty of friendship with Hanoi, it did not give military aid to Vietnam against the Chinese punitive expedition of 1979.

And on each of these occasions there was a nervous chorus in the West saying, You're completely crazy; what is the point of trying to defend yourself? The Soviets will make a meal of you. But the nomenklatura does not make a meal of those who resist; that only applies to those who give in. Dubček, who dared not oppose the Soviet invasion, now lives the life of a persecuted little clerk. Tito stood firm, and they ended by exalting him while he was still alive and expressing deep sorrow at his death.

The nomenklatura attacks the weak and fears the strong; it kicks the timid and retreats from the resolute. It remembers the Russian proverb that Lenin quoted: If you're given, grasp; if you're beaten, run fast. The whole political wisdom of the nomenklatura as an aggressive class is based on that principle. It is ready to conquer the world if it is allowed to do so, and to extricate itself if it meets resistance.

6. PEACEFUL COEXISTENCE AND DÉTENTE

If the path to world domination on which the nomenklatura has set out is not that of war against the west, what is it? The answer is that it is "peaceful coexistence between states with different social systems."

That fear of war has led the nomenklatura to adopt the principle of peaceful coexistence is of course a good thing. But it should not be imagined that it is a guarantee of peace and harmony and idyllic international relations. The nomenklatura should be given credit for never having claimed that it was. The program of the CPSU defines peaceful coexistence as a "specific form of the class struggle in the international arena."

In speeches, books, and articles intended for the foreign public, nomenklatura politicians and ideologists try to obscure that definition. In the Lenin manner, they mention the class character of peaceful coexistence only incidentally, drowning it in a flood of verbiage about peace and friendship. A book published in Austria by the Soviet journalist Vladlen Kusnetsov, *The Policy of International Détente from the Soviet viewpoint,* is an excellent example of this. It was written in Moscow for Western consumption and has not been published in the Soviet Union.[9]

I myself met with disapproval on the part of the Soviet authorities when I wrote some articles for the West German press accurately explaining the official view of peaceful coexistence.[10] The chief purpose of the term détente is to camouflage the real meaning of "peaceful coexistence" as conceived by Lenin. Nowadays it has become so current that no one takes the trouble to think about its real meaning. The statesmen of the most varied countries insist that there is no alternative to détente but many of them would be embarrassed if they were asked to explain exactly what they mean by it. What does it mean, and how does it differ from peaceful coexistence?

The latter is defined as the form of class struggle prevailing between two conflicting systems, and that accords with Leninist theory. But détente is a deliberately vague term, not linked with the class struggle; it ignores the question of between whom and why international tension exists and how relaxation of that tension is to be achieved. The politicians who launched it are well aware that there is nothing Leninist about it, and it would not be tolerated in the Soviet or the Communist press in general if its vagueness were not deliberate. The term comes from the tactical arsenal of the international Communist movement; it belongs to the category of "programs and slogans acceptable to all democrats." The tactical principles of the movement require such programs and slogans to be launched when it is necessary to secure the cooperation of forces that would not support an openly Communist program. Points are selected from the Communist program, which, while serving the aims of the Communist leadership, can be isolated from their context in the plans of the nomenklatura and interpreted in terms of non-Communist principles (such as pacifism, for instance). They are then restated without reference to the idea of class in such a manner as to facilitate a non-Communist interpretation. That is what is meant by détente, a form intended to conceal the substance and to be taken literally by the West, causing it to relax its efforts, to regard the Communists with confidence, and to overlook the fact that peaceful coexistence does not mean harmonious understanding between friends, but confrontation between two opposing systems.

Let me repeat that détente is preferable to cold war, and that it is not détente as such to which I object, but to a misunderstanding of its meaning. I am not arguing that an end should be put to détente, but that it should be properly identified as a formula, "acceptable to all democrats," that has been substituted for that of peaceful coexistence. It is intended to conceal the fact that the latter does not imply just peace and friendship, but is a special form of the class struggle in the international arena, i.e., in the nomenklatura struggle for world hegemony.

7. THE LIMITS OF PEACEFUL COEXISTENCE

It is not surprising that strict limits are set to peaceful coexistence as so understood.

The first is ideological. The Soviet people are continually reminded that in the ideological field there can be no peaceful coexistence between the two systems. That is a limitation of great importance.

The principal aim of the ideological warfare that the nomenklatura wages against the West is certainly not to establish the superiority of real socialism by means of irrefutable arguments, for it realized long ago that it can hope to convince only small groups that for various reasons desire the collapse of the Western system and are therefore willing to accept the other side's propaganda at its face value. The object is to maintain the combativeness of the nomenklatura's subjects and the Communists of the whole world at a high level by keeping the capitalist bogey continually before their eyes. This unceasing anti-Western propaganda ensures that both foreign Communists and their own people do not take talk of peace and friendship with the West seriously, but realize that the West is the enemy and that professing friendship with it is a tactical maneuver. In the nomenklatura's own words, peaceful coexistence does not reduce the intensity of the ideological struggle. The nomenklatura believes this state of ideological mobilization to be essential, for it still remembers the mortifying setback of the winter of 1939–40, when it launched the Soviet Army against Finland without ideological preparation, starting a war that the troops did not understand, for in the preceding months there had been talk of a Finnish-Soviet pact of mutual assistance. Similarly the lack of anti-Fascist propaganda between the autumn of 1939 and the German invasion on June 22, 1941, had serious consequences in the first phase of the war with Hitler's Germany.

One may ask, What is the point of such propaganda if the Soviet nomenklatura does not intend to make war on the West? It is certainly afraid of a war, but only because of the present balance of power: if it could change the latter so much to its own advantage that it could attack without risk, it would cease to be afraid and would attack. By excluding ideology from peaceful coexistence, the nomenklatura clearly shows that it seriously envisages the possibility of war on the West. Two other limitations reinforce that conclusion: its refusal to include in peaceful coexistence struggles for national liberation and for social emancipation.

In regard to the former, the nomenklatura claims that the armed conflicts to which it gives military support in the Third World do not conflict with détente. Now, its purpose in these confrontations is to strengthen its position by shifting the balance of power in favor of the socialist countries. Not extending the idea of peaceful coexistence to struggles for national liberation thus amounts to encouraging the West to continue with détente, while at the same time trying to upset the balance of power to the latter's disadvantage. As for struggles for social emancipation, the Soviet Union has not yet thought fit to explain what it means by the term. It seems to refer to social conflicts in the West. If it is taken literally, it apparently means that the nomenklatura reserves the right to intervene militarily to support such struggles.

Thus everything depends on the balance of power, for the nomenklatura itself admits that peaceful coexistence is a function of the relations of strength between the two systems.

8. THE INTERNATIONAL BALANCE OF POWER

Since peaceful coexistence is a form of the class struggle, the balance of power must play a decisive part in it, as in all struggles.

In the West, what generally springs to mind in this connection is the relative strength of the armed forces of NATO and those of the Warsaw Pact. The nomenklatura takes a wider view; it takes into account the economic, political, military, structural, and moral strength of the two parties. Thus the nomenklatura has substituted the idea of global class strength for that of purely military strength.

That is more realistic than the Western approach, even when applied to military matters. In spite of its overwhelming military superiority, the United States actually managed to lose the war in Vietnam—to the pleasant surprise of the Soviet nomenklatura. On the other hand, it is impossible not to have doubts about the extent to which the troops of the "people's democracies" can be regarded as increasing the strength of the Soviet divisions stationed on their territory. It should not be forgotten that one of the vital functions of the latter is to keep an eye on allies who, in the last resort, cannot be relied on.

Newcomers from Eastern Europe note with surprise the learned speculations by journalists and politicians in the West on whether the Soviet Union does or does not aim at establishing its superiority. Those newcomers are puzzled by other questions. Why, they want to know, have Westerners not yet realized what every Soviet schoolboy knows, namely, that the U.S.S.R. obviously wants to overtake the West in every field? How can they be so blind as not yet to have realized that that has been its officially proclaimed objective for more than sixty five years? Those questions are indeed difficult to answer.

The constantly pursued, deliberate aim of the Soviet ruling class, and the ruling class of its satellites, is to strengthen their position to the maximum possible extent in the military and all other fields and to weaken the West to the maximum possible extent. They do not always succeed, far from it; the nomenklatura is hampered in the pursuit of its aims by the clumsiness and poor productivity of the socialist economic system; and the discontent of its subjects is an additional handicap. In short, its efforts are ill rewarded. But, as these efforts persist, in the course of decades it has scored successes. Though the balance of power is not what Soviet propaganda claims it is, since Lenin's time it has unquestionably shifted to the nomenklatura's advantage.

The nomenklatura tries to persuade the world that there is a kind of mystic, irreversible law by virtue of which the balance of power in the world is constantly shifting in favor of the socialist camp. That is a product of the imagination; there is no such law, and the balance of power fluctuates. It reached a high point for the nomenklatura at the end of the fifties, during the first phase of the Khrushchev government. Stalin's death and the progressive abandonment of the worst of his methods led to temporary popular support for the Soviet regime, the alliance with China was still in existence, the international Communist movement was still monolithic, and the nomenklatura had military successes to its credit—in particular, it acquired intercontinental ballistic missiles before the United States. Moreover, further favorable developments seemed to be in store. The nomenklatura felt entitled to expect that the imminent breakup of the colonial system would lead to the establishment of more "people's democracies," and it looked forward to desirable developments in Europe also, i.e., to Spain, Portugal, and Greece becoming such "democracies." The balance of power nevertheless developed to its disadvantage, not compensated for by the intensification of arms manufacture.

But the West should not believe there is an opposite historical law favoring a miraculous growth of its own power and a corresponding weakening of the Soviet Union without its making the slightest effort. No such law exists. In every balance of forces, as in every competition, the advantage goes to the side that makes fewer mistakes and shows more foresight and resolution while having larger reserves to draw on and knowing better how to use them. Taking into account the disadvantages inherent in socialist society and the policy of the nomenklatura, the West should have no difficulty in winning such a competition. But it is hampered by weaknesses inherent in Western society.

9. VICTORY OF REAL SOCIALISM ON A WORLD SCALE

That is the declared aim of the nomenklatura. It follows Lenin's principle of seeking out the "weakest link in the chain of world capitalism" and then concentrating its attack on it. It tries its chances in many parts of the world, but most methodically, though cautiously, in Europe. Europe is not the weakest link in the chain, but (still according to Lenin) "it is the particular link in the chain which you must grasp with all your might in order to hold the whole chain."[11]

The socialist countries are now responsible for more than a third of the world's industrial production. This proportion would be greatly increased if Western Europe came under the control of the nomenklatura, which would then have an absolute preponderance in that most important indicator, as well as in skilled labor and scientific potential.

If Europe went over to the nomenklaturist camp, the balance would swing decisively in the latter's favor; Europe really is the most important link in the chain. Americans who talk of barricading themselves in "fortress America" in case of need should ask themselves what prospects the United States would have, confronted by a nomenklatura that was mistress of the Eurasian-African landmass and conducted intensive subversive activity in the Latin American countries and the United

States itself. In the present balance of power in the world, Western Europe, with its wealth, its industry, and its skilled work force, is of vital importance in answering the question, put by Lenin, of who will beat whom.

That does not prevent the nomenklatura from being simultaneously on the political offensive elsewhere in the world. The vast expanses of the countries of the Third World lie to the south of Europe and the Soviet republics of Central Asia, and the nomenklatura is on the offensive there, too, the object being to install regimes of the "people's democracy" type (in the Third World, Moscow calls them "national democracies"). If that is not yet possible, it hopes to resort to a "Finlandization" adapted to Afro-Asian conditions.

In the course of recent years Africa has seen the birth of a number of governments of the "people's democracy" type. Third World countries have to fulfill few conditions to have their "socialist orientation" accepted by the nomenklatura. Neither the level of development of the productive forces nor the size of the working class nor even its existence is taken into account; the criterion is whether the regime adopts a pro-Western or a pro-Soviet stance. That is the explanation of the frequent changes in nomenklatura propaganda descriptions of Third World regimes. For a long time the Ba'athist Party, in power in Syria, was denounced as Fascist, while at the time of writing it is described as revolutionary-democratic. Colonel Qaddafi used to be denounced as a Fascist reactionary and a religious fanatic, but has since been transmogrified into a progressive socialist statesman. On the other hand Modibo Keita and Sékou Touré, who used to be the object of fulsome praise as socialists or even almost Communists, have been regarded very skeptically by Soviet propaganda since Chinese influence grew strong in Mali and Guinea.

In the countries of the Third World, a great deal depends on the governments' actual behavior. Thus the Central African Republic might have been a perfectly acceptable national democracy in Moscow's eyes if President Bokassa had appointed himself secretary-general of the party, condemned American imperialism, and proclaimed his unalterable devotion to socialist ideas. Instead he proclaimed himself Emperor, thus demonstrating the unsocialist attitude of his regime.

It would be a mistake to dismiss Soviet nomenklatura policy in these countries with an indulgent smile, for it plays skillfully on the hostility felt in Third World countries to their former colonial masters and their tendency to regard Western countries, whether they possess colonies or not, as potential recolonizers. It is curious that the world's last colonial empire, the Soviet Union, should be regarded by the politicians of the Third World as a bulwark of anticolonialism. The chief problem of most of these countries is that of economic development, in which the West could do much more to help them than the Soviet Union. The West is consequently the Third World's natural ally. But the nomenklatura's sloganizing to the opposite effect is taken seriously by Third World politicians. That has been one of the greatest successes of nomenklatura diplomacy and propaganda, enabling it to secure the systematic support of many Third World countries in the United Nations and other international bodies. The Soviet intervention in Afghanistan brought about a certain change in the matter, and voices in the Third World are beginning to be raised against Soviet neocolonialism in underdeveloped countries. But obviously there is still a long way to go before this realization is permanently reflected in the foreign policy of those countries.

Latin America has a special importance in the plans of the Soviet nomenklatura. It regards that region as a United States sphere of influence, and its object is to infiltrate it with a view to opening up a new front there without being caught red-handed by Washington. Cuba plays an important part in these plans, and high hopes were also had of Chile. It has long been remarked in Moscow that, because of its geographical position, that thin strip of territory stretching from north to south along the western border of Argentina would be an ideal base for a Communist partisan movement in the countries of South America.

Not content with seeking to establish the real-socialist system in the countries of the Third World and Western Europe, the nomenklatura also has its eyes on North America, Australia, and New Zealand. Official documents of the CPSU and other Communist parties insist that socialism will not stop at the frontiers of any country in the world, but represents the radiant future of the whole of humanity. That is not just Marxist verbal radicalism; it is the real intention of the nomenklaturist class. Under the cover of real socialism for all, its aim is hegemony over the whole world.

It is not deterred by the fact that, as its experiences with China, Yugoslavia, Albania, and North Korea show, the transition to real socialism does not always imply acceptance of Soviet domination. The view is often expressed in the West that, because of that, the Soviet leaders do not want to see socialism established in countries where it might not be accompanied by recognition of Soviet hegemony. That view is mistaken; it is based on the principle that the nomenklatura aspiration to world hegemony is mere boasting, while in fact it is a necessity to it, as we have explained. Another view that is occasionally expressed in the West is that the aggressiveness of the nomenklatura could be bought off by helping it to cope with the difficulties that face it in Eastern Europe, and also of course in the Soviet Union.

These arguments ignore the impossibility of buying off nomenklatura expansionism and aggression, for those things are part of its nature. At best it might be possible to gain a respite by abandoning nations or peoples—potential allies—to its hungry jaws, for devouring and digesting them would take time. But when this process came to an end and one found oneself at the edge of the abyss, no allies would be left.

An alternative policy is of course possible, but giving political advice is outside the scope of this book.

10. THE INTERNATIONAL COMMUNIST MOVEMENT

The international Communist movement, according to the official definition, consists of the socialist countries and the Communist parties in other countries. Nomenklatura ideologists call it the most influential political force in the world.[12] There are altogether about ninety parties, with a total of fifty million members.[13] This view of the movement reflects the nomenklatura nostalgia for a monolithic unity which in fact never existed, for the pretense that it did involves ignoring Trotsky's Fourth International and later the existence of Yugoslavia and its Communist Party. Nowadays the international Communist movement has disintegrated to the extent that Communist countries can make war on one another; thus the "international Communist movement" referred to in this book is all the Communist parties not in power, the leaders of which are loyal to the Soviet nomenklaturist class.

There are certainly fewer than ninety parties in the movement as so described. Nevertheless there are a large number of them. The exceptions are countries such as China, Yugoslavia, and Albania, which, though ruled by Communist parties, have broken with the Soviet nomenklatura. The parties in the movement show varying degrees of dependence on the latter; most could not survive without Soviet support, but big parties such as the Italian, French, and Spanish are self-supporting and can afford the luxury of a Eurocommunism from which the Austrian and Dutch parties, for instance, have had to dissociate themselves. That, incidentally, was why the sudden change of line of the French party in favor of the Soviet nomenklatura surprised the Western world.

What do the leaders of all these parties want of the Soviet nomenklaturists? First of all, they want money in order to be able to live as comfortably as the latter; they want to be invited to the Soviet Union or some other socialist country from time to time to take advantage of the privileges that the nomenklaturists have succeeded in arrogating to themselves; and finally, above all, they passionately want Soviet support to enable them to gain power in their respective countries and live in conditions as luxurious as those of the Soviet nomenklatura.

Does that mean that among the Communist leaders in all these countries there are no genuine idealists who are in revolt against the injustices of modern society and want to fight for a better future for their people? I hesitate to give a categorical reply to that question. But in the Soviet Union and the other socialist countries, idealistic Communists died out long ago. I lived for many years in the Soviet Union, and it is only in the West that I have met convinced Communists; whether there are any among the leaders of the Western parties I do not know. There are of course idealists and honorable individuals among the members of those parties, but if the Communists took power in their countries, their fate would be that of the Leninist old guard in the Soviet Union. If I doubt the genuineness of their leaders' beliefs, it is because among the Communist leaders with whom I have had dealings in various countries I have always met the same desperate eagerness to follow the slightest variations in the general line of the CPSU. What they were really interested in was merely tactics and propaganda; the living conditions of their compatriots at best left them cold. At a lunch in the canteen of the institute of social sciences of the Central Committee of the CPSU, in Moscow, a leading functionary of the West German Communist Party who was taking a refresher course there complained to me bitterly that workers in the Federal Republic were much too well off to be interested in putting the party in power.

But the greatest doubts about the genuineness of the Communist beliefs of these leading comrades arise when one notes the servility with which they accept the twists and turns of Soviet policy and ideology. All these officials sang Stalin's praises, then joined in unmasking him, and then turned and rent those who had unmasked him; they all went into ecstasies about Tito's heroism before denouncing him as the leader of a Fascist clique and a spy and then rehabilitating him with touching unanimity before accusing him of revisionism; they all rejoiced when they were told that the advent of communism in the Soviet Union was due in 1980, which does not prevent them from now congratulating themselves on the unexpected arrival of a phase of "advanced socialism" that is still a long, long way from communism. We could go on like that for pages.

Are the leaders of these Communist parties naïve enough to be taken in by all this? Of course not, for they are anything but naïve. So the conclusion is that the only thing they really believe in is the impossibility of their attaining power without nomenklatura help. They are firmly convinced of that, and that is why they agree to pay the price demanded by the Soviet nomenklatura. They aspire to become leaders of future vassal nomenklaturas, and so they are docile vassals of the Soviet nomenklatura in the meantime.

Why they need the Soviet nomenklatura is clear, but why does the Soviet nomenklatura need them? They cost it dearly (incidentally in precious foreign exchange), and many of these parties are minute and have no hope of attaining power on their own. So is the expense worthwhile?

Yes, in at least two respects:

In the first place, the pattern intended to be followed in the acquisition of world power is socialist revolutions that will put Communist parties in power. Hence, these parties are indispensable, and as their leaders aspire to power with Soviet nomenklatura aid, the interests of the two coincide. The nomenklatura can therefore rely on these Communist leaders. Examples are the puppet governments that the invaders took with them in their baggage trains to Afghanistan and Cambodia. The nomenklatura uses them as a fig leaf to make the occupation of the country look respectable, and the puppets in power above all want the occupation to continue.

Secondly, these Communist leaders render invaluable services to the Soviet nomenklatura. It would be a mistake to underrate the advantages it derives from them. Other countries have only their official diplomatic missions in other countries, while the Soviet Union and its allies also have a party of their own. Small though they may be, their members arc natives of those countries and know all about them, are in contact with people of the most varied social backgrounds, and are thus able to collect valuable information, unlike Soviet embassies. These latter are staffed by nomenklaturists appointed for political reasons or for reasons of patronage and interested only in buying foreign goods and promoting their own careers; this last factor makes it advisable to avoid all contact with the local population, which is always regarded with suspicion by the KGB. The consequence is that, contrary to a widespread view in the West, Soviet embassies are very inadequately informed about their host countries. Most of their information comes from newspapers that could equally well be read in Moscow. That is why Soviet diplomats so often use the stereotyped phrase "We must discuss the matter with our friends."

"Friends" in this context is nomenklatura jargon for officials of foreign Communist parties, just as "neighbours" means thc KGB. These "friends" are consulted on the most varied matters, and contacts take place at all levels, right up to that of the Politburo. That does not mean that the tail wags the dog, but that foreign Communist parties perform an important function in providing the nomenklatura with information and advice. Such information, of course, is not objective, because it is dictated by the interests of the party leaders concerned, who are anxious to show how indispensable they are and how essential it is to give them full support. That is realized in Moscow, but the information provided is trusted all the same, for it is rightly assumed that the interests of the Soviet nomenklatura and those of the foreign party leaders coincide.

These advanced bases of the Soviet Union in foreign countries also fill in gaps in the work of Soviet embassies. To prevent the possibility that exposure of espionage activities by countries of the Warsaw Pact might harm the local Communist parties, these parties generally do not directly engage in such activities now. In 1960 the Central Committee of the CPSU again authorized the Soviet secret services to recruit agents among members of foreign Communist parties.[14]

The existence of Communist parties in nearly all the countries of the world also provides the Soviet nomenklaturists with magnificent opportunities for organizing and orchestrating international propaganda campaigns. It doesn't matter if these make no impact in countries in which the Communist Party is insignificant; the smallest meeting or demonstration is reported in millions of copies of Communist newspapers printed all over the world. Thus they create the impression that the "peoples of the world" (as nomenklatura jargon puts it) are demanding something (that has just been decided on by the Central Committee of the CPSU). To make these propaganda campaigns look like genuine, spontaneous mass movements (and to help pro-Communist organizations to seem representative in spite of their total and unconditional subservience), it is essential to secure the cooperation of public personalities or, better still, organizations well known not to be Communist. The value of these people generally increases proportionately to their distance from communism, for they bring their own supporters with them, as well as groups whose position is intermediate between theirs and that of the Communists. This intensifies public interest in the campaign and in general enhances trust in the movement.

An important part of the work of these parties is the type of activity we have just described; that's why responsibility for it is generally given to a senior party leader. Once the party is in power, interest in these non-Communist personalities fades rapidly: They have outlived their usefulness, and the security services see to their further fate. If, however, the international situation makes it seem advisable, the Communist leaders will set up a "national front" or some such body, certain members of which, having been specially reprieved for the purpose, will assure foreign visitors that, in spite of their active support of the party line, they are not Communists. Their fate, however, is merely postponed. But so long as Communist parties are not in power their leaders are charming and obliging to non-Communist personalities whom they hope to harness to the nomenklatura plans.

The devising of programs "acceptable to all democrats" is an important part of Communist tactics. Examples of slogans concocted by the international Communist movement are Peace and Disarmament, Ban the Bomb, Nuclear Freeze, Peace in Vietnam, and Out with Foreign Troops.

This last slogan has not been heard since the Soviet invasion of Czechoslovakia in 1968. It was taken up by many non-Communists, many of whom condemned the Soviet intervention in that year. The strange thing is that, since then, they, too, have given it up. Why?

To understand the process by which "programs acceptable to all democrats" are devised, you should try the experiment of launching the slogan: Ban the Tank, the Weapon of the Aggressor. First of all it will be gently pointed out to you, with no raising of the voice, that it is not a topical idea, that objectively it is an actually harmful one, for it distracts attention from the important thing, the banning of the bomb. But if you insist, and point out that it promotes the cause of disarmament, and that it is tanks that the people of Europe are most afraid of, they will raise their voices, shout at you, tell you that your slogan is a provocation, they will denounce you as a reactionary, an enemy of détente, a cold warrior and a Fascist.

Another example: If you were incapable of dropping a habit you had gotten into years ago and went on calling for an "end to the dirty war in Vietnam" after the Americans withdrew from that country and the North Vietnamese Army started its offensive against the South without troubling about the peace treaty, or again when it occupied Cambodia and Laos, the result would have been the same: You would have been denounced as an enemy of détente and a Fascist. But when the Chinese launched a "punitive expedition" against Vietnam in the spring of 1979, you would have had complete freedom to take your progressive and peace-loving slogan out of the cupboard and proclaim it as loudly as you liked.

The reason for these chops and changes is that the peaceful and democratic principles enshrined in these slogans are a fraud, merely serving the interests of the nomenklatura. When it says it wants peace, it means that it doesn't want war in a situation in which war does not fit in with its plans or might turn to its disadvantage. In view of the Eastern bloc's superiority in conventional weapons, banning nuclear weapons or the neutron bomb would mean shifting the balance of power in its favor. By disarmament, the nomenklatura means Western disarmament. All these "democratic" slogans serve the nomenklatura's purpose of attaining world hegemony.

What shall we say of the Western non-Communist personalities who adopt these slogans? The Bolshevik Lenin called them useful idiots; the German Social Democrat Mommer called them Trojan asses; it was not the purity of their intentions, but their lack of comprehension that they ridiculed. Such persons should be advised to consider for a moment what happened to their predecessors in countries in which real socialism has been established. Let them wonder whether it is wise to risk subjecting their party, their country, and themselves to the same fate.

So far they do not seem to have given much thought to the matter and thanks to their aid the international Communist movement continues to organize worldwide campaigns ordered by the Central Committee of the CPSU. There is no other political force that could do that, and from that point of view it is indeed the most influential force in our time.

It is not surprising that the nomenklaturist class has a high regard for foreign Communist parties and their leaders, for they do something that the nomenklaturists themselves cannot do now. Without the KGB, without labor camps, even without the power to deprive people of their livelihood, the foreign Communist leaders manage by the mere force of persuasion to turn rank-and-file members of their party—free men—into unpaid pawns of the Soviet nomenklatura, and are often called on to make sacrifices on its behalf. The secret lies in the ability to play on the huge gamut of human feelings: passions, prejudices, envy, conformism, conservatism, loyalty, submission to authority, dislike of admitting mistakes, shame and fear of being regarded as a renegade, of being condemned by the comrades, fear of isolation, of a break with Communist friends. When one joins a Communist Party and finds oneself caught in the net that extends to the humblest member, the easy course is to fall in with the majority, slowly acquire the seniority that is the pride of every good Communist, develop the feeling of belonging to the great army of the international Communist movement, and feel oneself a hero struggling against an unjust social order (which is easy in the West, because it is perfectly legal). It is much harder to find the inner resources needed to make a break and put up with the ostracism and vengeance of the party and its sympathizers, while being received with mistrust in the other camp for having been a Communist.

The virtuosity of foreign Communist leaders is rewarded by the nomenklatura in hard cash. They receive generous subsidies from the CPSU or parties in other real-socialist countries. The money is generally sent by courier to prevent its being traced back to its source through bank accounts. But the increase in the international operations of Soviet banks and the opening of branches in various countries have made other methods possible, and the nomenklaturists have begun to use the banking system for transferring funds by devious routes. The source of these funds is now an open secret. The West German press was not indignant, but amused, at the disclosure that the German Communist Party recorded in its accounting books a larger amount than any other party under the heading of "donations," surpassing in this respect the Christian Democrats, whom it nevertheless denounces as the chief party of monopoly capitalism in the Federal Republic. Everyone knows that the anonymous patrons are the central committee of the Socialist Unity Party (as the East German Communist party is called).

The leaders of the foreign Communist parties are well-paid vassals of the nomenklatura. They lead comfortable lives in their various countries, and when they go to the Soviet Union or to one of the countries allied to it, state dachas, cars with chauffeurs, the Kremlin hospital, or similar establishments are put at their disposal. Less important leaders are put up free of charge in the hotel of the international department of the Central Committee, in Plotnikov Street, or in similar first-class hotels in other socialist countries. Guests are taken around the country and put up in the best health resorts and rest homes and are given handsome presents. In short, it is not only disinterested love of the "fatherland of all the workers" that encourages foreign Communist leaders to visit the U.S.S.R.

The Soviet nomenklatura is lavish in its rewards to its foreign vassals, but if they are disobedient it is unforgiving. In Stalin's time there was little beating about the bush: the penalty was the notorious "nine grams of lead in [the back of] the neck." Survivors of the Great Purge have sufficiently described the wholesale arrests and summary executions to which foreign Communist leaders living in the Hotel Lux, in Gorki Street (the Comintern hotel that is now called the Central), were subject. But times have changed: foreign Communist leaders no longer live in Moscow, but in their own countries, and party officials who show too much independence are dealt with differently. The method now used by the nomenklatura is officially described as "consolidating the healthy forces." In plain language this means finding new faces to replace refractory leaders. "Healthy forces" are summoned to Moscow for an exchange of views and are assured of backing in their preparations to overthrow the leaders who are to be displaced. The Czech leader Smrkovsky has described an interview of this type: Brezhnev himself tried to persuade him to oppose Dubček by hinting that the post of first secretary of the Czech party would be his if he agreed.[15] Smrkovsky declined, but others, i.e., the present Czechoslovak leaders, accepted. Sometimes the initiative is taken by the "healthy forces" themselves. It is said in Moscow that Jeannette Vermeersch, Maurice Thorez's widow, presented herself at the Central Committee of the CPSU to give free rein to her indignation at the "revisionist" line of the French Communist Party and propose herself as a "healthy force."

The "consolidation of healthy forces" has been used a number of times. Kádár assumed the leadership of those forces during the Hungarian revolution in 1956. In Austria, in 1969, Friedl Fürnberg, who spoke Russian like a Russian and was formerly of the Comintern and longtime secretary-general of the Austrian party, was called on to form the nucleus of the "healthy forces"; but because of her advanced age, the presidency of the party was given to Franz Muhri, who had quickly changed his position. The same method led to the formation of a pro-Soviet party headed by Lister in opposition to the Eurocommunist leadership of the Spanish party. No doubt the nomenklatura will often use this technique in the future to keep its vassals in the international Communist movement in order.

That movement is the tool by means of which the nomenklatura hopes to realize its aspiration to world hegemony. By now it is a little worn and blunted, but it is still capable of being exceedingly useful.

Can I be said to be aiding and abetting what is called "primitive anticommunism" by this not very flattering description of the orthodox Communist parties? No. I believe the idea of a classless *communist* society as a free association of producers of material and intellectual goods free of all exploitation to be a fine one. But all that the nomenklaturists and their foreign acolytes have to do with it is the lip service they pay it while assiduously building up just the opposite: their own hegemony. The society they have created is in much more flagrant conflict with the Communist ideal than the capitalist system is. Real socialism is no way related to Marx's communism, and it is high time that that truth was realized. The real anticommunists are not the critics of the nomenklatura regime, but the orthodox Communist parties loyal to the Kremlin.

What is the role of the so-called Eurocommunist parties?

In the first place, the term is misleading. The European Communist parties are far from being all Eurocommunists; the Australian and Japanese parties should be included with them. It would be more accurate to talk of democratic communism, but the Eurocommunists have rejected the term, illustrating yet again the ambiguous nature of Eurocommunism, which never goes more than halfway in anything it says.

Objectively speaking, Eurocommunism is merely one of a number of branches that have grown from the trunk of the orthodox international Communist movement. The nomenklatura class has permanently discredited real socialism as a model to be followed. Communist parties looking for support other than merely that of the Central Committee of the CPSU and wanting to have a larger electorate are obliged to mark themselves off from that model, and in particular from the dictatorship of the nomenklatura, which masquerades as the "dictatorship of the proletariat." Lenin's contention that the "dictatorship of the proletariat" would be more democratic than any kind of parliamentary republicanism has lost its appeal. So the Eurocommunists proclaim that in the event of the triumph of Eurocommunism all the rights and liberties that their fellow citizens already enjoy would be preserved— and even increased—by the introduction of new rights in the social field.

So, is Eurocommunism merely a vote-catching stunt? Disillusioned Westerners who ask that question seem not to grasp the extent of the political change underlying the Eurocommunists' tactics.

The Eurocommunists are certainly Communists. They emphasize the basic differences that mark them off from social democrats. But they also mark themselves off from orthodox Communist parties. The latter display a thoroughly Leninist scorn for "parliamentary cretinism" and use parliaments merely as "legal platforms" from which to conduct political agitation. By their own confession, the principal task of the orthodox parties is to prepare "the political army of the revolution," so that it will be ready when a revolutionary situation arises (with the following combination of circumstances: weakness of the central power, severe economic crisis affecting the people's standard of living, popular discontent). It will then be possible to carry out the great leap that will lead to power. The chief concern of the orthodox Communist parties is to prepare the troops for that great day.

In today's West, that is not a very promising task, which is why the leaders of those parties rest all their hopes on Soviet nomenklatura aid. Eurocommunist leaders do not rest their hopes on a victorious advance of Soviet divisions, but (like all ordinary parties) on the votes of the electorate. To obtain those votes they are willing to repudiate the real-socialist model, knowing that this is bound to incur the wrath of the Soviet nomenklatura. Though Eurocommunism is a branch of the orthodox Communist tree, it *might* be independent of it. But its secession is ambiguous. A whole series of factors prevent the Eurocommunists from marking themselves off more definitely. The Eurocommunist parties have been Eurocommunist for only a short time, and nearly all their members were brought up in a spirit of orthodox veneration of the Soviet model. Because of the existence of that state of mind, it is always possible that a "consolidation of the healthy forces" might take place at all levels of the party from the summit to the base. Secondly, a great deal of mistrust of and skepticism about Eurocommunism exists in the West, thus depriving it of the possible support of many socially influential sections of the population.

In these circumstances the Eurocommunist parties remain doubly tied to the Soviet nomenklatura; in the first place psychologically, which is undoubtedly the more important, and in the second place materially, though this takes the most varied forms. The Eurocommunist leaders, knowing that the West will not help them into office, are unwilling to deprive themselves of the backing of that great world power the Soviet Union.

Such are the factors that account for the obvious illogicality and ambiguity of their relations with the Soviet nomenklatura. Though they never cease insisting that socialism is inconceivable without democracy, and in spite of their admission that democracy is in a bad way in the Soviet Union, they do not dare draw the logical conclusion that socialism in the Soviet Union does not exist. Instead they hedge; they say there is a primitive type of socialism in the U.S.S.R., or that there are as many kinds of socialism as there are countries (if they were consistent they would say the same of capitalism). That is why the Eurocommunist leaders have adopted a compromise in relation to the Soviet nomenklatura. The electorate in the countries in which they seek votes is principally interested in domestic questions, while the Soviet leaders are principally interested in foreign policy. So the Eurocommunist parties support the foreign policy of the Soviet nomenklatura, confining themselves to expressing reservations in flagrant cases of aggression and expansionism.

This compromise has turned out to be acceptable to the nomenklatura, whose criticisms of Eurocommunism are not to be compared to its past attacks on the Yugoslav Communists or their diatribes against the Chinese Communist Party. In spite of a widespread contrary view in the West, the Soviet Union would like to see Eurocommunists in power. Their willingness to conduct a pro-Soviet foreign policy would in the eyes of the nomenklatura mean a Finlandization of the countries concerned.

Finlandization means dependence on the Soviet nomenklatura, dependence less complete than that of a "people's democracy," but substantial nevertheless. Now, the nomenklatura deals pitilessly with "revisionists" who have the misfortune to be dependent on them; the fate of Imre Nagy, Dubček, and their followers will be recalled. The really imponderable thing about Eurocommunism is the fate that the Eurocommunist leaders expect after their victory, when they have put their countries in the hands of the masters of the Soviet nomenklatura. They know very well that neither a return to orthodoxy nor humble acts of contrition will save them from a settling of accounts. The Stalin purges showed that the nomenklatura never forgot or forgave even a venial fault committed in the distant past.

The leaders of the Eurocommunist parties are now faced with the choice between going back to the bosom of Moscow orthodoxy and sadly awaiting the hour of their punishment or going forward along a path enabling them to pass from the status of vassals of the Soviet nomenklatura to that of leaders of independent national Marxist parties. Parliamentary democracies include the most various political formations, and no one is forbidden to be a Marxist. Most Westerners mistrust Eurocommunists, not because they are Marxists, but because of the risk that they will implant themselves in the West like cancer cells, becoming the metastases of the Soviet nomenklatura.

Every Eurocommunist party will have to choose in the near future between the two alternatives open to it.

11. THE WAY TO WORLD WAR

The history of the twentieth century has shown that megalomania on a world scale leads not to world hegemony but to war. It is bizarre that some Western governments escalate the campaign of intimidation with the bogeyman of a nuclear holocaust and, simultaneously, try to play down the real risk of war by minimizing the ambitions of the nomenklatura.

A distinguished representative of the business world in a Western capital told me that in his view the Soviet leaders did not want to extend their supremacy to the countries of Western Europe. He had spent five days in Moscow, and his arguments were simple and irrefutable. He said that the Soviet Government consisted of intelligent people (I agreed); the things that the Soviet people could buy were in short supply and of bad quality (I agreed); the Soviet leaders were too intelligent not to know that that was the consequence of the poor productivity of the socialist economy (I agreed); if they extended their system to the West the same conditions would prevail, with the result that it would be impossible to improve the supply of goods to the Soviet population by means of Western credits and capital exports (I agreed). "The aim of the Soviet leaders," he said by way of conclusion, "is, as they say themselves, to raise the standard of living of their people, so they cannot want to transfer their system to the West. That means we have nothing to fear." That was the only point on which I disagreed. To understand why this conclusion is wrong, one has to have spent more than five days in the Soviet Union.

The indisputable facts of the situation are that: (1) the nomenklatura, not content with keeping the colonial empire of the czars, has enlarged it; (2) it has secured control of a whole series of countries in Europe, Asia, Africa, and America; (3) it does everything in its power to extend its control to all the countries of Europe and the Middle East, as well as to new areas in Africa and Asia; (4) it tirelessly tries to undermine the United States everywhere in the world, including Latin America; (5) it finances and controls Communist parties in nearly all the countries in the world and prepares them for a takeover of power in their respective countries; (6) it conducts a bitter campaign against Communist parties, whether in power or not, that are not prepared to turn their countries into satellites of Moscow.

There really is no reason to doubt the nomenklatura's often repeated statements of its intent to establish real socialism throughout the world.

When I search my memory of the many years I spent living and working in the Soviet Union I can find nothing whatever to cause me to doubt the seriousness of nomenklatura aspirations to world hegemony. On the contrary, the whole mentality of the nomenklaturists, their talk, their behavior, and their ideas, are evidence of those intentions, which to them seem perfectly natural.

Those intentions are especially dangerous because they have a dynamism of their own that is capable of unleashing a geopolitical hurricane that the nomenklatura itself might not want. Classes, like individuals, can get themselves into situations from which there is no retreat. In its stubborn pursuit of the aim of world domination, the nomenklatura has gotten caught up in a mechanism on the international plane from which it may have a great deal of difficulty in extricating itself unharmed. Consider the following:

1. The nomenklatura's megalomania has led to isolation. What allies has the Soviet Union today? The countries of the Eastern bloc are certainly dependent on it, but they are not real allies; as Poland, Czechoslovakia, Romania, Yugoslavia, and Albania have shown, the nomenklatura has to keep troops in socialist countries to ensure their loyalty. The People's Republic of China, formerly its principal ally, is now the Soviet nomenklatura's dangerous enemy notwithstanding the "normalization" talks. The euphoria about détente that prevailed in the West in the seventies is over. The nomenklaturists of course believe that this isolation is the product of a crafty "encirclement" movement, while in fact it is merely the logical consequence of their hegemonist policy.

2. In the course of the sixties and seventies the geopolitical balance of power shifted to the nomenklatura's disadvantage. It tries to com-

pensate for this by massive increases in its armaments and aggressive acts in the Third World, thus inevitably provoking defensive reactions that merely increase its isolation.

3. In this situation the nomenklatura sees a solution to the problem it has created for itself in the subjection of Western Europe, first of all by "Finlandizing" it. From this it hopes to secure (a) the stifling of internal opposition in the U.S.S.R. and resignation in the Eastern bloc; (b) a radical improvement in the economy of the Eastern bloc and the disappearance of the threat of a political or military second front in its conflict with the Chinese People's Republic. The disappearance of this threat might induce the Chinese leaders to change their minds and return to a Moscow-Peking axis. Having gotten thus far, the only remaining task facing the nomenklatura would be laying siege to and overcoming the encircled "fortress America." Its hegemonist aims would have been achieved.

That is why it concentrates on Europe. The distribution of Soviet forces clearly reveals the Kremlin's purpose. The forces deployed on the frontiers of Western Europe are nearly three times greater than those on the Far Eastern frontier, though that is where the military threat to the Soviet Union, if there is one, lies. The Soviet leaders have no understanding of the West; they are taken in by their own propaganda, and the information they receive from leaders of the Western Communist parties is tendentious and sometimes actually false. Like Hitler in his time, they count on the conciliatory spirit of Western governments and believe they will give in without a fight. Like Hitler, they risk going too far without realizing it and plunging the world into a world war they do not want.

As we have seen, they want, not war, but victory. Now, the road that leads to victory crosses the frontier between peace and war, and that is where the danger of another world conflagration lies.

The global balance of power gives the Soviet nomenklaturists no chance of victory in such a war. But they rest their hopes on the "contradictions of imperialism" and the "peace-loving and realistic-minded forces," in short, on dissension, defeatism, and shortsighted selfishness in the West. That is a dangerous calculation that in Hitler's case went badly astray, but when he realized it he had passed the point of no return and world war was raging. To prevent history from repeating itself the nomenklatura must be stopped.

Can it be claimed on the nomenklaturists' behalf that they are true patriots, that the greatness of the U.S.S.R. lies in its successes on the road that leads to world hegemony, and that they are acting in the interests of their people? Those are the ideas that they try to inculcate into their subjects.

Heads can easily be turned by chauvinist megalomania. Some Soviet citizens have succumbed to it, but they are far from being a majority, for the people of our time are generally well aware that a country's greatness lies not in expansionism, but in the freedom and prosperity of its inhabitants. What sort of greatness is it when a country's frontiers have to be hermetically sealed to prevent its citizens from escaping? What sort of greatness is it when the whole world knows that the Soviet population is not free and lives in poverty? Which is the greater, the militarist Japan of the thirties and forties or the thriving Japan of the present day? Ask the West Germans whether they would like to go back to the pseudo greatness of the Third Reich. A country whose ruling class aspires to world hegemony cannot be called great, for that objective conflicts with the interests of its people.

The nomenklaturists' aspiration is doomed to failure. In the course of history there have been several candidates for world hegemony: Alexander the Great, Attila, Genghis Khan, Napoleon, Hitler. . . . They failed. So will the nomenklatura.

NOTES

1. Lenin, *Collected Works*, Vol. 33, p. 218.
2. Winston Churchill, *The Second World War*, Vol. VI, p. 537.
3. Marx and Engels, *Collected Works*, Vol. 12, p.17.
4. Ibid., pp. 113, 114.
5. Ibid., p. 230.
6. Lenin, *Collected Works*, Vol. 23, p. 43.
7. Ibid., Vol. 44, p. 409.
8. Stalin, *Works*, Vol. 6, p. 52.
9. Wladlen Kusnezow, *Internationale Entspannungspolitik. Aus sowjetischer Sicht*, Wien, 1973.
10. Michail Woslenskij, "Friedliche Koexistenz aus sowjetischer Sicht," *Osteuropa*, 1973, Heft 11, Seite 848–55; "Klassenkampf, Kalter Krieg, Kräfteverhältnis, Koexistenz," *Osteuropa*, 1974, H. 4, S. 259–69; "Die DDR und friedliche Koexistenz," *Deutschland Archiv*, 1975, H. 10, S. 1030–34.
11. Lenin, *Collected Works*, Vol. 27, p. 274.

12. *Die kommunistische Weltbewegung. Abriss der Strategie und Taktik,* Frankfurt, 1973, p. 9.
13. Ibid., p. 42.
14. *The Penkovsky Papers,* New York, 1965, p. 81.
15. *Kontinent* (German edition), No. 5, pp. 271–316.

8

A Weakness
of the Nomenklatura:
Change at the Top

I was asked:
"Who will be the imam after Shamil?"
I answered:
"The one with the sharpest sword."
Leo Tolstoy. *Hadji Murat.*

Communist propaganda works hard to create the impression that the Soviet Union and its allies succeed in everything they attempt. But in reality this is not the case. The nomenklatura as a social organism has its own innate flaws, its own weaknesses and diseases.

A Western observer would say that the difficult problems of the nomenklatura are the economic underproductivity of the system, the dissatisfaction of the population, the risks of a worldwide expansion. But the nomenklaturists feel differently. They know: the most striking weakness of their class is its inability to guarantee an orderly and routine succession of power at the summit of the nomenklatura. In monarchies the change at the top proceeds by inheritance, in democracies by elections. In the dictatorship of the nomenklatura the change is only formally an election; as a point of fact, it is the sum total of a struggle for power within the Politburo and the Secretariat of the Central Committee.

The struggle shakes the entire nomenklatura in a feverish paroxysm.

The nomenklaturist, whose goal in life is advancement in the ruling hierarchy, turns out to be unintentionally a player in a game of chance. Its rules: to join the future victor as soon as possible even though it is not known who that will be. The stakes are high, and he cannot sit the game out, since the rule "Whoever is not with us is against us" is applied with an iron logic throughout the nomenklatura.

To explain how a change at the top of the nomenklatura takes place, I shall examine an example. Let us take the latest instance: the transfer of the position of Secretary-General of the CPSU Central Committee from Brezhnev through Andropov to Chernenko.

1. BREZHNEV'S TWILIGHT YEARS

We all remember the ridiculous figure with the immobile face of an old monkey that moved so slowly across our television screens; we remember too the last close-up, when, four days before his death, he went out as usual on the left wing of the Mausoleum to wave to the ambassadors at the diplomatic tribune—only, he could no longer raise his hand. But I see in my mind's eye the Brezhnev I once met: the dynamic first secretary of the central committee of Kazakhstan; a lively, agile man in the Kremlin, with alert eyes in a massive face, self-important in the nomenklatura style and with a typically southern joviality, constantly making faces and gesturing. Invoking fate, he liked to say that his forefathers had lived to a ripe old age, and so would he. He was worried about "Comrade Appetite," as he put it, for he did not want to put on weight. He chain-smoked and started a diet, in order not just to live longer but to remain the same lively person, with hair and eyebrows dyed black, just as he had always fancied himself.

All that came to an end in 1974. Brezhnev fell ill. There was a rumor that he had a slowly progressive leukemia. His periodic and lengthy disappearances and his puffy face, a sign of cortisone treatment, lent weight to the rumor. Before our eyes, the lively person turned into the slowly dying man that the world remembers.

He clung desperately to the life that was ebbing away from him, deserting him just when he had achieved complete success and had so much to savor. He held up well: he traveled throughout the country and even abroad, and stubbornly read his speeches, with a leaden tongue. Those who met him said that he had bursts of energy, when he talked and gesticulated, but he would suddenly sigh and go dead with an empty gaze, apparently no longer hearing or understanding what was being said.

When a childhood friend, the seventy-five-year-old colonel general Grushevoi died, in 1982, Brezhnev cried over the coffin with a bitter resentment in front of the Soviet television cameras that suddenly turned merciless: totally self-absorbed, he was mourning for himself, not his friend, resenting the inevitability of his approaching end.

And then the newspapers appeared with the black frames around his portrait, even here retouched to make him look younger. And the process described so well by Gogol in his *Dead Souls* began:

> All the officials walked bareheaded after the coffin. . . . They were not even indulging in the trivial talk which is usually kept up by persons attending a funeral. At that moment, all their thoughts were concentrated on themselves: they were wondering what the new governor-general would be like, how he would set to work and how he would take them. . . . So much for the prosecutor! He lived and lived and then he died! And now they will print in the newspapers that he has passed away to the grief of his subordinates and of all humanity, an honored citizen, a devoted father, a faithful husband, and they will write all sorts of nonsense; they will very likely add that he was followed to the grave by the lamentations of widows and orphans; and yet if one goes into the facts of the case, it turns out on investigation that there was nothing special about you but your thick eyebrows.[1]

Let us analyze our own reactions: what was our impression of Brezhnev during his last years? Sick, barely surviving, incapacitated, soon to die. We were constantly surprised that he was still living and breathing. Foreign politicians and reporters considered it their duty to report after each and every interview with the head of the Soviet state that he looked well and gave the impression of a healthy man. And all the while it would never have occurred to anyone to say such things after meeting with other heads of state, even if they, like the Italian President Pertini, were significantly older than Brezhnev.

Meanwhile, there was no basis for it. Yes, Brezhnev was old and consequently sick. But he died at age seventy-five, which exceeds the average life span for men in Western Europe, to say nothing of the

U.S.S.R., where it is sixty-two. In addition, he was active literally until his last days: three days before his death, on November 7, 1982, he stood through two hours of ceremonies on the wind-swept tribune at the Mausoleum, plus another few hours at a reception at the Kremlin Palace. Not every seventy-five-year-old is capable of such an effort only seventy hours before his death.

What, then, determined our impression of Brezhnev? Who was it who even several years before Brezhnev's death instilled the idea that the Secretary-General was on the verge of dying? Andropov's disinformation people. It was they who conducted an operation highly unusual in Soviet circumstances: persistently although not maliciously to leak information abroad that would create the impression that the Secretary-General was about to depart this world.

Indeed, which of the foreign correspondents in Moscow were expelled for discussing Brezhnev's illness? None. Imagine how a journalist would be thrown out if he had attempted to discuss Khrushchev's health during his rule—to say nothing of Stalin's! The state-security-controlled Soviet "acquaintances," as well as Soviet servants of Western diplomats and journalists in Moscow, seemed suddenly to grow daring by revealing "in secret" the Secretary-General's illness—a subject so prohibited that the ordinary Soviet citizen would know absolutely nothing about it. The much experienced Soviet censors somehow could no longer prevent TV, film, or photo shots of the party leader that showed him looking helpless, an impotent old man. Tragicomic shots of Brezhnev appeared in Western newspapers: for example, how he, with an effort-strained face, tries to get up out of a chair while Gromyko pulls him by the arm. And somehow the guys from "the nine" did not screen out the photographer's lens with their well-trained backs and did not give the disrespectful photographer an elbow in the solar plexus.

The operation's organizers demonstrated great imagination in several cases. In 1977, Willy Brandt, about to set off on distant travels, was discreetly informed that if he stopped off in Moscow he would be received by Brezhnev. Brandt made the stop in Moscow, but it turned out that Brezhnev was in the hospital. This provocation called attention once again to the Secretary-General's illness.

When Brezhnev felt well and functioned adequately for a long time, a rumor—which became a standard feature—would circulate that he was preparing to retire with pomp and glory—either at a party congress or at a session of the Supreme Soviet, on his birthday or at the beginning of the new year. The rumor was intended for Westerners, who were used to politicians retiring, ignorant of the fact that no nomenklaturist, to say nothing of a Secretary-General, has ever renounced power voluntarily.

The impending change in Moscow was greeted in the West with curiosity and even impatience. For some unknown reason, a joyful expectation took root in the West that some sort of young, liberal technocrats with pro-Western sympathies would come to power, and everything would be fine and dandy. The nomenklatura viewed the prospects more realistically. The Politburo rapidly undertook the operation described above to remove Shelepin, for it was not mysterious young liberals, but the ex-chairman of the KGB with his cronies, who would attempt to take power.

The tactics of the Brezhnev group consisted of pretending that there was absolutely no change to be expected in the foreseeable future. With that in mind they began to blow up the laughable Brezhnev personality cult. The old man, who tried greedily to get as much as possible out of his last few years, pinned more and more medals on his chest with undiminished satisfaction and accepted literary prizes for brochures he did not write.

The priority goal of the Brezhnev group was to put forth a candidate for Secretary-General from within their own ranks. At first, Kirilenko seemed the natural candidate: he was the Central Committee Secretary for Organizational Questions, and therefore the second in rank in the Party Secretariat. Suslov, also considered a "second secretary" of the Central Committee, laid no claim to the position. Kirilenko had already chaired sessions of the Politburo and the Secretariat. It is difficult to say exactly what it was in his behavior that displeased the members of the Brezhnev group: his dictatorial manners or perhaps something else, but in any case his candidacy was abandoned.

After Kirilenko, Shcherbitsky was considered the candidate for a short while, but he, too, was unsuccessful; then the Brezhnevites got together behind Chernenko. And indeed he could satisfy everyone. Brezhnev had a lot of confidence in him, considering him an irreplaceable assistant. Others were attracted by a different merit: Chernenko had never been first secretary anywhere, ever; and it was too late in life for him to learn the tricks of the trade now, so he would turn out to be the kind of weak Secretary-General that all the members of the nomen-klatura elite preferred. In two years, Chernenko went from ordinary department head in the Central Committee to Politburo member and secretary of the Central Committee; that is, he was brought into the small circle of three or four people from whom the Secretary-General is chosen. During the SALT II negotiations, Chernenko was shown off to the whole world as Brezhnev's successor; without saying a single word during the negotiations, he sat there as the guarantee of the fulfillment of the obligations that the departing Brezhnev was undertaking. Chernenko began to demonstrate his special status: he published a book outside his specialty (the work of the party apparatus) and on a very provocative topic for the Soviet Union: human rights.[2] The leaders of small socialist countries, highly sensitive to any movement on the Moscow Olympus, began giving Chernenko medals and delivering glowing speeches about him.

It was clear who the Brezhnev candidate was. But who was the opposition candidate? The first signal reached the West in 1976. It consisted of a little-noticed release by a Western news agency. It reported that Soviet dissidents had received word of a dispute in the Politburo between First Secretary of the Ukrainian Central Committee Shcherbitsky and the head of the KGB, Andropov, because Andropov dealt with dissidents in the R.S.F.S.R. mercilessly and demanded the same treatment in the Ukraine. Shcherbitsky supposedly objected. The information was quite clearly deliberately leaked to the dissidents to be transmitted to the West. The dissidents had no real sources of information concerning discussions in the Politburo, and the persecution of dissenters was especially harsh precisely in the Ukraine. The purpose of the leak was to present the West with an image of the Brezhnevite Shcherbitsky as a liberal who made the Ukraine a haven for dissidents, and at the same time to tarnish Andropov's image by presenting him as a supporter of police repression. The fact that the information was transmitted by the only channel the KGB did not control—the dissidents—shows that it was directed against Andropov.

After this signal, it was clear that the rival of the Brezhnev group was Andropov.

2. ANDROPOV DURING STALIN'S RULE

One warm autumn day in 1957 I was walking with a friend from the International Department of the Central Committee through Staraya Square, past the imposing Central Committee buildings stretching along it. Near Entrance 3 we met a slowly moving, slightly hunched, middle-aged man wearing a high-quality light-brown suit. My friend greeted him with an exaggerated friendliness; the man nodded at us, and his cold, skeptical glance slid over us. "That's Andropov," my friend whispered to me. "He's the head of our new Department for Socialist Countries."

After that I saw Andropov many times: in the presidiums of ceremonial meetings, at the leadership table at large receptions, on the Mausoleum tribune. He was appointed a secretary of the Central Committee, then a nonvoting member of the Politburo and the chairman of the KGB. He became even more hunched, his features sharper, and his eyes colder. People joked uneasily that when he took over the KGB he started to look like Beria. Andropov was no Beria, but he was a man who managed to accomplish what Beria never did: to leap from the obscure chair of the chief of the secret police to the throne of the Secretary-General.

With Andropov's arrival at the summit of the nomenklatura, the Western press erupted with information and stories of varying age and —more important—varying degrees of reliability. Facts were piled over with invented detail. This unreliable information left such an unpleasant taste that the opposite tendency arose: to maintain that "virtually nothing is known about this man called Andropov."[3] That, too, is an exaggeration; things are known, if not a great deal.

Andropov's life is like a novel, only far more engrossing than *The Count of Monte Cristo*, that naïve fantasy of a peaceful century. There is something common in the younger years of Andropov and Stalin. Stalin studied to be a Georgian priest, worked as a bookkeeper in an observatory, and became the master of Russia. Andropov studied to be a telegrapher, worked as a film-projector repairman, then was a sailor— and occupied Stalin's position. Behind the seeming chaos of their biographies is hidden an inexorable logic. Both were completely indifferent to what they did in their ordinary, everyday existence. The meaning of their lives consisted only in climbing to the top—by any means possible, as long as they led to the top.

Yuri Andropov's career began early. It was helped along by events fatal to millions of other people: Stalin's repression and foreign conquests. As a twenty-two-year-old man, Andropov was appointed, in 1936, to the modest position of secretary of the Komsomol organization of a technical school in Rybinsk, in the Yaroslavl Region. The Yezhov terror had cleared the path upward, and within two years Andropov was first secretary of the Komsomol committee of the Yaroslavl Region.

He joined the party in 1939. That was the year Stalin began the annexations agreed upon with Hitler. After the war with Finland, the Karelo-Finnish Soviet Socialist Republic was formed, creating new vacancies in the nomenklatura, and the twenty-six-year-old Andropov was sent in as first secretary of the Central Committee of the republic Komsomol—that is, he entered the leadership group.

Consequently, during the Soviet-German war he was not sent to the front, but trained partisan detachments. In reality this work was conducted by the NKVD, so that Andropov entered into close contact with that organization.

In 1944 he was transferred to party leadership work, realizing the hidden dream of every Komsomol worker. Andropov became the second secretary of the party city committee in the republic capital, Petrozavodsk, and within three years, leaping over several steps, the second secretary of the central committee of the Communist Party of the Karelo-Finnish S.S.R. The first secretary in a republic is usually a Russified member of the local nationality, and the second secretary is a Russian, Moscow's eyes and ears. Appointment to such a responsible nomenklatura position required Stalin's personal approval. Andropov was then thirty-three.

The Stalin years were dangerous also for the nomenklatura. Later Andropov told that he, too, "awaited every day to be arrested," but "it did not occur."[4]

The leadership position in the Karelo-Finnish S.S.R. led to direct contact with at least one person close to Stalin: Otto Kuusinen, who was the chairman of the presidium of the supreme soviet of that republic. I would not want to exaggerate Andropov's closeness with this dynamic and influential person; Andropov probably never became one of his inner circle. But there is no doubt that Kuusinen supported Andropov. Apparently, with his help Andropov was transferred in 1951 to work in the center of nomenklatura power: the Central Committee of the CPSU. He became the head of a subdepartment. In the Soviet hierarchy this corresponds in level to the position of deputy minister of the U.S.S.R.—only, with fewer purely formal functions and more political clout.

After Stalin's death, in March of 1953, the nomenklatura organizations were reorganized and many directors were shuffled around. Brezhnev, for example, who only five months earlier had been admitted to the circle of the top leaders, lost his position as nonvoting member of the Presidium and secretary of the Central Committee and was demoted to the job of head of the Navy Political Administration. Even Suslov was out of the Central Committee Presidium. For a long time— until the June 1957 Central Committee plenary session—Kuusinen was out of both the Presidium and the Secretariat of the party Central Committee.

The organizational shifts also touched Andropov. From his leadership position in the Central Committee, he was transferred to a rather modest spot in the Ministry of Foreign Affairs. He also lost his place in the U.S.S.R. Supreme Soviet, which he had held as a Karelo-Finnish leader. The demotion was a significant one: Andropov was once more a rather ordinary member of the nomenklatura. Apparently, using his Central Committee connections, Andropov quickly corrected the situation: he was sent to the Soviet embassy in Hungary. Although by ministry standards it was not an enviable job, the position he received— counselor of the embassy—was quite high. And then he was named ambassador. The Soviet ambassador in a socialist-bloc country is the political commissar to the local government. In that way, his fall was overcome, and he was once again on the level he had reached under Stalin.

3. IN FOREIGN-POLICY POSITIONS

Who would have supposed that it would be the pleasant and quiet post of ambassador to Hungary that would land Andropov in a crisis situation? In any case, it was not something he expected, and according to Hungarians who knew him at the time, he sincerely enjoyed his ambassadorial functions: the receptions and the banquets, the festive environment of an ambassador's life.

In October 1956 the storm broke: the Hungarian revolution.

The event concealed a huge danger for the career of the Soviet ambassador. Khrushchev and his then favorite, Shepilov, the Minister of Foreign Affairs, were in the habit of making their ambassadors to socialist countries the scapegoats for the failures of Soviet policy. For precisely that reason, not long before the Hungarian revolution, Lavrishchev, the ambassador to North Vietnam, and Valkov, the ambassador to Yugoslavia, were driven out of the Ministry of Foreign Affairs, and what was worse, completely out of the nomenklatura. Andropov was in danger of just such a disaster, because he could easily be accused of not having given adequate warning of the imminence of "counterrevolutionary events," as they were then termed, and did not ensure that the Hungarian leaders took measures against the "antisocialist forces." In addition, as is clear from Khrushchev's memoirs, the Central Committee Presidium wavered on whether to intervene militarily in Hungary or not, and placed their trust in the ambassador: "Our troops were not in Budapest," Khrushchev noted, "but our people were there; our ambassador was right there in Budapest."[5]

In these circumstances the ambassador could not count on clear-cut instructions from Moscow and had to act to avoid losing, no matter what was decided.

I cannot help paying Andropov a compliment: he did this brilliantly, finding the one and only correct approach. That consisted of ceaselessly reassuring the Hungarians that intervention was out of the question and that Moscow was busy trying to find a way to withdraw Soviet troops from Hungary. That approach guaranteed an Andropov win. If Moscow did not go for intervention, the ambassador would have been correct. In case of intervention the old proverb would apply: "Victors are not judged."

It is hard to condemn Andropov for such a solution to the problem.

But we must not fail to notice the acting talent and laudatory self-mastery that Andropov demonstrated in the process. What else can we say about the way he acted during the last night of the Hungarian revolution, the so-called "night of betrayal"? On November 3, 1956, at two-thirty in the morning, a KGB operational group burst into the meeting of the Soviet-Hungarian commission working out the terms for the withdrawal of Soviet forces and arrested the entire Hungarian military leadership, including Pál Maleter, the Minister of Defense. But an hour and a half later, at four o'clock, as Soviet troops entered Budapest, attacked the center of the city, and neared the Parliament, Andropov sat with Prime Minister Nagy and assured him that there was some kind of misunderstanding, since the Soviet Government had not ordered an attack. And Nagy, who trusted Andropov, forbade the Hungarians to return fire against the Soviet troops. "The ambassador and I will try to get through by telephone to Moscow," he explained to a person who asked him to order the troops to open fire.[6]

Sándor Kopácsi, who was chief of the Budapest police at the time and who now lives in Canada, has the following to say about Andropov's behavior the next day. He knew Andropov as an affable ambassador who sang and danced at diplomatic receptions and asked for a gypsy orchestra that was at Kopácsi's disposal. On November 5, Kopácsi and his wife were arrested as they attempted to take refuge in the Yugoslav Embassy, and they were taken to Andropov. He even then greeted them cordially. When they were put in a car and driven off to prison, Andropov waved good-bye to them, smiling.[7]

Kopácsi spent several years in prison; Nagy and Maleter were hanged.

Andropov got a promotion. The Soviet leaders were satisfied with his maneuvering during the crisis. Under the influence of the events in Hungary and Poland in 1956, the Politburo decided in 1957 to create a department in the Central Committee on relations with the ruling Communist and workers' parties. Andropov was named its head.

It was an enormous leap upward. According to Soviet protocol, the head of a department in the Central Committee is above a minister. And it was just one step (although admittedly not an easy one) to the post of secretary of the Central Committee, that is, a member of the nomenklatura leadership. Circumstances permitted Andropov to take that step. In 1961 the head of the parallel International Department of the Central Committee, B. N. Ponomarev, who had uninterruptedly since 1937 been in charge of the world Communist movement, became a secretary. Discriminating against the Department for Socialist Countries was found to be awkward, so the following year Andropov was also named a secretary. Since then it has been customary for the "fraternal department," as it is nicknamed, to be run by a Central Committee secretary, either directly (Rusakov) or as a "curator" (Katushev).

In the Central Committee apparatus, people joked that Andropov managed to control relations with the socialist countries between one Soviet invasion and the next: after the suppression of the Hungarian revolution, in 1956, and before the occupation of Czechoslovakia, in 1968. But that does not mean that his ten years in the job passed by quietly. On the contrary, the events Andropov confronted were highly dramatic: the Sino-Soviet conflict, the establishment of the Castro regime in Cuba and the Caribbean crisis of 1962, and the Vietnam War. These years saw the split between the Soviet Union and Albania and, after several years of terror, the creation of the liberal Kádár model in Hungary. As far as is known, in all these cases Andropov conducted himself extremely cautiously, leaving it to higher-ups to make the decisions. He did not stand in the way of the International Department's taking over, for the most part, questions concerning relations with China. Andropov supported the Hungarian experiment, which was crucial, since in the nomenklatura circles any innovation is greeted with suspicion. However, the Hungarian model was never presented as a model for the other socialist countries.

Most likely, this combination of diplomatic caution and administrative efficiency led to the next stage of Andropov's career. In 1967 Brezhnev conducted a campaign to drive out Shelepin's group. Semichastny, Shelepin's man as head of the KGB, was ousted, and Andropov was named to replace him.

4.   CHAIRMAN OF THE KGB

The appointment to the KGB chairmanship demonstrated the confidence the Brezhnev group felt in Andropov. After all, he was sent over to the KGB to transform that bastion of Shelepin into a reliable instrument of Brezhnev power. The security agencies, subdued after Stalin's death and the liquidation of Beria, had begun to feel more independent after the overthrow of Khrushchev, undertaken with their assistance. Eight months after that change, a woman KGB officer said in my presence that in their organization "no one bothers with the opinion of any other organization except the Central Committee apparatus, and not all that much even with them." Apparently, that spirit was inculcated by Semichastny and other Shelepinites who had come over from the Komsomol central committee. Under Andropov the spirit changed. You began to hear that in the KGB "everything has become more stable after the departure of Semichastny, with his Komsomol fervor." Former CIA director Admiral Stansfield Turner said on German television that the KGB was a very well run and excellently managed agency and that that was undoubtedly due to Andropov.[8]

However, the appointment to the KGB had another, less pleasant side: Andropov was now away from the Central Committee Secretariat, one of the two centers of nomenklatura power. True, this disadvantage was compensated for by his becoming a nonvoting member of the Politburo—but only a candidate member. In the Secretariat he had been a member, with the right to cast the deciding vote. He was no longer one of the gang of omnipotent Central Committee secretaries. They spend the whole day in the same building, constantly calling each other up and meeting briefly to settle problems. And he was sitting over in Lubianka and had to protect their secrets and supply them with new ones, seek out and punish the enemies of the policies they determined.

To be brief, the transfer to the KGB was not a promotion. But it did give Andropov the kind of leverage that a skillful person could use to obtain an enormous success: to become the Secretary-General. The path was rocky: Beria had lost his life on it, Shelepin his career. And the examples in the other socialist countries were not comforting (for example, Rankovich, in Yugoslavia). Only Hua Kuo-feng, in China, had shown that it was possible. But that was in China, and nothing like it had ever happened in the Soviet Union.

5. THE COMPROMISE THAT WAS A COUP

The recurrence of events is a sign that laws are hidden behind them. With this in mind, let us look at how power was organized at the summit of the nomenklatura after the departure of each of its leaders. After Lenin's death a "troika" held power: Stalin, Kamenev, Zinoviev. After Stalin's death it was another troika: Malenkov, Beria, and Molotov. After Malenkov's retirement, a "dvoika": Khrushchev and Bulganin. After Khrushchev's fall, another troika: Brezhnev, Kosygin, Podgorny. Each time, the Soviet propaganda machine began to drone away that collective leadership was the natural organization principle of the Marxist-Leninist party. We have already discussed the real reason for this: the new Secretary-General needs time to get his supporters into power, and until this is done he must be content with the role of member of a collective leadership, as first among equals. The hidden law was, as we have already seen, that in the nomenklatura environment, people do not move up alone, but in groups, and that between such groups there is a struggle for control of the commanding positions.

We have pointed out still another law: Politburo members are eager to have as weak a Secretary-General as possible. A quite human characteristic: life is easier when you have a weak boss.

That is why Chernenko's selection as the Brezhnev group's candidate was completely natural: he had had no experience in running a dictatorship, so he would fit into a troika easily, with Tikhonov and Suslov.

So then, Andropov's assumption of the position of Secretary-General was an anomaly. Andropov was the strongest of the potential candidates. In addition, he had been for many years the director of the security agency and the nomenklatura had cut short attempts by Beria and Shelepin to get the top job.

For the first time in Soviet history a troika or some other form of collective leadership was not formed. From the very beginning, Andropov turned out to be a Secretary-General who had a strong grip on his job.

Perhaps Andropov charmed the usually unsentimental Politburo members so much that they, despite everything, elected him? Not likely: the very same members did not elect him Chairman of the Presidium of the Supreme Soviet. The information, disseminated in the West almost immediately, that Andropov himself supposedly did not want the job was a cover-up: eight months later, he took the job. We can therefore infer that the Politburo was unable to make a decision about the appointment. Andropov did not have a guaranteed majority in the Politburo. So how did the Andropov anomaly come about?

Immediately after Andropov's election as Secretary-General, I pointed out that it was either a fascinating compromise or a coup.[9] It has gradually become clear that there was a little of both in the events: it was a compromise that was a coup.

For such a coup the KGB was not enough: the support of the military-industrial complex also had to be guaranteed. According to Roy Medvedev, Andropov and Ustinov reached an agreement to take concerted action against Chernenko in February and March 1982.[10] In May 1982, on Ustinov's motion, the Politburo, in a close vote, decided to recommend Andropov for the Secretary-General post.

Chernenko and his supporters made more than a few efforts to prevent the alliance between Andropov and Ustinov. A curious example of such an attempt is Brezhnev's last major speech, given at a conference of army and navy leaders on October 27, 1982. According to the prepared text, Brezhnev didactically declared to those present, "The Party Central Committee is taking steps to ensure that you will have no need of anything. And the armed forces must always remain worthy of this concern." Then followed the glowing praise of the high qualifications and rich experience of the members of the collegium of the Ministry of Defense, "the helm of which is in the trustworthy hands of a true son of the party of Lenin, member of the Politburo of the Central Committee of the CPSU, our friend in arms and comrade, Marshal of the Soviet Union Dmitri Fyodorovich Ustinov."[11]

But no exhortations or praise could help the Brezhnev group. At the Politburo session after Brezhnev's death, Marshal Ustinov put forth Andropov's candidature. A majority voted for him. To firm up his victory, the Andropov block passed a resolution that Chernenko would present Andropov's candidacy at the plenary session. Chernenko had no choice but to take this slap in the face.

How did it happen that a majority in the Politburo voted for Andropov when the Brezhnev groups had previously held a majority? Or, to put it differently, what methods did Andropov use to get his opponents to vote for him: did he persuade them or force them?

He persuaded them—and that is the compromise. But he persuaded them KGB style: that it would be better not to resist. And that is the coup.

The KGB method of persuasion consists of three elements: instilling almost hypnotically the belief (1) that a person can be convicted of a crime, the evidence being more than sufficient, (2) that no one will stand behind him, and (3) that his fate is entirely in the hands of the KGB.

As a rule the method works flawlessly. But in this case it was applied in a special way; it was not ordinary and powerless Soviet citizens who had to be persuaded, but their masters, the powerful members of the nomenklatura leadership.

6. A NEW METHOD: THE FIGHT AGAINST CORRUPTION

Stalin ousted the Lenin group and took power under the guise of fighting the intraparty opposition for "the purity" of Leninist doctrine. Khrushchev ousted the Stalin group and took power under the guise of "fighting against Stalin's personality cult" and the attempt of an "antiparty group" who wanted to return the country to those dark times. Brezhnev and his companions ousted Khrushchev under the guise of overcoming his "subjectivist errors" and eliminated Shelepin under the guise of avoiding a new Stalinism.

In each case, the individual's struggle for power was concealed in ideological dress as part of the party's fight for socialism. But in Andropov's case the U.S.S.R. had already been declared "a country with developed socialism," and the "irreversibility of socialist transformations" had been proclaimed even in Ethiopia and Afghanistan. To undertake once more the salvation of socialism in the Soviet Union would have been awkward. It was essential to find another problem to fight.

This problem was found in the fact that the nomenklatura had turned into a wealthy and privileged class, more and more sunk in corruption. Therefore there was logic to the idea that the whip to intimidate opponents would be not "the rescue of socialism" or the fight against deviations, but a campaign against bribes, pilfering on the job, and other forms of corruption. Such accusations could nearly always be supported by facts.

During an earlier discussion of nomenklatura baksheesh, I mentioned that Aliev, the KGB chairman in Azerbaijan, and Shevardnadze, the minister of internal affairs in Georgia, became first secretaries of their republics and even nonvoting members of the Politburo by applying exactly the same method: with the help of the police powers they had at their disposal they opened a campaign against bribery and corruption, as a result of which the previous secretaries and their helpers were forced out of power.

Who helped implement this curious form of the overthrow of a government in miniature? In the case of Azerbaijan, we know from a reliable source that Aliev was supported by the KGB chairman—Andropov—and his first deputy, Tsvigun, Brezhnev's brother-in-law.[12] It is also clear that Shevardnadze, in Georgia, could not have acted against Andropov's wishes. It is highly doubtful that these wishes are to be explained simply as the noble desire to punish vice and to assist the triumph of virtue: the practical result was only a change in the faces, and the bribery and corruption continued.

It is difficult to rid oneself of the impression that Azerbaijan in 1969 and Georgia in 1972 and 1973 were for Andropov experiments to determine whether it was possible by means of a campaign against corruption to force the first secretary to cede his post to the head of the police apparatus, who organized the campaign in the first place. In both cases the experiment gave positive results.

The time came to make use of the acquired experience. And so the "organs," who had always been content to leave cases involving corruption to the OBKhSS, the regular police department concerned with the theft of socialist property, suddenly sprang into action in the fight against corruption.

The nomenklatura always acts by employing a campaign against something or other. For a short period of time, a certain task will be singled out and nothing in the world is more important. It is harped on over the radio and at public meetings; it is written about in the newspapers and sung about in songs. Poets write poems about it, and fiction writers short stories. Then, suddenly, it is all over and the nomenklatura curses "campaignitis." When it starts the next campaign, it swears that this time the issue is a permanent direction in the party's work. But the nomenklatura has to have its campaigns!

What was the campaign against corruption really about? To eliminate corruption in the U.S.S.R.? For that it would be necessary to make larger capital investments in consumer goods, not run campaigns. No, the purpose of the campaign was to raise the fight against corruption from a police matter to a political one, to force the nomenklaturists to feel that they, too, were vulnerable.

But what about the ruling circle? In the hierarchical thinking of the nomenklatura, the old Roman saying *Quod licet Jovi non licet bovi* has taken firm hold.

Here the Andropov group had to demonstrate that no one, not even Brezhnev himself, would come to the aid of anyone accused of corruption. This was done with great resourcefulness. A search was conducted at the home of the Moscow playboy Boris Buryatov (nicknamed the Gypsy and Brezhnev's daughter's lover). Technically he was an actor but actually was linked to some very profitable speculations. During the search, diamonds stolen not long before from the famous animal trainer Irina Bugrimova were found. Diamonds had during the past few years become very fashionable in nomenklatura circles and Galina was crazy about them. In that way, the impression was created that Brezhnev's daughter was indirectly connected with the theft of the diamonds.

Of course, a more skeptical approach would lead to the question, Why would such rich and powerful persons as Galina and Boris, who undoubtedly had far more jewels than the retired lion tamer, get mixed up in some sleazy affair for a few stones? A skeptic would not be convinced by the fact that Bugrimova's jewels were found during the search: there have been too many cases involving dissidents in which weapons, American money, and narcotics were planted during such searches, all of which would be found and entered into the police report. The facts of the case will probably never be known: the healthy young playboy, thrown in prison after the search, died there that very night. There are two versions: One attributes Boris's death to the revenge of Galina's deceived husband, Colonel General Churbanov, at the time first deputy Minister of Internal Affairs. The other version attributes his death to considerations of high-level politics.

Politics, in any case, played a part in the whole matter. The Soviet acquaintances and employees of Western journalists and diplomats in Moscow quickly began to tell stories about the affair, which compromised Brezhnev's family. Even the Russian-language broadcasts of the Voice of America, ordinarily jammed, could be heard without interference when the details of the scandal were broadcast.[13]

How did Brezhnev respond to this operation, so clearly directed against his interests? By doing nothing. True, there was a jumbled story connected with the sudden death of General Tsvigun, which the same KGB-controlled "sources" persistently linked to the affair with Boris Buryatov and Galina Brezhneva. The sources maintained that Tsvigun had wanted to expose the couple, but he was summoned by Suslov and given to understand that henceforth his career was over and even, it is said, told that suicide would be appropriate—which recommendation Tsvigun followed. This version overlooked one fact: as Brezhnev's brother-in-law, Tsvigun was the Brezhnev group's eyes and ears in the KGB. If this oft-repeated version is true, then we must assume the following: coming to the conclusion that Andropov would become the Secretary-General, Tsvigun switched to his side and was then hunted down by the Brezhnev group. Support for this interpretation can be found in the fact that Tsvigun's obituary was not signed by Brezhnev and the majority of the Politburo, the Central Committee Secretariat, and leaders in the Council of Ministers, as would ordinarily be the case. On the contrary, it was signed by all the KGB leaders, some of whose names appeared in print for the first time.[14] But another interpretation is possible: that at the critical moment, Tsvigun, as the Brezhnev group representative in the "organs," was somehow compromised in the eyes of Brezhnev and his group and therefore eliminated.

7. INTIMIDATION IS INTENSIFIED

In October 1980 the nomenklatura was shocked by the announcement that Masherov, nonvoting member of the Politburo and first secretary of the Belorussian Central Committee, had died in an automobile accident.[15] It was the first time in Soviet history that a Politburo member had been in an automobile accident, let alone a fatal one. Even an insignificant incident, when Molotov's car went off the road, became history. The incident seemed so unusual that it was turned into a Trotskyite assassination attempt against "Comrade Stalin's closest friend and comrade-in-arms" (as Molotov was then referred to) and figured in one of the Moscow show trials.

And it is truly hard to imagine how an automobile accident could happen to a Politburo member. They have armored limousines made of special steel, highly trained chauffeurs, cars with bodyguards from the KGB's Section 9 who watch out for conditions along the route. Throughout the entire trip, police posts warn of the cortege's approach, give it a green light, and the car races down the center lane, where other cars are prohibited.

Rumors immediately spread about how Masherov died. They agreed in saying that the accident had happened at an intersection where unexpectedly there were no police directing traffic, and that Masherov's ZIL had collided with cars blocking the road. According to one version it was two police cars. Another version says that one of the cars accompanying Masherov raced ahead, and after passing the intersection, blocked the road. As the ZIL with Masherov approached, at a signal given by the first car a heavy truck going at high speed jumped out from behind the curve and hit the ZIL. Everyone involved died, including the truck driver.

However it may have been, stories started circulating that Masherov had been Andropov's rival. Attention was called to the similarities in their biographies: each had been first secretary of the Komsomol central committee in his republic, and both had trained partisans during the war.

Masherov's replacement as first secretary of Belorussia was Kiselev, a Brezhnev-group protégé, it is said. He became, like Masherov, a nonvoting member of the Politburo. But in 1982 he, too, died unexpectedly. Once more rumors spread, linking his death to the desire of the Andropov group to have their man at the head of the Belorussian nomenklatura. In fact, the next first secretary, Sliunkov, had worked in the "organs," according to informed sources.

Soon still another automobile accident occurred: the victim was Nikolai Suslov, second secretary of the Leningrad district committee and a member of the Central Committee. It was said that the circumstances surrounding his death were similar to those in the Masherov case. The story goes that the Brezhnev group wanted to make Suslov the first secretary of the Leningrad committee instead of Romanov, considered an Andropov supporter.

Other deaths in automobile accidents—a sudden epidemic ravaged the nomenklatura—included the chairman of the Council of Ministers of the Georgian S.S.R. and the deputy chairman in charge of the KGB's overseas forces. Members of the Central Committee died unexpectedly: Zarodov, the former deputy editor in chief of *Pravda* and editor in chief of the international Communist magazine *Problems of Peace and Socialism,* and the academician Inozemtsev, the director of the Institute of World Economics and Internation Relations. Both were Brezhnev-group underlings; although Inozemtsev had his problems (it is suspected that he built himself a dacha with official funds), a wreath "from the Brezhnev family" was placed on his grave.

In April 1982 Rasulov, the first secretary of Tadzhikistan, died suddenly, and the still-young first secretaries of the Tatar and Yakutsk parties and the just-appointed head of the Political Administration of Soviet Armed Forces passed away.

Very probably none of these deaths was an assassination. But this accumulation of deaths and the rumors that accompanied them played an important psychological role in the upper circles of the nomenklatura. Even Politburo members got the message: their lives were in the KGB's hands to a greater extent—not to a lesser—than were the lives of ordinary citizens. Such is the result of the system introduced by Stalin and accepted by the Politburo with great pleasure: the entire service personnel in their homes, including the cooks and chauffeurs, to say nothing of their bodyguards, consists of employees of the KGB. They are subordinate to their KGB superiors, and not to the Politburo members themselves. Everything is fine as long as those superiors order the personnel to lavish care upon their nominal masters. But if those superiors order some other kind of treatment?

It is quite possible that the rumors about the circumstances of Kiselev's and the others' deaths were spread by the KGB itself—precisely in order to force the top-level nomenklaturists to ponder the risks of fighting the Andropov group.

The grand finale of the intimidation suite, which was meant to (and undoubtedly did) produce a strong impression on the Politburo, was the banishment of Kirilenko. For the usual holiday on November 7, 1982, the portraits of the Politburo members were hung out—but no

Kirilenko. By way of explanation a rumor was let loose by all the "sources": Kirilenko's son had escaped abroad and Kirilenko had shot himself. But at Brezhnev's funeral he appeared in the group of personal friends of the deceased, and since the ceremony was being televised live from Red Square, the whole country saw him. The "sources" immediately came up with a new variation: Kirilenko had shot himself but he had been "reanimated"—as though a person could immediately set out for a stroll through Red Square after such a "reanimation" procedure. The important thing, however, was not these silly stories, but the fact that someone, not being a Stalin or a Brezhnev, could—without any resolution by the Central Committee plenary session—simply banish a Politburo member and a Central Committee secretary, one of the most influential leaders in the nomenklatura, who not long before had chaired the Politburo and the Secretariat. This demonstration of Andropov's power on the eve of the election of the Secretary-General apparently decided the outcome of the vote once and for all.

So, then, the goal was reached by somewhat unexpected methods: without resurrecting Stalin's terror (which the nomenklatura would never have permitted) to persuade the Brezhnev group that they would be better off electing Andropov. They were shown that, without any anti-Trotskyite hysteria, each of them could be accused directly or implicated indirectly; that even the Brezhnev clan was not safe; therefore there was no one to defend him; and finally, that their fate was in the hands of the "organs." On that basis there took place the compromise that was a coup.

The probability of Andropov's getting the Secretary-General job became significant, it was noticed even by a computer. In 1981 a computer at Iowa University predicted who Brezhnev's most likely successor would be. The result was, given the variables—age (sixty to seventy years) and nationality (Russian)—the number of candidates was limited to one person. That was Andropov.[16]

8. A LIBERAL IN POWER?

While all these events were taking place, the Andropov group was conducting a campaign to present him as a liberal and pro-Westerner. Soviets who had never before told stories about the nomenklatura leaders suddenly began to volunteer all kinds of details about Andropov to Western diplomats and journalists. All these town criers stressed the idea that Andropov, unlike the other members of the Soviet leadership (sometimes Chernenko was mentioned by name), was a person with liberal, open views, who liked the intelligentsia and was sympathetic to the West, and that his taking office as Secretary-General was a rare stroke of good luck that should be highly appreciated. The Western press, which swallows greedily any bit of news about nomenklatura bosses, was quickly filled with the news that Andropov read American novels, collected records of contemporary Western music, played tennis, drank whisky, had heart-to-heart talks with dissidents (these were never named), and—through his daughter Irina and her husband, the actor Filippov—was linked to the artistic world.[17] Even though an interest in pop music and a taste for whisky are no guarantee of liberal views, and Irina had long since divorced Filippov and remarried (a scientist with no connection with the artistic world), the image of an aging playboy, an ex-bohemian, in the position of Secretary-General aroused hope in the West that a new page in Soviet history was being turned.

The fact that a propaganda operation to popularize Andropov in the West was being conducted on the Soviet side was acknowledged by my old friend G. A. Arbatov, a member of the Central Committee, during a conversation with the American journalist Joseph Kraft. Arbatov did explain, however, that the operation was the "work of volunteers."[18] Arbatov himself belonged to their number, and the co-workers from his institute—but not only them! Among Soviet intellectuals there were of course volunteers who considered the pragmatic Andropov the best of possible candidates for Secretary-General.

Picked up by the Western media, the campaign produced results. Letters from the U.S.A. addressed to Andropov began arriving in Moscow. I quote them from the Russian translation in *Pravda:* "I have heard many good things about you," a fourteen-year-old schoolboy from Nebraska writes. "I believe you when you wish every American family a Happy New Year and sincerely wish them success and happiness," trustingly writes an American Legion member from Florida. A woman from Vermont, on the subject of the U.S. response to the deployment of the Soviet SS-20 rockets, appealed with enthusiasm to Andropov: "I want you to know that there are people in our country just like you, who not only protest against these plans but emphatically reject the insane logic that gives birth to this monstrosity." "Dear friend," a Miamian writes more simply, "what you have done is great!"[19]

Could it be that Andropov really is a liberal? In the Western sense . . . certainly not. In the Soviet sense . . . also not. Ever since Lenin's times the word "liberal" is an insult in the Soviet Union. Lenin would rage with a furious hatred whenever he spoke or wrote about liberals. An interested reader can use the index to Lenin's complete works and admire the richness of the abusive epithets applied to liberals. And it is a bit much to expect a liberal politician in a person who headed the KGB for fifteen years.

But, all the same, it is by the standards of that organization that Andropov was a kind of liberal. After all, he was neither a sentimentally fanatic killer like Dzerzhinsky, nor a psychotic monster like Yezhov or Beria. He apparently did not derive a sadistic pleasure from his work, although he was not all that bothered by it either. In the Kraft interview, Arbatov said that "he made the KGB different from what it had been. Under him, its reputation improved. It no longer fitted the stereotype of an organ of terror. Still, it is not a welfare organization."[20] The last remark is quite true.

For fifteen years Andropov occupied an enormous office: a huge room on the fifth floor of the well-known building on Lubianka. One of his predecessors in the job, Abakumov, enjoyed beating prisoners with a stick; to avoid splattering a carpet with blood, a special floor covering was installed.

With Andropov, KGB prisoners had a different kind of experience, although still not particularly pleasant ones. For example, Nikolai Sheragin, born in one of the Baltic states but a British subject residing in England, came to Moscow as part of a British delegation. The KGB arrested him and tried to force him to collaborate. Sheragin refused. He recalls how Andropov entered suddenly while he was being interrogated. Everyone in the room leaped to his feet. Andropov said casually,

"Please continue, comrades." Then he asked, "Why is no one taking notes?" Everyone began to feverishly jot down notes. When Sheragin announced that he would not answer any more questions, Andropov inquired whether the detainee had his papers. Sheragin took out his passport. "I stood in the center of the room," Sheragin relates. "Andropov jumped up from a sofa, grabbed the British passport out of my hands, and opened it to the page with personal data." Andropov told the others that I had been born in Russia and added, "Unfortunately, although you have a British passport, you were born here, and therefore you'll be dealt with according to our laws, and our will." Then he closed the passport, walked right up to me, and said in English, "The queen will not go to war with us over you."[21]

That prediction was correct, and Sheragin spent many years behind bars in the U.S.S.R.

Andropov (also in the English language) advised a Canadian professor who had become a Soviet agent to announce his candidacy for Parliament. Andropov offered to pay all the campaign expenses of "the people's choice" out of the KGB treasury. The Canadian became confused and rejected the offer.

It is known that soon after Andropov's arrival at the KGB, the agency's disinformation work was reorganized. In 1980, during the trial of the Soviet agent Pathé, a member of French counterintelligence quoted Andropov: "The U.S.S.R.'s political role abroad must be supported by means of the dissemination of false stories and provocatory information."[22]

More examples could be given, but there should be no need. From what has already been said it is clear that Andropov was no liberal intellectual.

It is to Andropov's honor that he was more concerned with the KGB's international activity than with the monotonous persecution of defenseless Soviet citizens. However, here, too, he did not introduce liberalizations—even expanding the practice of imprisoning dissidents in special psychiatric hospitals, those disgraces of Soviet medicine.

The war in Afghanistan provided the incentive for a new departure: Karmal's security forces, directed by advisers from the U.S.S.R., when interrogating those suspected of contacts with the resistance movement, began to use types of torture transported to our times from the

Asiatic middle ages. A single word from Andropov would have been enough to stop them, but he said nothing.

All of this should not obscure Andropov's positive features. Acquaintances who worked in his department in the Central Committee had a good impression of him: a reasonable person, not an arrogant bureaucrat, but a thoughtful manager who would listen to his subordinates' opinions. True, everyone noticed that he was aloof and cold. But he was businesslike, and he was a good person to work for. These comments were not the fawning glorification of a superior, but the honest opinions of people who said the same thing even after Andropov was no longer their boss.

What were the results of Andropov's fifteen-month tenure as Secretary-General? The account is lean: the worker-discipline and anticorruption campaign in domestic policy and the course of confrontation with the U.S.A. on the foreign side. Beyond that there were a few inconsequential economic experiments and the announcement of academic reform. Certainly a disappointment to the "free citizenry" of the U.S.S.R. and to those in the West who had hoped for more.

De mortuis nil nisi bonum. Now we know that Andropov was already terminally ill when he assumed power, and aware of the limited time left to him. The result was that all his sophisticated maneuvers served only one purpose: to leave his name in reference and history books. It is doubtful that one will actually want to look up the name Andropov in these books.

On an unusually sunny February day in 1984 the Kremlin elite carried him in slow pace across Red Square into oblivion.

9. THE PREPROGRAMMED VICTORY

It was obviously not the intention of the Chernenko group to watch Andropov's chess moves with resignation. The complicated position in which they found themselves was made tolerable by their awareness of the Secretary-General's poor health. The Chernenko group's tactic was probably to avoid serious confrontation and to marshal their forces so that, as Stalin put it, they could drag victory with them.

This tactic had promise, since Chernenko had time on his side. His group supported itself through the party leadership, the heart of the nomenklatura; whereas Andropov could only count on the KGB and the military-industrial complex, the stabilizers of the class. Of course the Secretary-General gained some influence in the party apparatus, particularly in the propaganda section. But in the long run the Andropov group was hardly secure. Even the post of Chairman of the Praesidium of the Supreme Soviet of the U.S.S.R. was granted Andropov only through compromise: Chernenko, in turn, rose to become second secretary of the Central Committee of the Communist Party. Responsible for organization and ideological matters, Chernenko had combined control over Suslov's and Kirilenko's power centers. This significant step made him the natural successor to the secretary-generalship after Andropov's death.

In the West there was surprise about Chernenko's comeback. In reality, his victory was preprogrammed: In the nomenklatura it is not the individuals, other than hidden powers behind them, that are of consequence. The party apparatus is, as the axis of the nomenklatura, the decisive power center, and thus Chernenko had to win.

Who is the victor?

Konstantin Ustinovich Chernenko is a short, stocky man, slightly stooped, with the swaying walk of an elderly person, but he is also robust and extremely concentrated. His broad face has unmistakable Mongolian characteristics, which is not rare among Siberians.

Chernenko's rise is breathtaking. Not only his ancestors, but he himself, were farmhands from the deep provinces, and he earned his livelihood as a dayworker for well-off peasants. Now he is the most powerful man in the immense Soviet Union and, to boot, in all the countries in the Soviet bloc. It's certain that such a life has had its dramatic twists, but we are told nothing of that: his official biography is logical, consistent, and actually boring.

Chernenko was born on September 24, 1911, in the village of Bolshaya Tes, in Novoselova district, Krasnoyarsk province. He is Russian even though his name is of Ukrainian origin.

Right from the beginning, Chernenko chose the secure path to success, which goes with the Komsomol and the party apparatus. At eighteen he was named leader of the department of agitation and propaganda of the Novoselova district committee. Thus already he was a nomenklaturist. At nineteen he entered the Army—the privileged Border Troop—and here too he soon became party secretary.

In 1933, Chernenko left military service. There are rumors that he entered GPU—the secret police—and served in Dnepropetrovsk, where he formed a friendship with the young Brezhnev, but the official biography reads that Chernenko returned to Krasnoyarsk province, again as director of the propaganda section in the district committee, but this time a party member. Later, he moved to the capital, Krasnoyarsk, where he became director of the House of Party Training. This position proved to be fortuitous. The thirty-year-old Chernenko rose to the rank of deputy leader of the propaganda section of the district party committee and then to secretary of propaganda of the committee.

Further advancement required higher education. In 1943 Chernenko was sent for two years to the Central Committee of the Communist Party. Although the level of education of the graduates was not extraordinary, a diploma guaranteed its owner a secure position in the nomenklatura. In 1945 he went to Penza as secretary for propaganda of the regional party committee. The Central Committee of the Communist Party advanced him in 1948 to Kishinev as director of the agitation and propaganda department in the central committee of the Communist Party of Moldavia. There Chernenko earned his university degree: he graduated from the Pedagogic Institute in Kishinev; incidentally, the institute came under his jurisdiction.

Much more important than this diploma was the fateful appointment of Brezhnev as first secretary of the central committee of the Communist Party in Moldavia in 1950. It was there that Brezhnev got to know and appreciate Chernenko. It is possible that the rumors in Kishinev about Chernenko's role in Brezhnev's drinking orgies and love affairs are untrue. What is true is that their inseparable friendship originated at this time. It was so inseparable that, from the Twentieth Party Conference (1956), at which Brezhnev was named Secretary of the Central Committee of the Communist Party, till the end of his life, a quarter of a century later, he always called on Chernenko. In his last years, Brezhnev even invited Chernenko to join him on vacations in the Crimea. Thus in 1956 Chernenko came to Moscow as chief of the agitation desk in the Propaganda and Agitation Department of the Central Committee of the Communist Party. We have already seen how powerful a section leader in the Central Committee is, and a further illustration appears at the end of the book. In 1960 Brezhnev, who in the meantime had advanced to the chairmanship of the Presidium of the Supreme Soviet of the U.S.S.R., made his friend Chernenko head of the Secretariat of the Presidium. And when, in 1964, Brezhnev became First Secretary, he took Chernenko back into the Central Committee—this time into the extremely important position of leader of the General Assembly. This office is the chancellery of the directive bodies, and here rests the entire decision-making process at the pinnacle of the nomenklatura.

Stalin evaluated correctly the position of Secretary-General of the Central Committee and used it as his stepping-stone. Chernenko also understood the value of the position and used it accordingly. Like Stalin, he worked late into the night, even on weekends. Once, on a Saturday, the director of the Institute of the Academy for Natural Science of the U.S.S.R. for the U.S.A., Arbatov, and I were working on a position paper for the leadership in the International Department of the Central Committee. Arbatov called Chernenko on his *vertushka*, and Chernenko was of course there, received the paper, and immediately ordered it "distributed in the Politburo."

In 1971, at age sixty, he became a member of the Central Committee. His meteoric rise since then is now well known.

In this manner, Chernenko rose step by consistent step in an almost prosaic yet also rather fantastic way from peasant to czar.

A czar? Not quite. Since Stalin, the Secretary-General of the Communist Party is no longer an autocrat. Even in his exalted position, Chernenko (as before him Andropov, Brezhnev, Khrushchev) does not make policy personally; that is left to the nomenklatura, the true ruler of the Soviet Union.

In the example of the transfer of the highest position in the nomenklatura from Brezhnev via Andropov to Chernenko, we have seen the most significant weakness of this class: its inability to find a regular procedure for the natural transfer of power. It is not an accidental defect. To a significant degree it has determined the entire history of the Soviet period. If you try to erase the struggle for power in the Kremlin from this history, the whole course of events becomes incomprehensible. In this organic flaw, the class essence is manifest: the readiness to seize power by any means, without regard for procedure or rules. This weakens the nomenklatura, because it makes plain to everybody that instead of fighting for the people's happiness, the nomenklaturists are fighting for power. But the nomenklaturist cannot help himself and will resort to it every time to achieve his dream: more power for himself.

NOTES

1. Nikolai Gogol, *Dead Souls,* New York, 1923, Vol. 2, pp. 37–38.
2. K. U. Chernenko, *KPSS i prava čeloveka,* Moscow, 1961.
3. *The New Republic,* Feb. 7, 1983, p. 21.
4. V. Krasin, *Sud.* New York, 1983, p. 73.
5. N. Khrushchev, *Vospominaniya,* Book 2, New York, 1981, p. 218.
6. E. Vasari, *Die ungarische Revolution 1956,* Stuttgart, 1981, p. 350.
7. See New York *Times,* Nov. 14, 1982, p. 39.
8. ARD (German TV) Broadcast, "Personalakte Jurij Andropov," Nov. 23, 1982.
9. See *Kurier* (Vienna), Nov. 14, 1982.
10. *The New Yorker,* Jan. 31, 1983, p. 106.
11. *Pravda,* Oct. 28, 1982.
12. See Zemtsov, *La corruption en Union Soviétique,* Paris, 1976, pp. 133–34.
13. *Harper's Magazine,* Feb. 1983, p. 24.
14. For more detail see *Der Spiegel,* Nov. 22, 1982, No. 47, p. 151.
15. See *Pravda,* Oct. 6, 1980.
16. E. Schneider, "Die zentrale politische Führungselite der UdSSR," Part 2, *Berichte des Bundesinstituts für ostwissenschaftliche und internationale Studien,* Köln, 15–1982, p. 111.
17. See *Harper's Magazine,* Feb. 1983, pp. 23–26; *The New Republic,* Feb. 7, 1983, pp. 18–21.
18. *The New Yorker,* Jan. 31, 1983, p. 109.
19. *Pravda,* Apr. 11, 1983.
20. *The New Yorker,* Jan. 31, 1983, p. 109.
21. ARD Broadcast, "Personalakte Jurij Andropov," Nov. 23, 1982.
22. *Le Figaro,* Apr. 6, 1983.

9
Parasitic Class

We dug and we toiled,
And we bit the iron,
We offered our chests
To the muzzles of submachine guns.
And you, driving past
In your Victory motorcars,
Shouted to us:
"Achieve your norm."
And we forgot
About sleep and food,
And you led us
From victory to victory.
Meanwhile you
Exchanged your Victories for Volgas,
And later
You exchanged your Volgas for Zims,
And later
You exchanged your Zims for Chaikas,
And later
You exchanged your Chaikas for ZILs.

And we wore ourselves to the bone,
We dug and we loaded,
And you led us
From victory to victory
And shouted toasts
To victory.

A. Galich, *Kogda ya vernus.*
Frankfurt, 1977, pp. 121–22

This last chapter will be devoted to the parasitism of the nomenklatura class and its morality—two topics that differ in kind from those we have discussed so far. The antagonistic nature of society under real socialism, the origin and development of the nomenklatura, the way it governs, its exploitative practices, its privileges, and its domestic and foreign policies are sharply defined realities. In contrast to that, in the present chapter we shall be dealing with things that are obvious enough in real life but do not lend themselves to treatment in the abstract. So, after a brief introduction, we shall provide some sketches from real life showing the nomenklatura in action. This will give the reader who has never met a nomenklaturist a more vivid idea of that class: its parasitism, its essential nature, its morality.

1. THE NOMENKLATURA BECOMES PARASITIC

We quoted the Marxist definition of classes in Chapter 1. As every class plays a definite part in the process of social production, parasitic classes should not exist. A class becomes parasitic when its social profitability dwindles; it begins to cost society more than it contributes to it. The process takes place at two levels: the privileges of the incipient parasitic class, the share of the national product that it arrogates to itself, increase, while its contribution to that product diminishes. At the point where the two vectors meet, its social profitability reaches zero. This rather geometrical pattern retains its validity in spite of the complexity of the social phenomena involved.

Why did the nomenklatura develop this parasitic trend? It is not the result of individual idleness; nomenklaturists as a rule are active, busy people. Their parasitism is of social origin, is a result of their class situation.

The parasitic tendencies of a ruling class are the consequence of its monopoly position.

In *Imperialism, the Highest Stage of Capitalism,* Lenin says that all monopoly . . . "inevitably engenders a tendency to stagnation and decay. Since monopoly prices are established . . . the motive cause of technical and, consequently, of all other progress disappears to a certain extent."[1]

Thus Lenin regards monopoly, not just capitalist monopoly but monopoly of any kind, as the principal cause of the parasitism of a ruling class. The degree of parasitic degeneration depends on the extent of the monopoly; the more complete it is (the weaker the competition—whether economic, political, or ideological), the harder it is to breach, the more accentuated does the parasitic degeneration of the ruling class become, and the more completely does it develop into a sclerotic caste that is a burden to society, robbing it of its substance and giving nothing in return.

Signs of parasitism are certainly evident in the capitalist system, but it is characterized by extremely powerful industrial groupings, rather than by true monopolies, and competition is not eliminated. Hence, in the capitalist society of the present day, parasitism manifests itself as a *"tendency* to stagnation and decay, which is characteristic of monopoly."[2]

The situation is different under real socialism, in which the nomenklatura monopoly is all-embracing. All competition with it is stifled at birth, with the result that parasitism and stagnation spread unchecked. Hence, in complete harmony with Lenin's view of the matter, the nomenklaturist class, though it appeared in history much later than the capitalist class, has already left it a long way behind on the road to parasitic degeneration.

Why should the nomenklatura work? It is a class of exploiters whose high standard of living is assured by the work of others. As the only employer in the country, it has millions of acolytes who manage the productive process on its behalf. The atmosphere of intimidation that it maintains by means of a huge police machine enables it almost effortlessly to do whatever it likes in domestic affairs. In foreign affairs it is not yet in that position, and feels that there is still a great deal of "work" for it to do. But that "work," like everything else it does, is in its own interest and not society's. With its unlimited power in the political, economic, and ideological fields, it has succeeded in so securing its position and so thoroughly isolating itself from the population that to remain in the driver's seat it no longer needs to do anything whatever on society's behalf; maintaining the mechanism of the dictatorship is sufficient.

Every social class defends its own interests; there is no such thing as an altruistic class. But a ruling class whose monopoly is incomplete has to do something for the other classes, to reconcile them to its dominant position. The nomenklatura has no need to do this, and that is the real reason for its rapid parasitic degeneration.

The dictatorship of the nomenklatura has cost the U.S.S.R. dearly. In the first place, there is the appalling loss of human life for which it has been responsible. Professor I. A. Kurganov has calculated the difference between the population level that should theoretically have been reached if normal population growth had taken place, and the actual figures for the period 1917–59; he puts it at 110 million. Such is the toll in human lives for which the dictatorship of the nomenklatura has been responsible. More than half the victims were murdered, executed, liquidated in camps, or died of starvation.[3]

The price paid also includes the poverty resulting from exploitation by the nomenklatura, and the inability of the latter to develop the country's economy and enable it to meet the population's demands instead of pursuing only its own class interests.

It also includes the continual increase in nomenklatura consumption; and here we refer not just to its gastronomic privileges and government dachas, but above all to the raw materials and labor wasted on behalf of its class interests: the gigantic war machine, the huge police and ideological apparatus, and its expansionist policy beyond the Soviet frontiers.

Also included in the price is the abolition of freedom, the stifling of all forms of independent thought, the brake on the normal exchange of ideas between citizens of the same country, and between them and citizens of other countries. All these imponderables have inflicted material as well as moral damage on Soviet society, as is especially evident in the field of science and technology.

The combined influence of these factors has prevented post-czarist Russia from joining the group of highly developed countries. Neither revolutionary slogans nor the creation of a powerful arms industry can conceal the fact that under nomenklatura rule the social and political backwardness of the country has been preserved. That is indeed a high price to pay for a country whose main problem is that of overcoming that historical handicap.

What benefits has the country had from nomenklatura rule?

Without the nomenklatura, heavy industry in Russia would probably not have reached its present level. The production of consumer goods and light industry, and the agricultural and food industries, would have been better developed. Nevertheless the establishment of heavy industry must be regarded as a positive achievement.

To the nomenklatura, this forced industrialization was not an end in itself, but the necessary prelude to the development of the arms industry. The present military strength of the Soviet Union is unquestionably due to the nomenklatura. If there were a real threat of aggression against the U.S.S.R., that would be a good thing. In its absence it is the reverse.

In certain matters the balance is favorable. In the Soviet Union rents and public transport are cheap; medical attention is free; convalescent and rest homes have been built; books, newspapers, theater, cinema, and concert tickets are inexpensive. All these things, of course, are merely a counterpart of the fact that wages are extremely low. But in themselves these are good things.

Scientific research is bureaucratically and expensively (but not badly) organized by the nomenklatura. Soviet education is in good shape, though Soviet students have a difficult time.

The favorable results of nomenklatura rule are more marked in the undeveloped than in the developed areas of the Soviet Union. There are also aspects of the system that call for a more ambivalent judgment. In contrast to the obvious unemployment in Western countries, for instance, unemployment in the U.S.S.R. is concealed. That has its positive aspects, but it also enables wages to be kept low and thus increases the exploitation rate. Attempts by the nomenklatura to put an end to certain offenses against public morality may have been inherently justifiable, but their effect is insignificant in comparison with the damage done by Lenin's relativization of morality and the persecution of religion. All such measures by the nomenklatura bear a striking resemblance to Hitler's attempts to give a healthy look to the Nazi regime.

Those are the things that can be put to the nomenklatura's credit, and they are certainly not to be despised. But they do not compensate for the millions of lives lost, the poverty, the suppression of freedom, and the consolidation of the country's backwardness.

Like every other country, the Soviet Union, of course, has its objective difficulties. But, in the West, there is a tendency to exaggerate these. How often have I heard it said that Russia has always been a poor country and cannot be compared with the West! As long as I lived in the Soviet Union, that is what I believed myself. But when I came to the West and saw countries almost devoid of natural resources whose economies were nevertheless flourishing, I realized that Russia is an immensely rich country that has always been wretchedly administered —first by princes and boyars, then by czars and nobles, and now by secretaries-general and the nomenklatura.

2. ORGANIZED FORMS OF PARASITISM

As evidence for his theory of the increasingly parasitic nature of the capitalist class, Lenin, in his *Imperialism, the Highest Stage of Capitalism*, mentions the increase in the number of persons living on unearned income, i.e., by "clipping coupons."[4] The claim is unworthy of Lenin's intelligence. It was obviously a hasty judgment (the work was written in six months) based on more or less chance observations made in Switzerland between 1914 and 1916. Investment is a form of saving that cannot be equated with parasitism. A society, any kind of society, can only congratulate itself if a large number of people invest their savings instead of spending them, thus contributing to the development of industry. That has nothing to do with parasitism.

But one can be much more specific about the parasitism of the nomenklatura, which has assumed organized forms. The most important of these is the system of dual control in the party and state apparatus.

Corresponding to every ministry, or at any rate every group of associated ministries, is a division of the Central Committee of the CPSU. According to the official ranking order, the head of a Central Committee division is senior to a minister of the Soviet Union; thus all a ministry's work is directed and supervised by the corresponding Central Committee division. The question arises whether one or the other is not superfluous.

Never mind how often it is repeated that the party organs consider questions from the party standpoint, while the state organs consider the same questions from the viewpoint of the state; in practice the same work is done twice. In other words, two people do it, one in the Central Committee division and the other in the ministry. This begins at the top, with the head of the division and the corresponding minister.

These important people do not, of course, do the work themselves, which brings us to the second form of organized parasitism. Many nomenklaturists have a number of deputies, and the higher up the ladder they are, the more deputies they have. The President of the Presidium of the Supreme Soviet has sixteen, the President of the Council of Ministers twelve, and the Foreign Minister ten. In scientific research institutes the director, who is the only nomenklaturist, sometimes has several. If he has one only, it is either because the institute is small or because he is a freethinker.

I remember a conversation I had with an Austrian high official when I was still in Moscow. I asked him who his minister's deputy was. He shrugged his shoulders and replied that no such post existed. "But who does the minister's work, then?" I asked in some surprise. "The minister himself, of course," he replied, just as surprised. The explanation of our astonishment was that we belonged to different worlds. It was obvious to me that a minister would not do the work himself, but would have someone to handle the files for him, while to my interlocutor it was just as obvious that a minister did his own work.

The official explanation is that the minister exercises "general supervision." That expression, like "party leadership," is nomenklatura jargon, but is more difficult to explain. Its meaning is suggested by terms such as "honorary president" and "under the distinguished patronage of." It implies that the minister lives in princely accommodation, is driven everywhere in a Chaika, attends Central Committee plenums and meetings of the Supreme Soviet, and has a seat on the platform at various ceremonial functions. He signs important documents drafted by his subordinates, takes part in meetings of the Council of Ministers, and when called upon to do so makes nervous appearances at the Politburo or Central Committee Secretariat when problems concerning his field of responsibility are discussed. He appears at banquets and receptions, goes abroad on delegations, and—rarely—makes purely formal tours of inspection of organizations or factories for which his ministry may be responsible in various parts of the country. But the important task is systematically to maintain the friendliest possible contacts with his counterpart on the Central Committee, the division head, and his first deputy, as well as with the vice-president of the Council of Ministers, who, as it is so elegantly phrased, is "in charge" of his ministry.

"To be in charge of," in Russian, *kurirovat*, is a piece of nomenklatura jargon that has been current since the middle of the fifties. The person "in charge" is a grade lower than the person who exercises "general supervision"; consequently it is not the head of the division or his first deputy who is "in charge," but the other deputies.

As we have mentioned, there are many deputies, and the work is shared among them. Ministries are "in the charge of" deputy presidents of the Council of Ministers, their principal divisions are "in the charge of" deputies of the minister, and the industries subject to the ministry are "in the charge of" deputies of the head of the division.

Thus, in practice, the work begins where the nomenklatura leaves off. There are of course exceptions to the rule, but generally speaking it can be said that wherever the nomenklatura is to be found, much giving of orders takes place; the real work is done by officials who are not part of the nomenklatura.

In the summer of 1957, the premises of the Ministry of Power-Station Construction, which had just been abolished by Khrushchev, were put at the disposal of the Institute of World Economy and International Relations of the Academy of Sciences, where I was then working. The ministry had occupied a big building in the Kitaisky Proyezd that now houses Glavlit, the Soviet censorship department. We went to have a look at the premises evacuated by the ministry: the minister's huge office with walls paneled in the Kremlin style, with rest room and lavatory and big anteroom attached; the spacious offices of his deputies, which were similarly paneled; the big offices reserved for less exalted members of the hierarchy; the small offices of the clerks, in which cheap desks and wobbly chairs were closely packed together. When we had sufficiently feasted our eyes on this anatomy of a Soviet ministry, we began curiously examining the registers that had been left on the desks. In conformity with Soviet practice, the secretaries had conscientiously noted down the remarks of their superiors. The minister's personal contributions were rather thin; they were limited to noting the name of the deputy who was to deal with the file concerned. The deputy passed it on to the head of the administration, marked "for examination and appropriate action." The head of the administration then passed it to his deputy, who in turn sent it to the appropriate office for action to be taken. As there were no more nomenklaturists to pass it on to, work then began. The abolition of the ministry caused all these minute-making nomenklaturists to lose their positions—in spite of which, power stations went on being built.

A thought flashed through my mind on that occasion. Were not all these nomenklaturist chiefs not parasites, perhaps? I now know the answer to that question.

3. THE BEING OF THE NOMENKLATURA DETERMINES ITS CONSCIOUSNESS.

According to Marx, "It is not the consciousness of men that determines their being, but, on the contrary, their social being that determines their consciousness."[5] It is the social being of the nomenklatura, which is an exploiting, privileged, and parasitic class exercising dictatorial power, that completely determines its consciousness.

The nomenklatura owes its moral principles to its two fathers, Lenin and Stalin. Lenin informed a Communist youth conference that "we reject any morality based on extra-human and extra-class concepts. . . . We say that our morality is entirely subordinated to the interests of the proletariat's class struggle," i.e., the struggle for the establishment of the dictatorship of the nomenklatura. "Morality is what serves to destroy the old, exploiting society and to unite all the working people around the proletariat,"[6] that is, for the establishment of a new exploiting class by a self-appointed vanguard of the proletariat, led by the nomenklatura. Stalin did less theorizing but put the new morality into practice in a most impressive way.

Works by Soviet sociologists in the twenties, that have long since vanished from Soviet libraries, noted a rapid moral deterioration among the population and a tendency to cynical egoism and careerism. Empirical studies (which were then still permitted) showed that this was increasing and was especially marked among the young; thus the phenomenon could hardly be said to be a relic of capitalism. What was to be the future development of this society in which only revolutionary, collectivist, and egalitarian ideas could be mentioned aloud? Research on this point was forbidden, and replaced by rhetoric about "the new

Soviet man," who was totally devoted to the party and its leadership and worked disinterestedly for the socialist fatherland.

To a Marxist, the phenomenon is easily explicable. Marx and Engels wrote: "The ideas of the ruling class are in every epoch the ruling ideas; i.e., the class which is the ruling material force of society is at the same time its ruling intellectual force."[7] The class morality of the nomenklatura spread through Soviet society. But however widespread the infection may have been in some social groups, it was only in the nomenklatura that it manifested (and still manifests) itself in its most concentrated form.

As we have pointed out, the privileges and favors that a nomenklaturist enjoys are not recompense for work done, but a mere consequence of a decision made by a directing agency of the party that appoints him to a position with the privileges attached. Only an ambitious and adroit schemer capable of climbing the hierarchical ladder can hope to secure such a decision. In a capitalist environment it is the spirit of enterprise that counts; the nomenklatura is dominated by careerism.

Careerism is the chief characteristic of its class mentality. All a nomenklaturist's thoughts and hopes are centered on his career. As in a game of chess, he must think continually about the move ahead, the step that will enable him to climb higher, or "grow," as they say in nomenklatura jargon. That is the ordinary state of mind of the nomenklaturist. Hence the golden rule of the nomenklatura is that you cannot be sure of keeping your job unless you have your eye on the next one above it; if you are satisfied with your present job, you are almost certainly heading for demotion. At the same time, promotion calls for superhuman efforts if you are not to be left at the post by a colleague.

In this rat race it is not surprising that anything goes, provided it is effective. I have never known an atmosphere so packed with intrigue, with so much hypocrisy camouflaged as loyalty to the principles of the party. The people who constitute the nomenklatura are, of course, too varied for it to consist solely of scoundrels; decent nomenklaturists also exist. But when it comes to the point, you have to stifle your scruples; otherwise you run the risk of expulsion from the nomenklatura, and nothing could be more disastrous to a nomenklaturist than loss of his status, the status that is his pride and joy.

We have spoken of the solidarity of the nomenklatura class, of the united front it shows to outsiders. But the medal has its reverse side, which is the solitude felt by every nomenklaturist: He is acutely aware that his class fellows are also his most dangerous competitors and that they support him only as long as it is in their own interest to do so. When this ceases to be the case, they are only too willing to drop him. He likes talking about capitalism, in which man is a wolf to man, but he feels himself to be merely a wolf in a pack of wolves, surrounded by his likes but nevertheless solitary and threatened. Such a situation is probably inevitable in every "new class" of parvenus who repudiate their class origins.

The philosophy of the nomenklatura has been summed up in a poem by Edward Bagritsky, who is considered a classic writer of Soviet literature:

> Stay loyal to the age we all live in;
> Your loneliness is to it akin;
> The hands you shake are not those of friends;
> About you are people you hate;
> And if the age says lie, lie to all ends;
> And if it says kill, don't hesitate.[8]

What this attitude means in real life is best illustrated by actual examples. So I shall conclude this chapter with two portraits. The first, which is historical, is based on documents; the second is contemporary and is based on personal observation.

4. DISTRICT COMMITTEE SECRETARY

I remember the growing sense of unease with which, when I was a young interpreter at the Nuremberg war crimes trials, I looked through the photostats of Nazi documents adorned with signatures, official stamps, and various annotations. Behind those documents I saw human lives broken by an inhuman administrative machine. Many years later I had the same feeling when going through other documents, this time not of Nazi origin, but coming from the western regional committee of the CPSU. They are now preserved in Washington in the so-called Smolensk Archive.

An excellent summary of them was made by the late American professor Merle Fainsod,[9] but it does not claim to be complete and does not exhaust the subject. I shall therefore concentrate on one aspect only, and try to revive in his ordinary, everyday reality a provincial nomenklatura personality as these documents show him to have been.

The scene is the small town of Kozelsk, one of many centers of districts in the western region, and the time is 1936, when the Stalin constitution was promulgated as a prelude to the Stalin purge. Dramatis personae: Piotr Mikhailovich Demenok, secretary of the Kozelsk district committee, address, the former Shchegolev house, Sovietskaya Street, Kozelsk; Joseph Petrovich Balobeshko, second secretary of the district committee and Demenok's deputy, who lived in the same house, evidently confiscated from its former owner; and A. Tsebur, second lieutenant in the security forces and local head of the NKVD.

These, then, are the leaders of 420 members of the local party organization. Their names also appear alone on a document rather puzzlingly headed: "List of leaders and deputies of the district committee of the CPSU, Kozelsk, to whom urgent telegrams about the declarational states of emergency, maneuvers and mobilization are to be delivered immediately."[10] So the two men are war lords also.

The secretaries of the western region of the CPSU, at Smolensk, are senior to these local leaders. These are Rumiantsev, first secretary of the regional committee, and Shilman, its secretary. (Shilman is a Jewish name; Jews had not yet been expelled from the party apparatus in 1936.)

But the horizon of the governors of Kozelsk is not restricted to the Olympian heights of Smolensk. Here is a file marked Secretariat of the Central Committee, Moscow, Staraya Ploshchad, House 4, no. OB/43/15. From the Orgburo of the Central Committee of the CPSU. To Comrade P. M. Demenok. He has been sent instructions and an extract from the minutes of an Orgburo meeting. Here is the full text of the letter in which some historical names appear:

Proletarians of all countries, unite.
Strictly secret. To be returned.
Special department No. P2600. Copy No. 2403.
Comrade Demenok,
By order of Comrade Stalin we are sending you a shorthand report of the

meeting of the Plenum of the Central Committee of the CPSU held on December 21 to 25, 1935.

A. Poskrebyshev
Head of the Special Department of the Central Committee.[11]

Here we plainly see the thread connecting the father of the nomenklatura to the nomenklaturists of Kozelsk. The hero of our story is not a mere provincial nobody responsible for a district lost in the vast spaces of Russia; he is an organic part of a system, the nomenklatura, that links him with Stalin.

We first come across him reporting to Shilman, the secretary of the regional committee, to which he returned on April 16, after recovering from an illness. The first task that awaited him was the renewal of the party cards. This was a process that enabled the administration of the nomenklatura to carry out purges. Yezhov, who was then an official of the Central Committee and had not yet been appointed People's Commissar for Internal Affairs, was in charge of this at Union level. Party cards were vetted for the purpose of getting rid of Communists whom the leaders disliked.

Expulsion from the party has disastrous consequences for a Soviet citizen. He is entitled not to join the party if he does not want to; in that case he will not have a very brilliant career, but he will be able to live. On the contrary, a person expelled from the party is branded. The sword of Damocles dangles perpetually over his head. The threat of expulsion is sufficient to impose obedience on party members.

Demenok is well aware of this and treats people in characteristic fashion. On the day after his return to work, April 17, 1936, five members or nonvoting members are expelled from the party.[12] Three weeks later, on May 8, he has the pleasure of informing the regional committee that he has expelled forty-six members and thirty-six candidates,[13] 20 percent of the local party membership.

Expulsion from the party is in any case a shattering blow, but with the Great Purge imminent, an expulsion for political reasons is practically equivalent to a death sentence. The secretary of the Kozelsk district committee knows very well what he is doing when he writes that a certain Ivan Gavrilovich Putsenin "is being expelled from the ranks of the CPSU because he comes of a Kulak family, had goats and a milking machine on his farm, and employed paid labor; and because of repeated desertions from the Red Army at the time of the civil war and concealment of all this on joining the party."[14] The phrase "repeated desertions from the Red Army at the time of the civil war" is worthy of note, for the penalty for a single act of desertion was death by firing squad.

Anyone expelled from the party for political reasons is a candidate for physical liquidation. Rumiantsev, the first secretary of the regional committee, sends the following strictly secret instruction to the secretaries of the district committees, on January 21, 1936:

> When you attend the secretaries' conference at the regional committee on January 29 the following information is to be brought to me personally: 1) Your view of the state of mind of those expelled from the CPSU in your district and what steps you are taking to keep informed of their state of mind; 2) what signs of counterrevolutionary activity there are among any group of expelled persons or individuals in your district; 3) what steps you have taken or still consider it necessary to take in relation to the expelled persons to prevent counterrevolutionary activity; 4) of those expelled, those whom you personally consider to be now politically or socially dangerous, how many there are whose continued presence in the district you consider to be dangerous, and why. In gathering this information I authorize you to consult only the second secretary and the NKVD representative.[15]

On April 29 the regional committee encloses with a secret letter a questionnaire about those expelled from the party at the time of the renewal of the party cards. The letter says:

> Exact and detailed replies are to be given to all the questions in the questionnaire. We draw attention to the fact that this information about expelled persons is being collected by order of the Central Committee of the CPSU. Completed questionnaires are to be returned to the regional committee, organization department, without further reminder, not later than May 7. Note that we are bound by a strict timetable.[16]

A secret letter of April 28 informs the district committee that

> those expelled from the party must be subjected to special surveillance. It is essential to know where they work and what their state of mind is and to keep hostile elements under surveillance. Secretaries of party committees and party organizations are to be instructed to this effect.[17]

The purport of these letters is not lost on the experienced nomenklaturist Demenok. In a secret letter to the regional committee "On Communists expelled from the party" he gives an assurance that he has warned the party organizations of the necessity of keeping expelled persons under surveillance, and takes the opportunity of making a denunciation:

At the meeting of workers at the glassworks on April 30 at which a representative of the regional committee was present, Kupreyenko, an expellee from the party who came to the glassworks from Belorussia a month ago, made an anti-Soviet speech. He said there was no difference in the life of the workers, it was just the same as before the revolution. There is information that this Kupreyenko is a former manager or deputy manager of a factory in Belorussia. We are making inquiries into exactly what sort of a man he is.[18]

The district secretary dutifully sets about drafting denunciations that send human beings one after the other to the hell of the Gulag Archipelago. Here is an example:

To the head of the NKVD, Comrade Tsebur. Copy to the regional prosecutor, Comrade Kochergin. From the district committee of the CPSU Kozelsk. Matveyev, Ivan Vasilyevich, formerly president of the New Life kolkhoz of the Beldinsk village soviet, a candidate member who was expelled from the party in 1934 for immorality, abuse of power, and other crimes, subsequently tried several times to strike the member of the Komsomol Mishin, president of the kolkhoz and an honorable, industrious comrade, and threatened to kill him. As before, he drinks and carries out subversive activity in the kolkhoz. The kolkhoz peasants are rightly incensed by his behavior. Also he is by origin a kulak and engages publicly in anti-Soviet activity. I urgently request that he may be proceeded against with all the rigor of the law. Please let me know the result of this request by January 10, 1936.

Demenok
Secretary of the district committee of the CPSU
January 3, 1936.[19]

In another secret letter to Comrade Tsebur, dated February 2, 1936, Demenok informs him that a portrait of Trotsky has been found in the home of the kolkhoz peasant Afanasy Khromov. "According to our information," he continues, "Khromov is a corrupt individual who engages in subversive activities in the kolkhoz. Because the kolkhoz peasant Ulzanov denounced him for this, Khromov physically ill-treated Ulzanov's father. I request that steps be taken to call him to account."

Not content with working havoc in his immediate environment, Demenok avenges himself on persons of whom he has lost sight but against whom he still has grudges:[20]

> After reading the secret letter from the Central Committee of the CPSU about the terrorist activities of the Zinoviev-Trotsky group [he writes to Comrade Tsebur], I remembered a certain Kovalev—his forename eludes me—who joined the party organization at Novozybkov in 1924-25 and was evidently acting on behalf of the Trotsky center in infiltrating into the party organization. He made Trotskyist speeches at a meeting of party activists. The party organization firmly rejected what he said, but it is possible that he is still a member of the party and has not yet been unmasked as a Trotskyist. I send you this information so that appropriate action may be taken. Kovalev was at the time a student at a Sverdlovsk higher school. He comes from the Klimovsk district (western region), where his father was a verger.[21]

Now, in 1924, a great all-party debate took place in accordance with a Central Committee resolution, and in taking part in it Kovalev was merely following the party decision. So how could he now be denounced by a party official for doing precisely that?

A nomenklaturist does not ask such naïve questions. Demenok is very well aware that, twelve years before, Kovalev would not have been sent to prison for making a Trotskyist speech. That is why he did not denounce him then. But times have changed, and he takes advantage of this to denounce him now; and others, too, as our next example shows:

> After reading the secret letter from the Central Committee of the CPSU on the terrorist activities of the Zinoviev-Trotsky group [he writes to the western regional committee], I remembered Trotskyists who actively opposed the party. I remember that in 1925-26, when I was secretary of the Novozybkov district committee of the CPSU, a certain Karkuzevich, forename Michael, I believe, a member of the CPSU since 1917 and a railwayman, was active on the committee as head of the agitprop department. At that time he was an active Trotskyist. Not only did he slander the party and its leader, Comrade Stalin, but went so far as demonstratively to decline to study the decisions of the Fourteenth Congress, as he

disagreed with them and believed them to be wrong. We got rid of him immediately, and presumably he received a party reprimand, but he is still in the party. I do not know where he works, but I remember that he was working as a railway watchman in Belorussia. It is possible that he has not been unmasked to the present day. I pass on this information so that appropriate action may be taken.[22]

That is how the nomenklaturist Demenok relentlessly pursues a man whose forename he is no longer sure of. The man has been a Communist since 1917 but has had to take a job as a gatekeeper, since Demenok had him thrown off the committee. Some might suppose that Demenok would be satisfied with that, but any such suggestion shows ignorance of the nomenklatura. Ten years later, an opportunity arises to liquidate a man whom our district secretary has already dragged in the mud, and the desk-bound murderer duly sends his letter of denunciation to the regional committee.

But does he perhaps believe he is merely warning the NKVD about a possible "enemy of the people" and that objective inquiries will be made before action is taken? Can he be as naïve as that? Hardly. Tsebur regularly sends him secret notes from the files about expelled persons. Let us take a look at them:

Strictly secret. Notes concerning expellees. Kozelsk district. Lagutin, Dimitry Ivanovich, born 1898. . . . Married, three children aged sixteen, fourteen, and eleven. Until his expulsion was head of the supply office of the tree-felling sovkhoz, now lumberyard watchman; wife is now a cleaner at the teachers' training college.

In other words, the man has already been crushed by Demenok. He has been expelled from the party, thrown out of his job, reduced to being a watchman and his wife to being a charwoman, and he has three children to keep. What more could a nomenklaturist want?

The man's physical liquidation. The note ends with the following paragraph:

After his expulsion Lagutin undertook counterrevolutionary activity against the party. In December he said in conversation with Granin, his colleague at the wood-felling sovkhoz, and another that the Bolsheviks recruited only their own people, he used an insulting expression about a party leader, etc. Subsequently, being without regular work, he took to drink and found a job as watchman in a lumberyard. He has a revolver of the Nagan type.

[signed] Tsebur.[23]

That is all. The man said that the Bolsheviks recruited only their own people—as if they ever pretended to do anything else! He also said something rude about a party leader. Which leader is not stated, and it cannot have been Stalin, because that would have been mentioned. No doubt it was Demenok himself. Not being able to think of anything else, the NKVD chief put down "etc." Then he mentioned the revolver, implying that he wanted to kill a leader, was a terrorist. Obviously he had a revolver because he was a watchman. But Tsebur wanted him to be arrested.

Here is another "note on an expellee":

Putsenin has a wife and children aged six and four to keep. When the case arose he was president of the Kozelsk consumers' cooperative. He is accused of coming of a kulak family . . . and at the time of the civil war in 1919 and 1920 he completely avoided military service and deserted several times.[24]

Now, if he completely avoided military service he cannot have deserted several times. But who cares? Logic is not the NKVD leader's strong point, and when he cannot think of anything else to say about an expellee he writes as follows:

At work [the note continues] he drinks and corrupts the kolkhoz peasants, he maintains relations with corrupt elements, thus causing disorganization in the kolkhoz. At present he is working as an ordinary peasant in a kolkhoz and his behavior influences the others.[25]

That is, of course, sufficient to condemn him. And this is what Tsebur has to say about another kolkhoz member who has been thrown out of the party, a man with a wife and three children:

Stepin drinks at work at the kolkhoz, works reluctantly, resulting in discontent and nonfulfillment of the state norms.[26]

This is what he concocts about the expellee Korotkov, formerly manager of the interdistrict training school for tractor mechanics:

When he was manager of the interdistrict training school he employed an engineer named Kapachinsky, a priest's son who had been expelled from the military academy. In Moscow he was in contact with Arsentyev, who was on the staff of the personnel department of the People's Commissariat for Agriculture, through whom he sought by bribery to secure an award for the school, though there were instances in the course of the school year in which students left their studies to go home. In 1934 there was great delay in the repair of tractors, thus sabotaging the opening of the tractor park. He has a dekulakized father and brother with whom he maintains contact, and he wants to buy a house. He has various possessions, and the expellees Kats and Danilkin have met at his house. What they talked about is unknown.[27]

The reader may be tempted to smile at this drivel from the pen of a second lieutenant in the security services, but he would be ill-advised to do so. This petty nomenklaturist has human lives in his hands, and he takes malicious pleasure in destroying them. Not content with the victims provided for him by Demenok, he also finds his own. Here is a letter to Demenok:

> Strictly secret. Series K. During the house search of the former member of the CPSU B. A. Gutovets a testimonial in his favor from Drozdov, head of the district finance department, was found. Gutovets was very proud of that testimonial and proposed to use it in the future.

A handwritten note by Tsebur follows: "Please take up the question of Drozdov at the meeting of the bureau," it says.[28] The testimonial provided by the unlucky Drozdov is not concerned with Gutovets' morals or political reliability, but says he is competent and has been sent on a course to the financial and economic institute at Leningrad.[29]

Meanwhile Gutovets has been sentenced by a special court to five years' imprisonment under the notorious Clause 58/10, Paragraph 1, and has written a denunciation of a witness who appeared on his behalf at his trial; he accuses him of having been the leader of a Baptist sect in 1926–27.[30] The court forwards this denunciation in a top-secret envelope to Demenok "to make such use of as he thinks fit."[31] Demenok "thinks fit" to have him expelled from the party. This delivers him into the hands of Tsebur, who sends him to the same special court. He, in his turn, writes a denunciation of a witness who appeared in his defense. Thus the victims of the Kozelsk nomenklaturists grow more and more numerous.

But they are not satisfied yet. Tsebur sends Demenok another strictly secret letter "on thefts and harmful actions committed at the Kozelsk cattle-procurement accounts office." He explains that the local NKVD is making inquiries about six persons, two of whom are party members. The "harmful acts" of which they are accused are that "in the course of 1935 they took to drink, cheated suppliers in weighing and counting cattle, fraudulently made fictitious lists of nonexistent cattle, received a loan from the State Bank, embezzled public funds, and permitted fraudulent slaughtering and death of cattle." Assuming that these charges were well founded, where was the subversion in them and what had they to do with the NKVD? The only discernible reference to subversive activity occurs in the following rather obscure sentence: "Rodin drank systematically with his subordinates and with outsiders . . . and this as a member of the staff of the cattle-procurement office. Things went so far that workers used swear words" (as if they normally expressed themselves in Turgenev's prose). The consequences of this rubbish were grim indeed: "In view of the fact that the criminal activity of the manager Rodin and the head of the storeroom Mishin is confirmed by documents and other evidence, I request that their expulsion from the party be discussed at the meeting of the bureau of the district committee."[32] As the four other accused are not members of the party, Demenok's approval of their arrest is not necessary.

There is no need to suspect Demenok of any idealism, for he is well aware that those expelled from the party have no hope of a fair trial. He remains on the lookout for more victims. Here is a letter in his own handwriting:

Strictly secret. Town committee of the CPSU, Kuznetsk.

According to information in our hands, the member of the CPSU Polosukhin, Nikolai Ivanovich, who from 1922 to 1923 was head of the organization department of the district party committee and now works here in the western region as head of the newly built Tula-Sukhinichi railway line, has taken part in Trotskyist activity since 1917. He told us nothing about this. We request immediate information on whether Polosukhin really took part in Trotskyist activity, and if so when, and of what this activity consisted.[33]

Demenok next expels from the party a kolkhoz peasant named Volkov, who has just been released from the Red Army. His crime is that he "actively defended his brothers, who have been sentenced for counterrevolutionary activity."[34] He also expels a man named Karasev for losing his candidate's card, though he has found it again; it is actually in his file. The expulsion remains in force in spite of the consequences that it involves for the unfortunate man.[35]

It would be unfair to completely blacken Demenok's character, for he is not totally immune from human feelings. These appear rarely, it is true, since in all these documents there is only one instance of his intervening to help someone, though the man who rouses his sympathy is a rogue.

The following document, which is marked secret, throws light on our hero's human qualities and on the independence of Soviet justice:

> Secret. To Comrade Adrianov, president of the assize court. By a decision of the Kozelsk district people's court, the president of the Bolshevik kolkhoz of the village soviet of Slobolsk, Aldonin Filip, was sentenced to two years' deprivation of liberty for malversation of kolkhoz funds and the attempted rape of two peasant women. I request you carefully to examine the charges against Aldonin.

A description follows of the kolkhoz's successes in the field of production, and it is stated now to be solidly based and on the high road of socialist development. But what about the alleged malversation of funds and attempted rape? Actually

> Aldonin was president of another kolkhoz, the Iskra, belonging to the village soviet of Dragunsk, where, under the influence of difficult material circumstances he embezzled about two hundred rubles from kolkhoz funds. . . . At the same time it should be borne in mind that he was not allotted bread or potatoes out of the kolkhoz produce. But it is true that he acted incorrectly in the matter of the distribution of funds.
>
> In regard to the alleged attempted rape of the peasant woman Anna Zenina, a former head of a brigade, we have looked into the matter at the district committee. . . . There are no grounds for imputing any such attempt to Aldonin. Zenina herself states that she slept soundly that night, though she made a different statement in court.

She may, of course, have been speaking the truth in court, but Demenok does not linger over that possibility, nor does he mention the other peasant woman. But it must be borne in mind all the same that Aldonin has held the office of kolkhoz president for six years. His is a strong and exemplary kolkhoz. The crops are excellent. The quotas are scrupulously fulfilled. I request you to make a deeper study of the charges against him.[36]

Such things are written, or, rather, telephoned, to the present day, and the independent Soviet courts still make deeper studies of cases and take "circumstances" into account.

On July 29, 1936, the Central Committee of the CPSU sends a secret letter to the party organizations "On the terrorist activity of the Trotsky-Zinoviev group." Discussion of this letter is to serve as prelude to the big Moscow trials, the first of which begins in the second half of August 1936. The Smolensk Archive contains the minutes of an extended meeting of the Kozelsk district committee held on August 4, 1936, at which the letter is discussed. This document is unfortunately too long for quotation in full, but here is a brief summary.

Those present include the members of the district committee bureau, Demenok, Balobechko, and Tsebur (who is of course a member); Kavchenko, the editor of the local newspaper; and Krutov, president of the executive committee of the district soviet. These are the fine flower of the district nomenklatura. Also present are twelve members of the plenum of the district committee, twenty-seven party organizers, twelve men who are on the so-called "active list" of the district, and finally the majestic figure of Fedko, the instructor of the regional committee. In accordance with the normal practice, Demenok reads the letter aloud. To the present day, secret letters from the Central Committee are read aloud in this way; those to whom the contents are to be communicated are not allowed to read them for themselves. Then the discussion begins.

Speeches on these occasions follow the same, unvarying pattern. Each speaker begins by saying that the Central Committee letter will give a fresh impulse to the party organization in its struggle against the enemies of the people and will lead to an intensification of political and class vigilance. After that, each speaker tries to outdo his predecessor in the matter of denunciation.

> Gorokhov: In the procurement organization there is a Communist named Kozin—he has had a party reprimand because of his conciliatory attitude to a Trotskyist. It is the duty of Communists in the procurement organiza-

tion to keep Kozin's activities under surveillance. It has come to my notice that there was a Trotskyist named Gleiser at the party school at Klintsy. . . . It seems to me to be essential that a report about him be sent to the CPSU regional committee.

District public prosecutor Kochergin: It has come to my notice that many kulaks and former employers are employed on the new railway, some of whom still employ workers. [What workers could a simple railwayman employ? Yet a public prosecutor could talk such nonsense.]

Girin, the secretary of the Komsomol district committee, has discovered counterrevolutionary matter in a program of pioneers' games that have been sent to him:

I have brought this to the attention of the Komsomol regional committee, and I think Comrade Fedko will bring it to the attention of the regional committee of the party.

Golovin, the local intellectual and head of the district department for popular education, is particularly zealous.

It has now become clear that there has been a group of Trotskyists in our local agricultural-machinery and tractor station.

He goes on to cast suspicion on a woman comrade present:

I believe that Comrade Sergiyuk, who works with them, knows something about their actual activities. She should report to the bureau on the matter.

Yes, of course I have my suspicions of the Communist Deikin. He is never seen anywhere, he does not mix with the people, he does not make speeches. . . . I knew Entish; he was manager of a factory at Bryansk in 1925–26; he was expelled for Trotskyism. A report about that should be sent to the CPSU regional committee.

Antonov, head of the district militia: Many strangers are going around the neighborhood. I think it essential to check their identity cards, as well as everyone else's. The recent forest fires suggest that all sorts of shady characters—people whose identity has not been checked—are employed on the railway. It is hard to believe that among these people there is no one who has anything to do with those fires. I talked to Polosukhin, the railway construction chief, about the frequency of fires along the railway line recently, and he answered that there have always been fires wherever they worked. I believe that answer to be incorrect. The district committee must take appropriate action in regard to Polosukhin.

Fedko, the regional committee instructor, incites those present to make still more denunciations:

There are many people in your district who have come from many other districts. They come because Bolshevik vigilance here is not yet sufficient. It is the duty of your organization to develop and increase Bolshevik vigilance in every way. Persons who in the past have had only the slightest connection with Trotskyism, no matter whether direct or indirect, must be boldly and resolutely unmasked. There is a certain Matyushin here with us. He is president of the kolkhoz and a party organizer. He has said himself that he once had the Trotskyist program in his hands. I am bound to say that he can no longer be tolerated as party organizer.

To conclude this witches' sabbath, Demenok spoke. He "appealed to the Central Committee to take the most resolute measures for the physical liquidation of their enemies" and, unconscious of any irony in what he was saying, added: "Life has become better, comrades, life has become more cheerful. Those true words spoken by our party leader Comrade Stalin apply completely to our district."[37]

Life must indeed have become more cheerful in the Kozelsk district. Demenok conscientiously sends longer and longer lists of victims to the regional committee. Here are some more examples:

Trubin, Philip Ivanovich, member of the party since 1918 [that is, since the beginning of the civil war], manager of the oil dump at the agricultural-machinery and tractor station, was accused of Trotskyism. The charge has been withdrawn and we are now rechecking.

Pomerantsev, Leonid. . . . after his Trotskyist activity in the holiday home was discovered he was dismissed. He is still working at a holiday home at Vyasma. He must be found.

Landyshev, Pavel Alexandrovich, doctor and party member, and M. V. Klimov, head of a special secondary school, nonparty. Both work in the Pokrovsky village soviet and in the evening meet to discuss obscure matters with unknown persons.

Lukyanov, head of train crew personnel at Kireyevka station, anti-Soviet. His case is being prepared.

Kozodoy, Komsomol member, forename and patronymic still unknown, present place of work unknown. In 1929 he worked in the canteen of the town consumer cooperative and had connections with a Trotskyist group. A Trotskyist program was found in his possession. We are searching for him and the ramifications [of the case].[38]

The ugly spirit of a medieval witch-hunt spreads from the local nomenklaturists, Demenok and Tsebur, throughout the neighborhood. Here is a quotation from a speech at a workers' meeting:

I suggest the firing squad is too good for bandits like Kamenev, Zinoviev, and the rest. They should be led through Moscow in chains, they should be made to dig their own graves, and they should all be hanged, for that is more disgraceful than shooting. . . . How are our enemies fed? Well, no doubt. But they should be fed on nothing but salted herring for a week, given nothing to drink, and then executed.[39]

But dissenting voices are also to be heard, and the secretary of the district committee notes them with alarm:

Voyevodin, of the Pokrovsky village soviet: I can't say anything about Trotsky. We're in no position to judge. You don't tell us the truth. You deceive us. There's nothing to wear and no shoes. Voyevodin walked ostentatiously out of the meeting.

At the Free Labor kolkhoz, belonging to the Maklinsky village soviet, Eremina said: You say life has become cheerful, but we have to hand over some of our cows, our pigs, our sheep, the products of our foundry and our farm. What is so cheerful about that? At the March 8 kolkhoz, belonging to the Grishinsky village soviet, Evkodia Savelyeva, a former party candidate who was deprived of her right to vote, conducts disgraceful agitation. You used to work for a landlord and get your pay promptly. Now you work the whole year for the kolkhoz and get nothing, she says.

Vasily Gorelikov, of the Free Labor kolkhoz, of the Machinsky village soviet, says: Pay no tax, it only goes to fatten the commissars.[40]

Some were even more outspoken:

Lagutin, who has been expelled from the party, says Bolsheviks are scum.[41]

In a conversation with kolkhoz peasants after Sergei Mironovich Kirov was killed, the wife of the teacher Akimov said: It's a pity they didn't kill Stalin.

Nikolai Novikov, of the Stalin kolkhoz, of the Machinsky village soviet, a former party candidate, said: If they now give us a weapon, we'll turn it against the party and the government.[42]

Those are sparks of the fire that is to flare up five years later, when invading German troops are met with offerings of bread and salt, soldiers of the Red Army surrender *en masse*, and tens of thousands volunteer for the anti-Communist army of General Vlasov.

The district committee secretary looks at the sparks with fear and hatred and drafts his denunciations and lists of proscribed persons, not suspecting that ten years later they will be read with revulsion in a free country.

5. A DAY IN THE LIFE OF DENIS IVANOVICH

And what are nomenklaturists like nowadays?

Solzhenitsyn has described a day in the life of Ivan Denisovich Shukhov, a Soviet camp inmate. Having spent years in the company of people like Shukhov, he knows what he is talking about.

My experiences were of a different kind, and I shall try to describe a day in the life of a person who is the antithesis of Solzhenitsyn's hero: the head of a desk of the Central Committee of the CPSU. We shall call him Denis Ivanovich and give him the Ukrainian-sounding surname of Vokhush (under Khrushchev and Brezhnev many Ukrainian comrades—whose loyalty to the party line has become proverbial—joined the Central Committee apparatus). Vokhush is a fictitious character, but everything that follows is derived from real life.

Denis Ivanovich awakened in the morning not by the blow of a hammer on a piece of railway line near the foreman's hut, but by the melodious ringing of an alarm clock recently brought back from Switzerland, to which he has paid an official visit. He has been having a pleasant dream: at an important meeting held in his office, the Secretary of the Central Committee ignored everyone else present, addressed himself exclusively to him, asked his advice, shook him by the hand, made him sit at his desk, and then suddenly he was no longer there; he had simply vanished. His colleagues rose to their feet and deferentially awaited his, Denis Ivanovich's, instructions.

Vokhush walks heavily to the bathroom in the light blue pajamas he recently bought very inexpensively at a Prisunic store in Paris. He dislikes striped pajamas, in particular those with blue and white stripes, which remind him of the uniform of prisoners in the special camps. Actually the apartment he lives in is not at all bad, though the sanitary fittings are all in a single room; his wife is perfectly right; they must think about moving. All he need do is go to the administrative department of the Central Committee and discuss the matter with them.

While his wife lays the table, Denis Ivanovich does some exercises, concentrating on the stomach muscles, because that damned tire around his waist keeps growing. At the Kremlin outpatients' department he was recommended showers and massage, but they didn't do any good. Might he have to go on a diet?

After having a shower, shaving, and applying some imported aftershave lotion, Denis Ivanovich proceeds to the dining room, where he takes a light breakfast: a little caviar, ham, a boiled egg, and tea. What a pity he can't have a glass of brandy now; for that he will have to wait till this evening. Above all, he mustn't eat too much, because soon it will be time for a second breakfast.

At eight thirty-five precisely he walks out the massive front door of the building. A Central Committee official car—a black Volga—is there to pick him up, and it is better to let the driver wait for the time it takes to go down in the elevator and not risk being seen by neighbors or colleagues waiting for it to arrive. That is something a man in his position cannot afford. The car is in fact waiting by the door. The driver remains at the wheel, for this is a democratic country, and Vokhush opens the door himself (even secretaries of the Central Committee do that) and sinks comfortably into the soft cushions of the front seat, next to the driver, with whom he very democratically starts a conversation. He tells him that when he was a young man working in the Donbas he always used to smoke two cigarettes on the way to the factory, but his wife has now forbidden him to do that. Actually Denis Ivanovich has never worked in a factory, and he gave up smoking of his own accord when he read in the weekly *Nedelya* about the danger of lung cancer.

Moscow glides past before his eyes: the Kutuzov Prospekt, the Moskva, the Garden Ring, the Kalinin Prospekt, the Kremlin Wall, the Riding School, the Bolshoi Theater, the monument to Fyodorov (the first printer), the somber mass of the Dzerzhinsky monument, the KGB building (neighbors, he says to himself with a warm feeling). Behind the Polytechnic Museum and the monument to the heroes of Plevna, the Boulevard begins, and on the right the massive outline of the Central Committee building appears. Here we are.

At the entrance a KGB officer politely but firmly asks for his pass, a small booklet bound in dark red leather, and examines it carefully. There is no need to take offense at this; it is a sign not of mistrust, but of order. It's true that heads of divisions—*sav. otdelom*—do not have to submit to this formality. The officer gives them a peremptory military salute. To salute the Secretary of the Central Committee he comes to attention.

There is a constant flow of officials into the big entrance hall. Vokhush exchanges friendly but brief greetings with his colleagues, who are solid, well-nourished men like him. Friendliness between colleagues is all right, but there must be no effusiveness of the kind that prevails among intellectuals.

After considering with carefully concealed envy the elevator reserved for the higher-ups—the *sav. otdelom* and, of course, the Secretary of the Central Committee have keys to it—Denis Ivanovich enters the ordinary elevator, which takes him smoothly to his office floor.

It is quiet and agreeable here. His vertushka is enthroned on a small table. In a middle drawer there is a little red book, the government telephone directory. Theoretically it would be possible to take his courage in both hands, pick up the receiver, and call the Secretary-General —familiarly known as the *generalny*—for the sake of hearing his deep bass voice with its lazy inflexions.

No, he will not call the *generalny;* what a childish idea! But there's a call he will have to make, whether he feels like it or not, because of a very stupid matter indeed.

Yesterday morning the first *zam. zav.*, the first deputy of the head of the division, signed a draft resolution concerning the sending of a delegation to Italy. It was a good delegation: two nonvoting members of the Central Committee, a member of the Central Control Commission, and some deputies to the Supreme Soviet. The first *zam. zav.* carefully examined all the signatures on the document, as was his habit. So far, so good. Then, when adding his own signature, he said, "A delegation like this ought to be approved by the *generalny* himself"; and Vokhush, always anxious to please, telephoned one of his friends in the general division and said, "We are going to send you a list of members of the delegation; the head of the division thinks it ought to be submitted to the *generalny.*" But the first *zam. zav.* had obviously not forgotten what he had said, and was worried. That evening, when he was leaving, he met Vokhush by the elevator and said, "We had such a high opinion of your delegation that we nearly sent it to the *generalny*. You realize that that was a joke, I hope?"

Vokhush mumbled something in reply, and the first *zam. zav.*, who was always in a hurry, disappeared into the elevator. Vokhush dashed back to his office to call his friend in the general division, but he had left. He then called the special desk of the general division and was told that the document had been sent to the Secretary-General's secretariat two hours before.

So he will have to telephone this morning. Not too soon, of course, or someone might suspect he has committed a gaffe, and not too late, or the *generalny* will see the document, which might well cause him to blow up (as happened from time to time). What's the meaning of this? he would shout. Has everything to be passed through my office nowadays? Even sending an office cleaner to a rest home? Who's the idiot responsible for this? Vokhush trembles at the thought; it wouldn't take them long to find out who was responsible.

But he must avoid doing anything that would arouse suspicion of himself. Where can the file have gotten to by now? It's an international matter, but too trivial for the *generalny*. So he won't approach his assistant, Andrei Mikhailovich, for the file won't be with him. Besides, the man has an extraordinary flair; he'd smell a rat immediately. Better ring the secretary, who has had an extraordinary career, the lucky fellow. He was a minor official dealing with Norway in the international division, but then he suddenly took off. Nowadays his name is mentioned in communiqués after negotiations in the Kremlin, and his picture appears on the front page of *Pravda*. All he does, of course, is to shuffle papers and deal them out to various people, but some of these papers make the world tremble.

Vokhush decides not to telephone at once, but to follow his usual routine. First of all he reads the newspapers, beginning with *Pravda*. The leader is about preparations for the spring sowing. That is something for the Agriculture Ministry, so there's no point in reading it; all that's necessary is to glance through it with a practiced eye to make sure that there is the usual reference to the *generalny*. Vokhush will never forget the day in October 1964 (he was not yet head of a department then) when he found confirmation in *Pravda* of the vague rumor about rumblings in the Central Committee, for Khrushchev's name suddenly vanished from the newspaper that day. But today the *generalny's* name is mentioned, so everything is normal, at any rate for the time being. There are announcements about awards and decorations for members of the Academy on the occasion of an anniversary, but not for anyone in the Central Committee apparatus. Let's have a look at page four. Appointment of a new ambassador to the Republic of Chad, the old one having been given new employment. How slow the Presidium of the Supreme Soviet is! The decision was made three months ago, and the Africans give their assent very quickly.

Page two is devoted to the "life of the party." Plenum of the Kustanai regional committee. Preparations for the spring sowing are mentioned here too, of course, but all that's necessary is to glance at the last two paragraphs to see if any organizational matters are mentioned and if any leaders were present at the plenum. No, it only says that the first secretary of the regional committee made a speech. The theoretical article, on "The Party as the Guiding Force in Soviet Society," requires more careful attention; it might contain interesting nuances and turns of phrase, for *Pravda* never publishes anything without a deeper meaning. But today it is not very interesting. In serious situations the subject of the articles is unity of party and people, but the view expressed today is that unity already exists and that there must be a further advance in consolidating the party's leading role.

Page three contains international news under headings such as "Successes for the Forces of Peace" and "Make Détente Irreversible." All perfectly normal. An American senator wants American troops out of Europe. Why don't the comrades in the international division put him on the Brussels Committee for European Security? He sounds like a good, realistic statesman. The next headline is neutral enough: "Press conference by Reagan." Nothing remarkable about that either, except for a casual remark toward the end that the American President favors the demands of the Israeli aggressors. To find out what Reagan really said, Vokhush can always look at the Tass bulletin *Vestnik.*

At the bottom of the page there are the usual comments on developments in China. An Arab newspaper is quoted as mentioning a secret agreement between the Chinese leaders, the military junta in Chile, and the racist regime in South Africa. Isn't the disinformation service going a little too far here? After all, a minimum of plausibility ought to be maintained. What could the Chinese be wanting in Pretoria? But perhaps the boys are right. People believe what they read; that news item doesn't originate with us; it's merely quoted from an Arab newspaper, so it looks trustworthy.

The internal telephone (the former K6 line) rings. Vokhush picks up the receiver. "Denis Ivanovich, Ivan Petrovich wants to see you about the delegation to Italy," the secretary of the first *zam. zav.* says. Vokhush manages to control his voice, but there is a lump in his throat. Has the bombshell burst while he has been sitting here like a fool reading the newspaper? Has an assistant of the *generalny's* been rebuking the first *zam. zav.* on the telephone, with the result that the latter will now be in a terrible rage? How is Vokhush to exculpate himself? To what god can he appeal to come to his aid?

He rushes to the door like a man who has been sprinkled with boiling water, but outside in the corridor he looks as calm and unruffled as usual, so that no one will notice anything. These people are his colleagues, of course (they go water skiing together on the Klyazma) but actually they are like rats: at the first sign of weakness they would pounce on him and gobble him up.

He walks calmly into the first secretary's antechamber, gives a friendly nod in the direction of his elderly secretary, and feels his heart sinking. The thought darts through his mind that it's at moments like this that cancer cells establish themselves in the human frame, but another thought chases away the idea of cancer. I'll be in his room in a moment, and what state of mind will he be in?

The first deputy is sitting calmly at his desk, so there's not going to be a row after all. What a relief! But Vokhush must control himself, show nothing.

The first deputy looks busy and self-assured—that is his style—and comes to the point immediately. "About that delegation," he says. "Wouldn't you like to join it yourself? We always seem to be sending consultants from the international department, but there's nothing obligatory about that. I'll mention the matter to Sagladin, and you can represent the apparatus."

Vokhush is torn by conflicting emotions. It would, of course, be delightful to go to Rome and do some shopping and also sightseeing, but a kind of reflex acquired in the course of many years in the nomenklatura tells him he must decline the offer, for he has only just come back from Switzerland. He is being put to the test. But then it strikes him that the man may be wanting him to go to Italy to bring back something for him. He promptly dismisses that idea, for any one of the members of the delegation would be only too happy to oblige the first deputy. If he really wants me to go, Vokhush says to himself, he'll insist.

"No, Ivan Petrovich, you had better count me out of it," he replies. "I've so much work at the moment that I can hardly keep pace with it. I can hardly take time off for lunch, let alone go to Italy. Besides, I'm not in favor of foreign travel except when it's absolutely essential."

If the first deputy says the trip's essential, it means he's personally interested, Vokhush says to himself. But the first deputy merely says, "As you wish. The work of the division must come first, of course." Then, in a more jovial tone, he adds, "I wanted to strengthen the delegation by putting you on it, but I see you don't want to."

Vokhush walks back to his office along the light pink carpet with its green edging. He feels pleased with himself, for he has reacted correctly. Ten days in Italy are not to be sneezed at, but he has higher ambitions. There is about to be a vacancy for the post of deputy to the head of the division, and if the first deputy supports his candidature something may come of it.

A pleasant thought strikes him. Perhaps it may not be a bad thing if the draft resolution about the delegation has landed on the *generalny's* desk. Its members have been carefully chosen, the *generalny* will sign it, and he'll be able to spread the news in the division that the *generalny* was pleased and complimented him on it. Perhaps the first deputy may be supporting his candidature at that very moment and he'll be promoted to *zam. zav.*, deputy to the head of the division. *Zam. zav.*, just think of it, a huge office, a secretary, a car with a driver for oneself instead of an ordinary Volga from the Central Committee pool, holidays in a dacha instead of the rest home at Klyazma, to say nothing of a higher salary and a more ample *kremliovka.* But the vital thing is the power, for the deputy to the head of the division has several desks under him; he sees the secretary of the Central Committee every day; he often attends meetings of the Secretariat; he's known by sight in high places. Oh, how marvelous it would be to be a member of that elite! The *zam. zav.* belongs to the top grade of the Secretariat nomenklatura. The next grade, that of first *zam. zav.*, belongs to the Politburo nomenklatura. So shall he take a risk and let the document reach its destination? Be bold, be brave, be resolute.

But his usual prudence, which has become second nature to him, prevails. When one has an objective in view, a frontal attack is best; a backdoor approach is always risky. The *generalny's* signature will be no sort of guarantee that he will be appointed, and if any difficulties arise he can be sure of not being appointed, and his mistake will be remembered for years. He must get back that file as quickly as possible.

As always before talking to an important person, Vokhush takes a pencil and notes down what he is going to say. Every word must be carefully weighed, and above all he must speak clearly, firmly, and respectfully, in a party-like manner, with no intellectual hesitations. Above all, he must let it be understood how greatly he deplores that the *generalny's* time should be wasted over such a triviality.

He concentrates before dialing the four-figure number on his vertushka, and the impassive voice of the secretary answers. Vokhush mentions his name and his division. He knows that the secretary will quickly look him up in the vertushka directory to find out his forename and patronymic, which he will subsequently use in the course of conversation to show that he knows and is well informed about everyone.

"Forgive me for disturbing you," Vokhush says in a confident but respectful manner, "but we have made a small mistake" (a little self-criticism is advisable, but saying "we" instead of "I" shifts the blame onto the first deputy, though as a loyal subordinate he, Vokhush, accepts full responsibility). "Yesterday we sent to the Central Committee a draft resolution about a delegation to Italy. We have discovered that the comrades in the general division were overzealous and forwarded the document to you directly. The delegation has not been at all badly selected, but the whole thing is not important enough to take up the *generalny's* time."

He pauses. He hopes the secretary will react in some way, but his only answer is a dry "Yes," leaving Vokhush to continue his monologue. How is one to tell what the man is thinking?

"You of course are in the better position to decide," Vokhush continues, slightly obsequiously, "but we thought it not worth troubling you with. So could you perhaps send it to the secretaries?"

Vokhush does his best to imply that he considers the *generalny* far superior to ordinary secretaries.

"Yes, I have the file here," the assistant says. "Tell me, Denis Ivanovich" (he must already have consulted the directory), "shall I submit it to the *generalny* or send it back to the general division?"

His tone is polite (that is the present style), but obviously he doesn't want to accept responsibility or to send the file to the other secretaries himself. It is always best to avoid exposing oneself. Vokhush replies in the same tone:

"Yes, I think it will be better to send it back."

"Very well, then," the other man replies in neutral tones.

Good. So that's settled. The only nuisance is that the general division will notice, but there won't be a fuss about it. It will be sufficient to invite his friend in the general division home for a drink (remember to offer him French cognac) and all will be forgiven and forgotten.

A plain young woman walks into Vokhush's with a file of Tass telegrams. To avoid any possible scandal, only rather plain young women are employed here. Quite right, Denis Ivanovich says to himself, glancing at her; this is not the place for that sort of thing. For that sort of thing the men at the top have their ballerinas. He, Vokhush, is not yet entitled to that; he shall cultivate his good Soviet family.

Great interest is taken in the party organization in anything having to do with women. When there is a scandal, the organization gloats over every detail. Vokhush recalls a fellow student of his who openly ridiculed this peculiarity of theirs. At the time, he, Vokhush, was only secretary of the university party committee, but he had the humorist expelled. That was in the spring of 1949, during the struggle against cosmopolitanism. After his expulsion from the party, it was impossible for the man to get a job and he had to go to Central Asia. He turned out to have a weak heart and died of heart failure in the summer heat. His mother went to the party committee and started weeping and shouting, "Murderers." Fortunately Sasha Krapulov, a former Chekist, who was his deputy for organizational matters, happened to be present, and he extricated Vokhush from her clutches. This Sasha was a splendid fellow. "If I have understood you correctly, citizen," he said quietly to the old lady, "it's the party committee that you're referring to, isn't it?" This silenced her; she sobbed and left. They wondered at the time whether she should be reported to the competent authorities. Sasha was in favor of this, but Vokhush felt the committee members would not understand. She was a mother, after all.

Sometimes small risks have to be taken. Not long ago a science student was sent to Prague on scholarship, but they didn't give his wife an exit visa. The young scientist was not a person of any consequence; he could be left to manage for himself. But his wife passionately wanted to go to Prague, and found out that it depended on him, Vokhush, whether or not her file was submitted to the foreign travel commission. He himself hinted as much when she came to see him, with her lovely gray eyes, shy and blushing, wearing a dress that showed off her attractive figure and her turquoise necklace. He explained that getting an exit visa was no light matter; he was far too busy to be able to deal with it in his office, but perhaps he might be able to find time after office hours, though she could not be admitted to the Central Committee building in the evening. . . . In her small, one-room flat in Profsoyuznaya Street he did not remove her turquoise necklace, but left the blue stones to shine against her soft skin. The look in her eyes was not exactly what he would have wished for; far from it. But now, walking on the banks of the Vltava or in the Old City, no doubt she was happy again.

Things are much easier with young women from one's own circle. At a Central Committee rest home he met a pert young instructress from the Voronezh regional committee. In her case there were no resentful looks. The only problem was satisfying her.

What harm is there in that? The fathers of Marxism had nothing against it. Vokhush was once a member of a delegation to West Germany. They had visited Marx's birthplace, at Trier, and it was there that he discovered that Marx had a mistress who bore him a son. The father of Marxism did not acknowledge the child. What a scandal there would be nowadays if Jenny von Westfalen came to the party committee and complained about her husband. Then there was Engels. Vokhush was once told at the Institute of Marxism-Leninism that he lived simultaneously with two sisters. Vokhush silenced the man who told him this with a look, but it was certainly true. And Lenin had his Inès Armand, whom he never addressed in the familiar form. Vokhush was not Lenin, of course, but when he went to see the girl in her room he, too, didn't address her in the second person singular.

But no more sentimental memories; it's time to get down to work. Let us see what Tass has to say.

Vokhush leafs through the poor-quality paper on which *Vestnik* is printed, but at the same time goes on thinking about the problems of the day. His thoughts and his reading intermingle. Protests by European socialist parties against the political vetting of appointments in West Germany. Refusing to appoint a judge because he's a Communist? Those rascals! Here we do the opposite; we don't appoint non-Communists. Incidentally, they must settle today that case of a non-party president of a committee. There are seventeen million members of the party, after all, so there is no shortage of comrades.

In South Africa marriages between blacks and whites are permitted. A nigger and a white woman. And the white woman agrees to it. But what's surprising about that? All the women students at the Lumumba University, here, would make a beeline for the black male students if we allowed them to. It will be opportune to discuss it with the prorector later in the day.

Eleven o'clock, and the Central Committee canteen opens. It is time for a second breakfast. Vokhush goes there, feeling pleased with life, for he has defused that little matter of the delegation and covered himself. What could be better than feeling safe?

There are already about fifteen people in the big, bright room, which gleams and glitters with cleanliness. Behind the glass-fronted counter there is everything the heart could desire. There are three girls behind the counter, and only two or three persons are waiting to be served by each of them, so he won't have to stand in line for long—this is in striking contrast to the lines at the Gastronom, where, moreover, customers are dealt with as quickly as possible. Here there's time to pick and choose and buy one or two little extras to take home; fruit or chocolates, for instance (Mishka or Nuka Otnimi chocolates—just you try and find them anywhere else; he had them as a child; they are relics of the NEP period). No, he won't have smoked salmon or caviar now; he prefers milk products such as *prostokvasha*, made of sour milk and sugar, or cream cheese, followed by sea kale with vegetable oil (warmly recommended by the Kremlin doctors as a protection against arteriosclerosis). And tea, of course, with two Mishkas. The buffet waitress gives you a little tea in a glass and you go to one of the small side tables and pour boiling water over it yourself. Once a week, when Vokhush has his weekly slimming session (that damned belly of his is a real disaster), he doesn't go to the Central Committee canteen, but has a light lunch here; he puts a small cube into a cup and pours boiling water over it. The result is a soup with a smell of mushrooms and specks of fat floating about on top.

Vokhush notices some members of his staff and greets them cordially, without actually fraternizing. That is the present style, for a certain sobriety in personal relationships has established itself since Stalin's time. In those days seniors treated their subordinates as if they were former comrades-in-arms in the Red Army, making jokes and slapping them on the back and being slapped on the back by them, or alternatively behaving toward them with condescension. Something of that still survives among the older generation, approaching retirement age, but nowadays you are expected to be sober, polite, levelheaded, and businesslike.

In Vokhush's desk it is understood nowadays that he must never be disturbed between 9 and 11 A.M. except in emergencies. But for that, on a day like today, for instance, they would all have come streaming into his office at that time to demonstrate their zeal; and how could he have telephoned the *generalny's* assistant if they had done that? So the arrangement is obviously a good one.

On his way back to his office, Vokhush as usual stops at the bookstall. He stops there for a minute and no longer, just long enough to see whether there is anything new. Some youngsters spend longer than that, looking at the books and browsing, but that creates a bad impression, suggesting that they have nothing better to do. The right impression to create is that you have a great deal to do but organize your time efficiently—thus combining Russian revolutionary drive with American efficiency, as Stalin put it. What a brain Stalin had!

Vokhush's subordinates will be popping in at any moment. Ah, here's one of them already putting his head around the door. "May I come in, Denis Ivanovich?"

Vokhush invites him in with a gesture. He is Shvetsov, recently transferred to the Central Committee from the Academy of Social Sciences. Vokhush has no particular liking for the young whippersnapper, whose father-in-law, however, is a colonel general on the general staff, so he treats him very benevolently.

Shvetsov presents a list headed "Composition of the Soviet-Bulgarian Biology Commission, submitted for consideration by the Academy of Sciences before confirmation by the Presidium of the Academy."

"Are there any signatories with it?" he asks cautiously. He will never forget the disaster that nearly occurred when he first became head of a desk. He very nearly approved the composition of a committee that included someone who had signed a petition in favor of Sinyavsky and Daniel. Luckily he was warned in time and crossed the name off the list. Otherwise he would have been in appalling trouble.

"No, Denis Ivanovich, there are no signatories," Shvetsov says with a laugh, "but it's possible that some comrades might leave the country."

So, there are some Jews on the list.

"Who?" Vokhush asks briefly. With the tip of his pencil, Shvetsov makes two almost invisible marks against two names on the list. They sound Russian, which shows how those people camouflage themselves. And this little son-in-law said nothing about it.

"Perhaps the list should be shortened, or other names might be suggested," Vokhush says politely. "If they take their departure, who will do their work on the commission?" he continues, at the same time saying to himself that if the two Jews are removed from the list they'll be saying at the Academy of Sciences that the apparatus is anti-Semitic.

Shvetsov merely shrugs his shoulders.

"The Academy proposed them," he says. Really, the Academy, which Khrushchev nearly closed.

Vokhush finds a way out. "We'll simply cross one name off the list and replace the other by someone else. There's a biologist named White at the Institute. He was a follower of Lysenko's, but that's no reason for overlooking his scientific qualifications."

Vokhush is delighted with his guile. White is a pure-blooded Jew, but not a member of that Zionist clique.

He smiles. "You know the joke, don't you? Love us if we're black; if we're white people love us anyway."

"Black or white, I don't love them in any case," Shvetsov says with a laugh.

Denis Ivanovich smiles. This young man doesn't like them, but in spite of that he put two on the list.

Vokhush assumes his official tone. "While we are about it, we may as well deal with another outstanding problem. How long is a nonparty man like Vensky to remain vice-president of the commission?"

The son-in-law smiles. "He's a nonparty Bolshevik," he says.

"That's a rather old-fashioned term, you know; it sounds like subjectivism" (he nearly said "the Khrushchev period," but used the official expression instead). "I'm told there have been protests and that the party secretary at the Biology Institute has been suggested as a replacement."

That is correct. Two women comrades came to see him about it. One of them had worked in the security services and the other for the World Trade Union Federation, and both said that biology was a science of concern to the party and that there was no place on the Soviet-Bulgarian commission for nonparty specialists. Neither mentioned the party secretary as a possible candidate, for the excellent reason that both had their eyes on the position themselves. But Vokhush has decided that this intellectual must be removed and replaced by the party secretary. There can be no question of appointing either of those overzealous women to the post.

Shvetsov, who at bottom is an "intellectual" himself, says a trifle hesitantly: "But he's a good specialist, and he talks Bulgarian."

"That's why we have kept him there all this time," Vokhush explains patiently. "He was useful in setting up the commission, but now we have passed that stage, and the Communists are complaining. So we must get rid of him."

Shvetsov is not completely convinced. "But what shall we tell him?" he says.

"Discuss the matter with the party secretary; it'll be strange if no deficiencies in his work come to light. There are spots even on the sun." Vokhush can no longer conceal his irritation. "If it comes to the worst, you can quote the opinion of the party organization. You could also say that the Bulgarian comrades are dissatisfied with him; he can't go there and check that for himself. There's no need to develop a guilt complex about him," Vokhush continues persuasively. "You're an inspector in the Central Committee apparatus; and he's not a member of the party and has no right to call you to account."

It's always the same with these scions of highly placed personages; they lack the Bolshevik fighting spirit; their mentality is petit-bourgeois.

Vokhush's favorite subordinate, Zinaida Ivanovna, the only woman in the desk, sweeps into the office. She is a serious person who came from the Komsomol central committee, and she is of good family; her husband works in the KGB. She produces a list of proposed publica-

tions by the Nauka (Science) publishing house. The political relevance
of the subjects dealt with is a matter for the publishing department;
here they are concerned with checking the authors.
"Who have we here?" Vokhush says jestingly. "Academician
Sakharov, perhaps? Or even Solzhenitsyn?"
"Yes, in the pornography series," she replies, and they both laugh.
No such series exists here, of course. When he was at Stockholm,
Vokhush could not resist the temptation of leafing through some maga-
zines at a kiosk; the experience was not at all disagreeable and re-
minded him of his instructress at Voronezh. She would have been a
godsend to those photographers.
"I've underlined seven titles that I think should be crossed off the
list," Zinaida says.
Zinaida never misses anything. In fact she's sometimes too strict.
The titles are not of proposed books, but of books ready for publication.
"Look, Lifshits, for instance," Zinaida goes on. "This is his fourth
book. Why help him to gain a phony scientific reputation?"
Quite right. Lifshits is crossed off the list.
"And who's interested in a subject like *Iconography and Iconoplas-
tics of Pushkin?* Priests and icon dealers?"
Quite right; cross it out too. What has Pushkin got to do with it?
"And here there was a grave oversight. The author is the daughter of
Rosengolts, who was sentenced at the Moscow trial in 1938. She uses
her husband's name."
What nerve her husband must have had, marrying such a person!
Cross her off.
"And this one is by a woman doctor of science whose son went to
England as a tourist and didn't come back."
What a villain! Just imagine it; he didn't come back to his country.
And now, no doubt, he's strolling up and down Regent Street, looking
at the shopwindows. So that's how his mother brought him up! Cross
her out.
What a splendid woman this Zinaida is! How does she manage to
find out everything? Perhaps her husband ran the list through the
Lubianka computer.
"These three each spent seventeen years in prison," Zinaida goes on,
a little less confidently.
"But they have been rehabilitated."

"So was Solzhenitsyn," Zinaida says, screwing up her nose. Yes, but now the books have been finished, and the authors will complain and write letters. It's a heavy responsibility to take.

"Zinaida Ivanovna, ask the secretaries of the party committee for their opinion," Vokhush concludes. "Don't forget that we have no views on the matter. The first four must be removed from the list. Tell the publishing department. They can be told we haven't any paper."

Zinaida needs to be supported, but also restrained.

Vokhush always leaves for lunch at a quarter past one, so he has just enough time left to read the minutes of the Central Committee Secretariat, every sentence of which has the force of law. Reading them is an elevating experience; it makes you feel identified with the sovereign power that makes these lapidary decisions.

At one fifteen precisely Vokhush puts on his comfortable llama-hair overcoat with its silky reflections (he bought it at Düsseldorf, where he stayed as a guest of the West German Communist Party; the street where he bought it had a strange name—Kö—but what lovely shops). He walks down the corridor with its light pink carpet in a dignified manner (he is, after all, a *sav. sektorom*, the head of a desk), but not with measured tread (he is not, after all, deputy head of a division). There's no hurry; he isn't really hungry. But he mustn't walk too slowly, either, for forty-five minutes is the proper time to take off for lunch. No one, of course, checks his timekeeping, but he is very conscious that it is in these minor matters that a Communist must demonstrate his conscientiousness. The party must not be deprived of a single moment of his working time. In any case, he'll be able to have a rest in his office after lunch.

He doesn't have far to go. There is that picturesque little church next to the new Central Committee canteen. Stalin had many churches of that type demolished. He was a genius, but he had his peculiarities. That he should liquidate his enemies was natural enough, but why destroy churches? It would have been better to use them to instill patriotism into the people, and then there would have been fewer deserters to General Vlasov.

At the glass door, he shows his dark red leather-bound identity book to a young man in civilian clothes, who examines it carefully, and he hangs his hat and coat on a hook. There's no risk of their being stolen; he's at home here. He goes to the cash desk and chooses the dietetic menu (he has to do something to counter this putting on of weight, and choosing the ordinary menu does not make the proper "serious" impression required of a *sav. sektorom*).

The dietetic buffet is on the second floor. He goes up in the elevator, which is tiny. Why did they build it so small? In the dining room everything is calm and quiet. While looking for a place to sit (at his level he must avoid mixing with junior personnel), Vokhush notices the head of the cultural division sitting at a small table, busily engaged in conversation. Vokhush goes and sits at a neighboring table as if by chance; it will be sufficient to catch his eye and greet him. Vokhush takes a surreptitious look at the man, with his still slim figure and carefully combed hair. He's in a difficult position, Vokhush says to himself. His subordinate, the Minister of Culture, is a nonvoting member of the Politburo, so how can he give him orders? But how can he avoid giving him orders, since the purpose of the division is precisely to do that? How does he cope with that situation?

Vokhush dislikes lunching with colleagues. If he always sat with the same persons, people would start talking of a clique, but it's impossible to keep changing all the time, for it would mean lunching with all the desk heads in turn; and mingling with junior staff is out of the question.

He takes his time. He begins with a glass of kumys (mare's milk), followed by sea kale in vegetable oil (to ward off arteriosclerosis; otherwise one might end up by forgetting the forenames and patronymics of one's own superiors), a half plateful of cream of carrot soup, steamed veal with rice, plums with cream and sugar (for the digestion), and black currant jelly with whipped cream (for the sake of vitamin C). He eats slowly, keeping a careful eye on what the head of the division is doing. By now he has finished his conversation and he looks around the room in an authoritative manner. Vokhush chooses this moment to smile politely at him and is rewarded with a good-natured nod. Splendid. Perhaps he'll remember Vokhush if he has to recommend someone for a responsible post.

It's eight minutes to two. Time to go back to the office. Vokhush could obviously take a short stroll along the boulevard facing the Central Committee building, as the first deputy generally does after lunch. But you never know what humor he will be in. He might engage you in conversation, or he might make a sarcastic remark such as: Going for a walk, are you? Have you finished all the work in your desk? So it's better to resist the temptation and go straight back to the office.

An idea flashes through his mind. Suppose my subordinates have the same feeling about me? And what of it if they have, he tells himself without hesitation. It's only natural.

Back in his office he allows himself a half-hour siesta. He does not have a rest room, not being a secretary of the Central Committee (though those who have such rest rooms have the least need of them, for after lunch they go back to rest in their sumptuous bedrooms at home). But his staff is understanding in the matter and never disturb him before two forty-five. So Vokhush snoozes on a hard chair (to avoid piles) near the table adorned with the vertushka, which is his pride and joy. If the bell rings—it has a subdued, sober note—he will be at his post at once.

It rings. The rector of the Lumumba University is on the line. It is not a big university, but it has its political importance. It is for students from developing countries and Japan; that was why Khrushchev allowed the rector a vertushka when it was founded. The rector, a serious person and a member of the nomenklatura, is not exactly a flatterer, but adopts a tone of extreme friendliness, and Vokhush does the same. That is not only because it is part of the new style adopted by the Central Committee in work relationships; it is also because Vokhush needs the rector, for he wants discreetly to remove his deputy Shabanov from the Central Committee apparatus, and the easiest way of doing so will be to have him appointed deputy rector of the "Friendship University." For this he needs the rector's backing.

Vokhush knows exactly what the rector wants of him. The present prorector is coming to see him at three o'clock. The latter is in fact a political commissar responsible for the students' ideological instruction. The rector wants to remind Vokhush that it is he, the rector, and not the prorector, who runs the university. This confirms Vokhush's feeling that there is conflict between the two. In other words, the rector is in a weak position, unable to cope with his ambitious second-in-command.

Vokhush dislikes the prorector. As a solid and self-confident man, he is not taken in by that tall and rather insolent individual, whose unpressed suit looks almost as out of place on him as it would on a donkey. His appearance is rather old-fashioned. There are, however, some influential people who like this thirties style, which reminds them of their youth. Whatever the case may be, this fellow has his wits about him. No sooner did he finish his course at a perfectly ordinary teachers college than he found himself a niche in the party apparatus and immediately made contact with the security services, who proposed him for the position of party secretary at the Friendship University, and he held the post for several years before becoming prorector. The students' section, of which he is the head, is practically a branch of the security services, with the result that he represents both the apparatus and the "neighbors." How can the rector, a mere engineer by profession, possibly cope with a man like that?

Actually the rector is more than just an ordinary engineer—he has been a deputy minister, and he has his connections. It will not be so easy for the prorector to get rid of him. Both must be given to understand that it is he, Vokhush, who holds the key to the situation; the winner will be the one whom he backs. This means that both will accept the person whom Vokhush proposes as an additional prorector. But it will be quite a good thing to take this prorector down a peg or two.

Working all this out takes Vokhush only a few moments. This speed of reaction is common to all the members of the apparatus; without it they would never survive in the nomenklatura. There are no violinists or Sunday painters on the Central Committee, but this quickness of decision and adroitness is shared by all.

The door opens, and the bald-headed prorector appears. Vokhush greets him coldly; the man must be intimidated.

First of all, he must be allowed to unburden himself, and in such a way as to reveal his trump cards. While he talks about his work with the students, Vokhush's face remains impassive. The prorector is an experienced person, and he is distinctly self-critical. "We overlooked this and we allowed that," he says, at the same time making it clear that it wasn't he but others, generally the rector, who were responsible. In other words, the correctness of Vokhush's appreciation of the situation is confirmed, and the time has come to strike a blow.

"Educational work among students," he begins in didactic tones, "is not limited to meetings, discussions, and film shows, or to talks to foreign students. Primarily it is the creation of an atmosphere of intolerance toward all breaches of Communist morality in the student collective. Above all, it is among Soviet students that we expect this intolerance to prevail. The Central Committee resolution says that joint education of Soviet and foreign students is an important means of exercising a positive influence on the latter. But [and here Vokhush raises his voice] this is not achieved, and we cannot escape our responsibility in the matter."

While speaking, Vokhush looks sharply at his prorector, who is obviously perturbed at his official tone and the political implications. This is what Vokhush wants, so he goes on to drive his advantage home.

"We have received information about bad and sometimes actually scandalous behavior by certain Soviet men and women students of the Lumumba University. Instead of setting an example and upholding the honor of Soviet girls and members of the Komsomol, some women students have been behaving actually indecently (I apologize for having to use that word)."

Vokhush modifies his official tone slightly and says, "One is reminded of Engels's *Origin of the Family:* Promiscuity prevails among you, too."

"Yes," says the prorector, accepting the criticism. "What is happening is absolutely disgraceful, that's what I always say. The district committees send us women students who—In the old days they would simply have been thrown out. But what are we to do? Make them wear chastity belts, as in the Middle Ages?"

Vokhush pointedly ignores this joke and goes on in the same official tone: "Possible mistakes by Komsomol committees do not excuse the shortcomings of educational work among the students. We cannot shut our eyes to the existence of a negative attitude among certain elements in the student body. It is not a matter of belts. The fact remains that some women students, far from thinking of founding a healthy Soviet family, try to take advantage of the time they spend at the university to get married to a foreigner and leave the country."

"It's a pity they repealed the 1947 law that forbade marriages to foreigners," says the prorector.

"It was repealed," Vokhush goes on dryly. "Various considerations led us to tolerate a number of marriages between Soviet students and students from the developing countries. But the Central Committee has never thought of the Friendship University as a matrimonial agency."

Vokhush now delivers the final blow.

"This is a serious matter," he continues. "Comrades have suggested the setting up of a Central Committee commission of inquiry into the level of the ideological work done at Lumumba University, both among Soviet and foreign students."

Vokhush notes with satisfaction the trace of anxiety that has appeared in the prorector's eyes. Both are well aware that a commission of inquiry would mean nothing but trouble for the prorector. Good! The man is intimidated. Now the thing to do is to backpedal a bit; otherwise he may hurry off to see his friends and patrons in the apparatus. Actually there's no one who wants such a commission.

"But the view, at any rate here, Vasily Pavlovich, is that we can manage without a commission," Vokhush continues, in more reassuring tones. "I myself am of the opinion that the student department does not bear all the responsibility and that the rector has not shown enough party spirit." Then, suddenly dropping into the familiar second person singular, he adds in a confidential tone: "The fact is that, apart from you, there's no one there from the apparatus. The rector and his staff are just specialists. It's a difficult job for a single man; you need help."

Anxiety vanishes from the man's eyes. His usual perkiness has disappeared, and he is full of gratitude. It is time to come to the point:

"If the university applies to the Central Committee through the ministry for a member of the apparatus to be appointed as an additional prorector, I believe the request would be granted," Vokhush goes on. "Your position would be strengthened, and there would be no point in setting up a commission."

"That is an idea completely in the party spirit," the prorector exclaims. "It should have been done a long time ago, Denis Ivanovich. It's my fault; I should have raised the question sooner. I shall have no difficulty in securing the agreement of the party committee, but won't the rector be against the idea?"

"We shall discuss the matter with him," Vokhush says suavely. "He will see the necessity of the step. Why should he want a commission?"

Vokhush knows what the bald-headed prorector is thinking: that a Central Committee commission would not forget that the rector was ultimately responsible for whatever happened at the university.

The prorector takes his departure after warmly shaking Vokhush by the hand. The man is obviously not to be trusted, but he won't take the risk of going to see his friends to check the accuracy of what Vokhush has just told him. In spite of his uneasiness at the idea that the new prorector might usurp his place, he will avoid all risk of conflict with the Central Committee apparatus.

The next step is to dial the rector's number on the vertushka. His tone is amiable and friendly again.

"Your deputy has just been to see me, as you know," he says. "We had a long talk about certain deficiencies that have come to light in the ideological work of his department, and he will certainly be telling you the substance of our conversation himself. Here, at desk, we do not think it necessary that a commission of inquiry be sent to the university [the rector wholeheartedly agreed], but on condition that Vasily Pavlovich confine himself in the future to his own department. If you asked for it, we could no doubt let you have one of our comrades to act as an additional prorector; I know there's a vacancy. If you think it a good idea, I suggest you submit an application to the Central Committee through the ministry. If the application succeeds, the question of a commission of inquiry would no longer arise."

The rector unhesitatingly and gratefully accepts this proposal. What else could he do?

The next task for Vokhush is to prepare the ground with the first deputy. Otherwise that brazen prorector might get his oar in first. What a shock that would be to the first deputy, who knew nothing about the whole thing. It's always like this; the people from whom you have most to fear are those who have worked in the apparatus; your own people, in fact.

Vokhush has timed the whole thing precisely. The first deputy is always most approachable at the end of the day, when he likes talking to the heads of departments. Denis Ivanovich picks up the receiver of his vertushka and slowly and deliberately dials his number.

"Ivan Petrovich, this is Vokhush troubling you; can you spare me a few moments?"

Once more he makes his way along the carpeted corridor. The anteroom is large, but smaller than that of the head of the division. Vokhush greets the secretary again. During the war, when she was a girl, she was a crack shot, a sniper with 209 Fritzes to her credit. She is a good, understanding comrade.

The first deputy is seated at his desk, at the other end of the room.

The Central Committee telephone list is open under a piece of glass. "What brings you here?" he says, indicating a chair with an energetic movement of his head.

Vokhush respectfully but confidently sits down. He is very well aware that nothing escapes the first deputy's notice. He assumes a slightly anxious expression, at the same time taking care not to overdo it.

"Ivan Petrovich, I'm worried about the situation at the Friendship University. I've just been talking to the prorector about the work with the students. They are completely out of control—"

"Politically?" the first deputy interrupts sharply.

"No, Ivan Petrovich, morally." (The first deputy's face relaxes.) "But morality is politics." (The first deputy again pricks up his ears.) "The view at the university is that party representation there needs strengthening. The rector told me they intend to apply through the Ministry to the Central Committee for a member of our staff to be appointed to the vacant position of prorector for social sciences."

"And what did you answer?" the first deputy wants to know.

Vokhush has been expecting this question and is ready for it.

"What could I say, Ivan Petrovich? I said that if they thought it advisable they should go ahead and apply to the Central Committee. It would then consider the question."

Vokhush is now covered, particularly in regard to his talks with the rector and the prorector. That was indeed the only positive suggestion he made to them; anything else was merely a subjective impression on their part.

"Who do you have in mind?" asks the first deputy, whose interest is now aroused. "Or are you thinking of strengthening the university yourself?" he continues half seriously.

The look of horror on Vokhush's face makes the first deputy realize he is on the wrong track, and he hastens to reassure him.

"I was only joking," he says. "We have no intention of letting you go." (Vokhush's whole frame assumes an expression of blissful relief.) "Do you have anyone to suggest to me, then?"

"I haven't considered that yet," Vokhush says modestly. "First of all, I wanted to find out what your attitude in principle was."

"And what is your attitude in principle?" says the first deputy, refusing to let go.

Good; matters are coming to a head.

"I don't think there should be any difficulty, Ivan Petrovich, in finding a suitable candidate in one of the desks that work closely with mine."

A hard look comes into the first deputy's energetic eyes.

"You really are a sly one, Denis Ivanovich," he says. "In one of the desks that work closely with yours. Why don't you suggest someone from your own desk? Haven't you anyone suitable?"

He has swallowed the bait. Vokhush must now put up a smoke screen to prevent him from seeing his real purpose.

"There's absolutely no one I can spare, Ivan Petrovich. The work load in my desk is as much as we can cope with."

The first deputy's tone becomes sharper.

"And do you think the others are any better off? Suggest one of your own people and I'll back you."

Vokhush now has to put his cards on the table.

"The prorector has to be someone with high academic qualifications. There's only one man on my staff with a doctor's degree and that's Shabanov, but we really can't spare him."

"Why not? He's certainly an able man, but people like him can be equally useful at the university. The title of professor goes with the prorectorship. And it's a big university, and he might very well become a corresponding member of the Academy of Sciences eventually. As soon as the letter from the ministry reaches the Central Committee I'll talk to him and we'll appoint him."

"Ivan Petrovich, you're breaking my heart," Vokhush exclaims, doing his best to make his despair sound genuine. "How can I let Shabanov go? And who is there to take his place?"

"You'll find someone," the first deputy replies reassuringly and, while Vokhush shakes his head disconsolately, goes on:

"Well, so that's settled, then. Is there anything else?"

"No," Vokhush says in a piteous tone, rising to his feet. The first deputy suddenly smiles.

"You're letting your Shabanov go very easily," he said. "Don't you get on with him?"

This was totally unexpected, and Vokhush expresses his horror.

"But, Ivan Petrovich," he exclaims, "I ask you to leave him with me and you say I suggested him for the job."

The first deputy is still smiling.

"No, you didn't suggest him for the job. But I agree with you completely." Then he goes on in a schoolmasterly tone: "I'm not interested in Shabanov as an individual, but in the smooth working of the desk for which you are responsible, and I have nothing against your choosing the people with whom you can work best. Is that clear?"

Sadly Vokhush goes back to his office. No, it's no use trying to pull the wool over the first deputy's eyes; he sees through everything. Otherwise he would never have become first deputy. Those who fight their way up the ladder to the Politburo or the Central Committee Secretariat are real geniuses. Stupid intellectuals tell one another that this member of the Politburo is a complete blockhead and that one is weak in the top story, but actually it's they who are fools and simpletons. The geniuses are the members of the Politburo.

Yes, but even they sometimes trip up. Who would ever have supposed that Malenkov, that brilliant tightrope walker who managed to skirt every pitfall in his perilous ascent, would not remain in power even for two years? Or Beria, who spent decades climbing to power over piles of corpses, and when he almost got there, did not last for four months? Or Khrushchev—but he wasn't really a serious person, and Stalin put him in his place: he sent him from Moscow to the Ukraine, and even there he dismissed him from his post as first secretary because he didn't take those strange "agricultural towns" seriously. Later on, of course, Khrushchev got his own back on Stalin, but only after he was dead. In his lifetime no one would have dared.

What a great man Stalin was! So, too, was Lenin, but his destiny did not permit him really to enjoy power, for paralysis struck him as soon as the civil war was over. But Stalin really knew the meaning of power.

The working day is nearly over, and Vokhush walks around the various offices of his desk (that is democracy). Each office is shared by two members of his staff, each of whom has a personal telephone and an internal telephone. Vokhush briefly discusses the next day's work, but by this time everyone is thinking about going home, and Vokhush is looking forward to it himself.

He generally remains seated in his office for twenty minutes after office hours. No one works in the evening now, but it wouldn't do to be seen leaving the building with the ruck of officials. The twenty minutes go by; no one telephones. The big chiefs have no more need of him, so he calls for a car.

He doesn't have to wait long. The Central Committee pool is close at hand, so he can start putting on his silky overcoat, then make his way toward the exit in the slow and self-assured manner appropriate to a responsible Central Committee official. The pink carpet on the shiny parquet flooring, the massive staircase, the second, noisy vestibule. Officials are still emerging, but most of them have already left. The KGB officer politely but carefully examines his little red leather pass book.

Outside it is dark, windy, and snowing. There is no ice outside the building. It has been carefully removed by cleaners with pointed tools, and as an extra precaution, red sand has been strewn on the pavement, for it wouldn't do to have a Central Committee secretary slipping and falling while getting into his car.

The black Volga draws up. He gets in, and once more the tires crunch through the Moscow snow. Once more he passes the Plevna memorial, the Polytechnic Museum on the left, and the Komsomol central committee building on the right, then the buildings on Dzerzhinsky Square, the Lubianka, which houses the KGB and the MVD. They go down a wide avenue. A glimpse of the Children's World shop, then a corner of the Maly Theater, the colonnades of the Bolshoi Theater, the Dom Soyuzov, and the building of the Soviet Council of Ministers. Then he catches a glimpse of the shining lights of Gorky Street, and the car passes the National Hotel, the Intourist house (the former American Embassy), and the old Moscow University. On the left there is the Kremlin, momentarily hidden by the Riding School building.

Vokhush doesn't feel like talking to the driver. After a few remarks about the weather and the snow, he sinks into a reverie.

Here he is driving through Moscow while she is walking about in the night somewhere in Prague. The lamps are alight in Wenceslas Square, and the clock strikes on the Old Town Hall. Why does he think about her and not about the sunburnt body of the instructress from Voronezh? Simply because, that day, her eyes went right through him. Denis, be honest with yourself; admit that she looked at you with revulsion, as at a repulsive animal. There was also helplessness in her eyes and an unsuccessful effort to conceal her revulsion, for she feared that if she upset you you might go back on your promise, for she badly wanted that trip to Prague.

But what is the point of these memories? For all her princess-like airs she's merely the wife of a wretched little student with a scholarship. She ought to be proud of the fact that the head of a Central Committee desk took an interest in her.

How often he has seen that look of despairing helplessness in people's eyes—in the eyes of that mother who shouted, "Murderers," in the eyes of persons whom he criticized or expelled from the party; they all looked at him with that expression.

But it's a good thing that they should do so, after all. A few weeks ago he had a horrible dream. He was in the Central Committee building, and he suddenly realized that the whole place was empty. He went downstairs to the vestibule, and there were no guards. He was seized with panic. People might come flooding in from the street at any moment. And in fact there they were. He made toward the elevator as if everything were normal, but it was upstairs and the one reserved for secretaries was closed. Meanwhile a crowd of people from the street had gathered around him and were silently gazing at him with a revulsion just like hers, as if he were a louse or some other sort of vermin. But there was no helplessness in their eyes; on the contrary, there was strength and power in them. He awoke sweating with anxiety and with a pounding heart, and it took him a long time to calm down again.

So it is right that things should be like that—to them the impotence, to us the power. Away with troublesome thoughts; why not think of something pleasant? In a few minutes he will be home, where his wife will certainly have an appetizing dinner waiting for him: smoked salmon, caviar, a roast, cheese, pineapple. He would have some Armenian brandy; he didn't like that Bulgarian Liska or Arab brandy, but only Armenian, and also Georgian brandy—as well as French cognac, of course. He would talk to his children, and also chat with his wife.

They might go out, as was appropriate to persons of culture. As head of a Central Committee desk he could go to any private film show at the Ministry of Culture or the House of the Film. These shows are a very good idea. You can see the most varied films from the most varied countries. Actually, from a strictly legal point of view these are stolen property; they are pirated copies of films loaned to the State Committee for the Cinema by international organizations with a view to possible purchase—which in fact seldom takes place. Obviously it would be very stupid to hand over foreign exchange for them to capitalists, since for ideological reasons the films can never be shown to the general public. So a few copies are made for top people only, and what harm is there in that? The atmosphere at these shows is very agreeable. You have the feeling of being among your own kind, among nomenklatura people, apart from a few artists or representatives of the creative intelligentsia. But Vokhush is not in a film-going mood this evening.

Foreign films withheld from the general public are also shown at the Central Committee on Thursdays, but Vokhush has no use for them. Like the canteen in the evening, they are intended for typists and secretaries. It would be dreadfully embarrassing for him to be seen there.

Perhaps he and his wife might go out for dinner and then go to the theater. Tickets are cheap; the most expensive seats at the Bolshoi cost only three and a half rubles. Those tickets are not, of course, on sale to the public. It's a very convenient arrangement; you are given seats in the first or second row of the orchestra from the quota reserved for the Central Committee, and there, too, you have the feeling of being among your own kind, though sometimes foreign ambassadors are present as well. And it must be confessed that that has a certain attractiveness, for it makes you aware of your place in society.

But Vokhush has had enough of theater and concert going; as part of his official duties he has to attend them after meetings or conferences, or has to accompany foreign delegations to them. No, tonight he won't go anywhere. He'll rest and use the time to think about the best way of getting the promotion that he wants so much. He'll go to bed at ten o'clock—for health is the *sine qua non* of all promotion.

While the elevator mounts noiselessly toward his flat, and then when he goes in and hangs his llama-hair coat with its silky reflections on the hook, Denis Ivanovich sums up the events of the day as usual. On the whole, it has been a satisfactory, almost a happy one, for nothing disagreeable occurred. He averted the risk of trouble about that delegation to Italy, resisted the temptation of going there himself, and removed undesirables from the Soviet-Bulgarian commission and doubtful authors from the publishers' list. He made the Friendship University apply to the apparatus for the appointment of a new prorector, and he obtained the first deputy's consent to his getting rid of Shabanov. If only he could do as much useful work every day.

For this day's work, Denis Ivanovich is paid ten times as much as an ordinary Soviet worker.

NOTES

1. Lenin, *Collected Works*, Vol. 22, p. 276.
2. Ibid., emphasis supplied.
3. Cf. I. A. Kurganov, *Nacii SSSR i russkij vopros*, Frankfurt, 1961, pp. 30–31.
4. Lenin, *Collected Works*, Vol. 22, p. 277.
5. Marx and Engels, *Selected Works*, Vol. 1, p. 329.
6. Lenin, *Collected Works*, Vol. 31, pp. 291, 293.
7. Marx and Engels, *Collected Works*, Vol. 5, p. 59.
8. Eduard Bagrickij, *Stichotvorenija i poemy*, Moscow-Leningrad, 1964, p. 126.
9. Merle Fainsod, *Smolensk Under Soviet Rule*, Cambridge, Mass., 1958.
10. National Archives, Washington, D.C., "Smolensk Archive," Microfilm RS 921, Folio 100 (American Historical Association, Microcopy T 88, Roll 123, Reel 57).
11. Ibid., Folio 76.
12. Ibid.
13. Ibid., Folio 95.
14. Ibid., Folio 12.
15. Ibid., Folio 131.
16. Ibid., Folio 94.
17. Ibid., Folios 97–98.
18. Ibid., Folio 96.
19. Ibid., Folio 1.
20. Ibid., Folio 271.
21. Ibid., Folio 123.
22. Ibid., Folio 124.
23. Ibid., Folios 133–34.
24. Ibid., Folios 134–35.
25. Ibid., Folio 138.
26. Ibid., Folio 142.
27. Ibid., Folio 139.
28. Ibid., Folio 65.
29. Ibid., Folio 66.
30. Ibid., Folio 35.
31. Ibid., Folio 34.
32. Ibid., Folios 43–46.
33. Ibid., Folios 223–24.
34. Ibid., Folio 157.
35. Ibid., Folio 153.
36. Ibid., Folio 204.
37. Ibid., Folios 277–83.
38. Ibid., Folios 303–4.

39. Ibid., Folios 306–7.
40. Ibid., Folios 307–8.
41. Ibid., Folio 300.
42. Ibid., Folio 305.

Conclusion

The Program of the CPSU promised that in all essentials the classless Communist society would be constructed by 1980. Since 1936, Soviet society has been described as a society without antagonisms. But classes and class antagonisms have not been abolished, and Soviet society remains antagonistic.

Lenin and Stalin created a new class, the nucleus of which was Lenin's organization of professional revolutionaries. After the seizure of power by that organization, Stalin's nomenklatura arose and became the ruling class in the Soviet Union.

The nomenklatura is a class of privileged exploiters. It acquired wealth from power, not power from wealth. The domestic policy of the nomenklatura class is to consolidate its dictatorial power, and its foreign policy is to extend it to the whole world.

The nomenklatura has some positive achievements to its credit, but it is becoming more and more parasitic. Its contribution to society is nil and its stubborn desire for world domination involves the grave danger of world war.

To banish the danger, the world not under Moscow domination needs a determined, unblinkered, and fearless policy of peace and security. The formation of such a policy requires knowledge of the nature of the nomenklatura. If this book makes a contribution to that knowledge, it will have served its purpose.

Let us take leave of the nomenklatura at one of its finest hours.

On November 7 in Red Square, to the accompaniment of military music and the firing of salutes, the nomenklatura celebrates another year of power by a military parade that lasts for several hours. Normally you catch only occasional glimpses of them as they flash by in their ZILs and Chaikas, or (in magazines) in their sumptuous homes or on the platform at important ceremonies. This is a unique occasion to see them *en masse*. Where else would you see so many nomenklaturists gathered together than on the stands by Lenin's Tomb on this solemn day?

There they are, standing on the light gray stone steps of the stands, solidly built men with coarse, authoritarian faces, accompanied by their dumpy, aging wives and well-nourished, red-cheeked children. They are all warmly dressed. The wind sweeps through the square, raising the flags, and small November snowflakes make their cheeks tingle. Their overcoats are made of best-quality English material; you are surrounded on all sides by soft furs, Persian lamb coats, fur hats. But an unwritten nomenklatura law is scrupulously observed here: all these luxurious items of clothing must not fit too well or be worn too smartly; on the contrary, they must hang badly, and the women must not be made up. It is a last, modest tribute paid to the mythical proletarian origin of the nomenklatura, the democratic ideal it pretends to respect.

Three minutes to ten. All heads turn toward the Tomb, and nomenklaturist fathers lift their children onto their shoulders. The heads of the nomenklaturist class are about to appear on top of the mausoleum as on a captain's bridge. There they are. First of all, the Secretary-General, then the others, a short distance behind him in strict hierarchical order. The nomenklaturists at the foot of the Tomb applaud and wave to their overlords, with whom they feel closely linked, and when the world looks at that handful of dignitaries, what it sees is, in fact, "the cream of" the nomenklatura.

KGB officers in civilian clothes with red armlets politely but firmly prevent less important nomenklaturists who have been put in distant stands from finding their way into the stands reserved for their superiors. One is allowed to go from one stand to another, but in one direction only—away from the Tomb. The tip of the nomenklatura pyramid is clearly on top of the Tomb.

At ten o'clock the march-past begins, followed by the procession of loyal "representatives of the toiling population" carrying huge portraits of nomenklatura leaders and banners with slogans and figures illustrating the success of the Five-Year Plan. Later there will be a reception in the Kremlin, with nomenklatura officials seated in impeccable hierarchical order and ambassadors from nearly all the countries in the world celebrating the anniversary of the October Revolution.

But, for the nomenklaturists, the high point of the day is now. For fifty glorious minutes they admire the precision of the marching troops, the huge rockets, the tanks that rattle by. How they smile, how delighted they are at the sight of those huge rockets. It is their strength that roars past with the power of an avalanche and forces the whole world to look toward Red Square, listen to their voices, and tremble.

Let us take leave of the nomenklatura at this ecstatic moment. Let us wave good-bye to these boyars who crowd around the pyramid of the mausoleum in which a mummy rests against a background of medieval ramparts. There they are, fascinated by their own power, standing in front of the tombs in the Kremlin wall as in a cemetery, while the November wind tirelessly spreads snow over their world as it slowly declines into autumn.

Index

A

Academy of Sciences, 99, 135
Administrative Management, 1
Afghanistan, 329, 338
Africa, 336
Akhminov, G. F., 7
Albania, 338, 340, 352
Alienation of workers, 173–75
Alliluyeva, Svetlana, 54, 56,
    230–34
Amalrik, Andrei, 8
Andropov, Yuri, 88, 359
    and climb to top post, 361–
    81
Angle of Descent, 60
Animal Farm, 6
Anti-Semitism, 291–95
Armand, Inès, 31, 32
Aron, Raymond, 109
Artsimovich, Lev, 301

Axelrod, P. B., 14
Azerbaijan Republic scandal,
    188–92, 372

B

Bagritsky, Edward, 396
Bahro, Rudolf, 8
Balance of power, 334–36
Berdyaev, Nicholas, 5
Beria, L., 68, 83, 86, 226, 368
Bolsheviks, 25–26, 28, 31, 41,
    45, 50, 261
    and Marxism, 62–63
    Stalinist purge of, 52–59, 86
Bourgeoisie, 71, 72
    control of, 37–42
    and revolution, 28–37
Brezhnev, Leonid, 7, 68–69,

74, 251–54, 256, 258–60,
357–61, 370, 373–74, 383
Bukharin, N. I., 47, 55, 60,
269
Bureaucracy. *See* Nomenklatura

C

Capitalism, 129, 174
in Russia, 15, 17, 21, 29
Careerism, 395
Carlo, Antonio, 7
Censuses of 1959 and 1970,
92–95
Central Committee of the
CPSU, 39, 47, 102, 103,
261–62, 270, 325, 391
apparatus of, 271–78
power of, 71–74
Secretariat, 247–48, 266–68
Secretary-General, 249–54,
357–85
staff selection process, 48–51
Stalin's purges, 52–62
Chauvinism, 290–91
Cheka (All-Russian
Extraordinary Commission
for the Suppression of
Counterrevolution and
Sabotage), 39, 57, 278–83

See also KGB
Chernenko, Konstantin, 252,
360–61, 369, 370
and climb to top post, 381–
84
Children, 155–56, 219–21
*Classes, Social Grades, and
Groups in the U.S.S.R.*,
10
Colonialism, 284–88, 338
Communist Manifesto, 19
Communist movement
(international), 339–51
Communist parties, 339–47
in Europe, 348–51
Communist Party of the Soviet
Union (CPSU)
fate of those expelled from,
398–400
and nomenklatura, 96–100
organizational hierarchy, 79–
80
Program of, 2–3
See also Central Committee
Cooperative property, 114–17
Corruption, 188–97, 372–74
Council of Ministers, 104–5,
247–48, 268–70
*Critique of Political Economy,
The*, 16, 19, 37
Cuba, 330, 338
Czechoslovakia, 144, 311, 329–
30, 344, 352

D

E

Dachas, 205–6, 227–36

Das Kapital, 30, 118–19, 140, 146, 154

Day in the Life of Ivan Denisovich, A, 152, 411

Decision-making process, 104–5, 384

Demenok, Piotr, 397–409

Democracy, 23–24

Détente, 331–32, 334

Deutsch, L. G., 14–15

Developed socialism, 3, 246

Dialectical and Historical Materialism, 288

Dictatorship, 278

    of nomenklatura, 243–317

    of proletariat, 37–42

Dissidents, 7–9

District committee secretary, 396–411

Djilas, Milovan, 4–8, 68, 74, 141

Dnepropetrovsk, 251–52

Dogmatism, 18–22

Dual control, system of, 391

Dudintsev, Vladimir, 91, 135

Dzerzhinsky, Felix, 279

East Germany. See German Democratic Republic

Economic History of the USSR, The, 121

Economic planning, 125–29, 136, 142–45

Education, 219–21

Effective wage, 162–63

Elite, 109–10

    See also Nomenklatura

Émigrés, 7–9, 315

Engels, Friedrich, 3, 112, 118–19, 395

    on dictatorship of the proletariat, 37

    theories on the working class, 14–22

Estonia, 329–30

Eurocommunist parties, 348–51

Exit visa, 302–12

Expansionism, 320–23, 325–27

Exploiting class, 112–75

Expropriation, 121–24, 146

F

February Revolution, 31, 33–36

Federal Republic of Germany, 165

Federated republics, 284–88
Finland, 315, 329, 333
Finlandization, 350, 353
Five-year-plans, 125, 126, 142–45
Foreign Ministry, 94, 109
Foreign-policy planning, 324–25
Foundations of Leninism, The,
28, 50
Freedom of movement, 297–312
Frontier, 312–17, 323

G

Georgian Republic scandal,
138, 192–95, 372
German Communist Party, 346
German Democratic Republic,
165
Gorky, Maxim, 25
Gosplan (State Planning
Commission), 132
Government. *See* Central
Committee of the CPSU;
Federated republics;
Politburo; Soviet
constitution; Supreme
Soviet
Great Britain, 16
Great Purge, 52–59

Gulag Archipelago, 400
Gulag Archipelago, The, 152
GUM (department store), 180,
238

H

Heavy industry, 141, 389–90
Historical materialism, 19–20
*History of the Secret Diplomacy
of the Eighteenth Century,*
289
Hitler, Adolf, 321, 329, 353,
390
Hospitals, 216–17
Housing, 201–4
*How We Should Reorganise
Workers' and Peasants'
Inspection,* 42
Hungary, 329, 365–67

I

Ideological front, 295–97
Ignatov, V. N., 14
*Impending Catastrophe and
How to Combat It, The,*
141
Imperialism, the Highest Stage

of *Capitalism,* 129, 140, 387, 391
Industrial development, 15–17
Intelligentsia, 2, 6–7, 10, 20, 110, 319–20
Invisible earnings, 185–87
Iskra (The Spark), 25–26, 261
Izvestia, 102, 115, 187

J

Japan, 326
Jasny, Naum, 139
Jasulich, V. J., 14
Jews, 45, 291–95, 397

K

Kapitsa, Piotr, 301
KGB (Committee for State Security), 54–55, 79, 87–88, 106–8, 278–84, 303, 306–8, 315–16, 371, 379–80
See also Cheka
Khrushchev, Nikita, 55, 56, 60, 68, 74, 83, 87, 114, 117, 144, 167, 270–71

downfall of, 255–61
secret report on Stalin, 86
Kirov, S. M., 54–55, 60
Kochetov, Vsevolod, 60
Kolkhoz (collective-farm) property, 114–17
Kolkhoz peasants, 319–20
Kollontai, Alexandra, 32, 33
Kommunist, 89, 102, 149–50, 186
Komsomol (Young Communist League), 92, 151–52
Kraft, Joseph, 378, 379
Krassin, Leonid, 24
Kremlin hospital, 216–17
Kremliovka (coupons), 182–83, 199
Kudirka, Simas, 315
Kurganov, I. A., 389
Kuron, Jacek, 7, 124, 164, 169
Kuusinen, Otto, 363–64

L

Labor, 146–52
compulsory labor, 170–73
wages, 152–55, 156–64
of women and children, 155–56
Labor camps, 152
Latin America, 336, 338
Latvia, 329–30

Lenin, V. I., 3, 4, 53, 62–63, 119, 122, 129–30, 134–35, 141, 148–49, 180–82, 272, 289–91, 387, 391, 394, 420

  and career bureaucrats, 43–44, 75–76

  on class, 10–11

  dictatorship of the proletariat, 39–42

  on dogma, 18–22

  model for soviets, 243–45

  and professional revolutionaries, 22–28

  on revolution, 26–37

Leningrad Program, 8, 85

Leninism, 289–91

Liberals, 378–79

Lithuania, 329–30

Litvinov, Maxim, 24

Lubianka, 279–80

M

Malenkov, G. M., 269–70

Man Does Not Live by Bread Alone, 91, 135

Martov, L., 25

Marx, Karl, 3, 288–91, 394, 395, 420

  dictatorship of the proletariat, 37

  exploitation of workers, 146–47, 154–55, 170–71, 173–74

  on property, 113–14

  on revolution, 30–31

  ruling class, 70–71

  surplus value, 118–20, 160–61

  theories on the working class, 14–22

Marxism, 3, 63, 64, 113–14

Mensheviks, 25, 261

Mikhalkov, Sergei, 181

Mikoyan, A. I., 258

Military, 107–9, 390

Ministry of Defense, 107

Modzelewski, Karol, 7, 124, 164, 169

Moldavia, 252

Molotov, V. M., 83, 374–75

Monopoly, 387–88

Morality, 394

Morosov, Savva, 25

Moscow, housing in, 201–4

Moscow trials, 55

MTS (machine and tractor stations), 114

MVD (Ministry of International Affairs), 106–8

N

Nagy, Imre, 366
Narodnaya Volya, 22, 27
Narodnik (populist) movement,
    16, 18
NATO (North Atlantic Treaty
    Organization), 334
Nazi Germany, 88, 106, 108,
    321
NEP (New Economic Policy),
    123–24
New Class, The, 4–5, 68
"New class," Djilas's view of,
    4–5, 141
New Course, The, 49
Nineteen Eighty-four, 6, 26,
    278
Nomenklatura, 1, 4–5
    and Bolshevik downfall, 52–
    62
    and career bureaucrats, 75–
    81
    and Communist Party, 96–
    100
    creation of, 46–52
    dictatorship of, 247–317
    hereditary posts, 100–2
    numerical strength of, 92–96
    parasitism of, 387–439
    power as ultimate goal, 70–
    74
    power transfer at the top,
    356–85
    social structure of, 102–10
    three-stage process, 62–65
    See also Privileged class;
    Real socialism
North Korea, 338
NOT (scientific organization of
    labor), 148–49
Nuclear war, 328–29

O

Oboyma, 77
October Revolution, 2, 4, 219
    Lenin's role in, 35–37
    postrevolutionary period, 41–
    42
Oformlenye, 302–12
On Good and Wholesome
    Food, 197
Organs of state power. See
    Central Committee;
    Politburo
Orgraspred, 50–51
Origin of the Family, Private
    Property, and the State, 14
Orwell, George, 6, 26, 278
OVIR (Visa and Registration
    Department), 107, 303

P

Panin, Dimitry, 7
Parasitism, 387–439
Paris Commune, 37, 244
Passport, 309–10
Paustovsky, Konstantin, 91
Peaceful coexistence, 331–34
People's democracies, 334–37
People's Republic of China,
    329, 335, 340, 352, 353
Personality cult, 249–54
Personal Opinion, 91
Planned economy, 125–29, 136
Plekhanov, G. V., 14
Poland, 7, 144, 164, 329
Police, 106–9
Politburo, 4, 49, 71, 103, 247–
    50, 268–71
  operation of, 264–65
  origins of, 261–64
Political class, 109–10
Political Dictionary, 1
*Political Economy of Socialism,
    The*, 127
Political selection, 46–51
Population loss, 389
Pörzgen, Hermann, 5
Power, exercise of, 70–74, 384–
    85
Pravda, 115, 180–81, 186, 414,
    415
Presidium, 247–48
Privileged class, 178–241

Professional revolutionaries, 22–
    23
  and bureaucrats, 43–46
  financing of, 24–25
  and the Great Purge, 52–63
  and the Revolution, 26–37
Proletariat, 2, 319–20
  dictatorship of, 37–42
  Lenin's theories on, 19–22,
    39–42
  in the nomenklatura, 88–90
  and revolution, 28–37
Propaganda, 109, 295–97
Property, 71–72, 112–18

R

Razumny, S., 9
Real socialism, 2–3, 7, 11
  control of means of
    production, 112–18
  and exploitation of labor,
    146–75
  and expropriation, 121–24
  fundamental law of, 124–25
  heavy industry and
    underproduction, 140–46
  planned economy and
    ultramonopoly, 125–29
  and surplus value, 118–21,
    146, 160–70

and technological stagnation, 129–39
Real wage, 162–63
Red Army, 46
Redlich, Roman, 7
Retirement, 82, 222
Revolution
  Lenin's theories on, 26–37
  Marx's theories on, 30–31
Ricardo, David, 152
Rizzi, Bruno, 6
Romania, 330, 352
R.S.F.S.R. (Russian Soviet Federated Socialist Republic), 285–86
Ruling class, 109–10
  See also Nomenklatura
Russia and Russians
  backwardness of, 15–18
  colonial empire of, 285–86
  tradition of barbarism, 323–24
Russian Marxism, 14–40, 288–91
Russian Orthodox Church, 75
Russians, The, 183

S

Sakharov, Andrei, 2
Sanatoriums, 216
Scandinavia, 33

Schools, 219–21
Scientific research, 390, 392
Scientific socialism, 20
Secretariat of the Central Committee, 247–48, 266–68
Secretary-General, 249–54, 357–85
  Andropov role as, 361–80
  Brezhnev role as, 357–61
  Chernenko role as, 381–84
  personality cult surrounding, 249–54
Secret Police, 39, 57, 278–84
Sejatel (The Sower), 9
Shelepin, Sasha, 256–60, 360, 367–68
Sher, Jacob, 7
Shevlyagin, Dimitry, 85–86
Shlyapnikov, Aleksandr, 36
Sik, Ota, 8
Smith, Hedrick, 183, 217
Smolensk Archive, 396–411
Socialism, 51–52
  See also Real socialism
Solidarity, 7
Solzhenitsyn, Alexander, 7, 152, 411
Soviet constitution, 75, 244–46
Soviet Peace Committee, 98
Soviets (councils), 243–46
Soviet Society 1965–1968, 9
Sovkhoz (state farm), 114
SOVNOT (Central Council for

the Scientific Organization
of Labor), 149
Stakhanov, Alexei, 151
Stakhanovite movement, 150–
51, 166
Stalin, Joseph, 7, 14, 28, 38,
40, 119, 123–26, 141–43,
184, 197, 231–35, 240,
262
and creation of
nomenklatura, 46–52, 62–
63
filing system, political
selection by, 47–48, 75–76
and purge of old guard, 52–
59, 86
Standard of living, 156–60
State and Revolution, The, 41,
126, 148
State Bank, 121–23
State property, 114–17
Steinberg, I. Z., 5
Story of the Great Plan, The
125
Stoyanovič, Svetozar, 8
Structure of the Party, 2
*Structure of the Soviet
Intelligentsia, The,* 10
Supreme Soviet, 75, 247–48
Surplus value, 118–21, 146,
160–70

T

Talantov, Boris, V., 9
Tax system, 166–68
Taylorism, 148–49
Telephones, as status symbol,
207–13
Terrorism, 16–17, 278
Thaw, The, 91
Third World, 326, 334, 337–
38, 353
*Three Capitals: A Journey
Through Red Russia,* 44–
45
Tito, J. B., 330–31
Trade unionism, 19, 21
Transportation, 217–19, 237–
37
Trotsky, Leon, 6, 41, 49–50,
54, 276
Tsebur, A., 397, 400–4
*Twentieth Century and Peace,
The,* 85

U

Uchraspred, 48–50
Ukraine, 361
Ulbricht, W., 84
Ultramonopoly, 127
Ulyanov, Vladimir (Lenin), 17

Underproduction, 140–46
Unemployment, 390
United Nations, 338
United States, 334, 336, 338
Universal Declaration of the
    Rights of Man, 298–99
UPVD (Department for the
    Planning of Foreign Policy
    Activities), 324–25
Ustinov, Dmitri, 370

V

Varga, Evgheni S., 9
Vestnik, 415, 420–21
Vietnam, 334, 344
Vyshinsky, Andrei, 55, 56, 60

W

Wages, 152–55, 156–64, 390
Warsaw Pact, 303, 307, 329–
    30, 334
Western Europe, 336–37, 353
Western journalists, 222–23
West Germany. *See* Federal
    Republic of Germany
What Is to Be Done?, 18, 21,
    23

*Will the Soviet Union Survive
    until 1984?*, 8
Women, 155–56
Working hours, 146–47
World hegemony (of the Soviet
    Union), 319–54
World war, specter of, 351–54
World War II, 321

X

Xenophobia, 291

Y

Yezhov, N. I., 52–60
Yezhovchina (the Great Purge),
    52–59
Yugoslavia, 5, 330, 338–40, 352

Z

Zavety Ilyicha ("Lenin's
    testament"), 227–28
Zhukov, G. K., 276